THE LAST COLONIES

This comprehensive and authoritative book is about the last colonies, those remaining territories formally dependent on metropolitan powers. It discusses the surprisingly large number of these territories, mainly small isolated islands with limited resources. Yet these places are not as obscure as might be expected. They may be major tourist destinations, military bases, satellite tracking stations, tax havens or desolate, sparsely populated spots that can become international flashpoints, such as the Falklands. The authors find that at a time of escalating nationalism and globalisation, these remnants of empire provide insights into the meanings of political, economic, legal and cultural independence, as well as sovereignty and nationhood. This book provides a broad-based and provocative discussion of colonialism and interdependence in the modern world, from a unique and original perspective.

Robert Aldrich and John Connell teach at the University of Sydney, the former in the Department of Economic History, the latter in the Department of Geography. They are joint authors of *France's Overseas Frontier*, published by Cambridge in 1992. They are inveterate travellers, and between them have been to most of the territories discussed in this book.

THE LAST COLONIES

ROBERT ALDRICH and JOHN CONNELL

CAMBRIDGE
UNIVERSITY PRESS

CAMBRIDGE UNIVERSITY PRESS
Cambridge, New York, Melbourne, Madrid, Cape Town, Singapore, São Paulo

Cambridge University Press
The Edinburgh Building, Cambridge CB2 2RU, UK

Published in the United States of America by Cambridge University Press, New York

www.cambridge.org
Information on this title: www.cambridge.org/9780521414616

First published 1998
This digitally printed first paperback version 2006

A catalogue record for this publication is available from the British Library

Library of Congress Cataloguing in Publication data

Aldrich, Robert, 1954–
The last colonies/Robert Aldrich and John Connell.
    p.   cm.
Includes bibliographical references and index.
ISBN 0-521-41461-X (hardbound: alk. paper)
1. Colonies. I. Connell, John. II. Title.
JV151.A5 1998
321'. 08–dc 21   97–39275

ISBN-13 978-0-521-41461-6 hardback
ISBN-10 0-521-41461-X hardback

ISBN-13 978-0-521-42490-5 paperback
ISBN-10 0-521-42490-9 paperback

Contents

Maps

Tables

Acknowledgements

In writing this book we have been able to visit more than half of the principal overseas territories which we discuss, and we would like to thank government officials, librarians, journalists and scholars in those places where one or both of us were able to do research – Jersey, Gibraltar, Ceuta, Mayotte, Réunion, Macao, New Caledonia, Wallis, French Polynesia, Guam, Saipan (Northern Marianas), Rarotonga (Cook Islands), American Samoa, Martinique, Guadeloupe, Puerto Rico, St Croix and St Thomas (United States Virgin Islands), Tortola (British Virgin Islands), Anguilla, Grand Cayman, Montserrat, Sint-Maarten/Saint-Martin, St Eustatius, Saba, Bermuda and Grand Turk. We are also indebted to the Australian Research Council for financial support and to several academic colleagues whose specialities are island micro-states and other territories, especially Stephen Royle, Gert Oostindie, Iain Walker and Paul Leary. Julie Manley deserves special thanks for a heroic job in deciphering scribbles, following arrows, cutting and pasting sections and revising drafts to produce the final manuscript. Margaret Connell provided sustenance and deleted commas during the last hectic revisions. We owe particular thanks to Phillipa McGuinness at Cambridge University Press, who waited with great patience and never-flagging encouragement for the submission of the manuscript.

NOTE: Unless otherwise stated all currency units are United States dollars.

Abbreviations

BIOT	British Indian Ocean Territory
BVI	British Virgin Islands
CEP	Centre d'Expérimentation du Pacifique
DOM-TOMs	*départements et territoires d'outre-mer*
	(overseas departments and territories)
EEZ	exclusive economic zone
FCO	Foreign and Commonwealth Office
FLNKS	Front de Libération Nationale Kanake et Socialiste
NAFTA	North American Free Trade Area
NATO	North Atlantic Treaty Organisation
TAAF	Terres Australes et Antarctiques Françaises
TTPI	Trust Territory of the Pacific Islands
USVI	United States Virgin Islands

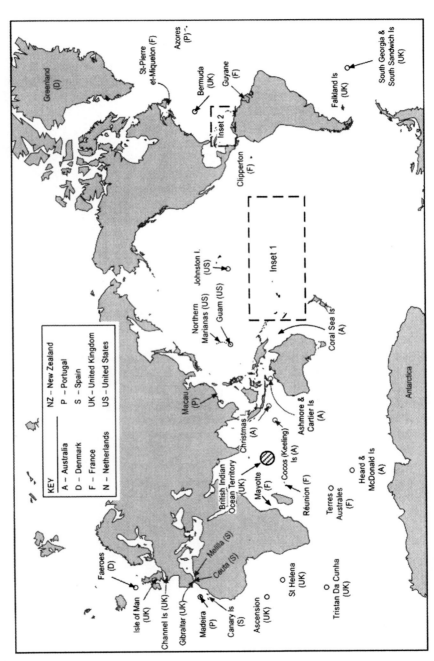

Overseas Territories

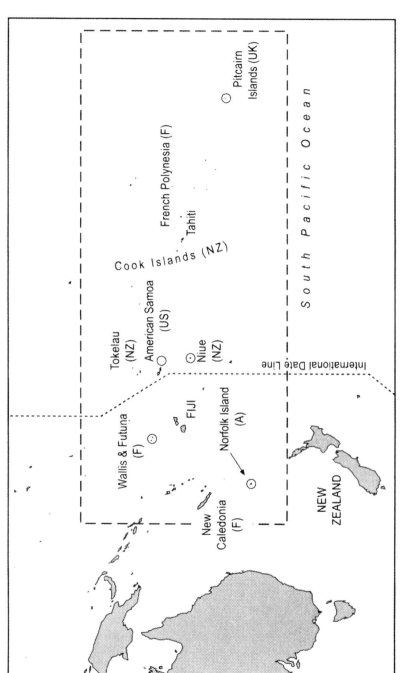

Inset 1 Central Pacific Ocean

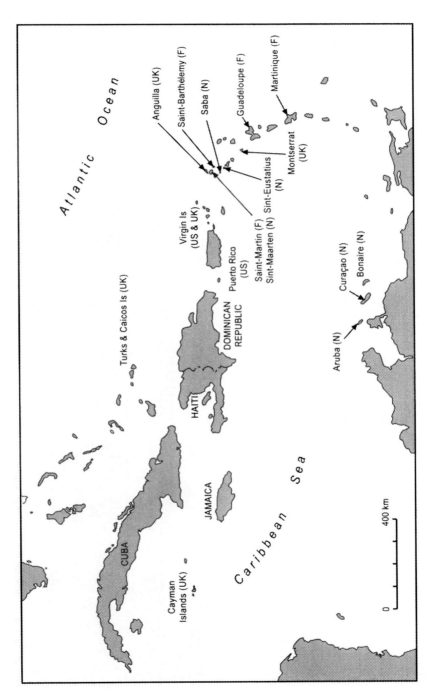

Inset 2 Caribbean Sea

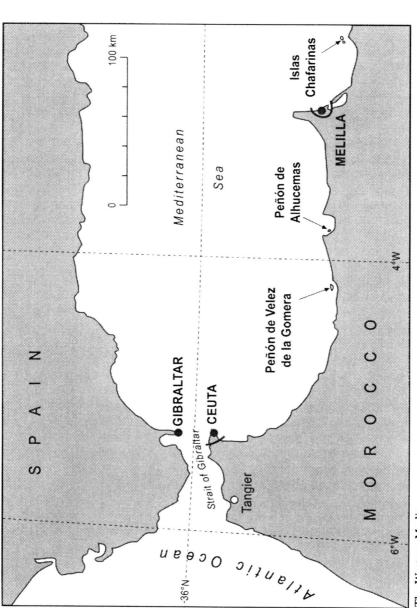

The Western Mediterranean

This year is already marked out as one of great significance for Britain, and not just because of the forthcoming election. In June Hong Kong, the last colony of any great strategic or economic importance, is to be handed back to China after more than 150 years under the Union flag . . . Once Hong Kong goes, there remains only a cluster of islands — once strategically important, now just dots in the oceans of the globe.

The Independent, 3 January 1997

CHAPTER 1

The Legacy of Empire

The actual liquidation of the remnants of empire will mark
the end of an era. It should improve the chances for a more
stable and peaceful world.[1]

In recent decades various books and numerous articles have examined
the political evolution of Britain's colony of Hong Kong, as it moved
closer towards reintegration with China in 1997. Several revived themes
of the 'last colony' and the end of empire.[2] H. A. Turner, in *The Last
Colony: But Whose?*, whilst recognising that a number of British colonies
remained, stressed that 'Hong Kong is by far the most lustrous jewel of
the once-Imperial Crown's otherwise residual adornments, and one
whose economic light bid fair to outshine its nominal possessor's.'[3]
Beyond Hong Kong, other enduring colonies were regarded as of no
political or economic significance, distant and quaint relics of Britain's
imperial past. Except when a crisis propelled them to the front page of
daily newspapers, as happened when Argentina attacked the Falkland
Islands in 1982, they were simply ignored. Whilst the actual political
status of 'colonies' is subject to dispute, there remain a substantial
number of distinct territories – not least Macao, just west of Hong Kong
– that are far from being independent, sovereign states. Though the
changing status of Hong Kong has intermittently focused attention on
surviving outposts of the British empire, other developed nations – the
United States, France, Denmark, the Netherlands, Portugal, Spain,
Australia and New Zealand – also have distant territories that remain, in
some way, politically dependent on the metropolitan power. These
territories are the subject of this book.

In an era that is bravely, and sometimes cynically, touted as one of a
New World Order, there is something seemingly paradoxical about the
continued presence of colonies in a supposedly post-colonial world. The
age of decolonisation is usually regarded as having peaked during the
1960s as the 'winds of change' swept through Africa. By the mid-1970s,
after the withdrawal of Portugal from Angola and Mozambique, African

1

decolonisation seemed complete; in 1980 Rhodesia became independent as Zimbabwe after fifteen years of white settler mutiny and civil
war, and a decade later Namibia also achieved independence. Even small
island colonies, once thought incapable of sustaining independence,
became nation-states, complete with flags, heads of state and seats in
international organisations. Sometimes the parting of the ways between
metropolitan powers and colonies had been difficult, as was the case for
the British in India and Rhodesia, and the French in Algeria and
Indochina; in other cases, independence occurred after mutual agreements, and 'mother countries' retained cordial ties with the states. In
rarer cases, imperial powers seemed anxious to divest themselves of
unprofitable and far-flung colonies; typical were Britain's Pacific
possessions, most notably Kiribati and Tuvalu.[4]

Yet Portugal did not withdraw from its oldest colony, Macao, nor from
its Atlantic islands. Spain remained in two North African enclaves and
the Canary Islands. Britain and France kept a scatter of possessions
around the world. Denmark continued to influence Greenland and the
Faeroes, and even the Netherlands held on to two groups of islands in
the Caribbean. European powers were not alone; the United States
retained 'territories' and 'commonwealths' in the Pacific and Caribbean,
notably Puerto Rico and Guam, whilst in the South Pacific, Niue and
Tokelau are New Zealand territories and Norfolk Island and the Coral
Sea Islands Territory are linked to Australia. Developing nations also
have dependent territories, such as Mauritius and Rodrigues, or Chile
and Rapanui (Easter Island). Even within some countries, like Australia,
particular states have overseas territories – for instance, New South
Wales and Lord Howe Island, and Tasmania and Macquarie Island – with
distinct administrative regimes. In many respects the permutations of
dependence and administrative difference are almost endless.

Defining 'Colonies'

These various territories – or some of them – may really be the last
colonies. Unfortunately, but significantly, there can be no precise definition of what is a colony. Dictionary definitions suggest a range of alternatives; one *Dictionary of Politics* provides the following:

> An area of land which, with its inhabitants, is entirely subject to the rule of an
> independent state, of which it does not form an integral part. It is not itself an
> independent state, though it may, according to its degree of political maturity,
> be given some self-government. A grant of self-government and of a representa-
> tive legislature does not prevent the ruling state from disallowing any legisla-
> tion of which it may disapprove. Colonies have usually originated in settlements
> by traders or explorers of territories unoccupied by any other independent
> states, or in conquests of territories already occupied by other states.[5]

Whilst there is some consensus that colonies are distant ('a new country', not 'an integral part' of the old country), established by settlers (including traders and explorers), and politically linked to an independent state elsewhere, the distances involved and the nature and significance of linkages can never be specified in formal definitions. Indeed, the *Dictionary of Politics* is ambivalent on the extent to which a colony might exercise independent political authority. Since political shifts are crucial to colonialism and decolonisation, any definition of a colony is condemned to flexibility and variable interpretations.

For this reason, and because the word 'colony' is laden with historically specific and emotionally heated connotations, this study largely avoids the word. The islands and enclaves discussed here exhibit the indelible imprint of a colonial past, and distinct traces of 'colonialism' remain in lack of political sovereignty, economic fragility, and social cleavages produced by disparities among ethnic groups. Yet almost none is a 'colony' in the rather simplistic vernacular understanding of a distant outpost lorded over by white foreigners who deprive local inhabitants of self-government and extract immense riches for their own profit. Indeed this book will suggest that, despite their dependent status, most (though not all) of the last 'colonies' enjoy a large degree of self-government and reap considerable economic benefits from their attachment to metropolitan states. Whether the costs – political, economic, social, cultural – outweigh the benefits, however, is a matter of often vigorous debate.

The choice of territories to examine here is, in some cases, clear. The French government officially considers ten outposts to be *départements et territoires d'outre-mer* ('overseas departments and territories', or DOM-TOMs) of the Republic: Martinique and Guadeloupe (and several islands administered as part of Guadeloupe) in the West Indies; Guyane in South America; the islands of Saint-Pierre-et-Miquelon off the coast of Canada; Mayotte and Réunion in the Indian Ocean; New Caledonia, Wallis and Futuna, and French Polynesia (as well as Clipperton Island) in the Pacific, and the Austral and Antarctic Territories.[6] The British government also has an official roster of 'dependencies' which is made up of Gibraltar; Pitcairn in the Pacific; the British Indian Ocean Territory (BIOT); the Falklands, South Georgia and the South Sandwich Islands, St Helena (and its dependencies, Tristan da Cunha and Ascension) and Bermuda in the Atlantic; and the British Virgin Islands, Anguilla, Montserrat, the Cayman Islands, and the Turks and Caicos Islands in the West Indies.[7] To these can be added the Isle of Man and the Channel Islands (Jersey and Guernsey). The Kingdom of the Netherlands is composed of three parts: the Netherlands itself, the Netherlands Antilles (the islands of Bonaire, Curaçao, Saba, St Eustatius and Sint-Maarten), and Aruba. The Faeroe Islands and Greenland are distant parts of the Danish kingdom. For the United States, official labels are also helpful: the commonwealths of

Puerto Rico and the Northern Marianas, and the 'unincorporated territories' of the United States Virgin Islands, American Samoa and Guam.[8] Australia's designated 'external territories' are Norfolk Island in the Pacific; the Cocos (Keeling) Islands and Christmas Island in the Indian Ocean; the uninhabited Coral Sea islands; the sub-Antarctic Heard and McDonald islands; and Australia's claim in Antarctica. New Zealand's links are with Niue and Tokelau, and also the Cook Islands, which adheres to a treaty of 'free association' with Wellington. This list favours official designations, but other territories are discussed here because their situations parallel those in the above group. The Spanish North African cities – more properly, 'autonomous communities' – of Ceuta and Melilla, and the Canary Islands are included, as well as Portuguese Macao (although it will be a Portuguese territory only until 1999), and Madeira and the Azores. In practice this book focuses on a rather smaller number, by effectively ignoring unpopulated territories (including Antarctica, and the Coral Sea Islands Territory, where the 1991 population consisted of three meteorologists).[9]

Though that already seems a lengthy list, many other areas might have been included. Northern Ireland and Corsica, at least in the views of nationalists in those two places, would be obvious candidates. Scotland has a distinct legal system and bank notes, stamps, a flag, a football team, a parliament (and a substantial independence movement). Some offshore islands in Europe – Sicily and Sardinia in Italy, the Balearic Islands in Spain, Svalbard (Spitsbergen) and Jan Mayen in Norway, and the Åland Islands of Finland – might also have been included because of the traits which separate them in important ways from nearby mainlands. The American states of Alaska and Hawaii, colonies in the past, are still considered colonies by Inuit activists and the Hawaiian 'sovereignty movement'. All have been excluded. This study also does not discuss peripheral regions, outlying territories and overseas possessions of non-Western states. To do so would be to venture into new fields with formidable obstacles and difficult terrain. Since many Third World states were designed by colonial powers, territorial disputes and ethnic rivalries have been endemic, often with tragic consequences. Furthermore, present-day independence movements in Bougainville, East Timor, Southern Sudan and elsewhere show that allegations of continuing colonialism are not restricted to Western countries.

The classification of overseas territories used here rests on certain broad principles. Firstly, territories are those overseas outposts that are, in some sense, recognised as constitutionally different from the 'mainland'.[10] Secondly, they are sufficiently distant from metropolitan states for there to be no obvious geographical basis for their attachment to a particular nation-state other than accidents of history; thus neither Tasmania nor the Shetland Islands is included (though they may have some 'colonial' characteristics) because proximity suggests that, if not independent states, they should logically be part of Australia and Scotland, respectively.[11] Thirdly, territories are politically 'dependent' to the extent that they are ineligible for membership of the United Nations; the Federated States of Micronesia is not a territory as considered here (though the United States can exert some control over its foreign policy), whereas the Cook Islands is.[12] The practice of the United Nations concerning the definition of statehood, and therefore potential participation in the United Nations, includes the basic criteria of a permanent population, fixed and defined territory, stable and effective government, and sovereign independence; these have been followed, but flexibly interpreted.[13] Of these characteristics the one most open to interpretation is that of a substantial degree of independence, the extent to which a state is effective in exercising sovereignty (mainly in the international arena) and consequently the extent to which states are recognised internationally.[14] The exact meaning of 'independence' or 'sovereignty' is as difficult to grasp as is the meaning of 'colony'.

In most respects any definition of an overseas territory should logically derive from that of a state: territories may also be expected to have reasonably defined borders, a permanent population and a more or less stable government (though with reduced authority and fewer spheres of action than a state), but there need be no requirement for any degree of sovereignty to be exercised. Indeed, the lack of sovereignty is the major trait of politically dependent status. In practice it is necessary for these various principles to be combined to produce a working classification. This classification thereby has excluded places with 'colonial' characteristics, such as Gaza or Tibet, that have at some point been incorporated into neighbouring states.[15] Further, it follows the UN position that 'colonies' are non-self-governing, geographically separate and ethnically and/or culturally distinct from the countries administering them[16] (though this definition might for example appear to rule out the Falkland Islands). Self-government may constitute either emergence as a sovereign independent state, or free association or integration with an independent state,[17] all of which are options taken by many colonies in the past. That no definition of self-government is possible ensures that any definition of 'colony' or overseas territory is ultimately arbitrary.[18]

Most attempts to define 'colonies' or territories focus on issues of political status and sovereignty; yet in various contexts, political units that may be regarded as 'colonies' actually act as states. Several territories are represented in regional organisations, such as the South Pacific Commission, as equal partners with independent states. Many territories have flags and anthems, issue postage stamps and use their own currency. Some are involved in the Olympic Games, the Commonwealth Games, the European football championship and even 'Miss World' competitions.[19]

Indeed, it is in these more informal contexts that overseas territories are much more likely to be indistinguishable from independent states.

Beyond scattered attempts at formal definitions,[20] these territories have more frequently been viewed in a diversity of contexts, with 'colony' (or colonialism) implying some degree of marginality or disadvantage and thus suggesting the need for resistance to this status. Consequently, the peripheries of many states have been viewed as 'colonies'; ethnic (or other) minorities have been perceived as 'colonised' people (whether or not located in national peripheries); and even women have been referred to as a 'colony'.[21] More generally, 'colonies' have been perceived to exist where distant places and 'other' minorities have been conquered, or settled, from beyond, and in a manner that has disadvantaged the colonised. Frantz Fanon's well-known critique of colonialism emphasises this context:

> Colonial administration, because it is total and tends to oversimplify, very soon manages to disrupt in spectacular fashion the cultural life of a conquered people. This cultural obliteration is made possible by the negation of natural reality, by new legal relations, introduced by the occupying power, by the banishment of the 'natives' and their customs to out-lying districts, by colonial society, and expropriation.[22]

This vision of colonial history, as one of violence and mistrust, racism and deceit, is certainly not true only of Algeria, the subject of Fanon's description. Similar situations were widespread, especially in Africa, the arena of much work on colonialism and decolonisation. It is this wholly negative construction of the phenomenon of colonialism that is the basis of much everyday parlance.

In many areas, colonialism was belated, brief and superficial. Whilst in certain cases, such as Namibia, 'Germany and South Africa, as late-comers to the colonial sweepstakes, were in general hastier and more brutal',[23] colonialists usually had slight interest in their new conquests in global peripheries. In the South Pacific, Britain only reluctantly took over the islands that became Kiribati and Tuvalu, and found few profits in these 'Cinderellas of the Empire'[24] (at least until the British were able to establish a phosphate mine on Banaba, the closure of which coincided with the independence of Kiribati). In Fiji, islanders were 'spared – by geography – the journey through hell of some African states',[25] and the same was true in other less distant British possessions. In the even smaller and scattered Cook Islands, where there were indeed expectations of economic gain, it quickly became apparent that welfare and protection – at some cost to New Zealand – dominated the island economic system; consequently, the material well-being of Cook Islanders increased rather than decreased, whilst land escaped alienation.[26] At the very least, colonialism was far from a homogeneous phenomenon, and indigenous opposition to it was, in some cases, weak or non-existent. Even where colonialism has been widely perceived as rapacious, as in late-nineteenth-century New Caledonia, during a major nationalist rebellion against the French in 1878, many Melanesians took the side of the coloniser against the colonised.[27] Whilst such *compradors* or collaborators may have been despised by the majority, in every colonial context there were winners and losers.

However defined, comprehended or experienced, colonialism reached its apogee in the first half of the twentieth century, following the last great Western scramble for empire, most obviously in Africa, Asia and the Pacific. The dominions of Canada, South Africa and Australia became independent, and, in the era after the Second World War, decolonisation moved towards a climax in 1960, when eighteen African dependencies became sovereign states. In the 1960s and 1970s decolonisation became a global phenomenon, as Caribbean and Pacific island micro-states took their places in the United Nations. By the 1980s, however, the pace of decolonisation had slowed. Only six entities – Brunei, Belize (British Honduras), St Kitts–Nevis, Vanuatu, Zimbabwe, and Antigua and Barbuda – became independent in that decade. When Eritrea's long war of independence finally succeeded in 1993, this seemed to mark the belated end of the process of decolonisation. Decolonisation was most rapid during a period of global economic growth that coincided with the diffusion and more widespread acceptance of notions of the nation-state.[28]

In many respects, colonialism has never been limited simply to those territories formally linked in a political sense to metropolitan nations. In the heyday of British colonialism, for example, there was also an 'informal empire' consisting of independent countries economically dependent on British trade and investment, and locked in by the international gold standard, which enabled the Bank of England to exercise some supervision and regulation of economic activity. Beyond that, more diffuse cultural influences have been exceptionally powerful elements in the development of global identities and linkages. In post-colonial times, neo-colonialism has been widely apparent in the economic activities of metropolitan nations, companies and institutions, in shaping trade agreements and aid policies, and in regulating (or failing to regulate) the activities of transnational corporations and such institutions as the World Bank and the International Monetary Fund. No country is beyond the reach of globalisation.

If it is impossible to make tidy general statements about colonialism, it is also impossible to say when it ended, or when it was transmuted into another phenomenon (as theorists of 'neo-colonialism' argue), or when it gave way to a sort of 'uncolonial' dependency. Furthermore, whilst the post-war era has largely been one of decolonisation, even in the most straightforward sense, the process of colonisation still continues in at least two distinct contexts. Most violently, in a number of areas, what are essentially colonial wars are still being fought in the struggle for access to land and resources (and, usually, in the name of reclaiming old empires, as in ex-Yugoslavia, Kashmir and the Caucasus). Many global political boundaries have come under threat, often in the name of liberation of a 'nation' from some 'colonial' master. Since the borders of many European states have fluctuated in the twentieth century, it is unsurprising that new political and economic realities there and elsewhere should result in challenges to old frontiers and continued charges of colonialism even in developed states of Europe. At the same time there have been renewed attempts to colonise the few 'uncolonised' fragments of the world, or at least those where claims appear tenuous, evident in the military manoeuvres of several Asian states to exert ownership of the unpopulated Spratly and Paracel Islands in the China Sea (the exclusive economic zone of the islands is considerable, and contains oil resources).[29] At a very different scale, Antarctica has also attracted much greater interest from metropolitan states, though the colonisation process has been carefully regulated by international legislation. In rather different ways, conventional processes of transforming geopolitics remain evident in a variety of global contexts.

Insofar as there is a new world order, it is partly linked to two related phenomena: the decline of ideological differences[30] and the revival of nationalism. Quintessentially the new nationalism has been based in Eastern Europe and the former Soviet Union, where political repression prevented expressions of cultural, religious or ethnic difference, and where the breakdown of communism responded to and revealed obvious failures of economic development. The political vacuum that ensued was quickly filled by nationalist movements that sought to return the map, and the lands, of the post-socialist states on the fringes of Europe and Asia to a form more like that of earlier centuries, the era before Russian, Soviet and satellite colonialism brought unaccustomed and distant centralism and control. Nationalist movements thus sought greater autonomy and sovereignty, economic development and recognition of cultural identity where all these had long been denied. These movements often achieved rapid success, especially in contrast with the consistent minority status of nationalist movements on the peripheries of Western European states, such as France, Spain and the United Kingdom. (In other cases too, like Quebec, they have failed.) The new world order thus spawned the genesis of new states, or, more accurately, the reappearance of many earlier states.[31]

In absolute contrast, the new world order in the dependent territories has brought virtually no change. Nationalist movements have either been absent, have lost vitality in the 1990s, or have sought limited cultural objectives. At the very time that new nations were being inscribed on the map of Europe, so the remaining territories, which might perhaps have been expected to seek a similar break from the political ties of the old order, largely acquiesced to their status. Meanwhile the notion of decolonisation has changed and been transformed. The simple, constitutional model of decolonisation which, in its last phase, took Namibia to independence in 1990, no longer encompasses more complex issues; Palau (Belau) chose independence in 'free association' with the United States in 1994. Decolonisation has now assumed various meanings in different contexts, from relatively traditional anticolonial militancy and secessionist nationalism, to quests for redistribution of land and economic benefits, and cultural recognition. This book seeks to explore and examine this diversity, at the core of which is an apparent paradox – the persistence of dependent overseas territories in a world where nationalism, in various manifestations, is pervasive and where independence is usually taken to be the endpoint of political evolution. Ultimately it seeks to examine why the processes of decolonisation have proceeded to a certain point, and no further.

The Overseas Territories

The territories discussed here are also interesting in their own right; to dismiss them as small, distant and inconsequential would be an error. Overseas territories are remarkably diverse (Table 1, pp. 12–15). Contemporary 'empires' vary greatly, from a mere 6000 people in the case of Australia, to over two million for France and more than four million for the United States. Though Britain has much the largest number of overseas territories, they include less than 400,000 people – even with the Channel Islands and the Isle of Man – but, like that of France, the 'sun never sets' on this empire. By contrast, the overseas territories of the Netherlands, Denmark and Spain are confined to restricted areas of the globe. Populations range from almost four million in Puerto Rico to much fewer than a hundred in the remote British island of Pitcairn; some territories are only sporadically occupied by small contingents of explorers, military personnel or researchers, such as the various zones claimed in Antarctica. Geographical size varies from the vast expanses of Greenland or Guyane to islands which measure only a few hundred metres in diameter and barely rise above sea level. The overseas territories are spread across the globe; many are situated in tropical or semitropical zones, but they extend to the cold ocean surrounding the Falklands and South Georgia, further south to the frozen continent of Antarctica, and north to the Faeroes and Greenland. Most of the territories are islands, but they also include the continental enclaves of Guyane, Gibraltar, Ceuta, Melilla and Macao. Residents of the outposts are often ethnically and culturally different from those of the 'mother countries', but Saint-Pierre-et-Miquelon, the Faeroes and the Falkland Islands are populated almost exclusively by descendants of European migrants. In still more outposts, distinctions between indigenous and colonial populations are hard to discern.

Overseas territories have strategic potential, both for military and commercial reasons, and they have not infrequently been flashpoints for conflict. The war between Britain and Argentina over the Falklands is the most obvious recent example of how a small possession – the Falklands have barely 2000 residents and cover 16,000 square kilometres – can become a battleground between two powers which claim sovereign rights over a territory. In the South Pacific, the struggle by indigenous Melanesians for independence in France's territory of New Caledonia erupted into violence in the mid-1980s. The status of Gibraltar has always been a sore point in relations between Britain and Spain. French nuclear testing in French Polynesia from the early 1960s to the 1990s was a highly controversial activity. The temporary revival of testing in 1995, after a three-year moratorium, prompted unparalleled levels of protest in French Polynesia and around the world, led to the condemnation of such tests by the United Nations, and provoked riots in Tahiti. Drug-running and corruption in several Caribbean territories have posed continuing problems. Small places can thus become sources of tension and conflict in international politics.

Some overseas territories contain useful resources, though their value is often exaggerated by lobby groups. The UN Law of the Sea agreement established exclusive economic zones (EEZs) around coastal and island nations, including their overseas outposts, and even uninhabited islands. Nations thereby retain a monopoly on the exploitation of maritime resources in the EEZs, and the possession of far-away islands gives such countries as Britain, France and the United States considerable options for fishing and the mining of submarine mineral deposits. Similarly, foreign claims to Antarctica hold importance partly because of the real or imagined profits of marine life, minerals or even fresh-water supplies frozen in Antarctica's glaciers. More prosaically, overseas territories are often duty-free shopping centres. Perhaps the most important visible economic activity throughout the territories, from Greenland and Antarctica to the tropics, is tourism. Landscape, in various forms, is the most valuable asset in many places. Less visible, but often more important, is the somewhat artificial economy stimulated by large bureaucracies, funded and subsidised by the metropolitan powers. It is this bureaucratic sector that has often become the leading edge of growth and development, rather than often elusive resources. Some territories, such as the Turks and Caicos Islands, the Cayman Islands and especially Bermuda, are havens for offshore finance and insurance, and useful locations for investments and liquid assets; in a number of contexts – including those where drug-trafficking occurs – these may be illegal.

Territories, furthermore, are pieces in geopolitical puzzles where rival powers try to secure military bases and intelligence stations to achieve their strategic goals. The United States, for instance, has used some territories as bases for a nuclear fleet, kept a tracking station in the British territory of Ascension, and leases the entire British Indian Ocean Territory as a military base. The closure of the British, Canadian and United States bases on Bermuda in the mid-1990s indicates, however, that the old order is declining, paralleled in the Pacific by a reduced American presence in Guam. During the Cold War, French, British, US, Portuguese and Danish overseas bases provided essential posts from which to monitor the activities of the Soviet Union, China and other perceived rivals and, at least according to some geopoliticians, to deter hostile attacks. The European space station at Kourou, in Guyane, and satellite tracking stations in other locations, provide scientific and strategic uses for overseas possessions. Seen individually, remote and diminutive islands might appear of minimal importance; as part of a global presence and strategy, they can be of considerable (even essential) value. The overseas territories ultimately have a particular, inestimable value to at least some metropoles: as symbols of their past glories, as stakes in their claims to the status of big (or, at least, medium-sized) powers in distant oceans, or as old 'family jewels'. Ceuta and Melilla have been Spanish since the 1400s, Macao and the Azores and Madeira Portuguese since the 1500s; London ruled Bermuda before it ruled Scotland; Martinique and Guadeloupe were part of the French kingdom before Nice and Corsica. The overseas territories remain outposts of national languages and cultures.

The overseas territories, therefore, are points of interest in geopolitics and international trade, tourism and migration. They are more significant in political terms, and could even constitute models for political evolution elsewhere; late in 1996, the Israeli prime minister envisaged the political status of Puerto Rico as highly appropriate for that of a Palestinian state, whilst, some months later, Portugal also perceived it as a potential model for East Timor.[32] At a time when nationalist movements are rampant in many parts of the world, yet when the spoils of political independence in a number of countries have been meagre, and European countries are facing the challenges of political unification or fragmentation, the territories provide insights. They illuminate the very definition of political and economic independence, the margins of manoeuvre and the constitutional variations between independence and dependence, the capacity of majority populations to incorporate those who are different by culture, skin colour or creed. The dependent overseas territories – dots on the map though many may be – provide a different dimension to discussions about the nation-state, international relations and the cultural contours which define any society.

Table 1 Overseas Territories[1]

Territory	Date[2]	Consti-tution[3]	Status	Location	Area (sq. km)	Population (official or estimated)
AUSTRALIA						
Ashmore and Cartier Islands	1931	1978	Territory	Timor Sea	5	No permanent population
Australian Antarctic Territory	1933	1962	Territory	Antarctica	5,896,500	No permanent population
Christmas Island	1958	1992	Territory	Indian Ocean	135	3,000 (1995)
Cocos (Keeling) Islands	1955	1984	Territory	Indian Ocean	14	593 (1992)
Coral Sea Islands Territory	1969	1969	Territory	Coral Sea	8	No permanent population
Heard and McDonald Islands	1947	–	Territory	Indian Ocean	369	No permanent population
Norfolk Island	1788	1979	Territory	Pacific Ocean	35	2,285 (1991)
DENMARK						
Faeroe Islands	1380	1948	'Home Rule' (self-government)	North Atlantic	1,399	43,719 (1994)
Greenland	1380	1979	'Home Rule' (self-government)	North Atlantic	2,175,600	55,117 (1993)
FRANCE						
Austral and Antarctic Territories	1924	1952	TOM[4]	Antarctica and Antarctic waters	7,822 (islands) 432,000 (Antarctic continent)[5]	No permanent population
French Polynesia[6]	1842	1984	TOM	Pacific Ocean	4,167	219,520 (1996)
Guadeloupe and Dependencies[7]	1635	1958	DOM	Caribbean	1,780	387,034 (1990)
Guyane	1817	1958	DOM[4]	South America	91,000	114,808 (1990)
Martinique	1635	1958	DOM	Caribbean	1,128	368,400 (1991)
Mayotte	1843	1976	Territorial collectivity	Indian Ocean	375	94,410 (1991)
New Caledonia and Dependencies[8]	1853	1988	TOM	Pacific Ocean	19,103	196,800 (1996)
Réunion[9]	1642	1958	DOM	Indian Ocean	2,512	630,700 (1993)

Table 1 (cont.)

Territory	Date[2]	Consti-tution[3]	Status	Location	Area (sq. km)	Population (official or estimated)
UNITED KINGDOM						
Anguilla	1650	1990	Dependency	Caribbean	96	8,960 (1992)
Bermuda	1684	1968	Dependency	North Atlantic	53	59,549 (1993)
British Antarctic Territory[5]	1908	1962	Dependency	Antarctica	1,710,000	No permanent population
British Indian Ocean Territory[11]	1800s	1965	Dependency	Indian Ocean	60	No permanent population
British Virgin Islands	1672	1994	Dependency	Caribbean	153	16,749 (1991)
Cayman Islands	1670	1994	Dependency	Caribbean	259	31,930 (1994)
Channel Islands[12]	1066		Crown dependencies	English Channel	194	144,369 (1993)
Falkland Islands	1765	1985	Crown colony	South Atlantic	12,173	2,704 (1996)
Gibraltar	1713	1969	Crown colony	Europe	6	28,051 (1993)
Isle of Man	1266	1919	Crown dependency	Irish Sea	572	69,788 (1991)
Montserrat	1632	1989	Crown colony	Caribbean	102	10,639 (1992)
Pitcairn Islands	1790	1964	Dependency	Pacific Ocean	5	54 (1995)
St Helena	1833	1988	Dependency	East Atlantic	122	5,700 (1992)
Ascension	1815	1967	Dependency of St Helena	East Atlantic	88	900 (1996)
Tristan da Cunha	1815	1967	Dependency of St Helena	East Atlantic	98	300 (1993)
South Georgia and South Sandwich Islands	1775	1985	Dependency	South Atlantic	3,903	No permanent population
Turks and Caicos Islands	1766	1988	Dependency	Caribbean	430	12,350 (1990)

			Status	Location	Area	Population (year)
Saint-Pierre-et-Miquelon	1816	1985	Territorial collectivity	North Atlantic	242	6,392 (1990)
Wallis and Futuna	1886	1961	TOM	Pacific Ocean	274	13,705 (1990)
NETHERLANDS						
Aruba	1636	1986	Autonomous part of the Netherlands	Caribbean	193	77,898 (1993)
Netherlands Antilles	1630s	1986	Autonomous part of the Netherlands	Caribbean	800	189,474 (1993)
Bonaire					288	10,187
Curaçao					444	144,097
Saba					13	1,130
St Eustatius					21	1,839
Sint-Maarten					34	32,221
NEW ZEALAND						
Cook Islands	1901	1965	Free Association	Pacific Ocean	237	18,500 (1994)
Niue	1900	1974	Dependency	Pacific Ocean	263	2,321 (1994)
Ross Dependency	1923	1923	Dependency	Antarctica	450,000	No permanent population
Tokelau	1926	1948	Dependency	Pacific Ocean	10	1,507 (1996)
PORTUGAL						
Azores	1450s	1980	Autonomous region	North Atlantic	2,330	237,800 (1991)
Macao	1557	1976	'Chinese territory under Portuguese administration'	East Asia	19	395,304 (1993)
Madeira	1420	1978	Autonomous region	North Atlantic	794	253,400 (1991)
SPAIN[10]						
Canary Islands	1476	1978	Autonomous community	North Atlantic	7,273	1,493,784 (1991)
Ceuta	1500s	1977	Autonomous community	North Africa	18	71,926 (1994)
Melilla	1500s	1977	Autonomous community	North Africa	14	62,569 (1991)

American Samoa	1899	1948	Unincorporated territory	Pacific Ocean	195	53,000 (1993)
Guam	1898	1950	Unincorporated territory	Pacific Ocean	549	152,695 (1995)
Johnston Atoll	1856	–	Unincorporated territory	Pacific Ocean	3	No permanent population
Northern Mariana Islands	1944	1986	Commonwealth	Pacific Ocean	464	59,000 (1994)
Puerto Rico	1898	1952	Commonwealth	Caribbean	8,959	3,685,000 (1994)
United States Virgin Islands	1917	1954	Unincorporated territory	Caribbean	347	101,809 (1990)

Notes:

1. The overseas territories in this table are listed according to the administrative units into which they are organised. The table does not include territories in the immediate offshore region of their metropoles, e.g. Corsica for France, the Åland Islands for Finland, and the Chatham and Kermadec Islands for New Zealand. Similarly it does not include Northern Ireland for the United Kingdom, or the Balearic Islands, which are part of Spain.

2. Date at which settlement or political sovereignty was established.

3. Most recent constitution or legislative act defining the territory's relationship with the metropole.

4. A *département d'outre-mer* (DOM) is constitutionally and legislatively fully part of the French Republic with the same regulations, in general, as the metropolitan *départements*. A *territoire d'outre-mer* (TOM) is covered by individual statutes and has a greater degree of administrative autonomy. The *collectivités territoriales* ('territorial collectivities') have a mixed system resembling both the DOMs and TOMs.

5. The territorial claims of France, Britain and Norway in Antarctica, like those of other claimants, are not universally recognised. The exact polar limits of Norway's claim have never been precisely defined. The French Austral islands are Saint-Paul, Nouvelle-Amsterdam, Kerguelen and Crozet; the French region of Antarctica is known as Terre Adélie.

6. Administratively attached to the TOM of French Polynesia is the uninhabited island of Clipperton in the eastern Pacific.

7. The dependencies of Guadeloupe are the neighbouring islands of Marie-Galante, La Désirade and Les Saintes, as well as Saint-Barthélemy and the French zone of St Martin, further north in the Caribbean.

8. The major dependencies of New Caledonia are the Loyalty Islands and the Isle of Pines.

9. Administratively attached to the DOM of Réunion are the Iles Eparses in the Mozambique Channel and Tromelin reef in the Indian Ocean; none has a permanent population.

10. The Spanish territories in North Africa also include several islands: Peñon de Alhucemas (366 residents), Peñon de la Gomera (450 residents) and Chafarinas (610 residents).

11. The territory is composed of the Chagos archipelago (which includes the atoll of Diego Garcia). Diego Garcia is leased to the United States as a military base. The original population was relocated to Mauritius in the 1970s, and the atoll's population is now made up of US military personnel.

12. Constitutionally, Jersey, Guernsey (including Alderney) and Sark are separate entities.

13. The United States also claims possession of several tiny reefs and atolls in the Pacific Ocean (Baker and Howland Islands, Jarvis Island, Kingman Reef, Midway Island, Wake and Palmyra Islands). None has a permanent population.

Source: Brian Hunter (ed.), *The Statesman's Year-Book* (London, 1996); *The Europa World Year Book 1996* (London, 1996).

CHAPTER 2

Constitutional Issues

The question of status – the exact constitutional relationship between an overseas territory and the metropole – is one of the keys to politics and development in the territories. In states governed by due process of law and administration and obliged to adhere to a constitution, judicial precedent and parliamentary legislation, the precise nature of a territory's status is crucial. It determines the legal personality of the territory, and opens or closes the door to social services, right of abode in the metropole, and financial subsidies. Status questions animate political life in some territories; in a few, practically every election is a plebiscite on status and every political forum a chance to debate the issue.

Options for changing status range from total integration to outright separation between overseas territories and administering states. Yet the choice is never so simple as those polarities, and many proposals advanced in recent years have outlined intermediate statuses between the two extremes. The exact nature of these – questions of citizenship, division of authority between national and local administrations, drawing of boundaries and definition of electorates, access to government transfers and social services – is both a highly complex legal and constitutional problem, and an issue filled with major political and economic repercussions. The case of the United States Virgin Islands (USVI) illustrates some of the options.

In the 1980s, officials in the USVI began the first serious discussions on a revised constitutional status for the islands, an 'unincorporated territory' of the United States. The local legislature appointed a commission to propose various options for submission to the electorate in a referendum. After several years, the panel set out three broad alternatives to be put to a vote in 1989; each broad category contained several more specific statutory arrangements, which citizens would consider once a majority had decided on the general direction of the territory's legal evolution. The three possibilities were:

1. complete integration into the United States through accession to statehood or by becoming an incorporated territory;
2. continued or enhanced territorial status through a compact of federal relations, the adoption of legislation making the USVI a commonwealth or the continuation of the status quo, with the islands remaining an unincorporated territory; or
3. withdrawal of United States sovereignty, with the USVI gaining complete independence or retaining ties with Washington through a treaty of free association.[1]

Another option not suggested to voters, for the simple reason that it would have been inconceivable in the USVI, was incorporation into a different state than the one to which it was currently affiliated. (Yet for other overseas territories, this is a real possibility, and for the two on which international arrangements have been concluded – the retrocession of Hong Kong and Macao to China – it is, barring unforeseen developments, a certainty.) A final possibility which was not suggested would have been the creation of a multi-state federation, perhaps a union of several territories sharing a common heritage and located in relative proximity. Efforts by colonial powers to form such unions, including British attempts to set up a West Indian Federation, however, were unsuccessful and, despite many links between the USVI and neighbouring islands, a new confederation would be highly unlikely.

The status options put forward for the Virgin Islands, though not exhaustive, indicate the varieties of relationships which are most probable between an overseas territory and a metropolitan state. The number of options points to the intricacies of constitutional and international law and the arcane nature of choices proposed to the electorate; the status commission in the USVI grouped some seven specific options into three broad categories precisely because it feared voters would have difficulty in understanding nuances between alternatives if confronted with such a range of choices. The commission also mounted a voter education campaign to explain the different alternatives and their potential impact. At least two of the choices, if adopted and approved by the US Congress, would be irreversible. Statehood would mean permanent integration into the United States – the only attempt at secession by American states resulted in civil war in the 1860s – whilst independence is a status which no sovereign state has voluntarily abandoned. Even options between these extremes would bring substantial changes in justice, representation in Congress, taxation and social services. Voters' choices, moreover, would amount to a statement of local identity and 'national' sentiment.

The referendum, finally held in the USVI in October 1993, produced straightforward results: an overwhelming 80 per cent of voters favoured retention of the Virgin Islands' status as an 'unincorporated territory' of the United States, a modest 14 per cent preferred statehood, and just under 5 per cent opted for independence. Ironically, however, only 27 per cent of registered voters went to the polls; since the rules of the referendum required a 50 per cent turnout for it to be valid, the results were technically invalid. The low turnout suggested that only one-quarter of Virgin Islanders were troubled by status issues, and only one-fifth of these wanted any major change. Moves for either statehood or independence, or indeed any dramatic revision in the constitutional status, consequently appear unlikely in the near future.[2]

Referenda have been organised in other overseas outposts, for example, in New Caledonia in 1986 and 1988, in Curaçao in 1993, in Christmas Island, Puerto Rico and the four smallest islands of the Netherlands Antilles in 1994 and in Bermuda in 1995. In 1998 voters of New Caledonia should again go to the ballot boxes to consider a revision of their constitutional status. By contrast, lack of opportunities to express an opinion on status has been a sore point in some territories. The decision to conduct a vote on status is a major step that not all wish to take: retaining the status quo seems the least troublesome alternative and ensures some degree of stability. Referenda themselves necessitate difficult decisions, such as on the composition of the electorate. In the case of the USVI, for example, no one contested the right of voters born in the islands to cast a ballot, but some queried those of the numerous Virgin Islanders residing on the American mainland, mainlanders living in the islands and other immigrants from nearby islands. In the case of New Caledonia in the 1980s, the question was whether only the indigenous Melanesian population should decide the future of the territory; or whether residents of European, Asian and Polynesian origin living in the territory – who, in total, outnumber Melanesians – should vote, and if so, how long they should have resided there to be eligible. Whether a local vote could and should be accepted by the metropole without the consent of the metropole's parliament or national electorate is another issue.[3]

Theories of Political Relations

The various options suggested by the USVI commission reflect different concepts about the organisation of the nation-state. For overseas territories, these ideas mirror varying views about the relationship between the metropole and its peripheral regions, between 'mother country' and 'colonies', between federal and regional governments, between majorities and minorities in the body politic. These views emerged during the heyday of imperial rule.

The British imperial tradition was historically one of gradual accession to responsible government then self-government for its settler dominions in Canada, Australia, New Zealand and South Africa; the incorporation of native elites into the administration under the guardianship of British officials, as occurred in India; or more direct rule, as was the case for the African and insular colonies. Self-government implied the election of local assemblies and control over colonial budgets and administration. It evolved into independence, although sometimes the exact date of independence is not easily identified, and London has retained vestigial symbolic or real powers in many former colonies.[4] Colonialists saw settler colonies as outposts of Britain overseas, bound to the British isles by ties of blood, politics and trade, but never envisaged the complete integration of colonies with the metropole. Nor did they allow the colonies parliamentary representation in London, though the Houses of Parliament enacted laws for the colonies. The British trained local administrators and supported the emergence of indigenous elites, but colonial theorists in Britain seldom thought that they were thus producing black or brown Britons; white 'colonials' might govern themselves but London would keep a guiding hand on administration. After the Second World War, British leaders accepted the devolution of administration to non-settler colonies as well, although within fairly narrow limits. Self-government became the goal, even when the authorities thought it lay far in the future.

A different strand of thought was represented by two French policies, although neither was uniformly applied. Since the French Revolution, France has been governed as a centralised state. The ideals of 1789 mandated a constitution and code of laws which treated France as a unitary and egalitarian whole, a state in which regional or provincial powers were severely curbed. The carving of France into *départements*, each administered by a prefect appointed by Paris, was meant to assure centralised uniformity; by tradition, the prefect was not from the *département* administered, a practice intended to ensure neutrality. Local councils were set up but enjoyed strictly limited powers, and their decisions had to be submitted to the prefect for approval.

This system was extended from metropolitan France to the empire. Colonial governors were proconsuls, their powers hardly tempered by consultative councils, and ultimately decision-making rested with Paris. Nevertheless, as France reorganised its empire after 1945, overseas territories were given representation in the national parliament with *députés* and senators chosen by electoral colleges or popular suffrage. The supposition was that such participation allowed the colonies a role in national politics, and representatives of the overseas domains had a voice in France's highest legislative bodies. The extension of the right to elect *députés* and senators in French territories in Africa, Asia and the Pacific islands followed the precedent of elected representatives from the *vieilles colonies*, Martinique, Guadeloupe, Guyane and Réunion, which have sent representatives to the national parliament since 1848. In 1946 these *vieilles colonies* became French *départements*, with administrative structures, laws and financial and monetary systems, in principle, identical to those of the metropole. (In practice, substantial disparities occurred, a point of contention for both advocates and opponents of *départementalisation*.) Such a degree of political integration was unusual, if not unthinkable, in other colonial systems; yet it corresponded to French ideas of the 'assimilation' of at least the 'evolved' populations of overseas domains, who, through acquisition of French language and culture, and after a suitable political apprenticeship, could be as French as their lighter-skinned European compatriots.

The ideals of both British self-government and French assimilation were often honoured in the breach in the age of empire, as London and Paris intervened in overseas domains as they thought fit, often using heavy-handed tactics. The margins of manoeuvre for colonial authorities depended on the goodwill of national governments to allow them degrees of autonomy. Rarely was self-government total (nor was it meant to be); areas such as defence and foreign policy were always excluded from local control. Moreover, only the elite of the colonies – usually European settlers – had any real political power. Few 'natives' sat on consultative or legislative councils, and few policy-makers believed that the masses of non-Europeans should play more than a token role in political life.

Imperial policy underwent various changes over the course of European expansion, and ideas of self-government, albeit in attenuated form, ultimately influenced French policy. Only in the 1980s, however, were they implemented and then somewhat selectively in the DOM-TOMs, where they provided a hitherto unfamiliar degree of autonomy. The British kept substantial control over their dependencies through appointed governors (who possessed important reserve powers) and ex-officio members of local assemblies.

The policies of the other powers exhibited variants of these traditions. Spain and Portugal accorded parliamentary representation to some of their colonies, whilst the power of often authoritarian governors and strong central governments (especially during the period of Franco in Spain and Salazar in Portugal) restricted local autonomy. The constitution and federal structure of the United States, by contrast, allowed considerable autonomy to local governments but restricted representation in the Congress. Denmark and the Netherlands, like other colonial powers, shifted from direct rule towards self-government for dependencies. Australia and New Zealand, which inherited their colonies from Britain, experimented with a range of alternatives.

Contemporary differences in theory and practice are apparent in the territories in terms of parliamentary representation. France's DOMs and TOMs enjoy full representation in both houses of the French parliament. The US overseas territories are represented only in the lower chamber of Congress, the House of Representatives, where their delegates can vote solely in committees and not in plenary sessions. The Spanish enclaves in North Africa, as well as the Canary Islands, the Portuguese islands of the Azores and Madeira, and the Danish territories, all have elected representatives in the national parliament, but also have strong, and largely autonomous, local governments. The British dependencies, by contrast, send no MPs to Westminster, nor are the New Zealand external territories represented in the parliament in Wellington; Macao does not elect a deputy to the Portuguese parliament. The Australian external territories, except for Norfolk Island, are incorporated into mainland electorates for electing members of parliament. The Dutch territories are represented in The Hague by official ministers plenipotentiary, who have the right to meet with the Council of Ministers on issues concerning Aruba and the Netherland Antilles; the Faeroes and Greenland are also officially represented in Copenhagen though their commissioners do not possess the privileges of their West Indian counterparts in the Netherlands.[5]

Legal Questions

Differences in political representation provide examples of the practical effects of legal and constitutional issues.[6] Such considerations are of great concern to residents of overseas territories, often much more so than in the metropole, although they occasionally inflame public debate in the metropole itself.

A primary question is that of citizenship. Countries determine this in various ways – the fact of being born in a country or of having a parent with that country's citizenship usually, but certainly not always, confers citizenship. Territories demonstrate the anomalies of citizenship. The United Kingdom recognises different categories. Those born in Great Britain are citizens; although the Channel Islands and Isle of Man are not technically part of the United Kingdom, their residents carry British passports and enjoy rights of British citizenship, including the right of abode, but not the right to elect members of parliament. Those born in the territories (or the children of residents there), however, do not enjoy all citizenship privileges, and most significantly, the right to live permanently in Britain. Britain tightened its nationality laws during the 1980s, a time of economic stringency, to limit the number of citizens of Commonwealth countries or Crown colonies and other dependencies who might claim such a right. This was of grave concern as Britain prepared to cede Hong Kong to China and feared that many of its six million residents would prefer to migrate to Britain rather than live under the rule of Beijing. The dependencies' residents, therefore, were given only a second-class form of citizenship (with, symbolically, a different British Dependent Territories passport). Exceptions were made, however, for the British subjects of Gibraltar and the Falkland Islands, the principal territories with primarily European populations, and those which have been the most politically contested; their residents maintain full citizenship status and right of abode. St Helena has been the most forthright of all dependent territories in arguing its claims to British citizenship, stating that its early fortress rationale made it an integral part of the United Kingdom as did the British identity of its settlers. A local commission on citizenship in the early 1990s argued that the United Kingdom was the only member of the European Union to deny full citizenship to overseas territories.[7]

Residents of most overseas territories, other than the British ones, are entitled to full citizenship and the same passport as those of their mainland compatriots. This is true of the citizens of US external territories, the Spanish North African *presidios*, and the overseas territories of Denmark, Australia, New Zealand and the Netherlands. (However, American Samoans are 'nationals' rather than citizens of the United States.) This does not mean, however, that they necessarily have full voting rights; residents of the US territories do not vote in presidential elections or all Congressional elections. An exception is Macao, not all of whose residents are Portuguese citizens. Nevertheless, Portugal has granted full citizenship and right of abode in Portugal to large groups of public servants and other residents (unlike the British in Hong Kong). In principle, some 100,000 residents of Macao thus have the right to migrate to Portugal before or after the retrocession of the territory in 1999. Yet China's attitude to Macao residents who hold Portuguese identity papers after Beijing's takeover in 1999 is uncertain.

Full citizenship does confer the much valued right of abode in the mainland or in other territories. This may be of little significance for residents of especially remote territories but has held considerable interest for residents of the French and Dutch Antilles and of Réunion, migrants from which are numerous in France and the Netherlands. It is even more significant for the large numbers of American Samoans who live on the US mainland, and for Niueans and Tokelauans, the majority of whom live in New Zealand. There are also substantial numbers of Azoreans and Madeirans in mainland Portugal, Canary Islanders and natives of Ceuta and Melilla in Spain, and, to a lesser extent, Greenlanders and Faeroe Islanders in Denmark. Migration between territories is less common, since the advantages are usually fewer, but there has been large-scale migration from Wallis and Futuna to New Caledonia, from St Helena to Ascension and the Falkland Islands, and from the smaller Netherlands Antilles into Sint-Maarten.

Financial benefits represent another aspect of status which enters into discussions over constitutional arrangements. In general, fully integrated territories – such as the French DOMs, the Spanish autonomous communities and the Portuguese autonomous regions – are subject to the taxes that apply in the metropole, whilst unincorporated territories, such as the French TOMs and the British dependencies, are exempt from certain taxes, especially a national income tax. (In the case of Puerto Rico and the US Virgin Islands, citizens pay income tax but the totality of revenue is returned to the territorial treasury.) In some territories, such as Puerto Rico, the Netherlands Antilles and Gibraltar, business taxes are substantially lower than in the metropole, a situation designed to encourage investment and employment. Several overseas territories – the USVI, both the Dutch and French sides of St Martin, Ceuta and Melilla, the Canary Islands and Gibraltar – are duty-free ports, an enticement to tourists and shoppers from nearby countries, and so collect few customs revenues.

Social welfare payments and similar services are also partially determined on the basis of status. They are usually lower in the territories than in the metropole; even in the French DOMs – despite their constitutional parity with metropolitan *départements* – the minimum wage is 10 per cent below that of the metropole. Welfare payments are lower in the US territories than on the US mainland, but a far greater proportion of the population receives such payments. Most territories have specific public welfare regimes which differ from those of the metropole.

Status is therefore a determinant in such benefits as citizenship, right of abode, tax and social welfare payments, but it is not a guarantee of privileges. Even supposedly complete integration with the metropole, as the case of the DOMs shows, does not provide absolute equality with such national standards as the minimum wage. Attachment to a metropole does not always secure the right to full voting rights or political representation, nor does it always entitle a citizen to reside there. Full integration may make certain financial and welfare concessions difficult to justify, although it may result in an increase in other payments. This question arose during the referenda in Puerto Rico and the Virgin Islands. If they became states, they would lose particular tax exemptions, and the national treasury would appropriate their federal income tax revenues; however, with statehood, citizens could argue through the courts and Congress that they had a legal right to the minimum wages and welfare payments of other states.

Unless independence occurs, status issues in the territories are never fully resolved. Statutes can be revised, negotiations reopened, referenda reversed, governments removed from office. As the cases of New Caledonia and the Netherlands Antilles, in particular, have shown over the last ten years, local inhabitants may regularly request that statutes be amended and regulations modified to correct perceived deficiencies or provide greater benefits. Continued demands for a variety of changes in the statute of French Polynesia, after a major overhaul in 1984 and amendments in 1990, led the French president to comment that Paris would not consider a perpetual round of changes just because of unresolved local grievances. Nevertheless, changes in the composition of local and national governments, and the vagaries of international affairs, prompt unending discussion about status revision; such debates can be acrimonious where no effective consensus about the future exists or where the metropole refuses to accept certain demands. Continued disagreement about status – and the continuing militancy of groups which adopt different status options as the basis of their platforms – is likely to endure.

Law and Administration

The French DOM-TOMs

The French outre-mer is divided into four départements d'outre-mer – Martinique, Guadeloupe, Guyane and Réunion – and four territoires d'outre-mer – New Caledonia, French Polynesia, Wallis and Futuna, and the Terres Australes et Antarctiques (TAAF). The two other outposts are Saint-Pierre-et-Miquelon and Mayotte, which are collectivités territoriales, a hybrid status.[8] The crucial difference is that DOMs are, in principle, identical to metropolitan départements, whereas each of the TOMs has a specific, and different, statute which varies from those of the DOMs.[9]

The vieilles colonies, those remaining from France's first overseas empire in the West Indies and Indian Ocean, became départements d'outre-mer in 1946. The move to obtain such a status, spearheaded by leftist parliamentary representatives, aimed to secure for the colonies political equality with other French départements and thus allow them to accede to the numerous economic and financial benefits of post-war planning, economic stimulus and social services. Départementalisation was also seen as a way of curbing the power of local elites, a measure of democratisation which would benefit the masses of largely poor voters. Politicians saw *départementalisation* as a recognition of political maturity and a mark of the 300-year-old ties which bound France with the West Indian islands, Réunion and Guyane. Combined with other measures, such as the abolition of Guyane's penal colony in 1945, *départemental-isation* represented the full entry of the DOMs into French life – a concession no other colonial power in the 1940s was willing to consider.

The DOMs have the same administrative structure as metropolitan *départements*. A prefect selected in Paris represents the national government and has responsibility for foreign relations, defence, law and order and the provision of national services. An elected *conseil général*, presided over by a president chosen from among its members, is the 'legislature' of the *département*. Its powers have expanded since the early 1980s, when the French government implemented a programme of administrative decentralisation; however, the powers of the *conseil général* are still less than those of a US state legislature or Australian state parliament. The *conseil général* holds responsibility for the local budget, many public works projects, certain economic initiatives, cultural activities and day-to-day administration. Furthermore, there is a *conseil régional* which covers the *département*, as a regional entity, in exactly the same way as the *conseil général*, although its members are elected in a different way. The division of responsibilities between the two councils is only vaguely defined, but, in principle, the *conseil régional* concerns itself with long-term projects of development and planning. Finally, there are elected municipal councils, each headed by a mayor. Local councils are often politicised and wield great power, since local government authorities are major employers and finance many development projects. The varying levels of authority do not always cohabit easily, yet they are interlocking. Most mayors serve on the departmental or regional *conseils* and some are *députés* in parliament; until a law in the late 1980s limited the number of offices a politician might hold concurrently, some individuals accumulated three or four mandates. Local office is a stage from which to put pressure on Paris (and the prefect who represents Paris) for changes in ordinances, increased subsidies or expanded services. Each DOM elects two senators to the French parliament, as well as a number of *députés* to the National Assembly according to the size of its population. They are elected in exactly the same manner as in metropolitan French *départements*. Such legislators participate in all parliamentary activities but, not surprisingly, also act as unofficial spokespersons and lobbyists for the DOMs.

In theory, metropolitan laws are extended in their entirety to the DOMs. Parliamentary legislation automatically applies there, though not in the TOMs, unless the parliamentary act specifically states the contrary. Systems of justice, education, and taxation are largely similar to those in the metropole, although judgements of France's constitutional court have permitted some divergences from national norms. The force of circumstance, and geographical distance, mean that the prefect and the presidents of the departmental and regional councils have a particularly high profile and assume certain powers, by law, custom or necessity, not exercised by their metropolitan counterparts.[10]

The degree of integration of the DOMs extends even to symbolic measures; none has its own currency, postage stamps or official flag. This appears of negligible importance to local residents, since the aim of *départementalisation* was to make the DOMs as much like the metropole as possible and thus to attract the benefits such status would provide. Anomalies between the DOMs and the metropole were (and still are) nevertheless often seen as a continued proof, or a threat, of second-class citizenship and 'colonial' treatment. There is a certain ambivalence about autonomy among politicians and administrators. Whilst many would like greater control of local affairs, and thus exemptions from certain ordinances, they generally reject any lack of uniformity which entails loss of benefits. Moreover, whilst a developing sense of cultural specificity is apparent in the DOMs, there is pride in access to the international culture provided by the French language and educational institutions.

Each TOM is governed according to a separate statute, and the underlying principle is that parliament must stipulate that general laws are applicable to the TOMs for them to be extended to the territories. The TOMs have somewhat different political administrations from the DOMs and the metropole, and they demonstrate several symbolic differences (such as the issuing of postage stamps).[11] More recently acquired by France, smaller, more distant, and in the colonial period considered to have populations less 'assimilated' and 'evolved' than the *vieilles colonies*, they retain many distinctive characteristics.

The TAAF, with no permanent population, is headed by an *Administrateur Supérieur*, based in Réunion, assisted by two advisory councils composed of bureaucrats and scientists. Administration of the territory, which covers a substantial slice of Antarctica and various sub-Antarctic islands, is relatively uncontroversial, although members of parliament, public interest groups and foreign governments have occasionally raised questions about French policy, such as the construction of an airstrip in Terre Adélie, the French sector of Antarctica.

The other three TOMs are located in the Pacific. Until the 1950s French Polynesia was administered by a governor, assisted by an elected council whose powers were largely consultative. In 1958, a referendum organised throughout the empire to approve the Constitution of the Fifth Republic gave French Polynesia, and other colonies, a choice of becoming *départements* or '*territoires d'outre-mer*' or of gaining independence. Although a Polynesian nationalist movement campaigned for separation from France, a large majority opted for continuity. The Territorial Assembly gained expanded powers in day-to-day administration, but decision-making remained with the retitled French representative, the *Haut-Commissaire de la République*. French Polynesians of different political orientations continued to demand greater autonomy, although for almost thirty years Paris refused to provide for decentralisation and self-government. Following the installation of a nuclear testing facility in French Polynesia in the early 1960s, Paris kept tight reins on the territory, especially as neighbouring governments in Oceania protested against the tests, other Pacific colonies gained independence, and new nationalist movements in the French territories called for independence there.[12]

In the 1980s the government of François Mitterrand agreed to greater administrative decentralisation, both in France and in the DOM-TOMs. A new statute legislated for French Polynesia in 1984 gave it a greater degree of self-government than any other French overseas territory. It confirmed earlier recognition of Tahitian as one of two official languages, and authorised a new territorial flag (which nevertheless always flies alongside the French Tricolour) – important symbolic gestures in the face of Polynesian nationalist claims. The law granted the Territorial Assembly power over most routine matters, although Paris and its resident high commissioner retained powers relating to defence, international relations, currency, the nuclear testing facility, and a considerable list of other areas. But the Assembly became more of a legislature, with power over disbursement of government revenue, public works, education and local government; it elects a president of the government, comparable to a prime minister in independent states, and a council of ministers with designated portfolios. Despite the flux of French Polynesian politics – marked by a changing constellation of coalitions grappling for power, vicious personal disputes, rampant clientelism and allegations of corruption – the statute assures French Polynesia considerable autonomy.[13]

In New Caledonia, political controversy, the militancy of a strong independence movement and the reaction of the 'loyalist' population of European ancestry provoked a rapid series of changes in the 1980s. Until that decade, New Caledonia, like French Polynesia, had been administered by an appointed high commissioner and an elected assembly with limited powers. In the early 1980s the Territorial Assembly and its head were accorded greater powers, but violence and a stand-off between *indépendantistes* and *anti-indépendantistes* prompted Paris to assume direct control of the territory. A series of different statutes then divided New Caledonia into regions with largely autonomous executives who dealt directly with the high commissioner; a renamed Territorial Congress was reduced to a nominal role. Yet the geographical boundaries of the regions were redrawn on several occasions with the blatant intention of reinforcing or minimising the powers of one or other of the two main factions. Finally, after considerable violence and many deaths, a compromise was reached in the Matignon Accord of 1988. New Caledonia was divided into three autonomous 'provinces', with elected councils and an executive responsible to the high commissioner. Meeting together, the three provincial councils constitute the Territorial Congress, though it lacks substantial power. The provincial councils remain the organs of elected power, but Paris still controls affairs in New Caledonia in a more direct way than in French Polynesia.[14]

Wallis and Futuna continues to be governed under a 1962 statute which made the islands a TOM. However, a unique system of power-sharing applies. A prefect exercises the powers of the French state, and there is an elected Territorial Assembly. The traditional king of Wallis, and the two kings of Futuna, nevertheless exercise much unofficial authority on issues of land use and Polynesian custom. Their role is recognised by the state, and they are paid a salary by Paris.

All three territories in Oceania elect *députés* and senators to the French parliament, although pro-independence movements in French Polynesia and New Caledonia have episodically boycotted elections. New Caledonia and French Polynesia, although not Wallis and Futuna, also have municipal councils. The situation is much the same in Saint-Pierre-et-Miquelon and Mayotte: a prefect presides over the government and represents the state but an elected assembly oversees much of the administration, and the powers of local officials have increased over the last decade. Both these *collectivités territoriales* are represented in the national parliament.[15]

Disparities between the TOMs and the metropole are significant. In New Caledonia, Wallis and Futuna and Mayotte, indigenous islanders can choose to be judged according to traditional law rather than French law in certain civil disputes (although not criminal cases). This is particularly important for the population of Mayotte, an overwhelmingly Islamic territory where polygamy is permissible. Other disparities in law, tax and military service are more easily accommodated by the much more flexible and variable French system in the TOMs than in the DOMs, constrained by their status to conform to the administrative regulation and structures of the metropole. Even among the TOMs, variations are considerable between French Polynesia and its largely autonomous government, New Caledonia, which is carved into provinces, and Wallis and Futuna, where three kings, a prefect and an elected assembly share power.

The French parliament alone can change the statute of the DOM-TOMs, and the president of the republic, without consent of local assemblies, can issue ordinances which have great import in the *outre-mer*. As the events in New Caledonia in the 1980s dramatically showed, Paris can intervene with formidable political, military and economic powers, and even assume direct rule, when it is deemed necessary. The parliamentarians and members of local bodies form a large group of elected officials with broad administrative powers and a base for lobbying the central government. According to French law, the councils in the DOMs can petition the National Assembly, which, in theory, is obliged to consult them on matters pertaining to their *départements*. Furthermore, the constitution gives the TOMs the right of independence, prescribing only that a majority of local residents must favour independence and that the French parliament must agree to the action. Yet, for a variety of political reasons, outright independence is improbable for the TOMs and even less likely for the DOMs.

The decades since 1945, and especially since the early 1980s, have seen a substantial devolution of power in the French *outre-mer*. There is now universal adult suffrage. Local governments have been granted greater administrative powers than ever before. But the DOM-TOMs do not enjoy sovereignty over domestic or external affairs. The metropole coordinates policy through a department for DOM-TOM affairs that has existed since the disbanding of the old colonial ministry, although its status (whether as a ministry or a lower-ranking secretariat of state) has varied. The duties of coordinating and regulating administration, finance and other areas have not altered. Nevertheless, other ministries and departments also play a role in DOM-TOM affairs.

The British Dependent Territories

Britain has never successfully undertaken a wholesale systematisation of territorial administration comparable to that of France. In the late 1940s the British government reviewed the future of small territories, and a report prepared in 1951 recommended that each should be given the status of 'Island and City State', which would allow considerable self-government within the Commonwealth. The proposal was greeted without enthusiasm by officials in London and the territories. In 1955 the Colonial Office suggested the creation of a 'statehood' status for the smaller territories to make them self-governing but not independent entities. No action was taken. Britain then toyed with the idea of creating federations of smaller territories (as had previously been undertaken – in much larger territories – with the self-governing federations of British colonies in Australia, Canada and South Africa). In 1958 a West Indian Federation of eleven territories was formed but, from the outset, suffered disunity and a lack of common interests among members. After four of the territories gained independence, the West Indian Federation became the Eastern Caribbean Federation, but faced the same obstacles and was abandoned in 1965. A conference convened by British authorities in the following year studied the possibilities of creating 'freely associated' states, and the next year saw a proposal for 'associated states'. Neither option was implemented, nor have there been subsequent efforts to harmonise administration, partly because of the assumption until the 1970s that all but the tiniest colonies would ultimately gain independence.[16]

Britain was confronted with the manifest desire of a number of dependencies not to become independent. The Cayman Islands had been part of the colony of Jamaica, but did not accompany Jamaica into independence in 1962. Nor did the Turks and Caicos Islands become independent along with the Bahamas, to which it was previously joined. Anguilla had been a part of the colony of St Kitts–Nevis, but when that colony moved towards independence in 1967, Anguilla's leaders, fearing domination by a distant island, unilaterally separated it from St Kitts–Nevis. After disturbances which necessitated sending in British police officers, Anguilla remained a British dependency. Such residual colonies had smaller elites, fewer national resources and less possibility of sustaining independence than larger outposts, a situation which helped thwart the desire of British leaders to complete the decolonisation process in the Caribbean (and possibly elsewhere) by the 1970s. By the 1980s – and in a change of heart not unconnected to both Conservative rule in Britain and the Falklands War – Britain seemed resigned to keeping its remaining dependencies. The under-secretary of state responsible for Caribbean affairs stated that Britain would remain aware 'of our commitment to the principle of self-determination and our determination to live up to our obligations under the United Nations charter, and our responsibilities for the good government and development of our dependent territories'. Nevertheless, he added: 'we should not seek in any way to influence opinion in the territories on the question of independence. We would not urge them to consider moving to independence, but we remain ready to respond positively when this is the clearly and constitutionally expressed wish of the people.'[17]

That statement symbolises a major difference between British and French attitudes. France argued that the DOM-TOMs were necessary to national security and status in world affairs and they provided advantages to the nation. The British seemingly accepted continued administration of at least some of their outposts as something of an obligation that they would shoulder, though without great enthusiasm or sense of national purpose. The French may have reluctantly granted independence to some of their outposts in the 1970s; the British rather reluctantly agreed to retain some of theirs. Moreover, the British have not claimed that any of their overseas outposts are constitutionally identical to an administrative entity of the British isles; there is no British equivalent of the French *départements d'outre-mer* (though the Isle of Man and Channel Islands come closest). In the mid-1950s, the government of the British colony of Malta expressed interest in full integration with Britain. A parliamentary round table considered a formal request from Malta's chief minister, which received a sympathetic hearing since Malta appeared so strategically important that it could be dangerous for British interests if it became independent. The round table recommended integration, with Malta receiving three seats in the House of Commons. In a referendum held in Malta in 1956, only a minority (albeit a substantial one) supported the plan; Maltese authorities lost interest, and Malta gained independence in 1964. The option of integration into the United Kingdom was never otherwise seriously considered by London, and Britain's overseas territories are not represented in the national parliament.

The legal instruments under which Britain's overseas territories are administered are their constitutions – in contrast to Britain itself, most have written constitutions – which are formulated and adopted as acts of parliament at Westminster and which receive the sovereign's assent. Only the British parliament has the right to amend or rewrite such constitutions. These constitutions date from various periods, and are constantly being reconsidered. Most have been revised since the 1960s, and also amended on various occasions. Bermuda's constitution of 1968, for instance, was amended in 1973 and 1979; the Cayman Islands' constitution of 1959 was revised in 1972, 1992 and 1994. The constitution of Gibraltar dates from 1969, the Turks and Caicos Islands' from 1976 (amended in 1988), and Montserrat's from 1989. The administrative structure of the British Indian Ocean Territory was established when that dependency was created (from islands previously attached to the Seychelles and Mauritius) in 1965, and a new administration was designed for South Georgia and the South Sandwich Islands when they were detached from the Falkland Islands in 1985. Something of an anomaly, the constitution of Pitcairn dates back as far as 1940. The Crown Dependencies (Fiefdoms) of the Channel Islands and the Isle of Man have laws and administrations inherited from the Middle Ages, yet

which can be changed only in certain circumstances by the British
parliament and government.[18]

The British sovereign is the head of state for each of the territories,
and her 'heirs and successors' automatically accede to that position. (In
the Isle of Man, the queen bears the official title Lord of Man.) The
queen is represented by a governor, appointed 'at the queen's pleasure'
(but generally for five years) by letters patent from the monarch on the
advice of the British and local governments. In the smallest outposts,
titles vary slightly. The queen's representative in Pitcairn is a commissioner, who since 1970 has been, ex officio, the British high commissioner in New Zealand. Few have ever visited Pitcairn. The governor of
the Falkland Islands is, ex officio, the commissioner for South Georgia
and the South Sandwich Islands. In Tristan da Cunha and Ascension,
which are technically 'dependencies' of St Helena, the British Antarctic
Territory and the British Indian Ocean Territory, the senior official is an
Administrator.

In the past, colonial governors were sometimes members of the royal
family or aristocrats. They are now almost always senior public servants,
although occasionally former political figures (such as the last governor
of Hong Kong, Chris Patten, former chair of the Conservative Party) are
appointed; the governor of Gibraltar has generally been a retired
military officer. Governors carry out the duties of the head of state. They
commission ministers, summon legislative assemblies, give their assent
to legislation, administer the public service and serve as commanders-
in-chief of local military units. As representatives of the Crown – occasionally wearing an official uniform and even a plumed helmet – they
also perform ceremonial functions.

Britain – nominally, the Crown; in reality, the British government; in
day-to-day practice, the governor – retains authority over crucial areas of
policy in the territories. International relations and defence are Crown
prerogatives, although local ministers are often delegated with authority
to represent territories at international conferences. Financial and
monetary policy generally fall under the authority of the Crown, which
in recent years, following a number of scandals linked to misuse of
funds, shady offshore banking, money-laundering and other allegations,
has tightened financial controls in the West Indies, sometimes transferring certain powers away from elected officials to the governor (as in
both Montserrat and the Turks and Caicos Islands). Matters relating to
immigration and emigration are usually the responsibility of Crown
officials who supervise distribution of the financial transfers which are
of great importance in smaller resource-poor territories. No written
agreements set out these relationships.

The governor presides over a consultative body, generally called the
Executive Council (although it is called the Gibraltar Council in that

territory, and the Senate in Bermuda). That body, in addition to the governor, usually consists of the deputy governor (where there is one), and several other ex-officio members, such as the attorney-general, financial secretary and chief secretary, and a varying number of nominated members selected by the territory's legislative body. (The Legislative Council of the Isle of Man includes the Lord Bishop of Sodor and Man.) The duty of the Executive Council is to advise the governor.

British colonies have traditionally had some sort of elected or appointed assembly – Bermuda prides itself on an assembly which first met in 1620. In the colonial period, officials and appointed members dominated such bodies, and elected members came largely from the expatriate European elite. In more recent times, they have been democratised, though only one is composed entirely of elected members. The names of the assemblies, the number of members, their terms of office and the extent of their powers vary. In Montserrat, for instance, the Legislative Council comprises twelve members: a speaker, two 'official' members (the attorney-general and the financial secretary), two nominated members and seven elected members. The Gibraltar House of Assembly includes a speaker appointed by the governor, four ex-officio members (including the governor and the attorney-general) and fifteen elected members. In the British Virgin Islands there is a Legislative Council of fifteen members, all elected except for the speaker and one ex-officio member. In the Falkland Islands Legislative Council there are two official and eight elected members, whilst in the Legislative Assembly of the Cayman Islands there are three official and fifteen elected members. The Island Council of Pitcairn comprises the island magistrate, five elected and three nominated members, and the island secretary. All forty members of Bermuda's House of Assembly, however, are elected. The lower house (the House of Keys) in the Isle of Man has twenty-four elected members. In the Channel Islands, particularly complicated systems of political representation have been inherited from the Middle Ages.[19]

All the territories, with the exception of some of the tiniest dependencies – St Helena, Tristan da Cunha, Ascension and Pitcairn, the BIOT, British Antarctic Territory, but also the Cayman Islands – have the equivalent to a prime minister in an independent country. The title, however, varies. Most often, the official is known as Chief Minister, although he or she bears the title Premier in Bermuda, Chief Executive of the Falkland Islands Government and Leader of Government Business in the Cayman Islands. Whatever the name, the chief elected official acts much as a prime minister, although with circumscribed powers. He or she is thus the head of government and leader of the majority in the assembly, with responsibility for day-to-day running of the territory. The division of authority between the governor and the chief minister (or equivalent official) is not always clear, and the personal views – and personalities – of the two officials often determine the level of cooperation or tension which exists between them.[20] Of all the metropolitan states, the diversity of colonial administrative structures is greatest for the United Kingdom, reflecting the number, and also the diverse geographies, histories, economies and societies, of the overseas territories, and of the intent that they develop their own particular political identities.

The British dependencies display not only significantly different forms of administration but varying degrees of political 'dependency' on Britain, although Britain can and does intervene in most of them, as in 1991 when the British parliament banned capital punishment in five Caribbean territories. (It has subsequently encouraged Bermuda to abolish capital punishment.) Of the northern Atlantic and Caribbean outposts, Bermuda is undoubtedly the least 'dependent'. A key distinguishing feature of Bermuda's constitution is 'the omission of any reserved right to the Crown to legislate for the peace, order and good government of the territory'.[21] Bermuda is the only territory with a premier, cabinet and bicameral legislature. Although the Senate is an appointed body, all members of the House of Assembly are elected. There are no ex-officio members of the cabinet, and the governor does not preside at cabinet meetings; the premier chooses the cabinet and retains the right to dismiss members. (The governor can, however, constitutionally act contrary to cabinet's advice.) Indeed, Bermuda is 'one step away' from full self-government, and British officials said in 1988 that there was no remaining possibility for further devolution of authority without a move towards independence. In the Caribbean, Montserrat is the least constitutionally 'dependent' of Britain's territories, followed by Anguilla and the British Virgin Islands. The Cayman Islands – which has no elected or appointed chief executive – is technically the most 'dependent'.[22] Among other British territories, the Falklands and Gibraltar enjoy a large measure of autonomy, though seemingly paradoxically their residents are the sole ones with right of abode in Britain. Pitcairn lives in a form of autonomy imposed by isolation.[23] The BIOT is, for practical purposes, under foreign administration, though not constitutionally so. Ascension and Tristan da Cunha, as well as South Georgia and the South Sandwich Islands, are doubly dependent, in that their administrations are legally subordinate to those of St Helena and the Falklands respectively.

Britain's policies in its empire (except for India) were traditionally coordinated by the Colonial Office, although by the 1960s the name 'colonial' seemed anachronistic. In 1966 the Colonial Office merged with the Commonwealth Relations Office to form the Commonwealth

Office, bringing Britain's dependent territories together with independent members of the Commonwealth under one umbrella. Two years later, that office merged with the Foreign Office to form the Foreign and Commonwealth Office. A Dependent Territories Division was responsible for Britain's overseas outposts, until it was disbanded in 1980, leaving the territories divided among six regional directorates.[24] The lack of a single government department to oversee the territories – any parallel to the French overseas ministry – itself indicates that the British, unlike the French, had no unified global view of their overseas territories and the way in which they ought to be administered.

The Territories of the United States

The United States exhibits a variety of constitutional and administrative structures in its overseas outposts.[25] Puerto Rico and the Northern Mariana Islands are Commonwealths of the United States; the Virgin Islands and Guam are 'organised', 'unincorporated' territories of the United States; and American Samoa is an 'unorganised' and 'unincorporated' territory.[26] The differences reflect the varying ways in which Washington acquired the territories, their population and size and the interests of US legislators. The United States acquired American Samoa in 1899 by cession from local chiefs and an agreement between the United States and Germany to divide the Samoan islands. Washington purchased the USVI, a former Danish colony, for $25 million in 1917. Puerto Rico and Guam came into US hands as booty after the Spanish–American War of 1898. The Northern Mariana Islands in Micronesia had been at various times a colony of Spain, Germany and Japan. After the Second World War, the United Nations gave Washington a mandate over the Trust Territory of the Pacific Islands (TTPI), which allowed the United States to administer the Marianas, as well as Palau, the Caroline Islands and the Marshall Islands, though without the United States being allowed to claim sovereignty over the archipelagos. By the 1970s all parties wished to wind up the Trust Territory, although various island groups preferred different options.

The basic legal and historical difference in American outposts has been between 'incorporated' and 'unincorporated' territories, although all current territories fall into the latter category. At the beginning of the twentieth century, federal courts, based on precedents of nineteenth-century mainland 'territories' that were later admitted to statehood, ruled that 'incorporated' territories were those which Congress intended eventually to become states. They were thus subject to the same laws, customs regime and administrative system as the US mainland. 'Unincorporated' territories were not necessarily destined for statehood, although that option was not ruled out; Puerto Rico was the obvious example, and questions about its import duties had provoked the court case. It has been assumed that a territory could become a state when it had a sufficient population, and the local electorate and federal Congress gave their approval. However, those territories outside the 'continental' United States, inhabited by quite different populations, were seldom seen in the same way as territories on the US mainland; Alaska and Hawaii, states since 1960, have been the only territories to gain statehood since New Mexico in 1912.

The constitutional history of Puerto Rico has passed through various stages since the island was taken over by the United States. The Foraker Act of 1900 placed Puerto Rico under the administration of a governor appointed by the president, an executive council in which the majority of members were American businessmen or civil servants, an elected House of Delegates and an elected Resident Commissioner who sat in the House of Representatives in Washington but had no vote. Any laws passed by the legislative assembly in Puerto Rico could be vetoed by the US Congress. In 1917 a Revised Organic Act conferred US citizenship on Puerto Ricans, proclaimed a bill of rights for the territory, and allowed members of the executive council to be elected rather than appointed. The next few decades saw increased activity by political parties in Puerto Rico, most of which advocated a closer, more democratic relationship with the United States. In a series of Congressional acts passed between 1950 and 1952, and approved by the island's population, Puerto Rico was made a Commonwealth of the United States.

The status of commonwealth, or *Estado Libre Asociado* (Freely Associated State) in Spanish, was agreed by all parties to be unique in US law. One resolution of the Constitutional Convention of Puerto Rico in 1952 defined it as 'a state which is free of superior authority in the management of its own local affairs'; another resolution stated 'that by the approval of a constitution we attain the goal of complete self-government'. The US government reported to the United Nations that 'Congress has agreed that Puerto Rico shall have . . . freedom from control or interference by the Congress in respect of internal government and administration' subject to compliance with the US Constitution and Congressional acts. The Puerto Rican governor, who had led the campaign for commonwealth status, concluded: 'There should be no doubt that all traces of colonialism have disappeared in Puerto Rico because this is a union by compact.'[27]

A number of judicial decisions have since defined the parameters of commonwealth status. The 1952 laws remain the legal framework under which Puerto Rico is governed, although some modifications have occurred, notably an act of Congress which changed the governorship from an appointed to an elected position. Puerto Ricans are US citizens with the right of residence anywhere in the United States; similarly, any American can move to Puerto Rico, open a business, buy property and, after a short period, register to vote. Puerto Ricans elect their own legislators and governor, as well as a Resident Commissioner in the House of Representatives. However, they cannot vote in presidential elections, and Americans who change their legal electoral residence to Puerto Rico thereby lose the right to vote in presidential elections. According to US legislative practice, all federal laws which do not specifically state the contrary are applicable in Puerto Rico. Federal authorities are responsible for defence, customs and immigration, currency matters and various other areas, just as for the mainland states. Nevertheless, Puerto Rico has a different system of taxation and social security payments from the fifty states. Labour in Puerto Rico is substantially cheaper than on the mainland, and tax and welfare concessions were designed to stimulate economic growth in an island where' the standard of living remains significantly lower than that on the mainland. Locally manufactured goods and agricultural products enter the US mainland without incurring customs duties.[28]

Political debate in Puerto Rico since the 1950s has centred on retention (or revision) of the commonwealth status, accession to full statehood or independence. Lack of consensus in both Puerto Rico and the mainland contributed to maintenance of the status quo. Most US presidents looked favourably on statehood for Puerto Rico but did little to achieve that outcome. Republican politicians were concerned about the votes their rivals would gain from resolutely Democratic Puerto Rico. Manufacturers and investors feared the loss of tax privileges which would cease with statehood. There was general concern with the cost that statehood would entail, as social service payments and other federal expenditures would attain higher national levels. Statehood advocates argued that integration would give Puerto Ricans full participation in national life and access to greater social security benefits. Commonwealth advocates claimed that the island would exchange present benefits for limited advantages. Pro-independence politicians charged that American companies were the prime beneficiaries from Puerto Rico's status, and that national identity, political integrity and economic emancipation demanded sovereignty.

Puerto Rico finally held a referendum on its status in November 1993; 48 per cent of the voters favoured the commonwealth status, 46 per cent preferred statehood, and a mere 4 per cent supported independence. The tiny proportion of votes for the independence option – in a record 80-per-cent turnout – made it unlikely that Puerto Rico could in the foreseeable future separate from the United States. Since the commonwealth alternative failed to win a majority of the votes, statehood supporters will probably continue campaigns for the complete integration of Puerto Rico into the United States.

The treaty which transferred the Virgin Islands from Denmark to the United States placed it under the control of the Department of the Navy; until 1931 naval officers were appointed by the president as governors. Under US sovereignty, as under Danish administration, the islands had two legislatures, one in St Thomas (which also covered St John), the other in St Croix. Electors were obliged to prove a property qualification. The question of whether Virgin Islanders were US citizens was left undecided until 1927, when they were formally granted US citizenship. In 1931, the president transferred the islands to the jurisdiction of the Department of the Interior and appointed the first civilian governor. Five years later Congress passed an Organic Act which instituted universal suffrage and extended the Bill of Rights to the islands. Island municipal councils were established, the three councils meeting together constituting a new unified legislature. The governor, still an appointed official, no longer had power to dissolve the assembly but could veto legislation; the veto could be overturned by a two-thirds vote in the assembly. Congress maintained a right of ultimate veto on legislative acts.

The Revised Organic Act of 1954, the basis for present-day relations between the USVI and the United States, defined the islands as an 'unincorporated territory' of the United States. It set up a unitary legislature to replace the municipal councils. (There is no municipal government or separate island government.) The act stipulated that the legislature could pass laws on 'all subjects of local application', although either the president or Congress could disallow legislation. A further change came in 1968, when Congress authorised Virgin Islanders to elect their own governor. Virgin Islanders do not vote in presidential elections but since 1972 have elected a delegate to the House of Representatives. Islanders are US citizens and can reside at will on the mainland or in other US territories.[29]

In the case of both Puerto Rico and the Virgin Islands, a number of matters which remain unclear are resolved by Congressional legislation or court judgement. Until an act of Congress has deemed it so, various portions of the US constitution and federal laws do not automatically apply in the Virgin Islands; until Congress so legislated, for instance, trial by jury was not an inherent right for accused persons in the territory. The federal government is responsible for areas over which it holds competence elsewhere in the United States, such as defence and taxation, and the Secretary of the Interior retains residual administrative rights in the USVI. Otherwise, there is considerable local autonomy, just as in the American states.

In the late nineteenth century, British, German and American missionary and trading interests established bases in the Samoan islands of Polynesia. American interests dominated in eastern Samoa, where chiefs ceded their lands to the United States in 1904. American Samoa became an unincorporated territory of the United States, which appointed a governor and set up a legislature; from 1978, the governor has been popularly elected. The legislature (*fono*) consists of an upper house, or Senate, of eighteen members elected by traditional chiefs (*matai*); women and commoners have no vote for the Senate. The House of Representatives is composed of twenty members chosen by universal suffrage. Since 1980 American Samoa has elected a delegate to the House of Representatives.

American Samoa is unique among US 'flag territories' in that it is both 'unincorporated' and 'unorganised': the US constitution applies only insofar as the Congress and courts determine, but also (in contrast to Puerto Rico and the USVI) no 'organic act' has been adopted by Congress to codify administration. It is the only US territory not formally integrated into the federal court system, and with a legislative chamber not elected by universal adult suffrage. Furthermore, its residents are US 'nationals', not citizens, though they may be naturalised if they migrate to the mainland, as many have done.

During the 1980s, moves were made to codify the status of American Samoa through a constitutional convention. A draft constitution was completed in 1986; although not officially approved by the US Congress, it was accepted by the Department of the Interior, which oversees territorial affairs. Samoan political leaders appear satisfied with the status of unincorporated territory, however, and there has been no concerted move towards statehood (which, in any case, would be unlikely to gain American support), commonwealth status or independence. Indeed at conferences of US overseas territories in 1993 and 1994, American Samoa was the only territory not preoccupied with status questions, despite the disparities which exist between the islands and the mainland.[30]

The United States has constitutional links with Guam and the Northern Mariana Islands in Micronesia. These islands became Spanish possessions in the 1500s; the Spanish colonial presence, except for Catholic missionaries, had most impact on Guam. In 1898, after the US victory in the Spanish–American War, Washington claimed Guam as war booty, and Spain sold the Northern Marianas (as well as Palau, the Marshalls and the Carolines) to Germany.

In 1950 Guam became an 'unincorporated territory' of the United States, but only after a walkout of members of the Guam House of Assembly in protest against the inadequacy of Guam's political status. The walkout, which also promoted US citizenship and civil government for the people of Guam, was the climax of half a century of Chamorro political resistance to naval rule.[31] The Department of the Interior subsequently held responsibility for the island and appointed its governor. Since 1970 the governor has been popularly elected, and from 1972, Guam has had a delegate (with limited voting rights) in the House of Representatives. In 1976 voters in a referendum in Guam opted for close ties with the United States. Seven years later, choosing among six proposed options, the largest number (though slightly less than a majority) favoured the status of commonwealth; however, little more than one-third of eligible voters had cast ballots. The US government did not act on the result. Voters provided similar support for a commonwealth option in 1987, but Washington again failed to change Guam's status, causing frustration in the island. The governor of Guam introduced himself at a 1993 conference in Washington:

> Good morning, everyone, I am Joseph F. Ada, the Governor of the American colony of Guam. . . . Today, I will not engage in the farce of calling Guam's status by other than its rightful name. . . . I will not engage in the deception of calling Guam an unincorporated territory. 'Unincorporated territory' is such a meaningless term because it can mean anything.

Ada went on to say that Guam is a colony because 'it is ultimately ruled by a government that we have no part in constituting' and which 'rules us without our consent', because Guamanians, though US citizens, cannot vote in presidential elections and have a representative with only limited voting rights in the House of Representatives and no senators. He asserted:

> The Federal government has unlimited power over us. . . . Tomorrow, if it chose to, the federal government could take away our civil rights, abolish our elected government, restore us to navy rule, even tear up our US passports and sell us, lock, stock, and barrel to another nation.[32]

Indeed no 'organic act' or similar legislation recognised by Congress ensures Guamanians control over their island or systematically divides powers between federal and local authorities, and Guamanians play no electoral role in selecting the federal government. Nevertheless, Guam is administered by an elected governor and a unicameral legislature of twenty-one members.

Though Guam has been a US outpost since the end of the nineteenth century, other islands in Micronesia did not come under US administration until nearly fifty years later. In 1914 Japan captured German possessions in Micronesia and administered them, from 1921, under a mandate from the League of Nations. During the Second World War US forces captured and occupied the islands. In 1947 the Northern Marianas came under US-administered TTPI; in 1975 it voted to become a Commonwealth of the United States, choosing a status similar to that of Puerto Rico. A constitution approved in 1977 provided self-government, but commonwealth status did not formally take effect until 1986. The Northern Marianas have a popularly elected governor and lieutenant-governor, and an elected bicameral legislature.[33]

US overseas territories have certain administrative similarities, whatever their exact constitutional status. Each has a significant measure of self-government under an elected governor and legislature. Most have constitutions, although the US Congress retains ultimate legislative power. Each has restricted representation in the lower house of Congress, but no representation in the Senate. Residents cannot vote in presidential elections unless they establish residence on the mainland. Local laws in the territories show a number of particularities, but there is a right of appeal to US federal courts and the Supreme Court. Residents of the unincorporated territories and commonwealths are (except for American Samoans) full citizens; all have the right of abode elsewhere in the United States and its territories. Their status provides various – and often beneficial – tax concessions and trading privileges with the United States which would probably be incompatible with statehood and would be lost with independence. The status quo in the overseas territories does not attract universal support, but in 1993 and 1994, respectively, the majority of voters in the USVI and Puerto Rico favoured their current statuses, and no appreciable moves in the Northern Marianas or American Samoa have sought to change the situation.[34] Only in Guam do political leaders press for a change; most favour the establishment of a commonwealth.

The Dutch Islands

The overseas outposts of the Netherlands are six islands in the West Indies – the Leeward Islands of Saba, St Eustatius (Statia) and the Dutch part of Sint-Maarten, and the southern islands of Aruba, Bonaire and Curaçao.[35] The considerable distance between the two groups and differences in size – Curaçao has 144,000 inhabitants, Saba little more than a thousand – partly account for both the difficulties in administering the territories and contemporary divergent responses to 'colonial' rule. Until 1936 the possessions were ruled directly by a governor, appointed by The Hague and responsible to the Dutch Crown and government. The governor of Curaçao, as the entire set of islands was then called, was assisted by an appointed consultative council. Lack of possibilities for political participation sparked the rise of political

sentiment, as did the central role of Curaçao, whose dominance was
resented elsewhere – particularly in Aruba, despite, or perhaps because
of, its proximity. Legislation in 1936 permitted the election of two-thirds
of the members of the Colonial Council and authorised the governor to
issue orders on his own initiative without reference to The Hague. This,
however, only aggravated reformist sentiment, as critics maintained that
the non-elected governor held near-dictatorial powers.

Politicians in general sought a greater voice in local government and,
especially in Aruba and Sint-Maarten, greater autonomy from Curaçao.
During the inter-war period some considered more radical changes; in
the 1920s Sint-Maarten politicians requested the United States to assume
control over the island, whilst a prominent Curaçao politician suggested
that the group become a province of the Netherlands. By the 1940s the
islands had an increased economic role through oil refining in Aruba
and Curaçao. During the Second World War, islanders actually sent food
parcels to the Netherlands, and the Dutch queen announced in a
wartime radio broadcast that it would befit the islands to have greater
autonomy after the war. In 1945 the first of a series of commissions to
study the question of the Netherlands Antilles – as the 'Curaçao' colony
was renamed – was set up; it adopted the principles of self-rule in
internal matters and increased participation in Dutch politics. Yet a
delegation of Antillean politicians went to the Netherlands and warned
of the danger that the entire group would separate from the Netherlands. Their statement was repudiated at home, and the Dutch government, embroiled in the Indonesian war of independence, was not
moved to draw up a new statute.

During the next few years, discussions on self-determination and
decentralisation were almost continuous. The Dutch reported to the
United Nations in 1950 that the Netherlands Antilles was not a colony.
In 1951 a Dutch court ruled that the islands should be given autonomy,
and the negotiations produced a 'Charter of the Kingdom', adopted in
1954. It made the Netherlands, the Netherlands Antilles and Surinam
(or Dutch Guyana, then a possession in South America) equal and
autonomous parts of the Kingdom of the Netherlands, bound to render
mutual aid and assistance but enjoying decentralised government. Only
those domains which were explicitly designated as joint areas of
concern, such as defence and international relations, were handled
exclusively by The Hague. Island councils and a central parliament,
elected by universal suffrage and based on proportional representation
for each island, were set up. The governor of the Netherlands Antilles
and the Crown's representatives on each island continued to be
appointed officials. The Netherlands Antilles was represented in The
Hague by a minister plenipotentiary, who had the right to meet formally

with the Council of Ministers when matters concerning the islands were under consideration.

The 1954 charter seemed a welcome compromise to all parties. Antilleans were now Dutch citizens with unrestricted right of abode in the Netherlands. Though without representation in the Dutch parliament, they sent an official delegate to The Hague. They enjoyed home rule under a prime minister selected by due parliamentary process, and there were regular elections in which all could vote. The Netherlands provided substantial aid to supplement local sources of finance, but otherwise assumed a low profile in the West Indies.

In the 1960s discontent revived, partly activated by the decolonisation sweeping other colonies. Leaders sought expanded powers, and a greater role in international affairs. Antilleans in the southern 'ABC' islands – Aruba, Bonaire, Curaçao – also wanted more official use and teaching of Papiamento, the local lingua franca, and a greater proportion of local people in the public service. In 1969, a labour dispute degenerated into serious riots in Curaçao; The Hague sent Dutch troops to the island, an action hotly resented by local residents, who considered this an unacceptable intervention in local affairs. In 1970 another commission convened to consider alternatives to the status quo. Among other options discussed were a British-style commonwealth, the special constitutional arrangement between the Channel Islands and the United Kingdom, and the French precedent of *départementalisation*. Some political figures demanded outright independence, although a 1974 opinion poll found that only one-fifth of the population preferred such an alternative. The situation of the islands thus differed from the Dutch colony of Surinam, which gained independence in 1975, though rapid economic decline, and the later installation of a military dictatorship, served as a warning about the dangers of ill-prepared secession.

Nevertheless, Aruba – and, to a lesser extent, Bonaire and Sint-Maarten – chafed under the rule of the central government in Curaçao. Aruban politicians, who felt that their interests seldom received just due from the central government in Willemstad, more interested in the island of Curaçao than in the Netherlands Antilles as a whole, demanded a separate status in the kingdom. Claims for a direct relationship with The Hague had been voiced in Aruba since the 1920s, but the Dutch government reluctantly agreed to the break-up of the 'Antilles of Six' only in 1984. The Dutch accorded Aruba a separate statute (*status aparte*), which took effect in 1986; Aruba would thenceforth have its own prime minister and parliament, currency and flag. The Kingdom of the Netherlands, since the independence of Surinam, had been a compact of only two nations; it once again became a kingdom of three parts: the Netherlands itself, Aruba, and the 'Antilles of Five'. Aruba was also set, with Dutch encouragement, to gain independence in 1996; although Aruban officials had hardly been adamant about outright independence, the Dutch wanted independence to signal that further autonomy or fragmentation in the Antilles would have a cost.

Autonomy in Aruba unsettled the Dutch islands. Several politicians in Sint-Maarten soon called for a separate, direct relationship between that territory and The Hague. Claude Wathey, the longtime leader of Sint-Maarten's major political party, in 1988 said he wanted Dutch Sint-Maarten to become independent, a stand which failed to win the support of his own party. Some politicians in Bonaire meanwhile suggested that their island should become a fully-fledged province of the Netherlands. The tiny islands of Saba and St Eustatius, though sometimes dissatisfied with administrative dependency on Sint-Maarten – each had a lieutenant-governor and island council but only a limited separate administration – proclaimed loyalty to Holland. The prime minister of the Netherlands Antilles strove to keep the group of five together, but also made ambiguous statements concerning eventual independence. Meanwhile, by the end of the 1980s, it became clear that the majority of Arubans opposed independence in 1996, and some local figures argued that it would be a violation of the right of self-determination contained in the 1954 charter if The Hague forced the island into independence – a neat reversal of usual arguments about decolonisation.[36]

The Dutch were manifestly disconcerted by these demands. By the early 1990s, the minister responsible for the islands discreetly said that the Netherlands would not force Aruba to accept independence, and in 1994 Dutch and Aruban authorities formally agreed to abandon the move to independence, though not ruling it out for some later date. The Dutch government said that it would be willing to agree to a new administrative arrangement whereby Curaçao and Bonaire would share a central government, and Sint-Maarten, St Eustatius and Saba would also share a separate administration; like that of Aruba, each would maintain certain direct links with The Hague. The Dutch government resolutely refused, however, a structure in which each of the five islands had its own government and a 'direct line' to the Netherlands, despite some demands to this effect in Bonaire and reservations in the two smallest islands about being ever more closely tied to Sint-Maarten. The minister replied that all three smaller islands lacked the population and infrastructure for separate status, and that the Dutch would not accept the complete fragmentation of the Antilles simply because of the precedent of *status aparte* accorded to Aruba.

The situation became further complicated in 1992 when the Dutch government decided to exercise stronger supervision over the island council of Sint-Maarten. Faced with allegations of mismanagement, corruption and financial irregularities, The Hague dispatched bureaucrats to verify budgets, administrative procedures and government conduct, and put the island on 'constitutional hold'. Wathey was jailed for eighteen months for fraud, forgery and perjury. Islanders baulked at this so-called 'higher supervision' as a reassertion of metropolitan control, and some spoke of 'recolonisation' of the Netherlands Antilles. Others suggested that the Dutch government was simply concerned about financial irregularities, and had decided to 'straighten things out' in the West Indies. The move, in a similar if much less dramatic fashion than the dispatch of troops to Curaçao in 1969, gave evidence of the powers of the metropole to intervene, just as discussions about further fragmentation in the 'Antilles of Five' showed that ultimate decisions on status are made in the metropole, despite the large degree of self-government which characterises the Netherlands Antilles.[37]

In October 1994 a referendum was held on the future of the four smallest islands: Bonaire, Saba, St Eustatius and Sint-Maarten. Voters were offered four options: independence; independence in association with the Netherlands (*status aparte*, as had previously been chosen by Aruba in 1986); transformation into a province of the Netherlands; or continued membership of the Antillean federation. Exactly the same issues had been voted on in Curaçao a year earlier, where a surprisingly high 73 per cent of voters sought to keep the federation intact, 18 per cent wanted secession from the other islands, 8 per cent wanted to be a province of the Netherlands, and a mere 1 per cent chose independence. In the smaller islands the vote favoured the status quo even more strongly – 91 per cent on St Eustatius, 88 per cent on Bonaire, 86 per cent on Saba – but support was 60 per cent in Sint-Maarten, where 39 per cent sought autonomy (*status aparte*). Only in Sint-Maarten was there even slight support for independence.

The case of the Netherlands Antilles represents an unusual variation on the phenomenon of decolonisation. The metropole was willing to grant independence to Aruba, yet local sentiment has been markedly opposed to it; a poll in 1985 showed that only 10 per cent of the population in Aruba, and 12 per cent in Curaçao, favoured independence. The islands' leaders were more frustrated with the central government in Willemstad than the Dutch government in The Hague. That frustration arose partly because most good jobs, investments and political appointments accrued to Curaçao – the 'capital' island. Aruba resented what was perceived as the burden of its tax profits being drained to Curaçao, although, ironically, Aruba gained *status aparte* in 1986 just when its oil refineries closed and revenues plunged. Sint-Maarten, by contrast, became restive in the 1980s, as its tourist industry grew rapidly, and it was obliged to pay increased taxes to the central government in Curacao. The larger islands also felt that they were required to support the smaller islands. The 'problem' in the Dutch outposts was not so much one of nationalist sentiment, and demands for either greater incorporation or independence; rather, the conflicts were about the organisation of the administration and centralisation at the level of local government which controlled geographically separate, economically different and historically distinct islands.

Denmark, the Faeroes and Greenland

Having sold its Virgin Islands colony to the United States during the First World War, Denmark was left with two overseas outposts, the Faeroe (or Faroe) Islands and Greenland. Since the Second World War, both have been granted self-government and, of all overseas territories, enjoy the greatest autonomy.

The Faeroe Islands, a Danish possession since the late fourteenth century, was administered as a Danish county until 1948. The Home Rule Act of the Faeroe Islands, passed by the Danish parliament in that year, made the islands 'a self-governing community within the State of Denmark'. It set up a legislative assembly (the *Løgting*); twenty-seven members are elected from seven constituencies; as many as five extra members may be appointed to rectify disparities between the popular vote and the distribution of seats by electoral district. The act also established an executive for the Faeroes, a government (*Landsstyri*) headed by a president (*Lagmand*) and five ministers. It gave Faeroese full Danish citizenship and the right to elect two members to the Danish national parliament (the *Folketing*). A high commissioner (*Rigsombudsmand*) represents the central government in the Faeroes, and Faeroese affairs come under the prime minister's office in Copenhagen.

Copenhagen transferred a number of affairs to the Faeroese Home Rule government in 1948 or subsequently, including local administration, public works, health, taxation, education, cultural affairs, and agriculture. However, it specified that the Faeroese authorities would have to assume financial responsibility for any matters over which they took control. Matters which were not specified in the act, such as the judiciary and police, as well as foreign affairs and defence, were reserved to national authorities. Nevertheless, the Danish government created a post for an adviser on Faeroese affairs in the Ministry of Foreign Affairs, and gave the Faeroes the right to station experts on business matters at Danish overseas legations where their interests might be of concern. Danish legislation relating exclusively to the Faeroes must be submitted to the Home Rule government for consideration before it is tabled in the Folketing, and other legislation must be put before the Faeroes government before it comes into force in the islands. In matters where the division of responsibility is unclear, a joint committee of Faeroese and Danish officials (joined by three High Court judges if necessary) resolves disputes.[38]

Greenland, like the Faeroes, traditionally came under the direct rule of a governor appointed by Copenhagen. Municipal elections, first held in the 1850s, marked the entry of Greenlanders into Danish politics. In 1911 the Danish government established two regional councils (merged into one council in 1950) with limited powers. In the 1940s, Copenhagen informed the United Nations that Greenland remained a non-self-governing territory. A new Danish constitution in 1953, however, gave Greenland full status as a region of Denmark and extended Danish citizenship to all Greenlanders; Greenland was given two seats in the Folketing and, in 1955, a Ministry of Greenland was established.

In the early 1970s Greenland politicians pressed for greater autonomy, especially as Denmark prepared to enter the European Community, a move which Greenlanders opposed because of fears about the potential effects of EC regulations on fishing. After several years of negotiation, the parliament passed a Greenland Home Rule Act in 1978. Of the almost two-thirds of eligible voters who participated in a referendum, 70 per cent voted in favour of Home Rule, whilst 26 per cent opposed it. Coming into effect the following year, the Home Rule Act recognised 'the exceptional position which Greenland occupies within the Realm nationally, culturally and geographically' and acknowledged that 'Greenland is a distinct community within the Kingdom of Denmark'. Modelled on the Faeroes Home Rule, it set up a Greenland legislature (*Landsting*), with twenty-three members elected by proportional voting in eight constituencies, plus as many as three extra members appointed, as in the case of the Faeroes, to rectify differences between the popular vote and proportional representation. There is an executive (*Landstyre*), headed by a chairman, generally known as the prime minister, and seven ministers.

The Home Rule government in Greenland assumed control over, and financed, a range of affairs similar to that in the Faeroes, whilst Danish national authorities retained control of constitutional matters, foreign relations, national finances and defence. A high commissioner represents the national government in Greenland's capital, Nuuk. Greenland's authorities have the right to examine Danish parliamentary bills concerning the island. Disputes between Copenhagen and Nuuk are resolved by a joint committee, which can call on High Court judges to arbitrate. A specific section of the Home Rule Act addressed the delicate question of natural resources and affirmed that 'the resident population of Greenland has fundamental rights to the natural resources of Greenland'. A joint council of Danish and Greenlandic authorities, established in 1979, makes policy for prospecting and exploitation of minerals and oil; the Greenland and Danish governments each have a veto over major decisions.

Since the establishment of Home Rule, the Danish national government has transferred a considerable number of matters to the Greenland government, including education, transport, telecommunications and electricity. In 1987, the Ministry of Greenland was disbanded, and the prime minister's office took over remaining administrative responsibilities. Greenland decided to withdraw from full membership in the European Community in 1985; it now has associated membership as one of a number of Overseas Countries and Territories.[39]

Portugal, Macao and the Atlantic Islands

In the colonial period the Portuguese state consisted of mainland Portugal, 'insular' Portugal (the islands of the Azores and Madeira), and Portuguese overseas colonies. In the mid-1970s Portugal retained the largest number of continental colonies of any European power, as well as various islands: Angola, Mozambique and Guinea-Bissau in Africa, Cape Verde and São Tomé and Principe off the African coast, Macao and East Timor in Asia. The dictatorial governments of Prime Ministers Salazar and Caetano were regularly accused of unrepentant colonialism, and militant independence movements were active in several colonies. Indeed, conflict over Portuguese opposition to a guerilla movement in Angola – which had produced episodes of violent protest and political crackdowns in Portugal itself – played a crucial role in bringing about the 'revolution of the carnations' in Lisbon in 1974 and the end of the authoritarian governments which had ruled since the 1920s. Portugal moved quickly to withdraw from its remaining colonies other than Macao, where China opposed withdrawal because of the destabilising effects it might produce on neighbouring Hong Kong. Decolonisation, however, did not bring peace and prosperity; civil war raged in Angola and Mozambique, Indonesia invaded and annexed East Timor, and the other African colonies fell prey to poverty and strong-arm rule.[40]

The revolution produced a democratisation of Portuguese life and inspired animated political debate; its effects were felt on 'insular' Portugal. The Azores and Madeira had been Portuguese outposts since the early fifteenth century; previously uninhabited, the islands had a population of entirely Portuguese descent. The islands had been important stopping-off points for ships and aeroplanes travelling from Europe to the Americas, and produced a variety of agricultural products, the best-known of which was the wine of Madeira. They remained poor, however, and massive migration to the United States (especially New England and Hawaii), mainland Portugal, Bermuda and other destinations had taken place. Political activity was greatly curbed under the Salazar and Caetano regimes; a very brief period of autonomy occurred in 1930 when an 'Atlantic Republic' survived in the Azores and Madeira for several weeks. The liberalisation of politics in the mid-1970s permitted a flourishing of dissident opinion in the islands.

In 1976 the Portuguese parliament adopted a new constitution, which also applied to the islands, where separate statutes were subsequently adopted. The Azores and Madeira are 'autonomous regions' of the Republic of Portugal. The second article of the 1980 Azorean statute says: 'The political, administrative and economic autonomy of the Region of the Azores does not affect the integrity of the sovereignty of the State.' It adds: 'The autonomy of the Region of the Azores aims at the democratic participation of its citizens, the economic development and social integration of the Archipelago, and the promotion of the defence of the values and interests of its people, as well as the reinforcement of national unity and the solidarity ties among all Portuguese people.' The status of Madeira is couched in similar terms.[41] The Azores and Madeira each have a Regional Legislative Assembly of elected members and a Regional Government. The president of the Regional Government and its ministers are appointed by a resident Minister of the Republic, who represents the Portuguese national government in each island group. Islanders also elect deputies to the parliament in Lisbon. The 'autonomous regions' have their own flags, coats of arms, seals and anthems. Residents are Portuguese citizens.

The Portuguese first established a settlement in Macao (Macau) in the mid-sixteenth century; not until 1783, however, did Portugal claim sovereignty over Macao, which was ruled as a Portuguese province from 1951 until the revolution of 1974. Two years later an Organic Statute turned Macao into a 'special territory', which remains the context under which Macao is administered. It granted autonomy to the territory in almost all matters except defence and foreign policy, which remain the responsibility of the Portuguese president. The president appoints the governor of Macao, the territory's chief executive, after consultation with the territory's Legislative Assembly. The governor serves at the president's pleasure and is responsible to him. The governor is assisted by several appointed under-secretaries responsible for such portfolios as economy and finance, transport and public works, and public services.

Most of the senior public servants are Portuguese expatriates, though the 1990s have seen a greater effort to 'localise' administration by appointment of ethnically Chinese public servants. A Consultative Council of elected and appointed members advises the governor.

The Legislative Assembly is composed of twenty-three deputies (*deputados*); seven are nominated by the governor, eight are chosen by direct universal suffrage, and eight are elected by various economic, cultural and welfare organisations. Macao has no political parties; civic associations and 'candidate committees' nominate candidates for election. All persons over the age of eighteen who carry a government-issued identity card (whether of Chinese, Portuguese or other nationality) are eligible to vote, as are Macao-born residents of Hong Kong. Since 1990, the assembly has chosen its own president. There is, however, no equivalent of a prime minister. The Legislative Assembly debates in both Chinese and Portuguese; laws and other official documents have traditionally been written in Portuguese, but are now published in Chinese as well. In addition to the assembly, there are two municipal councils, one for Macao itself (dating back to 1583) and one for Taipa and Coloane islands. Macao has an independent judiciary, and appeals can be made to higher courts in Portugal.[42]

In 1986 and 1987, Portugal and China held negotiations which resulted in an agreement for Portugal to retrocede Macao to China on 20 December 1999. As was the case with Hong Kong, Macao will become a 'special administrative region' of China, and Beijing has promised to maintain its economic and social structures for a fifty-year period after takeover.[43]

Spain, Ceuta and Melilla, and the Canary Islands

Spain was once master of an enormous empire, but it lost most of its American colonies in the early 1800s, and defeat in the Spanish–American War in 1898 deprived it of the Philippines, Cuba, Puerto Rico and a number of Micronesian islands. Only a few small outposts in Africa remained, and an attempt to carve out a larger empire in the Maghreb in the early twentieth century proved short-lived. Spain retained only Equatorial Guinea in sub-Saharan Africa, the Rio de Oro on the north-western coast of Africa, and several enclaves in Morocco. It granted independence to Equatorial Guinea in 1968 and withdrew from the Rio de Oro after the end of Franco's rule in 1975.

Meanwhile, the democratisation of Spain led to the creation of 'autonomous communities' with regional governments and legislative bodies. Such a measure of decentralisation represented a response to long-standing grievances of Catalans, Basques and other groups which had bitterly resented the authoritarian centralism of the Falangist regime since the late 1930s. Provisions of the 1978 constitution gave varying degrees of self-government to different regions, including the Canary and Balearic Islands, but did not include Spain's remaining North African enclaves, Ceuta and Melilla, among the new autonomous communities.

Ceuta and Melilla are fortified enclaves (*plazas de soberanía*) over which Spain claims full sovereign rights. (Spanish sovereignty, however, has regularly been contested by Morocco.[44]) Each had a municipal council and mayor, but from 1981 onwards local residents demanded greater autonomy. In 1985 Madrid approved plans for the creation of local assemblies with control over agriculture, tourism, local trade and public works, but with less legislative autonomy than accorded to mainland regions. This sparked protests by *Ceutís* and *Melillenses* on several occasions during the following years, including a general strike in Melilla in 1992. Negotiations on administrative arrangements for the cities dragged on, aggravated by disagreements between local politicians and national leaders, and between Spain's two major political parties. There was also controversy about the status of Muslims, many of them illegal migrants from Morocco.

In late 1994 the Spanish parliament (Cortes) adopted Statutes of Autonomy for Ceuta and Melilla which made each an 'autonomous community' in the Spanish kingdom. Unlike other regions in Spain, each 'autonomous community' comprises only one municipality. The new Legislative Councils for Ceuta and Melilla superseded the former municipal councils. The first elections to the 25-member councils were held in May 1995, and the autonomous governments of Ceuta and Melilla, each headed by a president, were subsequently constituted. In addition, Ceuta and Melilla each elect one deputy to the lower house and two senators to the upper house of the Cortes. A delegate (*Delegado del Gobierno*) represents the national government in each city, and a commandant-general has responsibility for the large military bases in the territories.[45] Such arrangements brought Ceuta and Melilla into line with Spain's other autonomous communities. The Canary Islands, also an offshore autonomous community, is composed of two provinces, Santa Cruz de Tenerife and Las Palmas. The autonomous community has an elected Legislative Council and government, which exercises a considerable degree of self-government on such matters as finances, public works and day-to-day administration. Responsibility for other areas, such as international affairs and defence, remains with the national government.

Australia's External Territories

The complex administrative structure of Australia's external territories mirrors their tangled colonial history. Christmas Island in the Indian Ocean was taken over by Britain and attached to the Straits Settlements, British outposts in Malaysia, in 1889, then later ruled as part of the colony of Singapore; in 1958, Britain transferred sovereignty over Christmas Island to Australia, after several requests from Australia. The uninhabited Cocos (Keeling) Islands, also situated in the Indian Ocean, were settled by a British citizen, John Clunies-Ross, in 1826. Britain annexed the islands in 1857 but gave Clunies-Ross title to the entire land area. The Cocos (Keeling) Islands was placed under the control of the British colony of Ceylon in 1878, was transferred to the Straits Settlements in 1886, to Singapore in 1903, and to Australia in 1955. In 1947, Britain ceded its claims on the uninhabited sub-Antarctic Heard and McDonald islands to Australia. The Australian Antarctic Territory was established in 1933. North of Australia, the uninhabited Ashmore and Cartier Islands in the Timor Sea were annexed by Britain in 1878 and 1909, respectively, and transferred to Australia in 1931. Australia claimed sovereignty over the Coral Sea Islands Territory, also uninhabited atolls, in 1969. Norfolk Island in the South Pacific was taken over by Britain in 1788, the same year as the British settled New South Wales, and was then administered at various times as part of New South Wales, Van Diemen's Land (Tasmania), or as a separate colony. In 1914, Norfolk Island became a separate territory of the Commonwealth of Australia.

Federal laws passed by the Australian parliament automatically apply only in the territory of Ashmore and Cartier Islands, whilst they must be officially extended to the other territories, usually by provisions contained in the acts themselves. Laws of the Northern Territory nominally apply in Ashmore and Cartier Islands, those of the Australian Capital Territory in the Coral Sea Islands Territory. The legal system in the Indian Ocean territories was highly confusing, and many anomalies have existed; in Christmas Island, for instance, there was no trial by jury in criminal cases until 1987. There and in the Cocos (Keeling) Islands, laws of the old British colony of Singapore had remained in effect, as did Australian parliamentary acts extended to the islands, ordinances made by the Australian governor-general and, in some cases, British laws of the 1820s. In 1992, in an effort to simplify legal regimes, the laws of the state of Western Australia were made applicable in the islands.

Norfolk Island has its own legislative assembly, which passes laws for that island, although some Australian parliamentary acts, ordinances proclaimed by the governor-general and various English statutes remain part of the island's body of law. An act passed by the Australian parliament in 1979 clarified the administration of Norfolk Island. An Administrator, appointed by the Australian government, is the senior official of the Commonwealth of Australia on the island and must give assent to legislation passed by the Legislative Assembly. The assembly is composed of nine members elected by island residents (those who have established legal right of residence, usually after three years on the island). It has plenary powers to legislate – 'to make laws for the peace, order and good government of the Territory', according to the 1979 legislation – and raise revenue; the Norfolk Island assembly cannot authorise maintenance of defence forces or the coining of money. International relations, defence, monetary policy and customs remain the province of Commonwealth authorities. A special parliamentary statute, slightly different from that of the Commonwealth, covers matters relating to immigration. Norfolk Islanders are Australian citizens with right of abode on the mainland. Settlement on the island, except for a short period, however, is highly restricted for non-islanders (including other Australian citizens). There is no Norfolk Island representation in either house of the Australian parliament; island residents may voluntarily enrol to vote in a mainland federal electoral district where they have a 'community of interest', or in the Australian Capital Territory.

The senior Australian representative in the Cocos (Keeling) Islands has borne the title of Administrator since 1975. In 1977 the Australian government purchased almost all of the land and other interests belonging to the Clunies-Ross family for $A6.5 million. Two years later it established the Cocos (Keeling) Islands Council. In 1984, in a referendum under UN supervision to determine the future of the islands, 90 per cent of the votes favoured integration with Australia. The islands thus officially became part of the Commonwealth, and islanders acquired full Australian citizenship. In 1992 the Islands Council was transformed into an elected Shire Council (modelled on local government in Western Australia). Islanders cast ballots in federal elections in a constituency in Western Australia.

Legal authority in Christmas Island also resides with an appointed Administrator and an elected Shire Council constituted in its present form in 1992. The laws of Western Australia apply in Christmas Island, although the island forms part of the Northern Territory seat in the national parliament. In 1994, an informal referendum was held in conjunction with local elections; more than 80 per cent of voters favoured greater local government control, but there was no support for secession from Australia. Migration, residency and citizenship requirements in Christmas Island, as in the Cocos (Keeling) Islands, are the same as on the Australian mainland.[46]

New Zealand Associated Territories

New Zealand's associated territories are the Polynesian island groups of
Tokelau and Niue, as well as the Cook Islands, which is linked to New
Zealand by a treaty of free association. Britain established a protectorate
over the three Tokelau atolls in 1877; New Zealand assumed administration in 1926 and sovereignty in 1949. The territory is now the
responsibility of the NZ Ministry of Foreign Affairs and Trade, which
appoints a non-resident Administrator. Day-to-day administration is in
the hands of an Official Secretary who, until 1993, was located in an
Office for Tokelau Affairs in Apia, Western Samoa; the office has since
been moved to Tokelau. New Zealand is responsible for international
relations, defence, monetary and financial policy, and many other areas
of administration for the tiny, resource-poor and isolated islands.

Each of the three atolls, which are largely autonomous in local affairs,
has a Council of Elders (*Taupulega*) formed by the heads of family
groups, although the qualifications differ between atolls. Two other
members are elected by universal suffrage: the *Faipule* (the presiding
officer, who represents the atoll in its relations with New Zealand) and
the *Pulenuku* (a official similar to a mayor, who looks after village affairs).
Fifteen members from each *Taupulega* meet together as Tokelau's
general assembly (*Fono*), which is chaired by the three *Faipule*, one of
whom is elected for a one-year term as the Head of Tokelau (*Ulu-O-
Tokelau*). The Ulu is Tokelau's de facto prime minister, and the three
island leaders act as unofficial cabinet members. The *Fono* is required to
inform the New Zealand government about any matter 'with international implications', or which requires the 'approval or the assistance
of the New Zealand Government'. Under a parliamentary act adopted
in 1992, the New Zealand administration can delegate all or part of its
powers to the *Fono* or the *Faipule*, although the Administrator had the
right to intervene in local affairs 'should the need arise'. During regular
consultations with the United Nations Special Committee on Decolonisation in the 1970s and 1980s, Tokelauans expressed satisfaction with the
political status quo. In 1994 they advised a new mission that they were
ready to assume greater self-reliance or, in the words of the 1996 New
Zealand Tokelau Amendment Bill, Tokelau wished 'to paddle its canoe
to the greatest extent possible . . . to come together and become
stronger, on the basis of their shared language and culture, as one family
and nation'. The 1996 bill gives the *Fono*, for the first time, the right to
pass legislation. It is anticipated that the next stage of political evolution
will be a referendum to choose the nation's new political status, and
probably confirm self-government in free association with New
Zealand.[47] Evolution may be slow because, although the three atolls

share customs and language, there has been no tradition of political unity, and rivalry between them has often been bitter.

The Cook Islands became a British protectorate in 1888 and was transferred to New Zealand in 1901. In 1965, it became a self-governing territory in free association with New Zealand; the relationship is regarded as a 'partnership' from which each partner can withdraw at any time. The constitution gives the Cook Islands the right to move to full independence at any time by a unilateral decision of the islanders. Cook Islanders have NZ citizenship and two-thirds live overseas, mainly in New Zealand. New Zealand takes official charge of the territory's defence but, since 1992, 'all legislative and executive powers, whether in the fields of defence, external affairs or any other, are vested exclusively in the Government of the Cook Islands'. In 1995 the Cook Islands government sought, through negotiation with New Zealand, to gain membership of the Commonwealth and the United Nations, and to obtain separate passports and separate diplomatic accreditation, but none of these goals was achieved. The head of state is the British sovereign, who names a queen's representative in the islands; the New Zealand government appoints a high commissioner. The 25-member parliament includes one member elected by islanders resident outside the country. There is also an advisory council of up to fifteen hereditary chiefs (House of Ariki). The head of government bears the title of prime minister, and several members of the legislature hold ministerial portfolios.[48]

Niue was placed under British protection in 1900, annexed by New Zealand as part of the Cook Islands territory in 1901, and then separated from the Cook Islands four years later. In 1974 it attained 'self-government in free association with New Zealand'. Since 1993 it has been emphasised that New Zealand's responsibility for external affairs and defence 'do not confer on the New Zealand government any rights of control'. There is a New Zealand high commissioner on the island. An elected assembly (*Fono Ekepule*) is composed of twenty members: fourteen village representatives and six members elected from a common roll. A cabinet comprises the premier and several other ministers. Niueans are New Zealand citizens; indeed, about five times as many reside in New Zealand as on the island itself.[49]

Dependent Territories and Regional Cooperation

The various overseas territories associated with Britain, France, the United States, the Netherlands, Denmark, Portugal, Spain, Australia and New Zealand show a wide variety of administrative and constitutional arrangements. They experience (and desire) different degrees of autonomy. Their systems of government are modelled on those of the metropole. All, however, are – to different degrees – constitutionally dependent on the outside governments or legislatures, which have the right to change their systems of government, alter their laws, appoint at least some of their officials, intervene in their internal affairs and contract international treaties on their behalf. None displays the level of servitude of 'classical' colonies, yet none claims the outright sovereignty associated with independent nation-states.

Dependent status brings with it a number of advantages, but it sometimes places territories in an ambiguous constitutional position. Politicians and jurists argue over the division of authority between local and national governments. Central governments grant greater autonomy to territories but then – as evidenced by 'higher supervision' of the Netherlands Antilles or British intervention in Pitcairn and the Turks and Caicos Islands – are able and willing to rein in local authorities who exceed their powers or engage in questionable conduct.

The anomalous position of overseas territories can be clearly seen in terms of their international legal situation and their participation (or lack of it) in international agencies. For instance, dependent territories in Oceania have little voice in the most significant regional organisation, the Forum Secretariat, which convenes regular meetings of heads of governments of independent states to discuss issues of regional cooperation and development. New Caledonia, Wallis and Futuna, and French Polynesia are excluded from membership, as are Norfolk Island, Pitcairn, American Samoa, Tokelau, Guam and the Northern Marianas, but Niue and the Cook Islands are members. By contrast, both independent states and the dependent territories (except, now, Norfolk Island) are represented in the South Pacific Commission, set up by colonial powers in 1947 as an advisory and consultative body to aid member states in development and regional coordination.

In the Indian Ocean, France was a major force behind the establishment of the Indian Ocean Commission, the members of which are France (representing Réunion), the Comoros, Madagascar, Mauritius and the Seychelles; the BIOT is not represented, and because of conflict between France and the Comoros, Mayotte is not separately represented. However, neither France and Britain, nor Réunion and the BIOT, were included among participants in conferences of Indian Ocean states held in Mauritius in 1994 and Australia the following year. In the West Indies, the overseas *départements* of France did not take part in the American Caribbean Basin Initiative programme of the Reagan administration. In the Caribbean Community and Common Market (CARICOM), the BVI and Turks and Caicos Islands are associate members, and Anguilla, Aruba, Bermuda, the Cayman Islands, the Netherlands Antilles and

Puerto Rico have observer status. Martinique, Guadeloupe, Montserrat and the USVI are not represented. France, Britain and the Netherlands are not members of the Organisation of American States, despite their sovereign territories in the West Indies and, in the case of Guyane, on the South American continent. Both Greenland and the Faeroe Islands are represented in the Nordic Council.

Dependent status thus sometimes implies a reduced official role for local governments in international relations. Overseas territories are not eligible for membership in the United Nations unless they are considered independent nations which have established covenants of free association with other nations. Thus, the Federated States of Micronesia has a seat at the United Nations, but the Commonwealth of the Northern Marianas and the Cook Islands do not. Niue is a member of both UNESCO and WHO, but when it sought to be a full member of the Asian Development Bank in 1996, the United States opposed this, arguing that it should be represented by New Zealand. The rather larger Cook Islands is a member of four UN agencies, including the Food and Agriculture Organisation and the International Civil Aviation Organisation, and has signed various multilateral treaties (mainly relating to environmental matters) and more than twenty bilateral treaties or agreements, to the extent that 'the Cook Islands membership in these UN agencies, and the international agreements it has entered into constitutes recognition of the Cook Islands nationhood by virtually every nation in the world community'.[50]

'Belonging to' another nation can create close links with other international bodies, however. The British territories are part of the Commonwealth, although they have no separate representation at the Commonwealth Heads of Government summit meetings. The French DOMs are fully integrated into the European Union (formerly, Community), whilst most of the other Overseas Countries and Territories – the nomenclature used by the European Union – are associate members and have access to development funding and preferential trading access. The populations of the French DOM-TOMs vote in elections for members of the European parliament; voter turnout, however, is generally very low. The confusion which the particular statuses of overseas territories can produce is evident in the links between the British Crown dependency of Jersey to the European Union. According to the chief adviser to the Jersey government:

> For the purposes of trade in goods the Island is 'within the community', for the movement of people, the common travel area arrangement with the United Kingdom provides for free movement between the Island and the United Kingdom but otherwise the free movement of persons between the Island and the Community is not provided for under the Protocol; for fiscal

and other measures such as the freedom of establishment and free trade in services the Island is treated by the Community as a 'third country'; for the free movement of capital the Island is also 'outside' the Community but these provisions are enjoyed by the Island because of monetary union with the United Kingdom.[51]

Such situations show the anomalous, but often significant, positions of territories in a world increasingly marked by moves towards regional collaboration. Yet that very collaboration inevitably blurs the boundaries between independent states and the dependent overseas territories.

Between Integration and Independence

The years since the Second World War, which have seen the decolonisation of most of the overseas empires, have witnessed remarkable constitutional and legal changes in the 'confetti of empire', partly as a response to decolonisation elsewhere but particularly as local populations claimed new rights. The *départementalisation* of the *vieilles colonies* of France in 1946 represented one response, that of wholesale integration. The Faeroes Home Rule statute of 1948, the Commonwealth statutes for Puerto Rico passed in 1950–52, official designation of the USVI as an 'unincorporated territory' of the United States in 1954, a new organic law for the Netherlands Antilles in 1954, and the acceptance of statutes of *territoires d'outre-mer* in France in 1958 – all these represented early attempts to find intermediate alternatives between integration and independence.

In most cases ministers and elected assemblies replaced appointed governors and privy councils, or at least shared power with prefects or appointed governors. Control of internal affairs and the budget came to be accepted as the brief of local governments. Universal suffrage has been established. By the 1980s, even the DOMs of France, the model for full integration in a centralised state, began to achieve greater autonomy, as did French Polynesia. Substantial decentralisation had already occurred in the mid-1970s for the insular regions of Portugal and Spain (and was extended to Ceuta and Melilla two decades later). However, greater autonomy in some cases sparked campaigns for independence, as happened in New Caledonia, or led to a fragmentation of island federations, as in the Netherlands Antilles. Continued demands for modification of statutes occurred almost everywhere, although occasionally metropolitan governments set limits to change. Examples are France's refusal to tamper continually with the statute of French Polynesia, and to 'departmentalise' Mayotte; the Netherlands' unwillingness to grant *status aparte* to each of its West Indian islands; and Britain's assertion that self-government could go no further in the Turks and

Caicos Islands and Bermuda without independence. Less frequently, metropolitan changes – notably the end of authoritarian regimes in Spain and Portugal – rather than local pressures promoted changes in the periphery.

Metropolitan governments and local political forces sometimes clashed on questions of status, as in episodes of violence in Anguilla in 1967, in Curaçao in 1969 and in Ceuta and Melilla in the 1980s. The French territories were particularly beset by unrest, including episodic pro-independence protests in Guadeloupe, Réunion and Guyane since the 1970s, a prolonged and bloody conflict between pro- and anti-independence groups in New Caledonia in the mid-1980s, and upheaval in Tahiti in 1987 and 1995. Yet in other situations, there was agreement on the terms of referenda; in these cases – most recently, the USVI in 1993, Puerto Rico and the Netherlands Antilles in 1994, and Bermuda in 1995 – voters favoured retention of the status quo.

The constitutional status of the overseas territories varies considerably. The French DOMs, the Azores and Madeira, the Canary Islands, Ceuta and Melilla are, in principle, the same regional administrative units as on the mainlands of their respective states, although there is some variation between areas of competence in each case. Here, parliamentary acts are automatically applicable to overseas areas. Other territories have greater or lesser degrees of autonomy, and national legislation does not automatically apply. Bermuda, the Faeroes, Greenland and the Cook Islands are not very different from independent countries, though they differ from each other and lack sovereignty and control of international relations, defence and monetary policy – quite crucial differences – and are unrepresented in significant international forums. All of the territories, however, have some sort of constitutionally responsible government which, by and large, runs local affairs. Such a situation represents an important transformation in the last half-century. Although national parliaments and heads of state still retain ultimate legislative and executive power over overseas territories, very substantial constitutional and administrative decolonisation has occurred.

CHAPTER 3

The Economic Transition

Mixed rationales accompanied early colonial endeavours, from the quest for grandeur and a global presence to the profitability that was, for some, the crux of empire. This economic rationale has outweighed other reasons to those who have sought decolonisation and opposed exploitation. Yet in every region, every period, and at every scale, the extent to which the colonies proved profitable has been contentious. Much evidence suggests that contemporary overseas territories have tended to be an economic cost to the colonial powers, most obviously in recent times. Nonetheless, varied geographies – in terms of the size, location of territories and distribution of various natural resources – histories and cultures have made general conclusions over the economic significance of empire difficult.

Over time, as colonial powers occupied smaller and more distant places, the economic rationale for empire became exceptionally weak. In the South Pacific, for example, the French bid for New Caledonia in the 1850s was greeted in Australia with uninterest. Australia was a vast continent still to be finally explored and conquered, and such small islands were of little consequence.[1] Britain took over the Gilbert and Ellice Islands (Kiribati and Tuvalu) without competition from other metropolitan powers; colonialism was a matter of duty rather than the acquisition of a valuable area, in either economic or strategic terms. There was little wealth or grandeur in this distant fragment of empire. Other colonial territories were acquired for non-economic reasons: for example, Britain deemed it necessary to claim Tristan da Cunha and Ascension, in case Napoleon were to escape from St Helena. By the twentieth century parts of the overseas empires had lost their mystique, and the prospects of profitability were slight. For the territories, colonial visions of profitability seldom existed or were short-lived. Perhaps their

60

most obvious characteristic is that most are small, if not in land area then in population; a few are so small that, but for natural hazards or quirks of history, they would remain unknown.

In a world where the compression of time and space is increasingly evident in the global economy, the role of locality (and isolation) is of prime importance for numerous territories. Some are accessible only by ship – including Pitcairn Island, Tokelau, South Georgia, St Helena and Antarctica – and then only infrequently. Tristan da Cunha lies 2000 kilometres from the nearest populated place (and more distant still from St Helena, of which it is a dependency), shipping connections are few – there are eight mail deliveries a year – and medical practitioners visit even more infrequently. The government ship calls just six times a year at St Helena, and other ships are rare. The total number of visitors per year is a few hundred, and potential visitors must book more than a year in advance. Great distances, too few people and too little trade prevent economies of scale. Access is invariably subsidised, connections are sometimes worsening, and none of these isolated territories has natural resources of great economic significance. Other territories are less isolated, but are distant from the metropolitan powers; Saint-Pierre-et-Miquelon is accessible by air only from Canada, the Falkland Islands from Chile or Ascension, and Wallis and Futuna from New Caledonia. Infrequent flights link Australia's Indian Ocean territories to the mainland, and the same economies of scale that hamper sea transport have prevented Niue negotiating reliable air services. Lack of physical links to the world system, and dependence on shipping, are measures of the extreme difficulty of developing economies of more than local significance, though these territories are not necessarily impoverished.

Not all territories are isolated. Some, such as Macao, Gibraltar, Ceuta and Melilla, have made virtues of their location, becoming entrepots, and later duty-free ports, and defence sites. Without 'colonial' status they would have been largely indistinguishable from neighbouring areas, and have built on this status to construct economies very different from those nearby; Macao and Christmas Island have legalised gambling, others (like the Isle of Man) have become tax havens and retirement centres, whilst most have promoted tourism. Few remain wedded to the regimes of agricultural production and mineral exploitation that often characterised nineteenth-century colonies. Typically there has been a transition from the primary sector to the tertiary sector, and from production to consumption, as imports (and aid) have increased whilst exports have decreased. Nonetheless considerable economic diversity is their most abiding characteristic.

The overseas territories experience a number of critical problems in achieving development. Most rely on a very small range of export products; some are monocultures. All have small domestic markets, few skilled workers, capital shortages, and high transport costs, and thus they depend on costly imports. They are poorly placed to benefit from growing excess capacity in ocean shipping and technological changes. Public administration is costly but inefficient, with duplicated facilities and 'under-employed' bureaucrats, and displays little neutrality, with politics centred on patronage rather than policy or ideology.[2] There exist minimal possibilities for economies of scale in administration and production,[3] few resources (including energy), dependence on external institutions and, especially in the tropics, intermittent natural disasters (with limited biodiversity increasing vulnerability). In some, such as the Canary Islands and the Cayman Islands, even water is often in short supply,[4] threatening the viability of the tourism industry. These constraints have emphasised the tendency of territories to maintain links with metropolitan states, to secure finance that would be difficult to generate locally.

The Fall of Production

A global shift from the primary to the tertiary sector has accelerated in the years since the Second World War; manufacturing and service sector activities usually dominate developed economies, with agricultural production more characteristic of the developing world. At the same time, internationalisation has become more evident in the expanding role and reach of transnational corporations, in every sector from primary production to finance, based on improved transport, organisation and communications, so resulting in diversification and fragmentation across continents and regions. These transitions are evident in the territories.

At a global scale, primary sector employment has continued to shrink, whilst manufacturing employment fell proportionately, but increased absolutely, until the early 1960s, when it began an absolute decline. Job creation in developed states was overwhelmingly concentrated in the service sector, initially in such areas as health care, education and public administration, and subsequently in the rapidly expanding 'producer service' sector, including information processing, communications and tourism. This shift has meant that continued growth in the capitalist world economy requires fewer raw materials than at any time in the past. Since the 1970s, the financial sector has universally grown: what has been termed the 'symbol' economy – capital movements, exchange rates and capital flows – has become the basis of economic activity, rather than the 'real' economy – the flow of goods and services.[5] Consequently core–periphery relations are much less defined now than in the 1960s, when distinctions between First and Third Worlds were relatively clear.

Agriculture

In most territories agriculture, including both food crop and export crop production, has declined, because of falling prices, conversion of land to other uses, preference for wage employment and increased food imports. Patterns of specialisation, developed in earlier years, emphasised a small number of crops; the decline in world prices created serious problems and diversification was not always easily achieved: disintensification of agricultural systems followed. Even the provisions of the Lomé Convention of the European Union, which effectively subsidised agricultural prices and production in some small island states, held little significance for the territories of European states.

Subsistence agriculture remains important in the more remote territories, partly because several are too poorly provided with transport to ensure that imports are consistently available. In distant rural areas, including interior Guyane and parts of Greenland and New Caledonia, food production retains its significance, because of its cultural role and ability to diversify diets. Elsewhere, as in Niue, government strategies have sought, with some success, to ensure that agricultural systems do not disintegrate, and in most territories there are food markets. In Wallis and Futuna, despite natural hazards and government incomes, agriculture remains extensive. The narrow coastal strips are planted with permanent tree crops (principally coconuts); kava, a root crop with mild narcotic properties, is important for ritual purposes; and pigs are ubiquitous. Agricultural production goes almost entirely for domestic consumption and sales are minimal.[6] In Greenland subsistence hunting for fish, seals and whales (despite international opposition to sealing) continues to underpin the social economy, especially in northern coastal areas.[7] On Tristan a partial subsistence economy is based on temperate crops, such as potatoes and cabbage, alongside sheep, a few cattle and fish, increasingly supplemented by occasional purchases from the sole island store.[8] Elsewhere the wage economy has discouraged food crop production.

Food gardens have shrunk in many territories, due to emigration, a stigma associated with agriculture, the loss of cultivation knowledge and changing food preferences. Yet in Montserrat more than one-third of households possess food gardens, which stimulate significant local economic activity, especially for otherwise unemployed older people, and provide a crucial source of food in the event of hazard, with various psychological and nutritional benefits.[9] Here, as in most territories where food crop production thrives, the non-agricultural economy is relatively weak.

Food production has sometimes fared better than commercial agricultural production, if only because of the tendency for many households to engage in some domestic activity. In the earliest colonial years agriculture (and usually fisheries) were extensively developed, as colonial interests sought to exploit the potential for primary production. Especially in the Caribbean, even small islands held promise for sugar production; elsewhere the rewards for agricultural development were less evident. Yet the promise was often short-lived, and agricultural production faded from the earliest years of empire through competition from better-endowed places. In the Canary Islands, the era of sugar production ended by the seventeenth century (though wine, and later cochineal, took its place). In the Caribbean some smaller islands also experienced early decline after the abolition of slavery. St Eustatius (Statia), a prominent tobacco and sugar producer in the seventeenth century, briefly boomed as a trading centre in the eighteenth century. In 1829 Statia had fourteen sugar plantations, but the abolition of slavery, the inability to obtain adequate labour, and competition from European sugar beet caused production to cease by 1863. Almost the entire population moved into the town of Oranjestad, the agricultural economy collapsed, and the government gradually became the only employer and benefactor. Attempts to produce sea island cotton failed after just a decade in the early twentieth century because of labour shortages, but destroyed subsistence production by taking the best land. Subsequent cyclones discouraged further efforts to revive agriculture.[10]

On islands with poor rainfall, such as Aruba, Bonaire and Curaçao and, further north, the Turks and Caicos and St Martin, commercial agriculture barely flickered into existence before it was extinguished. On Anguilla, the decline of agricultural production came even earlier than in Statia. By the end of the eighteenth century, sugar plantations had been neglected and abandoned, and years before formal emancipation slaves had already fled the island. Only some fishing and salt production replaced agriculture, hence emigration continued for over a century. In the Turks and Caicos the few plantations were replaced by salt-making, which collapsed in the 1960s. The plantation industry also collapsed in the British and United States Virgin Islands; almost all agricultural activity was abandoned by the 1950s, as employment in the government or tourism took over. Only when tourism stagnated, at a time of rapid inflation, did agricultural revitalisation prove possible.[11] On Saba, which had no plantation economy, production continued into the early twentieth century. In Bermuda, the trilogy of sailors, ships and salt (from Bermuda's own dependency, the Turks and Caicos Islands) dominated the economy in the eighteenth century, alongside military posts on this early strategic frontier. The nineteenth century was also 'the golden age' of Bermuda's agriculture: the lily-bulb trade flourished; potatoes and onions received such high prices in New York that Bermudians were known as 'onions', and in the 1920s Bermuda was seen as the 'market garden of New York City'. From then onwards, however, tariff barriers, low prices and increased competition from the US South effectively ended Bermuda's agricultural exports.

On the larger Caribbean islands, the situation was rather different, since plantation economies usually remained viable after slavery. In Guadeloupe, Martinique and Puerto Rico, plantations had expanded rapidly in the seventeenth century, to the extent that the domination of sugar discouraged diversification. The French islands especially, for more than two centuries, represented early and almost perfect examples of the classic structure of primary production for export, in return for manufactured goods and other services from the metropole. Agricultural problems became more significant in the twentieth century. In both islands, a crisis of sugar overproduction in the 1920s was minimised by France's willingness to guarantee a market. The quota system preserved the agricultural economy, even through the years of the Great Depression, because of French colonial preferences. Diversification into bananas and pineapples provided partial success, and no absolute fall in agricultural production occurred until the post-war years. In Martinique sugar production had almost ended by the 1960s, though it survived in Guadeloupe, and rum remains a valued export. Both banana and pineapple production declined, as wages rose, and on the outlying islands – such as St Martin and Saint-Barthélemy – tourism completely replaced agriculture. Guyane, despite its vast land area, never achieved agricultural success; sugar occupied only a tiny area, though some rum was exported. In the 1980s, irrigated rice seemed agriculture's last hope. However, labour was expensive, mechanisation costly, and self-reliance only achieved with considerable subsidies.[12]

Puerto Rico was also a major sugar producer long before the 1800s, but in that century the sugar industry waned, through labour shortages, limited capital availability and US tariffs. Coffee production increased, but in the twentieth century, with Puerto Rico a US territory, the process went into reverse; coffee declined, because of cyclone damage and foreign tariffs, whilst sugar production revived with American investment and tariff removal, as Puerto Rico became more closely integrated into the United States. Sugar – the 'white gold' – made the US presence exceptionally profitable, with exports valued at $53.7 million in 1925; Puerto Rico increasingly took on the more extreme characteristics of other Caribbean monocultures, with the rural population turned into agricultural labourers, a sometimes violent transition that produced dissent and resistance. The richest sugar, tobacco and coffee lands were bought up by American syndicates so that by 1930 the 'big four' US corporations operated almost half the island's sugar lands.[13] Puerto Rico provided substantial economic benefit for the colonisers, a situation that few other territories ever attained.

In the Indian Ocean, Réunion belatedly experienced similar changes to those in the French and Spanish Caribbean, becoming a 'sugar colony' in the early nineteenth century. Plantations expanded, immigration increased, and by 1860 two-thirds of the cultivated land was under sugar. When sugar production began its precipitous decline in the French Caribbean, it continued in Réunion, though the island moved closer to monoculture. French and European Union support, including direct subsidies to growers, enabled continuation of production, though by the start of the 1990s agriculture represented just 3 per cent of gross domestic product (GDP). It did however constitute 78 per cent of the total value of exports. Production of other traditional export crops, such as geranium, vetyver and vanilla, almost disappeared.[14]

Caribbean territories were usually less productive than nearby colonies, because of their smaller size, and in some cases because of topography, soils and rainfall. Thus the history of islands like Montserrat was 'largely one of increasing marginality in relation to overseas markets compounded by a series of natural disasters'. Such smaller islands could not compete with islands producing sugar more cheaply; moreover, lack of capital, conservatism and the difficulty of the terrain discouraged technological change. The introduction of sea island cotton in the twentieth century created some agricultural stability, until prices fell, labour shortages and militant unionism reduced profitability, and the cotton industry disappeared in 1962. At the same time, the Canadian government removed its regular refrigerated shipping from the West Indies, thus devastating vegetable exports.[15] Even before that, Montserrat had been unable to sell high-quality bananas because it grew too few to finance good harbour facilities or attract shippers bound by regular inter-island schedules, let alone afford disaster insurance or agronomic expertise. By the late 1960s the agricultural economy had been devastated, and Montserrat sought to develop limes and other niche crops to revive its agricultural sector. Despite ardent government promotion, agriculture's contribution to the GDP had fallen to only 4 per cent by the mid-1980s.

Outside the Caribbean, commercial agricultural production was rarely so important in early colonial history, but agricultural systems often fared better in the twentieth century, despite exceptions. Such territories as Ascension never had an agricultural economy, whilst isolated islands like Pitcairn and Tristan produced no exports. More frequently, agriculture provided a major form of livelihood, made some contribution – sometimes the only one – to exports, but declined in the post-war years. In Mayotte, for example, following secession from the Comoros, vanilla production declined drastically, coffee exports and copra sales ended, maintenance of coconut plantations was neglected, and the main export, *ylang-ylang*, experienced difficult market conditions, as labour costs rose and public service employment increased.[16] In more artificial conditions, plantation economies survived until relatively recently. On the Cocos (Keeling) Islands, copra exports increased until the mid-1960s, when cyclone damage caused problems. After 1978, when wages were raised, copra could only be sold at a loss, and output declined until 1987 when it was abandoned; alternative sources of income were unsuccessfully sought,[17] and emigration ensued. Territories with copra production all experienced sharp falls in agricultural production in the 1970s, during a global price decline. On Wallis and Futuna, copra had represented a key source of cash income; despite the introduction of hybrid coconuts, all exports ended and efforts to find replacements failed.[18] In the Northern Marianas, once a significant copra exporter, the agricultural area shrank from 15,000 hectares in 1937 to 240 hectares in 1980, and has now virtually disappeared. Neighbouring Guam experienced a similar transition compounded by poor soils, cyclones and labour shortages; the official launch of a 'green revolution' in 1975 did nothing to revive the defunct agricultural system,[19] and it is now one of the few places in the world with a development plan that mentions neither agriculture nor forestry.

On St Helena, after more than half a century of flax production, synthetic fibres replaced it in the 1960s. This marked the second phase of economic decline, after the transition from sail to steamships and the opening of the Suez Canal ended the island's strategic position. More frequently agricultural decline followed either the growth of tourism or a movement of the workforce into the government sector. In the Azores and Madeira, with few alternatives to agriculture and fisheries, and more restricted government intervention, agriculture has remained vibrant; despite fragmentation of holdings and low agricultural incomes, cattle in the Azores and wine in Madeira retain significant roles.[20] In the Canary Islands, where natural hazards – especially drought – made agriculture particularly difficult, the development of tourism in the 1960s marginalised agriculture; in just two decades the agricultural sector went from contributing over 25 per cent of the GDP to less than 7 per cent.[21] Bermuda experienced a similar decline, exacerbated by high wage costs, a growing population, and new housing demands. By 1983 the total agricultural area had fallen to only 285 hectares. Only in a few vegetables does Bermuda come close to satisfying its needs. (Much of the remaining agricultural land is owned by families who previously resisted the temptation to sell or develop and now find that planning legislation prevents them doing either.) Agriculture is important, however, not merely to give Bermuda some token element of self-reliance, but also because of its aesthetic value. Maintaining the agricultural system and the vegetation cover to provide a diverse landscape, incorporating citrus groves, banana plantations, and livestock, is crucial to retaining a rural character and a sense of place in several territories.

In the French Pacific territories agriculture has also slumped, though New Caledonia and French Polynesia have considerable local marketing, especially in the capital cities. In New Caledonia, Melanesian coffee and copra production have collapsed; coffee must be imported to ensure that local manufacturing be maintained. Cattle ranching also stagnated and, despite efforts at land reform, new tenure structures have not raised productivity. In French Polynesia agricultural decline occurred rather later than in New Caledonia, but the rapid growth of non-agricultural employment ensured that it was more comprehensive; coffee exports peaked in 1957 but had completely ended by 1964, and much the same occurred with vanilla.[22] Copra production survived, despite cyclone devastation in the 1960s; exports, valued at $19 million in 1993, come primarily from the Tuamotu atolls (and rely on extensive government subsidies).

In cooler territories, such as the Falkland Islands, only extensive agriculture has been feasible. In both the Falklands and the Faeroe Islands, sheep-farming has lost its earlier role despite attempts to improve stock quality. In the Falklands before the 1982 war, the economy had drifted into recession and the population fell – wool prices slumped, fuel prices increased, and there was uncertainty about the political future and the investment strategies of the principal companies. After the war, land tenure was reformed and new sheep stock was introduced; but world wool prices collapsed, and diversification was directed into dairying and vegetable production, with massive British government investment.[23] In the territories closest to the United Kingdom, agriculture and fisheries have survived with specialisation. Climatic advantages enable the Channel Islands to produce horticultural goods for British markets. The distinctive Jersey and Guernsey cows supply the local market, provide exports, and enable the islands to retain a distinctive rural image. On the Isle of Man the productive economy reached its peak in the 1880s, when the agricultural acreage was greatest, and both fishing and mining held considerable importance, but from the 1890s to the Second World War, there was recession and depression; tourism became the only sector of economic importance. Agriculture continues with difficulty, reflecting situations in other European peripheral areas.

Land shortages, land tenure constraints, difficult topography, poor soils and inadequate rainfall, high labour costs, a preference for white-collar employment, consumer tastes oriented to processed food, limited

and costly marketing infrastructure, and distant markets have all discouraged agricultural production. Where agriculture has survived, it has
economic and social utility, providing some food and limited exports.
More commonly, agriculture has been supported by government grants
and subsidies that often derive from metropolitan government assistance. Despite government support and rhetoric concerning self-reliance, agriculture has nowhere retained its pre-1945 role. Many of those
who once practised agriculture have sought alternative employment or
emigrated.

Fisheries and Forestry

A similar situation has been broadly true of fisheries, though three
territories – the Faeroe Islands, Tristan da Cunha, and Saint-Pierre-et-
Miquelon – are exceptional in that fishing dominates their economies.
Although most territories are islands, fisheries potential has largely been
unrealised, though fishing has nowhere declined like agriculture.
Economies of scale exist, but there are many obstacles: remoteness from
major markets, high labour costs, difficulties and high costs of transport,
poor long-term fish prices, and considerable competition. The massive
cost of modern vessels, fuel costs, and protected markets have generally
prevented effective local exploitation of often substantial EEZs.

Fisheries have only been economically successful in climatically temperate and cool territories. Even then, success has been intermittent.
South Georgia had an economy based on whaling; this collapsed in
1965, but fees from transhipment of fish catches provide the main
source of the territory's income.[24] In the Faeroes at the start of the
twentieth century, the fishing industry depended on distant fishing
grounds off Greenland, Newfoundland, Iceland and Norway, because
there was a 3-mile fishing limit around the Faeroes. The fisheries limit
expanded in stages, reaching 12 nautical miles in 1964, but the United
Kingdom – the largest market for Faeroese fish – then imposed a ban:
the Faeroes possessed new fishing grounds but a reduced market.[25] The
immediate outcome was over-capacity, followed by diversification into
salmon and trout fish-farming. Improved management and the expansion of fish-farming brought temporary stability. Then depletion of
stocks, a smaller catch, and a fall in prices led to a reduction in export
earnings and a financial crisis, averted only in 1993 when the Danish
government provided loans of 2700 million kroner ($465 million), to
prevent the collapse of the two principal Faeroese banks, conditional on
reductions in public investment and the size of the fishing fleet. Whaling
continues, despite international protests, though stricter regulations
were imposed in 1992. By 1993 fishing and fish-processing accounted for

16 per cent of GDP, employed a quarter of the workforce and produced almost all exports.

Fish absolutely dominates the productive sector in Saint-Pierre-et-Miquelon, where the climate prevents agriculture. Though inshore fishing has declined, deep-water trawling remains of great value (and a major cause of disputes with neighbouring Canada,[26] as some traditional fishing areas of both countries have been fished out). About 20 per cent of the workforce is in fishing, and a similar proportion is engaged in onshore processing. On a much smaller scale, commercial fisheries are important on Tristan da Cunha, where the sole export (and source of wage labour outside government) is crayfish, locally caught and processed in a packing plant owned by a South African company and registered in Bermuda.[27] Fisheries have been belatedly successful in the Falkland Islands, following the establishment of a Falkland Islands Conservation Zone, with a radius of 320 kilometres from the islands. In 1992–93 £28.3 million (57 per cent of all government revenue) came from the sale of licences to fish in these waters. Fears over the depletion of resources have introduced doubts over future success, and the fishing industry (like that of South Georgia) has been partly undercut by extensive Argentinian fishing operations close to the maritime boundary.[28]

Greenland also has a major fishing industry, which accounts for 80 per cent of all exports. Greenland departed from the European Community in 1985, whilst simultaneously negotiating associated Overseas Countries and Territories status, thus obtaining favourable access to European markets (in the same manner as the Faeroes). However, the fishing industry went through a severe crisis after the mid-1980s, due to European recession, mismanagement, uncontrolled growth of the fishing fleet and overfishing. Unemployment levels have risen and other alternative industries – including tourism and mining – are being sought.[29] The fishing industries of the Azores and Madeira are surprisingly small, given the extent of their territorial waters; because of competition from deep-water fishing nations, they grew slowly in the 1980s, with tuna a valuable export.[30] That of the Canary Islands continued to decline. In Guyane fishing, mainly by foreign vessels, has been moderately successful; fish are now the major export (though this is largely indicative of the failure of other productive sectors). Despite the size of the EEZs of French Polynesia and New Caledonia, high labour and fuel costs have prevented sustained growth.[31] Elsewhere attempts to develop a modern commercial fishery have rarely succeeded. In both Guam and the Northern Marianas, domestic fishing remains undeveloped, but is carried out, under licence, by Japanese and Koreans. Niue and the Cook Islands have shown no more success. Throughout the Pacific, licence fees provide the bulk of financial gains, but represent a small fraction of the value of the fisheries resource.

American Samoa is exceptionally dependent on fisheries, but through the indirect activities of Asian vessels and local manufacturing. Since the 1970s two fish canneries have been the only real source of private sector employment (though mainly of migrants from Western Samoa). The canneries are subsidised (with the largest – Star-Kist – having a twenty-year tax exemption), wages are barely half those in Puerto Rico, and there are no unions. The canneries exist because American Samoa was the lowest wage location within US tariff walls; otherwise they would probably not be viable. Since the industry employs 40 per cent of the territorial workforce, no island government has sought to impose extra taxation and it operates with some exploitation and great secrecy.[32] However, the North American Free Trade Agreement (NAFTA) may reduce tariff barriers for competitors and lead to a local slump.

In many regions, notably the Caribbean, overfishing has produced a loss of biodiversity and depletion in the availability of marine species for consumption or sale. Around Réunion, fishing yields fell by 50 per cent in nine years, causing the relocation of fisheries to sub-Antarctic waters.[33] Wallis and Futuna already saw a decline in catches by the end of the nineteenth century; by the 1930s any fish longer than 15 centimetres was exceptional, and tuna-fishing had virtually ceased.[34] Similar problems have been experienced in the Cocos (Keeling) Islands and Bermuda, despite conservation measures, and around British offshore territories; there have also been conflicts between Manx and Channel Islands fishermen and those of France and Britain. In Bermuda, fish production fell rapidly in the 1970s, probably through overfishing and the pollution of coastal spawning grounds. Entry into the fishing industry is now tightly controlled; there are restrictions on numbers of fishermen and on size and numbers of catches. Seasons are limited and a marine reserve of 30 to 40 square miles has been demarcated.[35] The same sort of problems have affected inshore fisheries in Tokelau, the Turks and Caicos Islands and Anguilla, whilst poaching and illegal fishing have threatened numerous territories – including the Azores and the French Austral and Antarctic territories.

Aquaculture has proved valuable only in rare cases, as in New Caledonia, with massive government subsidies, an affluent local market, and some exports. Spectacularly successful in French Polynesia and the Cook Islands have been pearl exports. In the Tuamotus (French Polynesia) the pearl industry began in the 1960s; by the 1980s pearls furnished the main export, valued in 1996 at $140 million (ten times the value of copra, the only other important export). Similar success was achieved at Manihiki (Cook Islands), where exports of black pearls were worth $NZ3.2 million in 1991, though the industry was in its infancy.

No territories have a timber industry. In New Caledonia, attempts to develop a pine forest industry and revive the sandalwood industry have met disappointment, and small-scale projects faced problems of land tenure and capital availability.[36] Development prospects for forestry in Guyane have yet to be realised because of forest diversity and difficulties of access. Most other territories are either too cool, lack the necessary land areas to develop forestry, or have long since exploited what little was there.

Mining

Mining occurs in a few territories, notably for nickel in New Caledonia. Gold and nickel attracted miners in the mid-nineteenth century, and the nickel industry created intermittent prosperity until the post-war years. The 'nickel boom' of the early 1970s produced considerable wealth and substantial immigration. After the Vietnam War, production fell and employment contracted but New Caledonia remained the world's second most important source. Production briefly revived at the end of the 1980s, when nickel consistently represented more than 90 per cent of all exports. Despite constant optimism, the industry contracted in the 1990s; mines of declining productivity were sold to Melanesian interests and there were ongoing disputes over ownership and operation of the mines. Nonetheless, no other territory has achieved comparable mining success.[37]

Phosphate mining, once successful on several tropical islands, is now largely a thing of the past. The Makatea mine closed in 1966, after more than half a century of operation, terminating the mining industry in French Polynesia.[38] On Christmas Island phosphate was mined throughout the twentieth century, until closure in 1984, prompting considerable concern over the island's future, since no other economic activity ever existed there. The Union of Christmas Island Workers battled against closure, finally winning permission in 1990 to reopen the mine and run it independently, probably into the next century. On Bonaire salt is still produced – perhaps the last Caribbean island where this continues (after Sint-Maarten, Anguilla and the Turks and Caicos all ceased production). It makes minimal contribution to the territorial income. Guyane, too, experienced brief success with mining; miners flooded into the territory in the nineteenth century, mainly for gold but also bauxite; there were 10,000 miners there in 1930. Numbers decreased, but alluvial gold mining officially contributes 10 per cent of Guyane's exports; the real value is probably much higher. Similar situations were earlier common elsewhere; on Puerto Rico the mining industry was already over by the 1530s, and on Aruba and Curaçao gold (and phosphate) had been exhausted by the end of the nineteenth century.

In Greenland interest in mining has grown, despite earlier opposition to exploitation of non-renewable resources. In the past, four significant mines and other smaller ones extracted a variety of minerals. Gold has been discovered in economically viable quantities and oil exists (but prices do not yet justify drilling). Mining generates 13 per cent of export revenue, and its potential remains considerable, but technical and environmental problems reduce the probability of successful exploitation.[39] More promising is oil offshore from the Falkland Islands, which might be worth as much as $4000 million, and thus have the capacity to transform the island economy.[40] Mining prospects elsewhere are associated with sub-marine activities, but the future of deep seabed mining remains uncertain. The prospect of manganese nodules being mined in the eastern Pacific provides a rationale for France's possession of Clipperton Island which, in another era, was a productive guano mine. Other territories, like Pitcairn Island, the Cook Islands, and French Polynesia, may also benefit. One further area where mining holds promise is Antarctica, but mining would require changes in present international agreements which favour conservation, an improbable shift.

Oil refining has held great value in the Dutch Caribbean islands of Aruba and Curaçao, especially in the absence of an alternative productive sector. Curaçao was once the political, economic and demographic centre of the Dutch Antilles but, like many other Caribbean islands, changed into an economically depressed colony in the nineteenth century. Aruba was even more depressed, used effectively as a Dutch penal colony for miscreants from Curaçao. The islands ceased being economic backwaters with the establishment of refineries processing Venezuelan crude oil for the American market; Royal Dutch Shell completed a refinery in Curaçao in 1918 and in the late 1920s the Lago refinery was built on Aruba by Standard Oil (Exxon). Both islands had good harbours, and they experienced political stability under Dutch rule and rapid economic growth, accompanied by massive immigration from other Caribbean islands. What little was left of the agricultural economy disappeared, and the government invested heavily in physical and social infrastructure, but labour shortages discouraged other initiatives. After the Second World War, concern emerged over the future of oil refining, as Venezuela sought to refine its oil, more refineries were built in North America and Europe, and automation reduced demand for labour. The number of oil employees fell from 20,000 (half the working population) in 1952 to fewer than 2000 in 1989. Exxon closed the Lago refinery in 1985, and Shell sold its refinery to the government (which then leased it to the state oil company of Venezuela, enabling it to evade OPEC quotas). An economic sector that had been of crucial importance to two island economies for most of the twentieth century became inconsequential.[41]

Industrial Development

Where it exists at all, manufacturing is either basic import-substitution (such as making beer and bread), small-scale handicraft production, or some subsidised assembly. Few resources, high energy costs, poor infrastructure and small markets constrain development, but open economies, enabling cheap imports, are more crucial inhibitors of industrial activity. These factors have discouraged industrial development, alongside the high cost of importing raw materials and equipment, a limited regional market, the lack of skilled labour, competition from the well-paid public sector and, above all, the relatively high price of labour, in terms of both wages and social security payments. In the smaller territories industrialisation is largely absent; only in a few exceptional cases have government incentives and subsidies enabled industries to thrive, though often for a brief period.

No territory has had more success with industrial development than the largest of them, Puerto Rico. Indeed, its experience was proposed in the 1960s as a model for developing countries; the model emphasised free enterprise, outside investment, free trade, the role of the state as a catalyst (through tax incentives, infrastructure and subsidy provisions and the extension of social services) and the centrality of growth. Before the Second World War, investment in Puerto Rico had almost entirely targeted the sugar industry, and there was virtually no manufacturing other than sugar processing and handicrafts. By the 1920s more than $1 million worth of manufactured goods, mainly cotton clothing, was exported. At the end of the Second World War, industrialisation was still limited, and almost all government-owned, but rapid privatisation then began. All government operations were sold, and mildly nationalist and redistributive policies gave way to policies seeking foreign capital and economic growth: the 'Operation Bootstrap' programme. The initial object was to attract labour-intensive industries through tax holidays; industries moved to Puerto Rico, attracted by low wages, tax concessions, industrial estate development, a relatively educated workforce, modern infrastructure, and easy access to American markets. Individuals and corporations earning income in Puerto Rico were exempted from income taxes. 'Industrialisation by invitation' brought in a diversity of industries, but increased dependence on the United States for capital, markets and imports. Initially new manufacturing enterprises were concentrated in clothing and textiles – the 'sweatshop' phase of export enclaves – followed in the 1960s by more capital- and skill-intensive industries, including pharmaceuticals and food-processing, electronics and telecommunications. From 1959 to 1968 an economic boom in Puerto Rico, associated with rapid industrial growth, compared to that in Hong Kong.[42]

With the partial application of US minimum-wage legislation, wages increased, giving Puerto Rico less comparative advantage with respect to the United States and to developing countries. In the late 1960s the focus of the industrialisation strategy shifted to construction of large petrochemical complexes, but little employment was created and linkages with other activities were few. In the following decade recession in the United States, high levels of external debt in Puerto Rico and increased overseas competition hampered industrial development; action by both the US and Puerto Rican governments failed to halt decline. Meanwhile industrial activity gradually shifted from relatively low-skilled assembly operations to high-technology manufacturing, with Puerto Rico becoming the specialised centre of less-skilled manufacturing activities decentralised elsewhere in the Caribbean.[43] By the mid-1990s the principal industries produced chemical products, mainly drugs and medicines, alongside electronics and computer parts. Though Puerto Rico continued to advertise itself as 'the only place [in the United States] strong enough to beat apparel imports at their own game', the clothing industry stagnated. Manufacturing industries employed about 16 per cent of the workforce and contributed 41 per cent of GDP. Whilst early successes had been blunted, manufacturing was established as the main source of income in the territory.

Though industrial development absorbed substantial amounts of labour in Puerto Rico, this occurred at the expense of the agricultural sector and the home needlework industry, and did little to stem emigration. Industrialisation drew capital and support away from agriculture; by the mid-1960s, despite industrialisation, the government had become the leading employer. Government assistance was an even more important source of household incomes. Unemployment grew to 23 per cent in 1977, alongside major inequalities in income distribution and regional growth. By the mid-1980s wage rates had increased to approximately half those of the United States, as minimum-wage legislation was extended to Puerto Rico, resulting in the loss of unskilled manufacturing activities; in the 1990s manufacturing losses continued with the Clinton administration's reduction of tax incentives on profits. The unemployment rate remained high, whilst more than two-thirds of the total assets of the Puerto Rican economy were externally owned.[44] Industrialisation was not without social and economic costs.

On a much smaller scale than neighbouring Hong Kong, Macao's industrial sector grew through the same key influences: market access, cheap semi-skilled labour and business acumen. Wages have been lower than Hong Kong, but Macao lacks land and comparable infrastructure; a labour shortage resulted in workers commuting from China, linking Macao and China in a way that never happened in Hong Kong. Most industries are standard component assembly industries; in 1992 textile and garment exports were valued at $125 million and toy exports at $96 million. Industrial production has subsequently slowed, with the continued rise of business and gambling, competition from other Asian newly industrialising countries and fewer trade quotas and preferences, on which Macao was heavily dependent. Economic and industrial diversification was expected to follow the opening of an international airport in 1995, as Macao positions itself as a finance and information centre for Guangdong, but China offers competition rather than cooperation.

Manufacturing sectors elsewhere are even more evidently propped up by a combination of government subsidies, often in conjunction with particular locational factors. Saipan (Northern Marianas) has a substantial manufacturing sector, entirely engaged in the production of garments from imported pieces for export to the United States. The industry grew rapidly in the 1980s and there were some twenty-six factories – all but one Asian-owned – in Saipan in 1993. The sole reason for growth was the ability to produce manufactured goods exempt from US import duties, a situation like that of the American Samoan canneries. Both territories were following the Puerto Rican model but with cheaper labour. Almost 8000 foreign workers, mostly young women from China and the Philippines, are employed in the Saipan factories (since local workers disdain this employment). Exports to the United States, worth $43 million in 1986, had grown to $279 million in 1992. The garment industry has been heavily criticised in the United States for its dependence on foreign workers (and exemptions from US immigration and minimum-wage laws), illegal operations, inadequate working and living conditions, and lack of unionisation. The Philippines eventually stopped the migration of unskilled women to the Marianas because of the extent of exploitation and violence. In 1994 the minimum wage was $2.45 per hour, substantially below the US level of $4.25. The island government agreed to amend wages legislation, under threat of reduced budgetary transfers, but the garment and construction industries blocked it. American Samoa has sought to follow the same broad strategy, though rejecting the 'sweatshop' image. In 1995 some 300 Chinese garment workers were brought in to 'train' local replacements, and establish a garment industry. The government actively recruited other industries that had reached their US quotas (outside US jurisdictions), though high freight costs were a disincentive. In these US territories, breaching the tariff wall was crucial to industrial development.

One unusual manufacturing activity that has created economic activity in many territories is the sale of postage stamps. In fact, these are often imported; they are marketed through overseas agents and are sometimes rare within the territories. Territories such as Tristan da Cunha and Pitcairn Island are known for their stamps rather than anything else.[45] Exceptionally, different islands within a territory have their own stamps, as do the Channel Islands and some of the Turks and Caicos and Cook Islands. The marketing of stamps provides some income and employment, and gives many territories a distinctive and unique presence in the world. Norfolk Island, for example, produced its first stamps in 1947, most being sold to tourists and overseas purchasers. Stamps immediately became by far the most important commodity, equivalent to about half the value of all imports. Although this was not sustained in subsequent years, new issues revived interest and by the 1970s stamp exports were valued at $500,000 per year.[46] The Channel Islands collectively earn profits of around £500,000 per year from philatelic sales. Proportionately, Pitcairn has probably benefited more from stamp sales than any other territory, with annual sales valued at over $35,000.[47] Commemorative coins are a recent and more restricted phenomenon; Gibraltar and the Isle of Man have an established coin trade, and the Cook Islands and other territories have followed. It is a measure of the small size or absence of other viable productive sectors that stamps and coins have attained such economic importance.

The decline, fall or absence of production in the primary sectors of agriculture, fishing, forestry and mining, alongside the widespread inability of territories to develop industry, even with substantial government support, emphasises the problems of economic development. Moreover, as exports have fallen, there has been no reduction in the volume and value of imports, as the territories have gone from production to consumption. Nowhere do exports exceed imports in value, and every territory shows a massive trade imbalance. Where production has almost disappeared, imbalance is exceptional. In St Helena at the end of the 1980s, the value of imports was more than forty times that of exports;[48] in Wallis and Futuna in 1984 the value of imports was 465 times that of exports. Only in 'good years' does St Eustatius have exports and, even then, the entire trade is organised by one person.[49] Whilst the situation in such very small territories is extreme, it is less critical than the substantial imbalances that exist in several territories, where the volume and value of trade are relatively high. Thus the Cook Islands, in 1991, had imports of $NZ94.5 million and exports of $NZ9 million, while French Polynesia in 1993 had a trade deficit of $821 million, with exports (mainly pearls) valued at just $148 million. Imports are everywhere considerable, often including the most basic commodities, such as food. Sustaining such trade deficits must come from sources other than local production.

Tourism: The Panacea?

In the absence of other resources, most territories – notably tropical islands – have held out great expectations for tourist development, and some have realised them. Except where visitors are discouraged – Ascension and the British Indian Ocean Territory – or access is particularly difficult, such as Tokelau or South Georgia – tourism has been welcomed. Most recently, this has incorporated such seemingly inhospitable places as Antarctica. Since the 1960s the advent of cheaper airfares and the growth of cruise-ship tourism in a leisure era have caused tourism to expand in volume, moving beyond earlier short-distance locations and transforming most territories. Tourism exemplifies the international orientation of territorial economies, their dependence on the fluctuations of the global economy, and their situation where one of few comparative advantages is an attractive environment. Tourism generates more income for most territories than commodity exports. Competition is intense, and tourism is subject to recession, the whims of fashion, and the schedules of connecting airlines and cruise liners. Hotels, transport services, travel agents and other activities are usually foreign-owned, and many of the goods consumed by tourists imported; despite a significant leakage of tourist revenue, the industry is crucial to income and employment in many territories, and of some value in most.

The Isle of Man had already developed as a major tourist centre by the mid-nineteenth century, receiving over 310,000 visitors (more than six times the resident population) in 1887, and numbers regularly exceeded a quarter of a million. A century later, numbers passed 400,000 in the 1980s, but the tourist contribution to the island economy had been eclipsed by the financial sector.[50] Tourism began even earlier in the Channel Islands; after the Napoleonic Wars British visitors began to cross the Channel, hotels were built, guidebooks written and railways constructed (on Jersey). Cruise-ship tourism began in the Azores, with the 1867 voyage of the *Quaker City* from New York to the Mediterranean; its first stop was Horta (Azores), it visited Gibraltar and on the return trip stopped at Bermuda. In the same period, affluent British were establishing a tradition of staying in residential hotels in the Canary Islands and Madeira. From the 1870s tourism took off in both places, with Madeira becoming a refuge for 'professional invalids'.[51] After a visit from Queen Victoria's daughter in the 1880s, Bermuda became known as an elegant winter resort for the leisured rich. Luxury liners eventually brought increasing numbers of tourists from North America, and before the Second World War tourism was the dominant sector of the economy.

In these few territories with easy access to the metropoles, where resorts acquired a particular elite ambience and the climatic and cultural differences were not great, tourism had an early start; in the more exotic territories it did not generally develop until the 1960s, when affluence and air transport created a global boom, above all in the Caribbean. One of the early centres was Puerto Rico, where the first modern hotel, the Caribe Hilton, opened in 1950. A few years later the tourist industry was thriving. The collapse of the Cuban industry, following Castro's revolution and American bans, an event with repercussions throughout the region, ensured rapid growth in the 1960s. Despite a decline in the 1980s, Puerto Rico receives more tourists than any other Caribbean territory; by the later 1980s visitor expenditure had passed $700 million, tourism directly employed 50,000 people and generated about 5 per cent of GDP. In 1993–94 tourist arrivals reached a record 4 million people, well in excess of numbers in any other Caribbean territory, generating a revenue of $1670 million. Puerto Rico is also one of the few territories where there is domestic tourism, with more than a quarter of a million local tourists stimulating the industry.

Elsewhere in the Caribbean, overseas territories experienced even more explosive growth; it was particularly dramatic where agricultural economies had all but disappeared and emigration had become common. Few islands displayed more rapid growth than St Martin, where the number of annual visitors rose from 5000 in 1964 to over a million in the 1990s. With few natural attractions, the existence of a good airport (built in 1943 by the United States), casinos and duty-free status were advantageous. The Dutch took the lead in tourist development, and focused on package, time-share and cruise-ship tourism, whereas the French developed smaller hotels and more exclusive restaurants. Growth on both sides of the island produced administrative and management problems (with corruption in Sint-Maarten). There was unmanageable pressure on roads, water, electricity and sewerage, and environmental problems for land, lagoons and seas, extending as far as neighbouring Anguilla.[52] With uncontrolled construction, increased crime (as two separate administrations were overstretched) and new competition, Sint-Maarten appeared to have come close to its limit.

Much of the same situation arose in both Virgin Islands groups, despite more controls on the British side, where the government eventually sought restrictions on cruise-ship visits and established conservation zones. Tourism in the United States Virgin Islands began around 1950, when about 15,000 visitors passed through on ships and 12,650 came by plane; their total expenditure was estimated at $1.8 million. In 1991 more than 1.9 million tourists, spending $708 million, passed through (almost two-thirds on cruise ships). On the British side growth was slower, with 295,000 visitors in 1991; tourism contributed 24 per cent of the GDP, but these islands too were reaching saturation point.

Other territories followed, but the cycle was more belated in small islands distant from the United States. At the start of the 1970s the Cayman Islands had just 22,900 visitors a year, all entering by air. By 1995 there were over a million tourists (two-thirds of them cruise-ship passengers). Tourism employed over 2000 people, from a total workforce of 15,000, and tourist expenditure had reached $436 million.[53] With the number of tourists more than twenty times that of the resident population, the Cayman Islands has the highest tourist-to-resident ratio in the Caribbean, just ahead of the USVI and St Martin. Anguilla, with few natural attractions, opposed cruise ships and mass tourism; it sought a more exclusive tourist scene, based on a number of small hotels which featured Mexican and Spanish themes. At the end of the 1970s Anguilla remained unknown as a destination, but tourist numbers jumped from 4900 in 1978 to more than 80,000 at the end of the 1980s. Anguilla achieved virtually full employment, reducing emigration (and commuting to St Martin) and stimulating return migration: the population increased by 50 per cent between 1984 and 1992. Tourism now contributes more than 76 per cent of GDP,[54] one of the highest proportions in the world.

In the Dutch ABC islands, tourism expanded following the decline of the oil industry, especially on Aruba. Cruise-ship tourism became more important in Curaçao, because of the attractiveness of the capital, Willemstad. Half of all tourists to Curaçao come from Venezuela, and a further quarter from elsewhere in Latin America, whereas Aruba has captured more of a North American market. Bonaire, ranked as the best destination for diving in the Caribbean, has developed a tourist industry that focuses on marine activities (with 49,500 tourists in 1991) after initially being disadvantaged relative to Aruba and Curaçao because of the absence of an international airport.[55] The ABC islands are relatively poorly situated for tourism, compared with the rest of the West Indies, since American cruise ships have concentrated on the northern Caribbean, whilst Latin American tourists are less affluent and their economies more subject to recession.

Tourism also grew relatively slowly in the French Caribbean, as agriculture remained viable; moreover, the tourism industry was ambivalent about Francophone islands where costs were higher. More than half of all tourists came from France rather than North America, the usual Caribbean source. Both territories have about one-third of a million tourists a year, substantially fewer than the principal Caribbean destinations. However on the small northern islands of Guadeloupe, St Martin and Saint-Barthélemy, where agriculture was dying, tourist growth was spectacular; it rapidly became a new 'monoculture', despite intermittent concern that the islands had become 'prisoners' of the tourist industry and the global economy that serviced them.[56] A similar situation was increasingly true of nearby Saba and St Eustatius, though the absence of good international airline connections and diverse onshore facilities slowed the transition from agriculture to large-scale tourism.

In the North Atlantic, tourism in Bermuda continued to grow; tourist numbers passed 600,000 in 1980, but have remained around that level, regarded as the maximum that Bermuda can sustain. Pressure on the island's infrastructure had led to a moratorium on hotel building, limits on the number of cruise ships, and rigorous controls over physical planning.[57] Tourism contributes two-thirds of national income and employment. Direct visitor expenditure in 1993 passed $500 million.[58] Visitor numbers have declined somewhat since the 1980s, because of high costs, but few other territories have come close to achieving comparable and sustained success with tourist development.

Though the South Pacific is widely regarded as a tourist haven, only a few territories have had comparable success to those of the Caribbean. Prominent among them are French Polynesia, Norfolk Island, the Cook Islands, the Northern Marianas and Guam. In 1961 fewer than 2000 tourists visited Norfolk Island, but at the end of the 1970s the total had passed 23,000 (stimulating population growth from 840 people to 2200 in the same period); the island was ranked first in the world in tourist arrivals per capita of resident population.[59] By the early 1990s tourist numbers stood at 30,000 per year. Tourism had rescued the island from considerable instability as a trivial producer of agricultural exports. Similar success was achieved in the Cook Islands. In 1973, the year the international airport was completed, there were merely 1800 visitors; at the end of the decade almost 10,000 arrived and that number had grown to 57,000 in 1994. Tourism concentrated on the main island of Rarotonga, but provided substantial employment and was the single largest source of national income.

Tourism has stimulated remarkable growth in the Northern Marianas and Guam. In the former it grew rapidly from 1978 when Continental–Air Micronesia inaugurated a direct air service to Japan, leading to an influx of Japanese tourists, alongside Asian and American capital. The strong yen led Japanese interests to begin a major investment programme in Saipan. In 1994, with over 600,000 visitors, tourist numbers reached record levels after a slump following the Gulf War. The tourist boom stimulated growth elsewhere in the service sector (to the extent that the WHO estimated over 3000 sex workers in Saipan in 1993, mainly Filipinas, alongside many other bar workers). The expansion of tourism put considerable pressure on land and infrastructure, and created tension over leasehold arrangements for foreign hotels, with disputes between traditional landowners and foreign investors.

In Guam tourism effectively began in 1967, with the first direct flight from Japan, and grew more rapidly in the 1980s, passing a million in 1994. More than three-quarters of tourists came from Japan, even after new direct air routes to Seoul and Taipei opened in 1993, as Guam sought to diversify the market (including, in 1993, gaining 'visa-waiver' status for tourists from Taiwan). Japanese tourists have spent around $400 million annually in Guam in the best years, and as much as 70 per cent of that – an unusually high figure – remained on the island. Tourism is much the most important component of the private sector, and has stimulated commerce, banking and the real estate industry. The tourism and construction industries generate considerable economic growth, though placing increasing pressure on land and labour resources.[60]

In French Polynesia, and to a lesser extent New Caledonia, tourism was similarly successful. The opening of a national airport on Tahiti in 1961 was the stimulus that the industry required, and enabled a renowned 'Pacific paradise' at last to be easily reached from North America. Though tourism spread to Moorea and Bora Bora, isolation and high costs slowed the rate of growth; numbers grew from just 1470 in 1959 to 78,000 in 1973 but subsequently slowed. Direct connections to Japan provided another stimulus, and numbers had been expected to pass 200,000 in 1995. The resumption of nuclear testing prevented the target being reached, though a record of 172,000 was set. Tourism is increasingly crucial to French Polynesia, being valued at $263 million in 1993, almost twice the value of exports. Tourism in New Caledonia was never so successful, though numbers grew from 16,000 in 1969 to 92,000 in 1984. By then it was the second most important component of the economy, but only a sharp fall in nickel prices stimulated official interest. The political upheavals of 1984 resulted in a sharp downturn, with numbers halving,[61] and negative perceptions and rising costs prevented numbers ever again reaching their earlier heights. The tourist industry is highly centralised in Noumea, with few benefits reaching areas of Melanesian population concentration.

Macao has also experienced remarkable tourist-led growth, primarily because of gambling. In the 1950s tourism ran at around 250,000 visitors per year, most of whom travelled by slow motor ferry on day trips from Hong Kong. In the 1960s new operators took over Macao's gambling monopoly, and tourism grew rapidly with new hotels and jetfoil connections to Hong Kong. Two decades later, gambling and tourism accounted for half the territory's revenue.[62] Less than one-third of tourists stayed overnight, but by 1996 numbers were over 8 million, the largest in any territory. On a very much smaller scale, Christmas Island adopted a similar development strategy, as phosphate mining faded. Casino development has created a steady stream of Asian tourists, mainly from Indonesia, to a place whose development prospects previously appeared exceptionally slight.

In other regions there have been success stories. In the Channel Islands the tourism industry is second only to the finance sector. At the end of the 1980s, Jersey had some 790,000 tourists and Guernsey 350,000. The smaller islands, despite smaller numbers – about 10,000 to Alderney and more than 65,000 day trippers to Sark (an island with just 500 residents) – have particularly benefited financially. Tourist numbers fell in the 1990s – as costs rose – and the industry has sought new European markets. Gibraltar, advertised in the United Kingdom as a destination with 'familiar language, money, policemen and pubs', had three-quarters of a million tourists in the early 1960s, until the land border with Spain was closed and numbers fell below 150,000. Improvement in relations led to a leap in tourist numbers in 1985, to 2 million in 1985 and 4 million in 1990. At this level – one of the highest tourist-to-resident ratios in the world – it then stabilised. Barely 1 per cent stay long enough for a night in a hotel.[63] The Canary Islands and Madeira have fared well from tourism; the Canary Islands had more than 2 million tourists in the mid-1980s, two-thirds from Spain itself. New coastal leisure-towns were developed, especially on Tenerife and Gran Canaria, and tourism accounts for about two-thirds of the island's GDP.[64] Madeira has evolved as a more elite tourist destination, though with more than half a million visitors per year in the 1980s; tourism is the most important component of the economy, alone almost balancing a substantial trade gap and bringing in as much money as migrant remittances.[65] Ceuta, to a much greater extent than Melilla, has gained from tourism, especially of Spaniards seeking duty-free goods. The Azores have benefited less, though there were 125,000 tourists in 1990, after a spurt of growth in the 1970s, when foreign exchange controls prevented Portuguese tourists going overseas but let them visit the Azores.[66] Otherwise on the fringes of Europe only the Isle of Man has failed to sustain earlier growth.[67]

The remarkable achievements of various, mainly exotic island territories with tourism, and the absence of realistic alternative local opportunities to earn income has suggested that tourism might be a panacea elsewhere. Indeed, a number of places have been surprisingly successful, even in the absence of obvious scenic, climatic or cultural attractions, alongside isolation and often high costs. In Saint-Pierre-et-Miquelon, tourist numbers reached over 13,700 by 1992 (about twice the local population). Numbers have also steadily risen in Greenland, to around 4000 per year in the early 1990s, mainly on cruise ships or specialised adventure holiday packages. There has been national interest in increasing tourist numbers to 35,000 by the year 2005, despite the substantial investment in infrastructure that would be required.[68] All too often, however, tourism has proved disappointing. In Niue, despite various efforts to make tourism the dominant non-government sector of the economy by 1987, annual tourist numbers have only once exceeded 2000; flight disruptions, regional competition and cyclone damage have reduced the limited attractions of the raised coral island.[69] Montserrat, where mass tourism has been limited, sought to introduce ecotourism based on the island's natural beauty, but without great success.[70] In some territories even government efforts have been absent; Mayotte and Wallis and Futuna had fewer than a hundred hotel beds between them at the start of the 1990s, whilst Guyane has been little more successful. Réunion, with spectacular scenery, has fared poorly (despite 242,000 visitors in 1993) compared with neighbouring and less costly Mauritius; the Turks and Caicos compared badly with the Bahamas; and Montserrat cannot compete with Antigua.

Few territories have been entirely without hope of developing tourism, but limited potential, high costs and irregular connections were drawbacks; successes were almost all in places easily accessible to metropolitan markets. In several places, the prospects are unpromising: 'The Falklands are rather bleak and are rarely warm. They are difficult and expensive to reach and are not of mass appeal to tourists.' The Falklands had just 131 land-based tourists in 1993–94; a ceiling of 500 a year is imposed on environmental grounds, but that figure has never even been approached.[71] Where tourism could be combined with another growing economic sector, such as the finance sector, or is associated with retirement migration, success was more probable and sometimes spectacular. Yet, as even the case of Bermuda indicates, it has been difficult to balance tourist growth, economic diversification and environmental management, and some territories have approached, or passed, the limits to sustainable tourism development.

Niches in the Worlds of Finance

Economically, the most successful territories have been those able to exploit new niches in the global circuits of capital, both legitimate and illegitimate.

> These places have set themselves up as offshore financial centres; as places where the circuits of fictitious capital meet the circuits of 'furtive money' in a murky concoction of risk and opportunity . . . essentially marginal places which have come to assume a crucial position in the global circuits of fungible, fast-moving, furtive money and fictitious capital.[72]

Financial service industries have particular attraction for overseas territories because other economic activities are weakly developed, and few local resources are required. There is little difficulty in designing a set of tax structures which broaden the tax base beyond what the local economy itself could achieve,[73] and they have minimal impact on the local environment and infrastructure. In the more established financial centres, such as Bermuda, financial management is subject to local and international scrutiny. More recent ventures have sometimes operated with a substantial degree of secrecy. Corruption has flourished and economies have collapsed following international crackdown on unscrupulous activities.

Some overseas territories have specific advantages for financial services. The Cook Islands occupies a particularly useful slot in the international trading day – the last centre to open for business. Otherwise location is less obviously a disadvantage than for most other economic activities, despite considerable competition within regions in the same time zone. Consequently, offshore financial centres have a global distribution. Some mainland states are successful players, but most are either micro-states (including Andorra, Liechtenstein, Monaco and San Marino) or territories (including Anguilla, Aruba, British Virgin Islands, Turks and Caicos Islands, Gibraltar, Guernsey, Isle of Man, Jersey and the Cook Islands). Each world region has something of a hierarchy; Switzerland dominates globally, and the Bahamas, Bermuda and the Cayman Islands dominate the Caribbean. In Europe several territories are challenging the more established players. Madeira became an offshore base for Latin American corporations doing business with the European Union, and has attracted some major banks.[74] In the Caribbean enormous competition between various entities seeking to establish centres resulted in dubious activities, but benefited from the reluctance of many investors to concentrate holdings in one place.

By far the most successful offshore financial centre has been Bermuda. It became the first international tax haven in the western hemisphere from the 1930s, though the most rapid growth occurred in the 1970s. Then 2000 companies were registered in Bermuda; two decades later the number had passed 8500 and was still growing.[75] The major speciality is insurance and reinsurance, a sector in which Bermuda is second only to New York. Though fewer than 10 per cent of the companies have office space and Bermudian staff, they nevertheless employ 10 per cent of the workforce, stimulate ancillary service industries and, through company taxes, contribute one-third of national income. Bermuda also has one of the largest flag-of-convenience fleets in the world, backed by British law but with fewer restrictions and regulations.

By the mid-1980s the Cayman Islands was the next most important financial centre. The number of registered companies exceeded the adult population; secrecy, accessibility and political stability enabled

early growth, whilst escalating costs in Bermuda and fears over the
Chinese takeover of Hong Kong stimulated new development. The
Cayman Islands has over 550 banks; just 69 maintain a physical presence
on the islands and only six 'high street' clearing banks exist in the
capital.[76] Beyond that some 34,000 companies are registered there,
alongside 350 offshore insurance companies and a shipping register for
flag-of-convenience business.[77] In a territory without taxes on income,
capital gains or inheritance, income is earned from company registra-
tions and their operations, which in 1992 reached some $25 million –
more than 15 per cent of total government revenue.

Financial centres have had some importance in the Dutch Caribbean,
especially in Curaçao, originating in a tax treaty between the United
States and the Netherlands, where companies paying Dutch taxes were
exempted in America. By charging the international finance sector only
2 to 3 per cent tax, Curaçao attracted hundreds of firms in the 1970s and
1980s. However, the United States revised its tax legislation in 1986,
forcing the Antilles to charge 10.5 per cent tax. Companies moved away,
and tax revenue from the finance sector dropped; nevertheless, in 1991
it still contributed 24 per cent of national income in the Netherlands
Antilles, second only to tourism. The situation is very similar in Aruba.[78]
Attempts to emulate Bermuda and the Cayman Islands have been
undertaken in the British Virgin Islands, the Turks and Caicos Islands,
Montserrat, Anguilla and Guam. In the BVI, the financial centre started
in the 1970s, quickly becoming one of the fastest-growing in the world.
Double tax agreements were concluded with both the United States and
the United Kingdom in 1984, and BVI was one of the principal beneficiaries from the Panamanian banking crisis in 1988. By 1996 as many as
178,000 companies were registered there (with the number increasing
by a reputed 150 per day). There have been constant concerns over
probity and the ability of the government to regulate the tax industry,
but it is the only offshore financial centre to achieve a five-star rating.[79]
The financial centre of the Turks and Caicos grew concurrently,
specialising in credit life insurance, with more than 700 companies
established at the start of the 1990s. It benefited from being a low-cost
location (relative to Bermuda), close to the United States and in the
dollar zone. Development slowed because of national corruption and
drug scandals in the 1980s, which placed the administration under considerable and continued international suspicion.[80] Anguilla's emergence
as a financial centre in the second half of the 1980s was belated, and also
marred by the British government's conclusion that there were illegal
operations.

Each of the United Kingdom's closest offshore territories – the Isle of
Man and the Channel Islands – is dominated by the financial sector;

Norfolk Island (and to a lesser extent the Cook Islands) have played a similar role relative to Australia and New Zealand. The Isle of Man became a finance centre in the 1970s, with a rapid growth in the number of banks; alongside the Channel Islands, it benefited from being within the immediate UK sterling area. Insurance companies were also attracted, alongside some operations of more dubious repute. In the Channel Islands the offshore finance industry grew at much the same time.[81] Initially some illegal operations existed, such as the notorious Bank of Sark, but gave way to more legitimate operations. Guernsey is the world's third most popular centre for offshore insurance, after Bermuda and the Cayman Islands, with 20 per cent of all employment in the financial sector. Both the Channel Islands and the Isle of Man experienced uncertainties in the late 1980s and 1990s, following the 1987 financial crash, which led to some closures. However, the islands weathered recession better than either France or the United Kingdom, because of their ability to negotiate special relationships with individual members of the European Union, unfettered by EU legislation, and to gain clients who sought access to European markets but wished to remain outside its fiscal and regulatory ambit. Gibraltar, specialising in asset protection trusts, and Madeira have taken up a similar position on the EU periphery. By 1992 more than 30,000 companies and more than thirty banks were registered in Gibraltar, which was gradually gaining in popularity relative to the Channel Islands.

Norfolk Island became an income tax haven in the 1960s, because it had no income tax and was regarded by Australia as a separate country in terms of income earned outside Australia. It also had a stable currency (and freedom of currency movements). By the end of the decade over 400 companies were registered on the island; in the 1970s new accountancy and legal practices were established and business tourism was stimulated. Tax avoidance activity declined in the late 1970s, following changes in Australian tax legislation, and the rise of less scrupulous tax havens.

Although Bermuda and the Cayman Islands expanded from tax havens to more diversified financial centres, other territories were less successful. Montserrat made no attempt to align itself with any major financial bloc (London, Tokyo or New York) and by offering banking secrecy, free of any regulation, attracted criminal money. Montserrat licensed about 250 banks in 1988–89 without enforcing regulations or monitoring operations. When illegality became apparent, the British government exercised its constitutional authority to transfer banking from the portfolio of the minister for finance to the (British) governor, and 300 banks were closed in 1992 due to questionable activities.[82] Attempts to use the Northern Marianas as a centre for suspect financial operations were discouraged by Washington. The Cook Islands' tax haven expanded in the 1990s; it was registered with the Hong Kong stock exchange and in 1991 was generating $6 million a year in fees, taxes, services and salaries. A year later the Serious Fraud Office of New Zealand discovered 'the biggest tax evasion scam' by NZ companies and individuals and uncovered a range of illegal activities in the Cook Islands. About half the 2000 companies established there, fearing investigation, fled the territory. New Zealand cut aid, and threatened to cancel it entirely. The tax centre experienced a massive downturn,[83] part of a chain of events that led to a major financial crisis.

Political stability has been of enormous concern to the financial centres, which emphasise solidity and good reputation, since 'money is very cowardly'. In the Caribbean, the BVI benefited from Panama's problems and the Cayman Islands gained from perceptions of instability in the Bahamas, and the hint of possible independence in Bermuda.[84] Illegality in Anguilla, Montserrat and the Cook Islands slowed or ended growth there. Bermuda and the Caribbean centres have gained from the movement of large companies out of Hong Kong. After the prestigious Jardine Matheson company transferred to Bermuda in 1984, nearly half the companies listed on the Hong Kong stock exchange had followed by 1996.[85] The Cayman Islands, like other centres, has sought to present an image of political stability and racial harmony, emphasising its colonial status: British responsibility for defence and external affairs, and English law and language. Even 'the pomp and pageantry of the colonial government, with its venerable yet quaint British customs, are used to sell the Islands as changeless (and hence stable) to both tourists and financiers'.[86] It has emphasised the lack of corruption and the legitimacy of business transactions – a situation which has demanded compliance with US legislation.

A more unusual niche in the global service economy is that represented by the 'casino-economies' of Macao and Christmas Island, which have taken advantage of opposition to casino development and gambling in nearby states: strategic locations were crucial. Though not the only territories where casinos exist, they have developed them to a greater extent. Casino gambling began in Macao in 1934 when a Chinese syndicate took over the monopoly rights of the colonial government. Gambling expanded further in the 1960s, with partial deregulation of the industry and the growth in tourism from Hong Kong and China. The government of Macao, the 'Monte Carlo of the East', derives half its revenue from taxation on gambling, but not without social costs, including prostitution and corruption.[87] The establishment of a casino on Christmas Island in 1993 transformed the territory. The Christmas Island Resort (with a 150-room hotel and a casino), largely owned by an

Indonesian entrepreneur, captured a substantial Asian market. (Four weekly flights link Christmas Island to Indonesia, compared with two to Australia.) A casino that was established on Tinian (Northern Marianas) in 1995 went broke, though another was under construction in 1996. Other territories are likely to follow the lure of gambling.

Whilst tax havens, and related activities, offer the most alluring possibilities for income generation, many territories have acquired duty-free status, a situation also designed to stimulate tourism. One outcome is that places like Gibraltar are distinctly 'nations of shopkeepers'. Other opportunities for relatively unusual financial flows have also been taken. In earlier centuries, such islands as the Channel Islands, Saint-Pierre-et-Miquelon, St Eustatius, Curaçao and the Isle of Man, were all involved in smuggling – benefiting from their strategic locations. Ceuta, Melilla and Macao have been similar conduits. Illegal trading activities continue.[88] More rarely, isolation may offer advantages, though the economic or other gains are usually fewer; the Canary Islands has an astronomy and an oil transhipment centre, Saint Pierre-et-Miquelon is a quarantine station for pure-bred cattle being shipped to Canada, as the Cocos (Keeling) Islands and Niue are for alpacas to Australia. St Helena, Norfolk Island, the Azores, Guyane and New Caledonia have been used for prisons in the past. With ingenuity, several territories have found other unusual niches in the quest for income generation. For example, the Netherlands Antilles and Niue are two of the world leaders in the provision of audiotext services (primarily 'telephone sex'); the BVI has specialised in cosmetic surgery; Montserrat's recording studios catered to Eric Clapton and the Rolling Stones; and until 1992 Saba was a popular destination for young Dutch citizens who travelled there to obtain driving licences without the strict and costly regulations of the Netherlands. As in this last case, some niches have been closed by metropolitan states concerned about financial losses and illegality.

Isolation has given some territories a strategic importance, analogous to the advantages of time zones for finance centres, that has sometimes proved economically beneficial. Mururoa, in French Polynesia, for thirty years was used for nuclear testing; this boosted employment and economic growth, but depressed local production, fostered massive migration and social tension, and stifled nationalist movements. In a rather different way, Guyane, once a small sugar and rum economy, is now dominated by the Kourou space centre, a site chosen because of its latitude and its location in a European territory, enabling the launching of European space satellites. Like the nuclear programme in French Polynesia, the space programme generated enormous infrastructure construction, and agriculture collapsed.[89] There are also non-economic gains from a military presence; in Bermuda the US armed forces freely

provided meteorological services, maintained the airport, and carried
out sea rescues. In New Caledonia, in the 1980s, French military constructed infrastructure in rural areas, and in Guam American forces
have been involved in disaster relief.[90] Parts of many territories – such as
Ascension, Guam, the Azores and (until recently) Bermuda and the
Northern Marianas – have been given over to military installations
(usually US), with some economic benefits. Other territories, such as
Christmas Island and the Cocos (Keeling) Islands, have gained improved airport facilities, though the military use of the islands has been
slight. The significance accorded the Falkland Islands has produced
massive British investment. Though military use has often been resented
and resisted, income from strategic land rentals is welcomed.

In the era following the Cold War, gains from strategic location
are likely to be fewer. The importance of Bermuda, for example, has
fallen substantially; NATO defence cuts caused the United Kingdom,
Canada and the United States to close their bases on the island. In
1992 NATO military stations and their personnel spent $53 million
there, and directly employed 126 Bermudians; hence the loss was
considerable.[91] US naval personnel were also withdrawn from Guam,
where 5000 defence jobs were expected to be lost between 1995 and
2000. In 1994 the US military contributed $734 million (including wages
and taxes) to the island economy. The French military presence has
declined in French Polynesia, and the end of nuclear testing brought
French offers of compensatory financial packages worth around
$220 million per year.[92]

Offshore financial centres, casinos and flag-of-convenience registries
point to both the place of the overseas territories in increasing global
integration, and the manner in which they are able to exploit particular
niches in world markets. That regional and global significance is also
evident in the strategic role, past and present, of numerous territories.
Though they may often be tiny and isolated, much of their economic
strength, such as it is, lies in the ability to manipulate and maximise links
with a wider world. Without substantial resources, developing these
seemingly artificial and sometimes transient linkages, alongside tourism
connections, has become the basis of economic stability. That economic
stability is highly dependent on political stability.

The Bureaucracy and the Tertiary Economy

Accompanying the emergence of a tertiary sector, increasingly divorced
from natural resources, has been the growth of the public service, a
result of the significance of financial support from metropolitan states.
In the smallest island economies the public service does not just

dominate the economy; it is the economy. On Pitcairn Island, there is no 'private sector' in the usual sense, but all adults receive some income as government officials (such as the radio operator and postmaster) and some have two or three such jobs. All men between the ages of sixteen and sixty-five are legally obliged to be available for public work, which may involve building, road work or boat repairs.[93] The island economy is sustained by the sale of postage stamps and British budgetary support. Even on the rather larger island of Niue, a similar situation prevails; it has proved almost impossible to stimulate private sector development, except where these activities, such as stores, printing or school buses, supply the government.

In other small territories the private sector is often directly or indirectly dependent on public expenditure. On Tristan da Cunha, where islanders are defiantly proud of their independent traditions and agricultural economy, the only wage employment is with 'the company' (a privately owned crayfish-processing factory which pays royalties to the government) or various government departments. All men on the island have at least part-time work with the government – ensuring full employment of men, and part-time employment for most women.[94] Moreover, in allocating government jobs, individuals' financial needs and family circumstances are taken into account, hence preventing poverty. In the Cocos (Keeling) Islands, apart from two oil company employees, everyone is employed by some branch of the Australian government. The government is also by far the largest employer on St Eustatius, employing over 50 per cent of the workforce; the Public Works Department 'functions as employer and as a safety net for the unemployed'.[95] Similarly, after the Australian government took over the plantation sector in the Cocos (Keeling) Islands, employment was guaranteed to all who wanted it. On St Helena, some 80 per cent of the workforce is employed by the government. In such circumstances, not only does the government provide virtually all employment, but it creates or maintains jobs and activities that have value in sustaining households rather than contributing to economic development.

Even in much larger economies the government is often the single most important employer, a trend that invariably accelerated from the 1970s. By the early 1960s the government was the largest employer on Montserrat. In Greenland two-thirds of employment was in the public service by the mid-1980s.[96] By the end of the 1970s, the public sector employed more than 500 people on Wallis and Futuna out of a total wage and salaries workforce of barely 600 people. A decade later the paid workforce had doubled but the proportion in the public service was just as high; a hundred of them were bureaucrats posted from France on extremely favourable conditions, which include double the standard

public service salaries, no income tax and a lump-sum payment at the
end of their three-year contracts.[97] In the Northern Marianas the public
sector similarly dominates employment through subsidised state authorities (such as water and power enterprises), 'for here government is
not the employer of last resort, but of first resort . . . working in business
. . . is considered demeaning, while working for the government is seen
as prestigious'.[98] In Macao, government jobs are seen as 'iron rice bowls'
– lifetime guarantees of support.[99] In most territories, wages and salaries
are higher in the public sector,[100] and there is a range of non-wage
benefits (including security of tenure); hence the locally-born dominate
government employment. Public sectors are often inefficient, have
limited policy-making capacity and cannot implement significant development projects, whilst poorly managed public enterprises have
increased national debt burdens.

The size of the public service is partly a function of the extensive
involvement of government in a range of economic activities and
services. Governments are often involved directly in market production.
On St Eustatius the government has run an agricultural project, with
Dutch technical assistance, producing vegetables for sale; it also acts as a
purchaser, at subsidised prices, of locally produced vegetables and a
middleman for exports.[101] Similarly in St Helena, agricultural production
is a result of extensive subsidies to small farmers (such as for government
pesticide spraying); the result is that prices are artificially low, satisfying
consumers but discouraging private investment.[102] In Niue the government controls alcohol distribution. In American Samoa the only
substantial hotel is government-owned. Even in larger territories, similar
situations exist; on Bonaire the local and federal administrations are
involved in many local businesses, including hotels and the yacht
harbour, and firms depend on work commissioned by the government.
There, as elsewhere, 'the involvement of the government in all kinds of
enterprises . . . is not the result of some brand of socialistic ideology, it is
simply the reflection of the lack of private investors. The aim of the
administration is to create employment.'[103] Only exceptionally has the
private sector been competitive and, where it has been successful, as in
tourism, wages are poor relative to the public sector.

Public sector wages have tended to increase relative to those in the
private sector. This situation has discouraged the latter and encouraged
migration into the territories, both of those willing to take up low-paid
and sometimes unpleasant work, and of metropolitan migrants who seek
government employment. Governments have been loath to reduce the
size of the public service (or cut public expenditure) because of its
importance in providing work, even when metropolitan governments
sought to withdraw financial support. Where bureaucracies have

diminished, the outcome has not always been straightforward or beneficial. In 1993 Niue laid off one-third of the 600 public servants (on an island of 2000 people) – a situation which, ironically, cut into government funds because income tax paid by public servants was the biggest source of government revenue. The unemployed public servants were then paid by the government to produce crops for export but, because guaranteed prices to farmers were too high, the scheme turned into a financial disaster.[104]

Lavish metropolitan support for territorial budgets has deterred attempts to enhance productivity and increase efficiency; many government agencies run at a substantial loss. In the USVI (as elsewhere),

> Despite criticism of waste and corruption from federal authorities and other outside observers, there seems to have been little local concern for the high cost of government or opposition to the unproductive use of indigenous labor. The inflated bureaucracy catered to, and reinforced, traditional employment preferences and small island personalistic policies.[105]

The pervasiveness of government provides both a stabilising influence and considerable inertia. Stability, however, has costs; on Tokelau, where the wages of public servants account for over 80 per cent of local income, they themselves were more responsive to external rather than local authority, which was increasingly eroded.[106] External conditions are, ultimately, the principal determinants of the extent of stability.

Most overseas territories have sought aid from the metropole as a means of solving development problems. Territories have particularly benefited from aid because of the 'small-country bias': donor perceptions of greater need and the 'visibility' of aid in small places. On a per capita basis, territories have invariably benefited more than independent states. Niue is usually regarded, in per capita terms, as the largest aid recipient in the world; but the Falkland Islands in the period immediately after the war, and such tiny territories as Pitcairn, probably fare even better. France classifies its aid to the territories as foreign aid, and thus emerges in the global scene as a particularly generous donor, with the DOM-TOMs privileged beneficiaries. The USVI receives more government funds per capita than any US state or territory except Washington, DC. Metropolitan governments are not parsimonious benefactors, and the territories of European states also benefit from EU support, either as Overseas Countries and Territories or, like the Azores, Madeira and the Canary Islands, as 'ultra-peripheral regions'.

The actual rationale for aid delivery is rarely more clear for territories than it is for independent states; thus in the 1980s the United Kingdom characteristically gave its Atlantic dependencies over £5 million each, compared with an annual grant to Caribbean dependencies of around

£2 million, a distinction probably tied to geopolitics rather than need or development potential. Nonetheless, aid to Montserrat was substantially above that to nearby independent states.[107] Many territories are exceptionally reliant on aid; on St Eustatius 'economic activity is largely determined by external aid', directly from the Netherlands Antilles government in Curaçao and indirectly from the Dutch government and the European Union.[108] Half of St Helena's budget is provided from the United Kingdom, and half of Niue's budget comes from New Zealand. A small number of territories, notably Bermuda, receive no aid; Bermuda meets the salary and expenses of the British governor and, when a navy frigate was last sent there in the 1970s, Bermuda was presented with the bill. Similarly the Cayman Islands, Channel Islands, the Isle of Man and Norfolk Island receive no aid.

In times of duress, support from colonial powers has been particularly valuable. Extensive destruction from Cyclone Hugo in Montserrat in 1994 resulted in massive British aid. So great was aid in reflecting the inadequacies and inefficiencies of the local government, that it may have 'bought off' independence.[109] This position was reinforced in 1995–96, when extensive assistance preceded volcanic eruptions that led to several deaths, abandonment of the capital, Plymouth, emigration of one-third of the population, a rise in unemployment from 5 to 50 per cent, and a pledge of $40 million from the British government. The hazard-prone northern Caribbean islands, especially the USVI and St Martin, were devastated by cyclones in 1995 with several deaths, enormous damage to hotels, transport infrastructure and various tourist and other facilities. In the USVI, federal agencies immediately began rebuilding and restoring electricity, water and telephone services. French army engineers were engaged in reconstruction in Saint-Martin and Saint-Barthélemy, where France donated 15,000 plants to help regenerate the landscape. Sint-Maarten saw similar Dutch government assistance and, in Anguilla, British support. In other regions natural hazards have tended to be less devastating, but Guam, Wallis and Futuna, French Polynesia and other Pacific territories have all received emergency aid on various occasions.

Some territories have experienced comprehensive metropolitan assistance for more than half a century. In the Dutch and American Caribbean, for example, the Great Depression was a period of impoverishment and the 1930s witnessed the first substantial metropolitan involvement in support of local economic and social systems. In 1930 a relief fund for St Eustatius began the process of Dutch government financial support: 'the start of a period during which financial support from the Netherlands and Curaçao became the sine qua non of the Statian population's relative prosperity compared to that of the English islands'.[110] Puerto Rico received extensive support, qualifying for most forms of assistance available in the United States. Various relief and public works projects provided funds to construct irrigation and water supply systems and develop forestry. The New Deal programmes of the Roosevelt era brought electrification to most of the island, new health schemes, land redistribution and economic restructuring. After the Second World War, US expenditure and transfer payments increased substantially, so that by the end of the 1970s, Puerto Rico was living under 'a mirage of economic affluence'.[111] Transfer payments had increased to 30 per cent of household incomes. More than half of all households received food stamps in the 1980s. Even when the local economy suffered decreases in production, individual purchasing power rose annually, a phenomenon also apparent elsewhere.

Beyond aid delivery at the territorial level, particular projects and programmes have received substantial funding. In French Polynesia, for example, a combination of programmes, including a subsidy to those seeking to return from Papeete to rural areas, subsidies to copra prices and transport services enabled population stability and development in outer islands, where it would otherwise have been unlikely.[112] On Tubuai, in the Austral island chain of French Polynesia, 92 per cent of the 190 jobs came from the government. For half the island families, government salaries provided the major source of income; government pensions followed in importance.[113] In the Dutch Antilles virtually all capital investments received funding through Dutch aid, and over the period 1962 to 1988 almost half went on infrastructure. At a different scale, as on St Eustatius, several aid-funded projects have been essentially 'pork-barrel projects' that have achieved little.[114] Even on the much larger island of New Caledonia, massive expenditure, in the aftermath of the Matignon Accord, resulted in construction of new infrastructure (especially rural roads) and thus created employment, but was unable to stimulate sustained economic development.

The provisions of metropolitan state welfare systems are also valuable, especially in the French DOMs and the Spanish and Portuguese Atlantic islands, where nationals enjoy the same rights as those in the metropolitan state. The Netherlands Antilles provides a general old-age pension from the Dutch government. There are also widows' pensions, and child supplements are available to government workers. In the Cocos (Keeling) Islands, islanders are entitled to the full range of Australian social security payments; welfare payments are a significant proportion of incomes, and the only source of income is the Australian government.[115] Various forms of government allowances have contributed to, and compensated for, the decline of commodity production; they have institutionalised employment and reduced the necessity for emigration. Tokelau, for example, came under New Zealand's policies of 'welfare colonialism' in the 1950s when the administrative costs of the group first exceeded locally generated revenues; in succeeding years the disparity grew much further.[116] In contrast, the taxation incomes earned by metropolitan states in the territories are either trivial or non-existent, since, in many cases, taxation is absent, tiny or paid to local administrations. In the Cocos (Keeling) Islands, for example, there are no taxes of any kind, and the only Australian government revenue comes from users of the airport.

The direction of financial flows has almost always been towards the overseas territories, even when the bulk of that finance returns to the centre, through company profits or purchases of goods and services. Greenland, it has been argued, 'is like a bottomless hole into which development money from Denmark and formerly from Europe, is poured . . . There is little doubt that Greenland would become a republic if there could be seen some light at the end of the financial tunnel.'[117] Similar metaphors recur elsewhere; St Eustatius 'is thought of as a parasite living off its economically stronger Leeward sister islands and the money spent on the island is described as disappearing into a bottomless pit'.[118] Despite the extent of financial assistance, demands for greater assistance have remained considerable because of the difficulties of achieving economic development, rising expectations and perceptions of uneven development. On Pitcairn, islanders have unavailingly sought an airstrip, an improved jetty and a resident doctor; they even turned to France, because of its presence in neighbouring French Polynesia, with similar requests. Despite unfulfilled requests and expectations, metropolitan support for projects and programmes has been the single most important influence on the direction of social, economic and political change.

After half a century of economic transfers, and little productive economic activity, the effects have been considerable. Again, this is evident in St Eustatius where, simply put,

> Modern Statia is a welfare state. Things are done for them and they in return are not expected to do anything . . . This welfare mentality permeates the whole social fabric, and deviation is minimal . . . Most of the able-bodied young men and women on the island are engaged in sinecure jobs, and the wages paid to them are not determined by the principle of economic rent. They receive money only because they have their names on the payroll.[119]

Consequently, there appeared to be little 'entrepreneurial spirit', no 'work ethic' and some tendency towards corruption.[120] This kind of 'welfare state' has also emerged elsewhere:

> [The] decline in St. Helena's ability to support herself necessarily raises the question whether British aid has not been wasted except as the means to a

respectable but parasitical standard of living for the islanders. The usual
answer is that . . . financial aid . . . weakens rather than enhances efforts to
achieve self-sufficiency.[121]

However, high levels of aid enabled development of health and education services, and infrastructure provision, beyond the level that exists in
otherwise comparable places, as the territories have gone from subsistence to subsidy.

The rise of migration and remittances in some territories, with employment increasingly concentrated in the public sector, has seen
Tokelau, Niue and the Cook Islands classified as MIRAB economies, that
is, as being particularly dependent on MIgration, Remittances and Aid,
thus sustaining the Bureaucracy.[122] This acronym can be applied much
more widely, as overseas territories overturn the classical theories of
economic development by moving into a post-industrial era, and from
productive to rentier status, an economic transition closely related to
political status. There are major economic advantages in metropolitan
colonial ties, but costs are also incurred: social, economic and political
change are driven by external forces.[123] Imports have crowded out traditional subsistence and export activities as the government sector has
triumphed.

In most contexts, more extensive government control of, and participation in, the economy has contributed to stability and provided some
guarantee of employment and social services. There have been exceptions. By the start of the 1990s international concern was mounting over
the national debt of the Cook Islands. The development of a major
luxury tourist project by a government-owned company resulted in the
government borrowing $46 million (for a project that was never com-
pleted); the telecommunications company was nationalised at some
expense; the government also took out loans from the Asian Development Bank for the construction of infrastructure (including $9 million
for a national cultural centre), increasing the already 'addictive' national
debt still further. By 1991 half of all employment was in the government,
and wages accounted for 40 per cent of the budget. On the outer islands
especially, family connections and political patronage directed public
service growth, the main source of wealth. Despite growing criticism
from New Zealand, government over-expenditure continued until 1996,
when the Cook Islands defaulted on loans, alongside the 'theft of public
money' from government superannuation funds, and New Zealand
refused to bail it out. National debt was estimated at $150 million,
though there were no national accounts. The arrival of an Asian Development Bank team resulted in the public service being cut from 3100
to 1200; the salaries of the remainder were halved, and the number
of departments reduced from fifty-two to twenty-two. Most overseas

diplomatic posts were closed, and various government agencies (including the liquor store, four hotels and all broadcasting services) were privatised, in a sharp transition 'from a big-government, welfare driven economy to a 90s style monetarist micro-state'.[124] One outcome was accelerated emigration to New Zealand.

American Samoa experienced similar problems in the 1990s, when government expenditure vastly exceeded the budget; projects were cut back, but the government failed to reduce employment or raise taxes to cover social service provision. In this context, US Vice-President Dan Quayle commented: 'You all look like happy campers to me. Happy campers . . . you are. Happy campers you have been, and as far as I am concerned, happy campers you will always be.' In 1993 the US Interior Department audited government operations, finding a $60 million deficit; though the government payroll was then reduced by 300 workers and most of the remainder were put on shortened hours, two years later the public service had returned to its old level of 4000. In the Netherlands Antilles too, government expenditure produced a similarly enormous debt, 'caused by the system of political patronage . . . and the allocation of funds towards a political clientele'.[125] In every case, stimulating the public sector was perceived to be the key to electoral success, to the point where national debt was excessive and metropolitan governments no longer willing to support over-expenditure and corruption.

The growth of the public service and the decline in production have usually coincided with centralisation and urbanisation of the population, as in French Polynesia, the Northern Marianas and Greenland. In some territories the centralisation of population was deliberately fostered. In Greenland the government G60 Policy in the 1950s and 1960s fostered a few large villages and towns, so that service provision could be centralised, reducing both the urban labour shortage and perceived rural unemployment. Housing was constructed in huge apartment blocks, very different from village housing; adaptation to urban life was difficult and later led to a range of social, health and environmental problems, including domestic violence, high infant mortality rates, alcoholism, HIV-AIDS and malnutrition. By the end of the 1980s Greenland had the highest suicide rate in the world.[126] Similar policies in the Northern Marianas resulted in high levels of unemployment, the demand for more welfare services and some urban squalor. Squatter settlements emerged in many territories, including the Canary Islands, Puerto Rico and several DOMs, even where emigration was possible,[127] accompanied by the growth of employment in the informal sector.[128] Moreover, the lack of development policies, or specific policies directed to the rural sector, enabled or encouraged rural–urban migration, producing environmental problems such as traffic congestion and water shortages.

Though migration into Nuuk, the capital of Greenland, has been remarkable, it has been more than paralleled elsewhere. In the Northern Marianas over 95 per cent of the population live on the narrow coastal plain of Saipan. In the Faeroes, the capital, Tórshavn, has grown at the expense of all other parts of the territory, having just over one-third of the population by 1993. In the very different Falkland Islands, Cook Islands and Cayman Islands, much the same is true. The two 'sister islands' of Grand Cayman have a declining proportion of the national population, despite government attempts to stimulate rural development. Even Saint-Pierre has gained at the expense of Miquelon. Thus the shift from production to consumption has been accompanied by a rural–urban shift; bureaucratic expansion is an urban phenomenon, but the weak urban economic base has contributed to difficulties of infrastructure and service provision that the establishment of a tertiary economy can rarely resolve.

Population and Migration

In a substantial number of cases, the territorial economies – despite their problems – have been much more successful than those of neighbouring countries. This has precipitated substantial immigration to take advantage of superior economic and social conditions. By contrast, some territories are marked by substantial emigration; in Pitcairn, Tokelau and Wallis and Futuna, populations are growing only slowly if at all, and in Niue the population is falling. In other places, including American Samoa, the USVI and elsewhere, there are complex bi-directional flows, associated with economic growth, employment opportunities, and the use of the territories as 'stepping stones' to metropolitan states.

In several European territories, emigration is an ancient phenomenon. As early as 1422 legislation existed in the Isle of Man to prevent emigration, but from soon afterwards until the late nineteenth century there was extensive migration to Britain and the United States. In the Azores and Canary Islands emigration to Spanish America had started before the end of the seventeenth century. There, and in Madeira, it intensified in the twentieth century – as rural areas stagnated – especially to the Americas and South Africa. Madeira experienced continuous steady emigration from the 1830s until long after the Second World War, mainly to South America and Portuguese colonies in Africa, though return migration brought capital inflows and some improvement in rural welfare.[129]

In the Caribbean, emigration from smaller to larger islands was evident early in the nineteenth century, particularly after emancipation.

Migration accelerated again at the end of the nineteenth century
because of European competition to local sugar production and
construction of the Panama Canal at the start of the twentieth century.
From the mid-nineteenth century onwards there was migration from the
British to the United States Virgin Islands, and from Saint-Barthélemy,
Saba and Sint-Maarten. Guadeloupe and Martinique, where sugar
plantations flourished, were places of immigration for the entire nineteenth century (as was Réunion on the other side of the world). Where
the sugar plantation system had completely collapsed, extensive emigration and population decline followed; St Eustatius, with a population of
8000 at the end of the eighteenth century, had just 1300 people at the
end of the following century.[130] Despite immigration, the USVI lost half
its population in the century after 1830, through emigration, high infant
mortality and natural disasters. By 1900 migration from Aruba had
become extensive, after bad droughts, the end of a short gold rush, and
the depredations on agriculture of an ever-increasing goat population.
There, and in Bonaire and Curaçao, more than half the male labour
force worked on South American farms and mines, or on the sugar
plantations of Cuba, leaving women to till the land and raise the
children. Wherever the Caribbean sugar industry remained viable, there
was immigration; elsewhere emigration occurred.

In the twentieth century the structure of Caribbean migration became
more complex, as larger islands also became sources of emigrants. Thus,
in Puerto Rico, large-scale migration began at the turn of the century, in
the first years of US control. Puerto Ricans left to work on the sugar
plantations of Hawaii, and in the inter-war years went to the US mainland. Within the Caribbean there was extensive migration to Aruba and
Curaçao in the half-century after the development of the oil refineries,
mainly from other Dutch islands, especially nearby Bonaire, but also
from British West Indian islands, Madeira, and even further afield. By
1940 the majority of the population of both islands was composed of
non-Antilleans; more than forty nationalities were represented on
Aruba. In the 1920s emigration from impoverished Saba, Sint-Maarten
and St Eustatius was substantial enough to provoke fears of depopulation. The populations of Sint-Maarten and Saba halved between 1900
and 1946; immigration from even poorer neighbouring islands such as
Nevis and St Kitts, and return migration during the 1930s Depression,
averted depopulation. In St Eustatius, despite the island's poverty, 'with
amazing optimism the inhabitants said that no one had ever died of
starvation on the Windward Islands because "the Queen will pay"'.[131]
The migrants themselves also paid. During the first decades of the
twentieth century, Saba earned a reputation as an 'island of women'
and a 'remittance society'. After 1945 a new 'money-order industry'

developed, with the further expansion of refineries in the Leeward Islands, and more permanent outmigration.[132]

Other Caribbean islands witnessed great diversity in migration flows. In the Cayman Islands, in the first decade of the twentieth century, many men signed on as crew on foreign ships or worked in the Americas; one-third of the population went away to sea. In Montserrat and St Martin, emigration in the twentieth century shifted to more distant destinations, including the United States and Canada, but also Cuba and the Dominican Republic. This pattern continued after the Second World War, with workers, as recently as the 1950s, going on six-month shifts to cut cane in the Dominican Republic. Similarly, in the British Virgin Islands, migration brought closer links with its American neighbour; by the 1950s, 'BVI mothers aspire[d] to outmigration for their children [and] practically everyone in the British islands depend[ed] on St. Thomas for full or partial employment during the year', though New York was also a favoured destination.[133]

After tourism took off in the 1960s, a number of territories – initially the USVI, Sint-Maarten, the BVI and the Cayman Islands, and subsequently Anguilla, Bonaire, the Turks and Caicos and, to a lesser extent, Montserrat – made the transition from being lands of emigration to places of immigration.[134] On a very different scale, the 1960s and much of the 1970s marked a new era of emigration. The long boom created a demand for labour; in the British transport industry, international migrant workers were actively recruited from the Caribbean islands; in the Pacific, temporary work schemes brought Polynesians to New Zealand. Similar situations existed in France, Denmark, the Netherlands (to a lesser extent) and the United States: most colonial empires saw a wave of migration to the metropole.

No territory has experienced more extensive migration than Puerto Rico; three-quarters of a million migrants left between 1945 and 1964, and, despite worsening economic conditions in the United States, the flow continued. The island government sometimes fostered migration, encouraging young women to go as domestic workers in the 1940s and 1950s to reduce unemployment and social problems. As early as the 1940s American employers recruited agricultural labour in Puerto Rico. By the 1970s these outflows were partly balanced by immigration from Cuba, the Dominican Republic and the United States. In 1970 almost a million Puerto Ricans lived in the United States, overwhelmingly concentrated in New York, but by the 1990s over three million of Puerto Rican descent were there, despite extensive return migration.[135]

Migration to the Netherlands from the Dutch Caribbean was initially encouraged in the 1960s by the Antilles government, which sought to export the unemployment that rationalisation of the oil refineries had produced. The Netherlands recruited labour between 1960 and 1970, and by the start of the 1980s there were around 30,000 migrants from the Antilles in the Netherlands. A decade later the number of people of Antillean origin there was 84,000, though one-third were born in the Netherlands, and the number was growing despite Dutch policies to subsidise return migration.[136] Montserrat was the British territory most affected by long-boom migration; population decline ensued and the population never again reached its 1946 maximum of 14,200, having fallen to barely 10,000 by the 1990s. For the first time, in the 1960s, there was also substantial migration from Martinique, Guadeloupe and Réunion to France. In 1963 the Bureau pour le Développement des Migrations Intéressant les Départements d'Outre-Mer (BUMIDOM) was set up to encourage migration in order to supply France with cheap labour (and reduce unemployment in the Caribbean and Réunion). BUMIDOM recruited, selected and rejected migrants for two decades, until sponsored migration declined at the end of the 1970s as unemployment rose in France. So substantial had migration been that by 1982 over a quarter of a million residents of France had left the three islands, though their populations remained more or less the same.[137] Subsequently they began to rise more rapidly.

Outside the Caribbean the situation appeared quite different. The northern 'old world' territories remained characterised by emigration, none more so than the Azores and Madeira, throughout the nineteenth and twentieth centuries. Bermuda, however, was relatively prosperous, and the other Atlantic territories were largely isolated from the ebb and flow of migration occurring elsewhere. Similarly, most Pacific territories were cut off from the 'modern' global economy; transport costs prohibited even inter-island migration. The global long boom transformed this phase of isolation, often dramatically. Only where opportunities were particularly limited had emigration begun in the pre-war years. Pitcairn Island achieved its historic peak of 233 people in 1937, followed by two major periods of population decline. By 1980 the population numbered barely 60 people, and the continuation of an island population was perceived to be threatened. British financial support enabled Pitcairn to remain populated, despite a continued slow population attrition, whereas other islands with similarly small populations, but less distinct political status, have become depopulated.

More affluent Norfolk Island and the Cocos (Keeling) Islands experienced significant emigration in the early post-war years. Emigration initially resettled islanders in Borneo but, after the islanders had voted for integration, shifted to Australia. Within a year of the referendum, almost half the Cocos Islanders had migrated there.[138] Emigration was almost as dramatic in several Pacific territories as a result of accelerating natural population increase, less costly air access to metropolitan states, and a demand for labour in New Zealand and the United States. Few migrants had previously left Tokelau,[139] but in 1963 the local administration arranged for ten single women to migrate with the support of the NZ government. After Tokelau had formally declared in 1964 that it wished to remain associated with New Zealand, Wellington devised the notion of relocating the entire population to New Zealand. Though this never materialised, migration accelerated to the extent that by 1972 as many Tokelauans lived in New Zealand as in Tokelau, and the population was falling: a trickle had become 'a rush to New Zealand'.[140] The situation stabilised in the mid-1970s, with recession in New Zealand and the provision of numerous government jobs in Tokelau.

In Niue, too, the prospect of depopulation has posed concerns, after a spectacular decline took the population from 5194 in 1966 to around 2000 in 1994. Cyclones, a modern airport and falling economic production all contributed to emigration. By the 1990s five times as many people of Niuean descent lived in New Zealand: the core of island life had shifted overseas. The Cook Islands has also experienced population decline for the same combination of reasons. It reached its maximum population of 21,323 in 1971 and fell to 18,552 two decades later; by then there were around twice as many Cook Islanders in New Zealand. Economic collapse prompted a new wave of emigration in 1996.

One other Pacific territory – Wallis and Futuna – went through a similar trajectory, in a different context. A flow of migrants in the 1950s and 1960s peaked with the labour demands of the New Caledonian 'nickel boom' at the start of the 1970s, when there were more islanders there than at home. Relatively few returned, but, as elsewhere, the rate of migration slowed.[141] This migration formed part of a deliberate French policy to ensure that French citizens satisfied labour demands in New Caledonia; migrants from Wallis and Futuna and French Polynesia were recruited 'both as docile labour and "reliable" voters at election times'.[142] The bias towards French citizens resulted directly from the increased value of nickel and the belief that New Caledonia should remain a French territory. No longer did the settler colony of New Caledonia merely attract migrants: it actively recruited those most likely to oppose Melanesian nationalism. International migration took on a political role unlike that in other territories.[143]

In American Samoa the situation was more complex. The population grew from 6580 at the start of the twentieth century to 32,300 in 1980 and as many as 53,000 in 1993. Growth was accompanied by the start of extensive migration to the United States in the 1950s; at the same time that American Samoans were emigrating, Western Samoans (and other Polynesians) migrated into American Samoa, especially in the 1970s and

1980s. By 1980 only 53 per cent of the local population had been born in American Samoa, and that percentage may have subsequently halved, as American Samoa became an 'underground route' to the United States. Similarly, both Guam and the Northern Marianas experienced immigration and emigration to the United States, like Puerto Rico and the USVI in the Caribbean.[144]

In numerous territories, migrant remittances have been of enormous consequence. This had long been so in the Azores and Canary Islands, and in the inter-war years in the small islands of the northeastern Caribbean, but by the 1970s many households in most overseas territories were at least partly dependent on remittances. In Tokelau, the per capita flow was as high as anywhere in the world. Remittances, and the incomes brought back by returnees, contributed to development, especially improved housing, better access to services, and purchases of land. Remittances reduced the necessity for arduous agricultural labour, and hastened the transition away from the productive sector. In Montserrat, the labour force dwindled, field crops gave way to cattle and coconuts, and scrub encroached on pasture, until more than half the arable land lay idle and production fell by two-thirds, yet remittances improved levels of health, housing, nutrition and education.[145] That situation recurred in many other island contexts, as migration and remittances both safeguarded and eroded the vitality of territories.

By the 1980s the most rapid phase of emigration from the territories had ended: the economies of metropolitan states faced recession, governments actively discouraged immigration and a conservative backlash threatened migrants. By contrast, relative economic stability in the territories, stimulated by aid and the growth of an 'artificial economy', resulted in return migration. In Anguilla and the Cayman Islands, many returned from the United States; migrants went back to the Faeroe Islands from Denmark. In the Pacific, with fewer opportunities, recession in New Zealand led to either unemployment or onward migration to Australia. However, where populations once seemed in free fall, with the 'end ever nigh', as in Pitcairn and Niue, the rate of emigration declined and a phase of relative population stability ensued. In the Caribbean, economic stability and growth resulted in new immigration, both from the metropolitan states (in the form of bureaucrats and entrepreneurs) and from neighbouring independent states. Sint-Maarten and the Turks and Caicos Islands grew rapidly; Gibraltar and the Spanish enclaves of Ceuta and Melilla experienced a substantial inflow, much of it illegal, from North Africa, whilst the French Caribbean departments and Mayotte all recorded unprecedented levels of illegal migration.[146]

In territories which experienced economic booms, population growth proved exceptional and changed the whole character of several places.

Christmas Island drew most of its population from Asia, when the phosphate mine was in operation; only 15 per cent of the 1981 population were born on the island, whilst two-thirds were citizens of Malaysia or Singapore. After the closure of the mine in 1987, the population declined to 1275, but the Malaysian and Singaporean percentage increased further. Macao's population grew from 250,000 in 1970 to over 450,000 in 1990 – a result of natural increase, industrialisation, and the legal and illegal immigration of Chinese refugees and workers, attracted by the new economic opportunities.[147] In the Northern Marianas, the tourism and manufacturing sectors simultaneously grew, and immigration followed. The population grew from 16,780 in 1980 to over 60,000 in 1995 – one of the fastest-growing places in the world. By that time almost three-quarters of the workforce were born elsewhere, and more single women and 'tourists' were giving birth than local women. In nearby Guam, growth was also considerable in the 1980s (from 106,000 to 133,000 in that decade), with more than half the workforce from elsewhere, mainly from the Philippines.[148] In Greenland, a combination of high birth-rates, Danish medical interventions and migration into the bureaucratic economy gave the island, for a time in the 1960s, the highest population growth rate in the world.[149] The explosive growth of tourism also led to exceptionally rapid population growth in Sint-Maarten; its 1972 population of 7800 had grown to 32,200 in 1992 (whilst as many as 30,000 illegal migrants from Haiti and the Dominican Republic may have been excluded from the census). On the French side of the island, population growth was somewhat less rapid, but it had more than quadrupled to 30,000 over the same two decades. Less than one-third (30 per cent) of the official population of Sint-Maarten were born there, whilst one-quarter were born in Haiti or the Dominican Republic; thus Sint-Maarten has one of the smallest locally born populations of any political entity (and less than half the population held Dutch citizenship).[150] Most of this immigration followed expansion of employment in tourism, but part resulted from retirement migration, mainly from the Netherlands, with the development of legislation to reduce income tax and remove wealth tax.[151] This pattern of 'retirement tourism' also existed outside the Caribbean; it had begun in the Channel Islands in the nineteenth century, and was evident in Madeira and the Canary Islands by the 1970s.

Few territories have been so characterised by immigration as the USVI, where between 1835 and 1930 the population fell by half. In the 1960s, the 'Development Decade', the USVI gained from its 'strategic position as a regional growth pole based on its capacity to draw upon relatively unlimited supplies of United States capital and expertise, and on its ability to attract a highly elastic supply of West Indian labor',[152] and the population doubled. Extensive immigration posed problems for infrastructure and service provision, and raised long-standing questions about identity and the role of aliens or 'down-islanders'. Between 1960 and 1976 the population density tripled, urban conditions worsened, and tensions between Virgin Islanders and others mounted; migrants experienced insecure legal status, persistent job and wage discrimination, grudging social acceptance, and political disenfranchisement, whilst uneven development intensified. Similar problems occurred in the Cayman Islands, which once sought to restrict employment to nationals. By 1989 barely half the population were born there, and migrants came from 117 distinct states, a measure of the extraordinary extent of migration stimulated by economic growth. Prominent Asian labour-exporting countries, like the Philippines, were well represented, whilst territories with similar economic structures to the Cayman Islands, such as Bermuda, the Channel Islands and the Isle of Man, were rather better represented than their size and distance would otherwise suggest.[153] Even where migration was less substantial, the population in many territories diversified; in New Caledonia in 1989 residents came from seventy-one other countries (and France and other DOM-TOMs).[154] In some cases, as in the Cayman Islands and Guam, political refugees from Cuba and from Vietnam and Kurdistan, respectively, added new dimensions.

Tax-free status has also stimulated immigration. Population increase in Norfolk Island since the 1960s was largely the result of the migration of a small but affluent group of retirees avoiding income tax, and death and gift duties. Often this combined, as in Sint-Maarten and Providenciales (Turks and Caicos), with property investment. In the Cayman Islands, the first modern international interest in the colony was the purchase in the 1960s of prime beach land and beach-front property by foreign investors. There, in Bermuda and elsewhere, the number of condominium apartment dwellings multiplied, contributing to capital inflows and creating jobs. Even on a much smaller scale, in Montserrat in the 1980s the expenditure of about 200 retiree households on goods, employment and services amounted to one-third of the value of commercial tourism.[155] In the Isle of Man and the Channel Islands, the impact of tax and retirement migration proved much greater. In the 1950s the Isle of Man government abolished death duties and reduced income tax, attracting more than 6000 'new residents' in a decade. Extensive immigration was opposed because of the rise in property prices, concern over the impact on Manx culture, and feelings that the island was becoming an 'offshore retirement home'. In 1989 Tynwald introduced legislation to control migration more carefully.[156] The Channel Islands experienced similar problems. Of Jersey's 1991 population, only half were born there, yet only those born in Jersey (or their descendants) may legally purchase houses. Migrant workers, including Madeira hotel staff, can acquire a stake in the local housing market only through marriage. Guernsey, by contrast, developed complex legislation to control migration, rather than intervene in the housing market. Migration is therefore highly selective, but there are no immigration or financial requirements for EU citizens and the absence or low rate of taxes attracts wealthy migrants. Throughout the Channel Islands, controls on migration have become as tight as possible without infringing human rights legislation.[157]

In many territories legal and illegal immigration, consequent on economic growth or taxation privileges, alongside natural population increase, created considerable pressure on infrastructure and resources. In Bermuda immigration and population growth have been compounded by a high divorce rate, with new pressures on housing. To prevent exceptionally high house prices, migrants can only purchase the more expensive houses. Hence immigration has created some degree of dualism in labour and housing markets, where established populations hold prestigious and well-paid employment in the bureaucracy, and many migrant workers are marginalised. Illegal Filipinos, Jamaicans and British, and especially Portuguese migrants, concentrate on office cleaning, landscaping and construction work, because Bermudians 'look down on manual labour'.[158] Similarly, in the USVI, 'expansion of government employment and its restriction to residents allowed native Virgin Islanders to escape low status jobs in the increasingly tourism-oriented private economy and to avoid its insecurity, competitiveness and greater demands for productivity'.[159] However, in other places labour markets became more complex, with metropolitan migrants moving into prestigious areas of employment. Greenland resisted and resented Danish immigration. The presence of Danes, paid 15 per cent more than persons born in Greenland for doing the same job, has emphasised income inequalities and placed indigenous Greenlanders in subordinate social and economic positions. Few Danes learn Greenlandic or interact with local people.[160] Even where new immigrants are ethnically indistinguishable from the local population, as on Norfolk Island, resentment festered at so many newcomers[161] who seemed to have superior access to certain services. Haitians have been deported from the Turks and Caicos, and in Guam and the Northern Marianas migration from the Federated States of Micronesia has caused concern. Although migrants experienced housing problems and unemployment, and received minimal support from public agencies, it was argued that there was a shortage of low-cost housing and medical facilities and schools were inadequate, and that migrants were a drain on welfare. Both states thus sought additional financial support from the United States to cope with the migration 'burden'.

The territories of rapid immigration and population growth experienced new tensions, with problems of infrastructure and service provision, and questions over the legal status, rights and access to services of migrants.[162] Rising house and land prices, and increased population pressure on scarce resources, contributed to environmental degradation; in the extreme cases of Gibraltar and Macao, land reclamation became necessary (though not primarily for residential development). In the Channel Islands, the Turks and Caicos, the USVI and American Samoa, efforts to restrict immigration, and to secure job opportunities for nationals, have intensified.[163] In the BVI, acquisition of citizenship is particularly difficult, and labour law mandates that all jobs first be filled by 'belongers' – BVI nationals. This has led to stratification of labour markets by nationality,[164] a situation that effectively applies in most territories and particularly affects prestigious government employment.

The tensions precipitated by immigration mark situations where employment opportunities have worsened, and emigration opportunities declined. In the mid-1970s, recession in New Zealand led to sporadic round-ups of illegal Polynesian migrants, though migrants from the territories remained; much the same was true in France and the Netherlands, despite policies aimed at stimulating return migration. In the British dependent territories, the situation differs; this was dramatically apparent during the last years of the colony of Hong Kong, as residents sought to flee future Chinese sovereignty.[165] Even in Bermuda and the Cayman Islands, which display no general resentment of the British presence and no great desire for migration, the absence of opportunities causes resentment, but nowhere is this such an issue as on St Helena and its dependencies. On tiny Tristan da Cunha,

> Some of the islanders, especially the young, would love to have the chance to experience the world outside. But their dreams and hopes are hampered by the astronomical cost of travel and by their status as British Dependent Citizens, effectively making them aliens, only able to remain in Britain for six months and without any hope of obtaining a work permit. As a result the islanders feel forgotten, betrayed and more deeply confined to their lonely exile. They long for a gesture that would acknowledge the warmth, generosity and loyalty always given towards Britain and the Crown.[166]

Whilst Tristan islanders also show no great desire to emigrate (and returned en masse after volcanic eruption and resettlement in England), most territories would prefer the kind of metropolitan access that is available to residents of French and other territories. Conscious of the disadvantages and difficulties of development in small territories, residents are centrally concerned that migration, so often crucial to economic development, should remain an available option, despite the skill-drain that ensues. In some cases, as in the Cook Islands, this is a key factor discouraging demands for independence.

Transfer Economies and Welfare State Colonialism

Most territories are economically handicapped by small size, isolation and inability to achieve economies of scale, alongside the concentration of economic activity in one sector such as fishing, tourism or finance. Production has declined and economic development, where it has occurred, has resulted from the stimulus of overseas capital, through investments in tourism or tax havens, or remittances and aid. Such strategies have demanded considerable political stability. Especially in the smaller territories, politics is characterised by patronage and opportunism, limiting opportunities for long-term development policies that focus on production. Development is constrained by many factors: a large, relatively well-paid but unproductive and inefficient bureaucracy; high costs of infrastructure; massive trade deficits; land tenure constraints; and vulnerability to hazard. The inherent problems of economic and social development are further complicated by rapid population growth through migration. Usually where economic growth has been successful, social friction and intense local rivalries result. Where there is potential for economic growth, shortages of domestic capital, skilled human resources or local institutions (such as tertiary education facilities) ensure considerable dependence on external support.

Economic success has resulted from location rather than resources. In earlier centuries, island territories such as the Azores, Canaries, Bermuda and St Helena presented strategic and trading value. So too did Gibraltar, Ceuta and Macao, the last of a long series of city-states established by colonial powers as entrepots and strategic toe-holds of empire. Much 'trade' was actually smuggling. In the twentieth century territories that were well placed for tourism, close to the American and Japanese markets, thrived, whilst changes in global communications eventually left others – like St Helena and the Azores – stranded. In an era of space exploration and nuclear testing, a few, including Guyane, French Polynesia, Greenland and the BIOT, acquired new strategic significance. Though finance centres were somewhat independent of location, despite the role of time zones, they nevertheless required accessibility to world cities; hence the most successful lay close to Europe or North America. In the more isolated and smallest territories, or the most remote regions, the challenges of conventional development have been acute. Success has followed integration into the global economy, evident where the twin pillars of finance and tourism form the core of economic activity. Otherwise, even territories like Puerto Rico, where both agricultural and industrial production are significant, have been described as being in a situation of 'total dependency': an 'economic "theatre of the absurd"'.[167] Whilst global recession threatens such dependent economies, the impacts of recession have been more apparent in the aid and remittance-dependent economies.

In most territories, expectations have risen to the extent that they are difficult to satisfy at home. Migration has followed, made easier by metropolitan ties, with a growing dependence on remittances. Ultimately, aid from the metropole, in one form or another, has almost always supported economic development. Both aid and migration have played a role in most territories, as in Puerto Rico, where 'the "safety-valve" of migration . . . removed the necessity for a time, to have to confront the failure of the growth model to provide adequate employment and income'.[168] Migration, remittances, aid and transfers of various kinds did not stimulate production; rather, they institutionalised unemployment and weakened agricultural economies. The shift into the 'symbolic' economy of the tertiary sector has resulted in inertia and stability: thus 'Statia does not produce anything at all, and in terms of economics, Statia is in the pre-industrial stage and belongs to the Third World group of underdeveloped nations. In terms of lifestyle and standard of living, it emulates Holland.'[169] In the French Antilles, the emergence of 'a pseudo-industrial society built on public transfer payments . . . has led to a cruel paradox, by which as each of these territories gets poorer and poorer, its inhabitants become more prosperous',[170] though several have more than one job. External financial support has enabled territories to weather the global economic stresses that have led to both increased unemployment in the North and impoverishment in many developing countries. In most territories residents have become dependent on external sources of income for employment, social services and a relatively satisfactory standard of living, otherwise impossible to achieve from local resources: a situation of 'welfare state colonialism'.[171]

Metropolitan financial transfers have supported, subsidised and transformed the overseas territories, ensuring that, as in Aruba, 'the public sector provides the "center of gravity" for the entire economic system'.[172] Moreover, to reduce dependence on metropolitan support and achieve greater self-reliance would involve unacceptable choices, especially where emigration provides an option, despite pressures from the centre. In American Samoa, such pressures have been resisted. Even attempts to diversify the structure of development have been resisted; Aruba, because of the 'relative affluence' that existed, showed no interest in shifting from an oil-refinery economy until there was no choice.[173] In Puerto Rico reliance on external resources has contributed to a sense of powerlessness, a feeling that local resources are inadequate and an unwillingness to contemplate alternatives.[174] Inertia has ensured reluctance to confront development issues. In a sense, the direction of development policy has not yet been established. The territories have reached an 'advanced stage' in development, in terms of the structure of employment, without ever confronting and considering basic questions relating to the nature of economic development. The ability and the will to effect significant changes appear limited. Though increased self-reliance is necessary rhetoric for territory plans, it has become little more than an attempt to establish a guaranteed income from any possible source.

In at least four cases – Bermuda, the Channel Islands, Macao and the Faeroe Islands – average incomes are higher than those in the metropolitan state. In the first three this followed economic growth, whereas the Faeroes received substantial Danish subsidies. More generally, metropolitan support for territorial economies has supported incomes and welfare systems that are much superior to those of neighbouring states. In some senses, again as in Statia, this is 'a fragile and superficial prosperity . . . pull out this source of life, and the island will flounder perilously into an uncontrollable economic disaster'.[175] Though seemingly superficial, this situation has been entrenched for many years as a result of a combination of the goodwill and perceived duty of metropolitan powers, the strategic significance of the territories, and the demands of residents. Where economic growth occurred, affluence and conspicuous consumption followed. The Cayman Islands already had the highest standard of living in the Caribbean by the mid-1970s. Although there are only about 200 kilometres of paved roads, there are 14,300 vehicles in the islands. More than three-quarters of households own a vehicle and over one-third more than one, but the accident rate is six times that of North America and Europe. Well over half the population have video recorders, microwave ovens and satellite dishes, all measures of the cultural transformations that accompany material prosperity.[176] In Macao the same sort of situation evolved; between 1985 and 1991 the number of vehicles increased by 41 per cent, producing almost continuous daytime traffic jams.[177] At least as important, infrastructure provision, health and education facilities are also usually superior in the territories.

This uneven economic and social development between the territories and nearby independent states has engendered return migration and extensive immigration, legal and illegal, from nearby independent states (and sometimes from the metropole). This has transformed the overseas territories in a way envisaged in the early post-war years, when metropolitan governments sometimes recommended that entire populations of smaller colonies be resettled elsewhere, because of the perceived non-viability of local society and economy. Pitcairn was actually depopulated in the mid-nineteenth century; Tristan da Cunha was depopulated in 1961 but, despite discouragement, repopulated two years later. There has been some consideration of the resettlement of even such large island populations as those of the BVI and Montserrat; with reference to Montserrat, academics have asked: 'Should Britain and the West Indies . . . try to revitalise Montserrat's economy or conserve scarce funds and skills, encourage Montserratians to move to Trinidad, and abandon the island to goats and beachcombers?'[178] In the BVI a 1962 study recommended that if tourism were not developed, the islands should be amalgamated with the USVI or simply evacuated.[179] Similar sentiments have been expressed concerning Saba,[180] and the Australian government sought to depopulate Christmas and the Cocos (Keeling) Islands, as did New Zealand for Tokelau. Perhaps surprisingly, such sentiments were rarely in evidence during the Falklands War.[181] In the end, the only colony depopulated in the present century has been the British Indian Ocean Territory, much against the wishes of its occupants. Elsewhere residents' aspirations to remain have prevailed and, however symbolic or superficial, their economies have ensured survival.

The central economic issue for many territories, therefore, is to preserve and enhance their status as rentier economies – ensuring a consistent external income – rather than to stimulate locally-based economic growth, which has only exceptionally supported development. Indeed, there is a lack of incentive to allocate resources to domestic activity, because wages are often driven up by the availability of better-paid overseas employment or, in extreme cases, by high unemployment payments, whilst capital is driven out by relatively high wage costs and low labour productivity. The transitions from production to consumption, and from some degree of self-reliance to greater integration into the global political economy, are seemingly irreversible. Finance and tourism have enabled some well-placed territories to avoid the drift towards the dominance of the government sector, but most are highly dependent on the metropole, which has given them an economic security that would otherwise be impossible.

CHAPTER 4

The Quest for Independence?

> The aspiration for independence is not simply reducible to
> economic categories or a history of development. Colonisa-
> tion and decolonisation remain fundamentally a question of
> dignity.
>
> *Paul Neaoutyine, President of the FLNKS, January 1993*

In no more than two decades between the 1950s and 1970s, vast colonial
empires that had taken centuries to assemble almost totally disappeared.
All the colonial powers witnessed, and sometimes expedited and encouraged, the disintegration of their global realms. The world map was
rapidly transformed. As decolonisation proceeded, it was initially
assumed that there were necessary limits to the process, limits that were
a function of size: small colonies, in population and area, would not have
the viability necessary for independence. Central to this was economic
viability, a hazy notion, but one that implied that independent states
should be more or less able to balance imports and exports, and that,
over time, their need for external assistance would disappear.

Elsewhere in the world, micro-states already existed. In Europe a few
tiny states retained independent status even when surrounded by a
larger state. Thus San Marino, encircled by Italy and with a population
of just 20,000, was a sovereign state, with all the panoply of statehood
(flag and stamps, if not currency, and diplomatic rights). Similarly
Monaco, the Vatican City, Liechtenstein and Andorra all had independent political status, though few were represented in the United Nations.
In Europe at least, size presented no deterrent to sovereignty. However,
where size was related to limited economic development and remoteness
(usually from Europe), there was often assumed to be some relationship
to political destiny.

The traditional criteria for statehood have specified the need for a
permanent population, a defined territory, a government, and the
capacity to enter into international relations with other states.[1] Size has
never been a criterion, though it was widely held that the era of decolonisation would end long before all colonies had achieved independence, since many were simply too small.[2] What this might mean was

never clear; in the 1940s Sierra Leone was considered a borderline case, but it and much smaller countries became independent between 1959 and 1965. By the late 1960s,

> the sights have been lowered and today it is impossible to tell how far and how fast the process of decolonisation will go on. What may be called the sound barrier of smallness has been broken and the only certainty in a confused situation is that decolonisation will continue. No one can predict the limiting instance or in what forms independence will appear.[3]

These issues became no clearer subsequently, even after decolonisation had largely run its course. Claims from small territorial units for autonomy and self-determination certainly posed problems for large states in the 1960s. This was emphasised by the 'secession' of Anguilla, and reflected in the views of some members of the United Nations that small and impoverished applicants for membership should be discouraged and excluded.[4]

In due course several very small states did gain independence, most successfully in the case of Bahrain (an oil-rich island in the Persian Gulf) and Singapore (though its population was large). Nauru, a phosphate-rich Pacific island, became independent in 1967 with a population of around 5000, whilst nearby Tuvalu and Kiribati became independent in 1978 and 1979. The former, with 7500 people, was exceptionally isolated; its economy was based on copra and postage stamp exports, and, like Kiribati, it was too impoverished to take its place in the United Nations.[5] In this case, at least, size and poverty were no obstacle to independence, the desire for national identity,[6] and the will to seek a new structure of development. By the end of the 1970s it was assumed that virtually any colony might accede to independence.

The colonial powers often had other perspectives. France never fully embraced the process of decolonisation; in Indochina and Algeria, only sustained warfare resulted in relinquishment of its colonies. In sub-Saharan Africa, France sought to weld the future independent states into a commonwealth, as Britain also wanted to do in east and central Africa; both colonial powers eventually left the region relatively quickly (though Zimbabwe posed problems for Britain). By the early 1960s all of France's larger possessions had gained independence. Only Djibouti, the Comoros and Vanuatu, alongside the DOM-TOMs, remained.[7] In Britain, by contrast, after several small Caribbean states led the way to independence, it seemed only a matter of time before even smaller colonies followed. Indeed, a Foreign Office conference in 1965 concluded that all five of the Caribbean dependent territories were candidates for eventual independence, provided that 'a suitable regional framework' could be devised; but Bermuda, along with Pitcairn Island and St Helena, was thought unlikely to achieve independence in the foreseeable future, since no regional context existed for these isolated islands.[8] Thus France's 'limit' to decolonisation was associated with what was perceived to be the 'special' nature of the DOM-TOMs, through their ties to France, whilst Britain's limit was more of a technical one that hinged on notions of size, isolation and viability. In Gibraltar and the Falkland Islands, ethnicity was also of some significance.

The other colonial powers, with smaller numbers of territories, rarely gave consideration to decolonisation. Portugal, Spain and the United States did not see themselves as colonial powers. The United States, despite granting independence to the Philippines in 1946 and acquiring the Trust Territory of the Pacific Islands after the war, remained aloof from debates on decolonisation. For Australia, Papua New Guinea was clearly a colony (though there were suggestions in the 1960s of its becoming an Australian state), but Norfolk Island had no colonial image; the other territories were too small to be of consequence. Western Samoa became independent from New Zealand in 1962, the first independent state in Oceania, and New Zealand encouraged its other territories to evolve as they saw fit. Of all the colonial powers, New Zealand was probably the most anxious to decolonise.[9] Denmark and the Netherlands took a similar position, willing to let their territories move to whatever political status suited them (except in the Dutch Caribbean, where acute fragmentation seemed imminent). In many large colonies, nationalist movements campaigned ardently for independence and gained it, yet in others, particularly those small and distant from metropolitan powers, interest in dramatic political change was minimal. In several, various forms of special relationship – based on some combination of ethnicity, proximity and colonial heritage – were invoked to ensure continuity rather than change. In most territories, independence has at some time been an important political issue, but only exceptionally has it fired imaginations and led to a sustained struggle. The diversity of the overseas territories, and the distinctive policies of the colonial powers, meant that there was little logic, consistency or inevitability to the process of decolonisation.

Towards Independence?

The final significant phases of global decolonisation saw moves towards independence in most territories. The late 1960s and 1970s were a time of global radicalism, marked by violent demonstrations in Europe and North America, the Vietnam War and the emergence of the 'New Left'.

A period of general euphoria in the newly independent states spread hopes that a more positive future was being created. Such trends proved contagious.

Of all the remaining territories, Puerto Rico, in some respects, is the one that most logically should have gained independence; large in land area and population, amidst numerous independent states, it has a relatively prosperous economy, though highly dependent on the United States. In 1952 Puerto Rico became a Commonwealth of the United States, a status that brought it more closely into the American ambit. Numerous subsequent attempts were made at redefining the status of Puerto Rico, as status became the abiding theme of island politics. In the early 1970s the Popular Democratic Party (*Partido Popular Democrático*, PPD) suggested a new relationship between Puerto Rico and the United States, based on the recognition of Puerto Rico as a separate entity with greater autonomy. However, the pro-statehood *Partido Nueva Progresista* (New Progressive Party, PNP) won the 1976 elections, which led to increased interest in closer ties, linked to a greater flow of federal funds, and coinciding with President Jimmy Carter's vision of a multicultural America.[10]

In the 1980s the search for alternative political arrangements took a new turn, with the victory of the Republican Party in the United States, which gave Puerto Rico an influential role in the Caribbean region (through the Caribbean Basin Initiative) and maintained the substantial inflow of federal funds. In 1989 the status of Puerto Rico emerged as a theme in the US Senate's Committee on Energy and Natural Resources, which became a forum for discussion of the island's political tendencies and metropolitan concerns over its status. At these hearings, emphasis was given to economic and cultural questions (rather than political and legal issues), with the Puerto Rico Independence Party (*Partido Independentista Puertoriqueño*, PIP) arguing that 'freedom and self-determination are on the march' in opposition to the political, economic and military presence of the colonial American state. After much debate, a referendum on political status was eventually held in 1993; it produced a mere 75,370 votes (just over 4 per cent) in favour of independence. One supporter of independence has argued that 'the 100,000 *independentistas* are the political tip of the nationalist iceberg'.[11] Puerto Rico had reached a political impasse; for the first time since 1952 commonwealth status failed to obtain a majority, as support for statehood grew, whilst support for independence remained as slight as ever.[12]

In the complex arguments over status, the option of independence was rarely of any consequence; yet this had not always been so. In the years between the world wars many prominent nationalists favoured independence, at a time when minority nationalist movements flourished in most of the larger Caribbean island states. Intermittent violent attacks on the symbols and representatives of US imperialism occurred, especially during the Great Depression and again in the 1950s (notably in 1954 when a nationalist gunman shot five US Congressmen inside the House of Representatives in Washington). Before the Second World War, the PPD, led by Luis Muñoz Marin, had broadly favoured independence, though he himself used independence as a political instrument rather than an end in itself. By the mid-1940s Muñoz Marin had deserted the independence cause, increasingly believing that to seek independence courted political disaster, because of the 'suicidal economic consequences'.[13] Consequently, *independentistas* gradually deserted the PPD.

The Puerto Rico Independence Party, founded in 1946, mainly by dissidents from the increasingly autonomist PPD, has participated in all national elections, achieving a peak of almost 19 per cent of votes in 1952. From 1960 onwards, it never received more than 6 per cent of the total vote, mostly from middle-class urban areas.[14] Low electoral support was argued by the PIP to be a function of fear, associated with concerted propaganda that correlated independence with economic decline, reduced investment, and the loss of rights to unrestricted migration to the United States. The PIP increasingly responded to such fears by arguing for a lengthy transition period towards an independent state. By the 1980s it espoused a loosely socialist position: popularism rather than class-based socialism. As the PIP became less radical, yet still continued to perform poorly in elections, more militant groups broke away, often advocating Cuban-style socialism. The most prominent such group, the *Partido Socialista Puertoriqueño* (PSP), established in 1972, never won significant support. Intermittently, tiny terrorist groups such as *Los Macheteros* (the machete-wielders, or canecutters) and the Armed Forces of National Liberation have used violence, within Puerto Rico and the United States, to draw attention to the 'colonial situation' in Puerto Rico.[15] Support for independence, in various forms, has remained strikingly consistent in the post-war years, but has always been tiny.

In the early 1990s, at much the same time as Puerto Rico, the United States Virgin Islands also conducted a referendum on its future status; the outcome – rejection of independence – was almost identical to that in Puerto Rico, though few voted. More divisive than the referendum itself were questions over who was a US Virgin Islander, and who might thus vote. Of those who voted, rather less than 5 per cent supported removal of US sovereignty. Just as there was silence before the referendum, there was silence afterwards, with minimal interest in and discussion of political status.[16]

In most other territories, support for independence has at some point been greater than in Puerto Rico and the USVI but has often been much less consistent, usually peaking in the 1970s, and then declining. In the Azores some consideration was given to independence in the nineteenth century, but it then seemed more likely that the Azores would be annexed by the United States (as Hawaii had been). An unsuccessful revolt against Portugal occurred in the 1930s. The revolutionary change in Portuguese policies in 1974 that led to independence in Portugal's African colonies, and the forced incorporation of East Timor into Indonesia, produced renewed demands for independence, especially in the Azores, and particularly on the main island of Saõ Miguel (which contained more than one-third of the population and half the land area). The violent summer of 1975 produced right-wing separatist movements in both the Azores and Madeira. On Madeira, an organisation called *Frente de Libertaçao Madeirense* (FLAMA) destroyed the radio station in Funchal and claimed responsibility for other acts of sabotage. On the Azores, the *Frente de Libertaçao Açoriana* (FLA) was more pacific, though the threat of secession was greater. The FLA announced the formation of a government-in-exile, headed by a high-school teacher in Massachusetts, and violent demonstrations broke out in some Azorean islands, mainly directed at left-wingers. Although the FLA sought full independence, others favoured Azorean political ties with the United States. After the threat of a Communist takeover in Portugal was averted, the confrontation between the islands and Lisbon gradually subsided. In 1976 both territories became autonomous regions and, despite continued opposition to the socialist government, the independence movements gradually became less visible.[17]

In the Canary Islands the first demands for independence came from Canary Island emigrants as early as 1810, and great pressure for independence and change came from Canarios in Central and South America in the nineteenth century. There was a brief insurrection in the islands in 1909. The long-standing independence movement was banned by Franco, and it languished in the 1950s and 1960s. A new independence movement emerged in the 1970s. *Movimiento para la Autodeterminación e Independencia del Archipiélago Canario* (MPAIAC) gained some support; Spanish withdrawal from the Sahara at the start of 1976 suggested possibilities for local change. The MPAIAC, based in Algiers and supported by Algeria, called for independence and the recognition of the 'Africanism' of the Canary Islands, and requested the Organisation for African Unity to declare the Canary Islands a territory subject to decolonisation; it organised concerted bombing campaigns in the late 1970s. The MPAIAC manifesto argued that 'opposition to Spain exists in our country not only because of historical reasons, but also through ethnic, political, economic, geographical and cultural differences that make Canarios a self-contained unity distinct from Spaniards'.

Greater autonomy from 1976 onwards in the Spanish territories put the islands in a relatively favoured position compared to mainland regions, and the MPAIAC faded away.[18]

On the other side of the world, Norfolk Island experienced some interest in independence in the mid-1970s, with islanders of Pitcairn descent supporting the status quo and more recent settlers, from both Australia and New Zealand, favouring independence. The former believed that retention of links with Australia would be more likely to lead to continuity of the existing, largely rural way of life, whereas those who supported independence sought to develop a finance-oriented economy. Though nothing then transpired, the demand for greater independence intermittently recurred. In 1991 some 81 per cent of Norfolk Islanders voted against an Australian government decision to enable them to vote in Australian elections, and even more overwhelmingly opposed changes in the island's constitutional status. Opposition centred on the possibility of taxation being introduced, with posters declaring 'Independence or Free Association, the only options' spread across the island. Few actually sought independence. The majority of the islanders again preferred retention of the existing status, with substantial self-government, and Australian financial support for major projects, such as airport extensions. Support for independence, as in the Azores, was not stimulated by radicalism; rather, it arose from conservative, and affluent, reaction against external control and possible financial legislation,[19] strengthened in Norfolk Island by claims to distinctive (if distant) Polynesian ancestry. In both the Danish territories, the achievement of Home Rule reduced demands for independence, and in the Faeroes, the initial success of the national football team in Europe proved a symbolic expression of independence. However, in both places there exists support for independence. In the Faeroes, two political parties advocate complete independence; one, *Tjódveldisflokkusin* (Republican Party), holds four of the thirty-two seats in the Løgting. In Greenland, the slowly growing *Inuit Ataqatigiit* (Inuit Brotherhood) party, which advocates eventual independence, won 20 per cent of the vote and six of the twenty-seven seats in the Landsting in 1995.[20]

Among the French DOM-TOMs, the earliest demands for independence came from one of the most remote territories, French Polynesia. In the years after the Second World War some politicians, led by the first prominent Polynesian leader, Pouvana'a a Oopa, began to seek greater autonomy. His party, the *Rassemblement Démocratique des Populations Tahitiennes* (RDPT), won fully 70 per cent of the votes in local elections in 1951, advocating transformation of the territory into a Polynesian republic, enabling greater autonomy, civil rights, and equitable treatment for Tahitians. Over time its programme became more radical and anti-French, as the party demanded that Tahitians replace expatriate bureaucrats and take over local commerce, that Tahitian be the official language and a Tahitian flag replace the French flag. Most support came from rural Tahitians, who believed that economic life would be improved because a more autonomous state could sell copra and vanilla directly to the United States. At a 1958 constitutional referendum, which allowed French colonies to vote on their future status, Pouvana'a campaigned for independence; but factional strife had divided the RDPT, Pouvana'a was denied access to government radio, and two-thirds of the electorate voted in favour of remaining with France. By then it had become apparent that the islands would be economically vulnerable without metropolitan subsidies. Support for Pouvana'a and the independence movement declined.

In the aftermath of the referendum, the local assembly solemnly stated that French Polynesia wanted to 'remain an integral part of the French Republic'. France, having lost its nuclear test sites in the Algerian Sahara, moved the site to Mururoa, though John Teariki, the RDPT member of the French National Assembly, strongly opposed its relocation. Opposition was ignored, and President de Gaulle dissolved the RDPT. Expansion of employment and incomes in the era of nuclear testing led to the decline of the independence movement in the 1960s. By the early 1970s there was no longer significant interest in independence, and only a minority expressed concern over either the extent of dependence or the impact of nuclear testing.

More overtly pro-independence parties emerged in the 1970s, all more radical than their predecessors. These included *Ia Mana Te Nunaa* (Power to the People), established in 1975, committed to socialism, independence and the end of nuclear tests, which pressed for economic independence as a precursor to political independence. Pouvana'a died in 1977, and new leaders temporarily came to the fore, including Pouvana'a's nephew, Charlie Ching, who was gaoled for breaking into a French army depot. In the French national elections of 1978, pro-independence candidates gained 15 per cent of the vote, and in the 1981 elections that proportion increased to around 20 per cent. Nuclear testing continued through the 1980s, accompanied by protests from Polynesians who had escaped any material benefits from the programme. *Ia Mana Te Nunaa* gained support, winning three of the thirty seats in the Territorial Assembly in 1982. Its elected representatives immediately transformed discourse in the assembly by speaking Tahitian rather than French. Meanwhile, Oscar Temaru had established *Tavini Huiraatira no Polinetia* (the Polynesian Liberation Front), which also sought independence by legal means. In 1983 Temaru was elected mayor of Fa'aa, a poor Papeete suburb on the fringes of the international airport, primarily because of his promises to reduce unemployment. The visibility of his party increased dramatically and, over time, these two new parties, once widely regarded as too idealistic, gained greater popular support, especially among urban Tahitians.[21] Further support followed the French Socialist government's emphasis on institutional rather than political reforms in the DOM-TOMs, and its unwillingness to adopt any policies that might put national defence policy at risk. Demands for independence were largely submerged in pressure for greater autonomy and the reduction and end of nuclear testing. *Ia Mana Te Nunaa* joined a largely anti-independence coalition government in 1987; following this grab for power, it lost all its seats in the 1991 territorial elections.

The struggle for independence was taken up by Temaru's *Tavini Huiraatira*, which had four deputies in the Territorial Assembly. Social unrest was considerable in the 1990s: there were general strikes against price rises, wage freezes and the installation of a territorial 'social contribution' (effectively the first direct tax), which resulted in a number of violent confrontations. Temaru took advantage of such disputes to strengthen his party and call for the extension of free social services; he renewed opposition to nuclear testing and land alienation, especially by big tourist hotels. His greatest support came from residents in the more depressed suburbs of Papeete, with persistently high unemployment levels.

The French resumption of nuclear testing on Mururoa in September 1995, after a two-year moratorium, gave a new focus to the independence movement. *Tavini Huiraatira* led the opposition. The first nuclear test stimulated two days of rioting in Papeete, with the airport set ablaze, many injuries, and considerable property damage. In the riots, and the debates that followed, denunciations of French colonialism and the symbolism of independence were much in evidence. However, after the first test and the riots, an opinion poll found that only 15 per cent of French Polynesians wanted independence in three years, 16 per cent preferred independence over a longer period, and 57 per cent did not want it at all. Those who opposed independence expressed concern over the decline of French economic support, though *Tavini* leaders insisted that a transition to independence would be gradual. In the territorial elections in May 1996, support for *Tavini Huiraatira* substantially increased, with Temaru's party winning ten seats in the 41-seat assembly. For the first time the party ran a joint electoral campaign with *Ia Mana Te Nunaa*, whose leader, Jacqui Drollet, won one of the seats. In the French national elections a year later, Temaru received 42 per cent of votes. The western constituency, though one-third of the electorate abstained, showed the strongest support for an independence candidate for more than a quarter of a century. Whilst support for *Tavini* is also linked to local social objectives, in a territory with restricted welfare services and no other effective opposition party, the demand for independence in French Polynesia is currently mounting – the only territory where this remains true.

In New Caledonia, the emergence of nationalism was contemporaneous with that in French Polynesia and, as in Polynesia, Melanesian frustrations with the slow pace of reform, racial discrimination, and centralised government produced a radical politics. Demands for greater autonomy paralleled those in French Polynesia, to the extent that in 1968 the two territories sent a joint delegation to Paris to present their grievances; the Minister for the DOM-TOMs refused to receive it. Continued rejection of demands for greater autonomy, and a growing pressure for land reform, were a catalyst for more radical, wholly Melanesian political parties led by Jean-Marie Tjibaou's *Union Calédonienne* (UC). The first demand for independence came in 1975 from Yann Celene Uregei, head of the *Front Uni de Libération Kanake* (FULK), whilst the *Parti de Libération Kanake* (PALIKA), founded in 1976, soon afterwards sought a 'Cuban-style socialist society' and 'Kanak independence'. In opposition to this radicalism, the fragmented conservative parties consolidated into the *Rassemblement pour la Calédonie dans la République* (RPCR), a primarily European party, and New Caledonian politics gradually polarised, as politics had done in Polynesia. By the end of the 1970s each of the predominantly Melanesian parties had come out in support of independence. Ethnicity was crucial in crystallising political identity, as nowhere else in the DOM-TOMs, because of the significance of land issues, the limited property ownership of Melanesians, and European dominance in the political, economic and social elite. Political and economic frustration brought direct action from pro-independence Melanesians (Kanaks) and confrontations with settlers; there was overt violence and, eventually, a bloody struggle for independence, without equal in other overseas territories.

Outside the two largest Pacific territories, demands for independence in the DOM-TOMs have been less strident and opposition to France has taken quite different forms. In the Caribbean and Réunion, only a tiny minority has ever voted for independence, in part because of 'an attitudinal framework emphasising security-mindedness and materialism, and the lack of a visible and charismatic pro-independence leader'.[22] However, there have been frequent demands for greater autonomy, and constant stress on distinctive cultures and identities, especially in Martinique and Guadeloupe, which were explicitly linked to nationalism. The first pro-independence groups in the Antilles appeared in 1959 in the wake of Castro's revolution in Cuba, the

Algerian War, and the steady progress of global decolonisation. These Marxist organisations, seeking local revolutions, had only brief periods of existence. Subsequently other pro-independence parties emerged, all strongly socialist in orientation.

In Martinique in the 1970s the principal independence party, and the only well-organised one, was the Trotskyist *Groupe Révolution Socialiste*, with links to a similar group in Guadeloupe. Primarily supported by young middle-class intellectuals, it enjoyed limited though not negligible working-class support. The most vocal of the legal pro-independence parties, the *Mouvement Indépendantiste Martiniquais* (MIM), founded in 1972 by a teacher, Alfred Marie-Jeanne, rejected both the Marxist analysis of the Trotskyists and the 'neo-colonialism' and 'reformism' of the autonomists, and boycotted French presidential and legislative elections in the 1970s. Intransigence to all other parties and its absolute and sole demand for unconditional independence marginalised the movement. The principal pro-independence party in Guadeloupe, the *Union Populaire pour la Libération de la Guadeloupe* (UPLG), was founded in 1978. Denouncing assimilation, emphasising the role of the Creole language, and calling for abstentions in French elections, it was no more successful than the MIM, despite an active campaign of land occupations and other forms of activism.

In the aftermath of the destruction caused by Hurricane Hugo in 1989, the UPLG stated that it would subsequently participate in elections, and seek associated status with France rather than independence for Guadeloupe. By contrast, a year later in Martinique, after another destructive hurricane, electoral support for pro-independence parties reached its highest level. In the 1992 regional elections, the MIM gained 19,000 votes (16 per cent of the total) and seven of the forty-one seats on the *Conseil Régional*. (Another pro-independence party, the ecologically oriented *Association pour la Sauvegarde du Patrimoine Martiniquais*, gained two seats.) A year later Marie-Jeanne stood for the French National Assembly (after previously condemning participation in French elections); he received 17,912 votes (42 per cent of the total) in the southern constituency, enough to claim a moral victory for the independence cause. In 1997, he was even more successful, with 28,916 (64 per cent) of the votes in his constituency. He became the first Caribbean independence supporter to be elected to the French parliament, and the only one since the New Caledonian deputy, Roch Pidjot, in the early 1980s. Apart from the local rise of the MIM, whose growth may be partly credited to its charismatic leader (and concern over the implications of EU legislation), support for independence in the French Caribbean appeared less than in the 1980s, when it was no more than slight.[23]

In both Martinique and Guadeloupe, independence parties had sought to gain new legitimacy in the 1980s by identifying Caribbean parallels with New Caledonia, but, beyond slogans, little united these disparate and fragmented movements in a struggle against French 'colonialism'. Unable to gain substantial popular support, and unwilling to recognise and participate in the existing democratic institutions, in the early 1980s many supporters of independence turned to violence. In Guadeloupe, where shootings, bombings and kidnappings have seemed endemic to the political scene, political violence was well under way by 1981. *The Groupe de Libération Armée de la Guadeloupe* (GLA) opposed 'French capitalism and colonialism', and argued that its revolutionary violence was a response to metropolitan institutional violence in education and language.

Luc Reinette, a leader of the now disbanded *Alliance Révolutionnaire Caraïbe*, articulated the sentiments of those who used violence:

> French colonialists in their souls remain racists and slavemongers. . . . If today we are runaway slaves, this is because a slave society still exists in Guadeloupean daily life, disguised by glittering facades and hypocritical institutions. No longer do physical chains shackle our bodies, but invisible chains bind our spirits. . . . Our cause is just: this land to which we were deported more than three centuries ago, that our fathers and mothers enriched with their sweat and blood, this land of Guadeloupe is ours, wholly ours. . . . Guadeloupeans are not French, they never chose to be so and cannot be so by history, geography or culture.[24]

Much of the literature of the independence movement in the Antilles has been expressed in similar vein: a powerful, rhetorical opposition to the trappings of colonialism, an assumption that merely false consciousness prevents the widespread recognition of injustice and the necessity for change, and the belief that only a socialist independence can genuinely transform the Caribbean. After two decades, and in opposition to different French governments, the aspirations and rhetoric of the independence movement had never changed.

In Guyane, the first small independence party appeared in 1974: the *Mouvement Guyanais de Décolonisation* (MOGUYDE). In the early 1980s a number of activists, mainly associated with another pro-independence group, the *Front National de Libération Guyanais* (FNLG), were arrested after bombings in Kourou and Cayenne. However, overall support for independence was no more than in the Antilles, and the structure of a post-independence Guyane was barely considered. In the 1983 *département* elections, pro-independence candidates won 9 per cent of the vote and four of the thirty-one seats. Much of this vote related to local issues, constituting a protest against the arrival of white migrants

from France, and the need for Guyanais to migrate there for employment, rather than 'a rejection of the French state cornucopia'.[25] Otherwise the struggle for independence appears over; 'gone are the days of
ideologies and aspirations to national dignity and pride'.[26] Nonetheless
two small independence parties, the *Parti National Populaire Guyanais*
(PNPG) and the *Mouvement de Décolonisation et d'Émancipation Sociale*
(MDES), control the main trade union in Guyane. After riots in 1996
and early 1997, ten independence supporters were arrested and gaoled
in Martinique, a situation locally regarded as deportation and an attack
on freedom of expression.[27] Significant cultural differences continue to
divide the population of Guyane; many are recent migrants from a
variety of places, and others are diverse groups of indigenous Indians. A
collective Guyanais identity is largely absent. However, pro-independence parties have stressed the role of Creole in cultural and
political consciousness in calling for the independence of 'Lagwiyann'.

In Réunion, equally tiny and radical groups also sought independence. In the 1970s Marxist groups argued strongly for independence,
but gained a much wider audience in radical African circles than
within Réunion; they ensured that there was occasional debate on the
idea of independence. However, since the autonomist *Parti Communiste
Réunionnais* already favoured nationalisation of the sugar industry, large-
scale land reforms, full employment and local control of the economy,
its programme left little place for the *indépendantistes*. For an island of its
population size, Réunion has been the least troubled by demands for
independence.

The British overseas territories have witnessed very different attitudes
to independence, though support was strongest in the early 1980s. In
the Caribbean island of Montserrat there was limited interest in
independence, after John Osborne, chief minister and leader of the
People's Liberation Movement, declared in 1979 that he would enable
Montserrat to achieve independence, though his priority was economic
development. Osborne raised the issue of independence more power-
fully in 1983, after the British government rejected the participation of
a small group from the Montserrat Defence Force in the joint US and
Caribbean invasion of Grenada. He criticised the situation where all
foreign policy initiatives had to be submitted to the governor, but won
limited support even within his government. Beyond Montserrat other
members of the Organisation of Eastern Caribbean States feared that a
declaration of independence would produce regional political instability. Osborne maintained his position, stressing the particular constitutional situation of Montserrat, which he argued gave it fewer privileges
than the Falkland Islands and Gibraltar, and maintained a definition of
Montserrat citizenship that was discriminatory and racist. In opposition

since 1991, Osborne continued to believe that Montserrat would be better off with independence, 'but I don't see us getting it without a fight'. He was particularly critical of constitutional and administrative changes introduced in 1990 and 1992 which strengthened British control over the political economy of the island, a process he saw as 'recolonisation'. Whilst there is some sympathy for these views in Montserrat, they have not convinced most Montserratians that independence provides the solution to political and economic problems.[28]

Opposition to independence focused on Montserrat's small size: 'the usual business sector's view that colonialism favours development since it creates a climate of political stability and confidence which attracts investors',[29] and thus the need for further economic and infrastructural development to precede independence. Howard Fergus, a Montserratian and the deputy governor of the island, argued:

> Constitutional independence cannot be postponed forever. It is a continuation of a journey from slavery to emancipation. ... It is my view that independence is necessary. But timing is important. Montserrat still needs critical infrastructure. ... It needs to seek the take-off of a couple of economic projects. It could not hurt if we are dependent for another two or three years, if that means ultimate independence.[30]

Ruby Wade-Bramble, a member of the Legislative Council, introducing a Position Paper to the UN Special Committee on Decolonisation, observed:

> Poverty is indeed a barrier to self-respect. Sovereignty based on poverty is a sham. Decolonisation that is a licence for mendicancy is a misnomer. So let the UN join us in a meaningful attempt to improve the economies of our small islands. Only then can we start to initiate meaningful discussion on the decolonisation process that will bring respect, dignity and happiness to the people of Montserrat.[31]

The island's chief minister, Reuben Meade, concluded in 1992: 'Independence is not a big issue for Montserrat. We are not going into independence unless we are going to get more jobs, more bread and butter on the table. We will not be pushed into independence. We will not be pushing that on the people.'[32] Concern has also emerged over the ethics of government and the need for responsibilities to accompany rights. Despite regular discussions of issues related to independence, there is minimal public support, particularly after British aid following the devastation caused by Hurricane Hugo in 1989 and volcanic eruptions in 1995.

In the Turks and Caicos Islands, a phase of interest in independence coincided, for a brief period between 1976 and 1980, with a new constitution and the political authority of the mildly populist People's Democratic Movement (PDM) led by the charismatic James (Jags) McCartney (who, however, died in a plane crash in 1980). The PDM was primarily interested in achieving full internal self-government, but both the British Labour Party and Conservative governments were willing to grant full self-government only on condition that this was a stage towards independence. A programme was devised for the Turks and Caicos to obtain full internal self-government as a UK-associated state in early 1981, and then move to full independence as early as mid-1982. The opposition Progressive National Party (PNP), a more conservative and business-oriented party, led by Norman Saunders, opposed independence on the grounds that the Turks and Caicos lacked the financial, institutional and defence resources to sustain it. In the next general election, in which the main issue was independence, eight of the eleven seats in the Legislative Council went to the PNP, with 59 per cent of the vote; 'the islanders made their verdict clear: the government was soundly defeated and all talk of independence ceased'.[33] In a period of benign neglect of the Caribbean by the British government, the Turks and Caicos had come the closest it has ever been to independence, much closer than any of the other Caribbean territories.

One of the most comprehensive statements concerning independence for the Turks and Caicos was made by Nathaniel Francis (later to be briefly the chief minister) in 1982, at a time when he, and most others, believed that independence was inevitable:

> As I study the independence of many of the countries of the West Indies . . . and when I see my own country and its own resources, I think that we will be safe to stay away from it for quite a few years. We need . . . to have our people trained in the field of medicine, in law, in architecture. We must have engineers. . . . The economy at the moment is far too low to speak about . . . if we went into premature independence . . . the masses will suffer and we will become professional beggars. People look for security; [they] will say they feel safe with you as you are; that they can invest in your country because you are under the umbrella of the British system and so their investing is safe.[34]

For the rest of the decade this perspective – that the economy was neither stable nor developed – dominated debate on independence. By the 1984 election the issue of independence, hitherto the most important in elections, had diminished in comparison with that of economic growth. The ruling PNP put independence in the distant future, whilst the PDM stated that it would not be an issue for another ten to fifteen years. This position has been subsequently maintained.[35]

No other territory has experienced such extensive and detailed consideration of independence in the last two decades as Bermuda. The first

stirrings of independence sentiment came in the mid-1960s, not much
later than in the larger now-independent British Caribbean colonies.
The Progressive Labour Party (PLP), almost entirely supported by black
Bermudians, swung broadly in favour of independence before the 1968
election, when it suffered defeat by the United Bermuda Party (UBP).
During the 1970s the UBP too began to contemplate the possibility of
independence, when Britain dissolved the sterling area and broke monetary ties with Bermuda; in 1977 the UBP government produced a Green
Paper on *Independence for Bermuda*, providing a detailed perspective on
the various costs and benefits of independence and colonial status. The
majority of UBP members opposed independence, pointing to negative
consequences elsewhere and arguing that the status quo contributed to
political, economic and social stability and avoided unnecessary costs;
the PLP argued that democracy and colonialism were incompatible. In
the 1980s interest in independence revived, with the accession to power
of John Swan, the first black Bermudian premier, and fear that independence might even be thrust upon Bermuda, as appeared to have
been the case in several British colonies in the South Pacific. Swan was
strongly committed to independence on the grounds that colonial status
was an 'affront to equality', despite considerable opposition within his
UBP party. The PLP, though still committed to independence, increasingly perceived that the position was not destined to win immediate
electoral support, in comparison to domestic economic issues. Throughout an extended debate, no arguments were produced that there would
be material gains from independence; support for independence followed ideological, psychological and cultural arguments and related to
the anticipated historical destiny of Bermuda. Opponents consistently
stressed solely economic arguments to suggest its impracticability.[36]

Independence was not put to the test of a referendum, mainly because
of widespread beliefs that inadequate information on the possible consequences prevented an informed choice. Though many in the UBP
continued to support the idea, it was a particularly divisive issue; nonetheless in 1988 Swan promised a referendum, arguing:

> It can be reasonably argued that Bermuda's ability to make its own way in the
> world and to take those actions which are in the best interests of the people
> of Bermuda – and which might not necessarily be in the best interests of the
> British government – can be secured only if Bermuda has the constitutional
> freedom to be able to exercise its judgement in its best interests.

Informal surveys found strong opposition to independence, and a
continuing divergence in opinion between black and white Bermudians.
Some UBP members formed a group to oppose independence; the PLP
opposed a referendum on the grounds that it was not part of Bermudian

tradition; a leading newspaper article quoted John Swan as saying in 1982, 'With the Americans to feed us and the British to defend us who needs independence?' The referendum was forgotten. At the 1989 general election, support for the UBP weakened, and subsequent discussion of independence was muted; the PLP leader observed, 'We still believe in independence but we believe Bermudians need to be educated. We recognise they have said they are not ready for independence at this time, so why should we push it down their throats?' The issues remained largely unchanged though cultural, social and psychological arguments gained prominence, with ethnicity becoming more significant than status. One independence supporter noted:

> To black Bermudians colonialism means chains, and puts them at a racial disadvantage. Independence would give black Bermudians a feeling of belonging and intellectual emancipation. It would benefit all races and be a catalyst for us to discover what is unique about Bermuda. Only independence can give us a sense of Bermudian nationality.

Such arguments were often ignored in an island where 30 per cent of the population were white, many of these were relatively recent migrants, and economic growth had substantially raised the standard of living.[37]

After the 1989 elections, as the issue of independence was scarcely discussed, a Committee for the Independence of Bermuda formed to ensure that debate and interest continued. The committee opposed various perceptions of independence: that it was too expensive and a disincentive to international investment and tourism; that security would be at stake; that poverty, corruption and abuse of power would follow; and that Bermuda was too small. It stressed the gains through Bermuda's ability to control its destiny and define its identity. The issue remarkably resurfaced after the 1993 elections, once again won by the UBP, when Sir John Swan declared that a referendum on independence would be held in August 1995. The premier emphasised rapid changes on the international scene – especially the growing strength of such major economic blocs as NAFTA and the European Union, and the preoccupation of the United Kingdom with European issues – alongside local changes, including the closure of the British and US military bases; these had combined to bring Bermuda to an important crossroads. Subsequent debate was complicated because of the unusual positions taken by the major political parties. The majority of UBP parliamentarians opposed independence, whilst the PLP, which had previously favoured it, called for a boycott of the referendum, on the grounds that the form of independence was uncertain and might disadvantage the PLP when prior electoral reform and constitutional change were required. This reversal of roles meant that much of the debate concerned participation in the referendum rather than the advantages and disadvantages of sovereignty.

In February 1995 the government published a Green Paper, *The Implications of Independence for Bermuda*, to allay perennial concern that citizens were inadequately informed. This reviewed the constitutional context, the implications of the transfer of reserve powers, and the costs of membership of international organisations, and concluded that political and social stability were unlikely to be affected.[38] The extended debate that ensued revisited old issues, and raised none that was new. Opponents of independence, whose advertisements dominated the media, stressed the costs of independence (and argued that these would inevitably blow out), expressed concern about patronage in key new appointments, argued that Bermuda would have less international weight (without British support), predicted that political and economic instability would result, feared for internal and external security, noted that any decision was irreversible, and maintained that pressing domestic problems should take priority. Supporters of independence recognised the costs, but stressed that these would not be great, and emphasised that Bermuda was now firmly established as a respected finance and tourist centre in the eyes of the world, hence political change would have no effect on global confidence. They argued both that it was time to emerge from the 'comfort blanket' (in Swan's words) and that independence would create a new sense of national identity, citizenship and 'belonging' in a racially divided island. These arguments were pointedly refuted by supporters of the status quo.

Colonial issues were defined in terms of the lack of identity, and the continued presence of antiquated attitudes; a racial slur was perceived in the notion that Bermuda, and thus Bermudians, were 'not ready' for independence. The chairman of the Committee for the Independence of Bermuda argued that Bermuda was an exceptionally fragmented society with people looking in every direction, to black America, white America, England and the Azores for some semblance of identity, inhibiting a Bermudian identity, whereas a new flag and anthem would provide real meaning, particularly for the young: 'We need symbols that everyone can relate to and give deference to, symbols that are far more potent and persuasive than those that are externally generated.' The most vocal UBP opponent of independence countered by asking, 'Independence from what? If you don't have national pride now, a new flag and national anthem won't do it.' Whilst most arguments were inevitably rhetorical, and were largely ignored by opponents of independence, some advocates pointed to the inequalities that existed between black and white Bermudians, the disproportionate black gaol population, an economy in which black Bermudians earned 30 per cent less than white Bermudians and more black households were on welfare, and where an electoral system disadvantaged black Bermudians.[39] The PLP, however, took the pragmatic view that such problems had to be addressed before rather than after independence.

Two polls, conducted prior to the referendum, indicated little support for independence, with opposition increasing as it drew closer; 24 per cent of black voters supported independence compared to just 5 per cent of white voters in one survey.[40] Some 59 per cent of voters eventually participated in the referendum; 74 per cent of these opposed independence, and 26 per cent supported it. Immediately after the referendum Swan resigned as premier, and the PLP emphasised that independence after constitutional reform remained on their agenda.[41]

In Bermuda, a substantial minority had continued to keep the dream of independence alive, principally by focusing on issues of national identity. With rare exceptions, however, independence movements that had been of significance in the 1970s had declined and even disappeared two decades later. Only exceptionally – and notably in two of the three French territories in the Pacific – were independence movements still active. Questions of identity, often of growing concern, held greatest significance where racial divisions were perceived to coincide with socio-economic inequality; nowhere was this more true than in New Caledonia.

The Question of New Caledonia

In most territories, the demand for independence was short-lived, supported by a small minority and conducted through the electoral process, with minimal bitterness and violence. New Caledonia was very different and unusual in the extent of conflict and bloodshed; the upsurge in nationalism prompted a sustained demand for independence, a more coherent political programme, and a mass movement that effectively challenged French hegemony. The roots lay in historical land alienation, emphasised by the failure of French authorities to carry out reforms. As other parts of the South Pacific became independent, especially neighbouring Vanuatu in 1980, and a Socialist government took power in France in 1981, Melanesian expectations for independence increased, though there was no indication that France would grant independence to New Caledonia. The pro-independence parties, united in the *Front Indépendantiste*, briefly gained power in the Territorial Assembly, in alliance with a small centre party, whilst tension and violence mounted. Kanaks were angry that no electoral reform was proposed (to disenfranchise recent arrivals who had turned Melanesians into a minority population) and there was no timetable for independence. A new coalition, the *Front de Libération Nationale Kanake et Socialiste* (FLNKS), formed in 1984 and demanded immediate independence for the state of Kanaky. As the Kanak position hardened, the conservative stand of the *Rassemblement pour la Calédonie dans la République* (RPCR) became increasingly extremist, and new right-wing parties formed to oppose the FLNKS.

Conflict escalated when Kanaks abandoned the unbalanced struggle for constitutional change, ignored the French government, and embarked on direct action to secure independence. The FLNKS boycotted elections in November 1984; the RPCR inevitably won. The FLNKS then occupied several town halls and gendarmeries, briefly held the small town of Thio, and declared a provisional government of the Republic of Kanaky with Jean-Marie Tjibaou as president. Violent conservative reaction followed; ten Kanaks were killed in an ambush at Hienghène, and ten more Kanaks and Europeans lost their lives in various incidents. New French constitutional proposals were devised for independence in association with France, with France retaining control of defence and foreign affairs, French citizens having special status, and New Caledonia moving to independence in 1986 if a referendum approved the plan. The proposals attempted to reconcile Melanesian claims to independence, the rights of French residents, and French strategic interests. The FLNKS perceived this to be a 'neo-colonial' solution and withdrew from negotiations after the death (in a police raid) of its most militant leader, Eloi Machoro. The French military presence was strengthened, and violent right-wing opposition to Kanak militancy grew.

New government proposals divided New Caledonia into four regions, each with a council responsible for a range of development planning issues; the FLNKS eventually accepted this, though continuing to distrust France. The FLNKS then withdrew from violent action and promoted a more self-reliant Melanesian society and economy in rural areas; it established alternative schools and encouraged cooperative agriculture in a bid to destabilise the economy of Noumea. In the elections for regional councils in September 1985, the FLNKS won three of the four regions, though the RPCR comprehensively triumphed around Noumea, so retaining control of the Territorial Congress. The election was fought solely over the issue of independence; in the highest turnout in history, 38 per cent of the voters, mainly on the east coast and in the islands, supported independence and 61 per cent were opposed. These proportions demonstrated the improbability of independence being gained constitutionally without some dramatic restriction of universal suffrage. Nevertheless FLNKS successes prompted renewed right-wing violence, with sporadic bombings, mainly of institutions favouring Melanesian development, and of the homes and cars of FLNKS supporters. In rural areas Kanak destruction of settlers' property also continued sporadically, and the new regional councils lacked funds to implement policy. The FLNKS coalition weakened, as the most important party within it, Tjibaou's *Union Calédonienne* (UC), chose a policy of greater compromise, whilst others, especially the *Front Uni de Libération Kanake* (FULK), maintained a confrontationist position.

The 1986 elections that brought Jacques Chirac to power as prime minister in Paris were boycotted by the FLNKS; hence the new and extremely conservative RPCR–*Front National* coalition swept the territory by gaining 89 per cent of the vote, though only half the electorate voted. The new government increased the authority of the French high commissioner and the RPCR-controlled Territorial Congress; though the regional councils remained in place, their funds were effectively frozen. This shift removed the possibility of the FLNKS regional governments adopting radical initiatives. The military presence was increased, and some of the 6000 troops in New Caledonia were dispersed throughout the countryside in a policy of 'nomadisation'. The FLNKS lost much of its power in the regions, the only places where it held legal and constitutional authority. Its minor achievements had largely disappeared, though its support had not been eroded.

Denied success within New Caledonia, the FLNKS switched to recruiting international support within the Pacific region and beyond. In March 1985 a delegation went to New York to attempt to have New Caledonia considered by the UN Special Committee on Decolonisation. However, only when the South Pacific Forum, an assembly of independent Pacific states (including Australia and New Zealand), agreed to raise the issue collectively after its 1986 meeting, did action appear likely. France launched a diplomatic offensive in the United Nations, aimed at countries sympathetic to the FLNKS (particularly Australia), but the UN General Assembly voted 89 to 24 (with 34 abstentions) in favour of referring New Caledonia to the Special Committee, effectively classifying New Caledonia as a colony. France rejected the decision, and refused the admission of UN officials to monitor developments.

The French government moved forward with plans to hold a referendum on independence in 1987. The FLNKS voted to boycott the referendum in order to 'destabilise the strategy of the colonial government', and embarked on a series of protests leading to strong repression from the French riot police. The referendum, held in September 1987, resulted in 57 per cent of the electorate voting in favour of remaining with France. Almost all the remainder of the electorate abstained. Once again, but for the first time in a referendum, the electorate had firmly voted against decolonisation; indeed almost 20 per cent of Melanesians voted against independence.

A new statute was introduced in New Caledonia which redrew the boundaries of the regions to produce quite different units, so that the FLNKS would be likely to control only two rather than three regions. The demise of the old regions, alongside Kanak electoral boycotts, left Kanaks powerless and with little incentive to take part in new political structures. Melanesians were no longer to have any distinct civil status but would be entirely subject to French law. Tjibaou bitterly accused France of 'cultural genocide', noting that the statute 'would mark the end of the Kanaks as people', and called for a 'muscular mobilisation' to oppose a statute that offered no concessions to Kanak aspirations. The political situation further deteriorated as land conflicts surfaced again on the east coast, and seven men accused of the murder of ten Kanaks in 1984 were acquitted by a jury which contained no Melanesians. Acute frustration and despondency had again brought the FLNKS to a position where it appeared that only a violent struggle could convince France of the gravity and legitimacy of its claims and again attract the attention of the world.

The French presidential elections and the New Caledonian regional elections were set for the same day in April 1988, a decision which angered the FLNKS. The secretary-general of the UC warned that 'the government will have to face the consequence of what will happen in the territory'. Two days before the elections, a commando group of Kanaks made a dawn raid on a gendarmerie on Ouvea island, killing four gendarmes and taking twenty-seven hostages. Some were released a few days later, but other police and officials who subsequently arrived were taken hostage, and transported to a coral cave. Kanaks demanded the cancellation of the statute and the regional elections, the withdrawal of the military from the island, and a new referendum supervised by the United Nations. As the hostages, deemed 'prisoners of war', remained in Ouvea, the first round of the presidential elections went ahead, disturbed by violent events in different parts of New Caledonia. Little more than half the population voted. The RPCR gained 64 per cent of the votes and thirty-five of the forty-eight seats in the Territorial Congress, whilst the *Front National* substantially increased its support. In the presidential elections, Jacques Chirac won 75 per cent of the vote in New Caledonia, Jean-Marie Le Pen of the *Front National* gained 12 per cent, and François Mitterrand received a derisory 5 per cent. Two days before the second round of elections, army units stormed the Ouvea cave, rescued the remaining hostages and killed nineteen Kanak militants. Two soldiers were also killed. Evidence trickled in that three militants were killed after their capture. The FLNKS promised that 'neither deaths, tears, suffering nor humiliation will stifle the cry for freedom'.

The re-election of President Mitterrand brought an end to the confrontationist policies of the Chirac era, and dismayed New Caledonian 'loyalists'. The new prime minister, Michel Rocard, held talks in Paris with the FLNKS and the RPCR, leading to the signing of the Matignon Accord. This established direct rule from France for a year, divided New Caledonia into three regions (two of which would be controlled by *indépendantistes*), established new economic development strategies, and proposed a second referendum on independence in 1998 under a different electoral system. Rocard described this as 'decolonisation within the framework of French institutions'. Much of the increased French financial support was directed at training Kanak bureaucrats. Optimists in the FLNKS, like Tjibaou, saw in the new regions the opportunity to demonstrate their legitimacy and effectiveness in power. A more cynical view was that, if further substantial economic resources were diverted from Paris to rural New Caledonia, an even more artificial economy would be created and many Kanaks would achieve positions of power, status and higher income in the emerging economic system. Whereas the previous FLNKS strategy was to set an independence date and then seek to construct the basis of a sovereign state before that deadline, the accord reversed this procedure and so reduced the probability of independence.

The proposal for a new referendum on independence in 1998 resulted in substantial debate on the formation of the electorate. The FLNKS sought to restrict the 1998 electorate to those born in New Caledonia, and requested a range of policies discouraging immigration from France alongside new measures to ensure that people would not vote against independence for economic reasons; these included the abolition of salary bonuses and supplementary benefits for metropolitan migrants to New Caledonia. There was also FLNKS concern that independence had been postponed for at least a decade. The small Kanak party FULK, often at odds with the rest of the FLNKS, was hostile to the accord, though most FLNKS supporters welcomed it, and applauded Tjibaou's role in achieving agreement.

Exactly a year after the events of Ouvea, following a period of peace in the wake of the Matignon Accord, the FLNKS leader, Jean-Marie Tjibaou, and the deputy leader, Yeiwene Yeiwene, were murdered by a dissident FLNKS supporter at a memorial service for the victims of the Ouvea violence. The assassinations pointed to divisions within the FLNKS, and these divisions increased further. The UC elected a new leader, François Burck, who stated that independence was not solely for Kanaks but would involve everyone and that 'independence means changing our relations with France – no longer colonial relations but a partnership. Independence means being able to choose

interdependence. And the partner that we must look towards is France.'
It appeared a withdrawal from earlier FLNKS aims. The loss of the sole
leader who had united the FLNKS emphasised the task of a divided independence movement, supported by a minority of the New Caledonian
population.[42]

Divisions were reflected in problems in selecting a replacement for
Tjibaou. Eventually Paul Neaoutyine, from the radical *Parti de Libération
Kanake* (PALIKA) was elected FLNKS president, and he rejected Burck's
position on interdependence. Consensus was lacking on whether the
FLNKS, or constituent parties, should boycott French national elections,
and electoral support for the FLNKS declined substantially. The *Libération Kanak Socialiste* (LKS) party, a signatory to the Matignon Accord but
outside the FLNKS, withdrew from negotiations, accusing both the
FLNKS and the French government of undermining Kanak culture and
tradition. French financial assistance to the regions meanwhile increased
substantially, raising expectations of employment and high wages,
though the economic gains were sometimes concentrated in the hands
of few; increased migration to squatter settlements on the fringes of
Noumea ensued. The public sector was further inflated, but production
did not significantly increase, though some tourism and mining projects
were initiated by FLNKS-controlled provinces.[43]

The UC, in 1993, called for accession to sovereignty in 1998, with a
timetable for the transfer of various administrative responsibilities
before full independence. Most other groups within the FLNKS had
separately called for a more concerted programme to ensure independence by that date. As the 1998 referendum drew closer, both the FLNKS
and the RPCR sought some means of achieving prior consensus to avoid
the possibility of another stalemate, or renewed violence. At the end of
1995 the FLNKS presented a proposal to establish a new state in 1998,
but with France retaining control of some areas (including law and
order, foreign affairs and defence) at least until 2001; the length of the
transition period would be open to negotiation, but it must lead to full
independence, and be accompanied by the 'rebalancing' of the economy, to enable New Caledonia to achieve 'economic independence' and
reduce the extent of uneven development. A parallel proposal from the
RPCR called for 'emancipation' and decentralisation of power from
France, other than defence, foreign affairs and public order, but recommended a thirty-year 'pact of peace and development' during which
New Caledonia would remain part of France; its leader, Jacques Lafleur,
warned of the danger of a 'racist independence'.

Talks between France and the two political organisations subsequently
suggested some possibility of a form of 'independence in association',
similar to that proposed in 1985. The French prime minister, Alain

Juppé, proposed a statute of internal autonomy – a clear indication that France did not accept ultimate independence for the territory. The new FLNKS president, Rock Wamytan, reaffirmed the basic FLNKS demand for a New Caledonian state, immediately after the referendum, that would then control immigration, island resources and education, whilst sharing sovereignty with France in other areas for as short a period as possible. The FLNKS, concerned over France's negative attitude towards independence, later withdrew from negotiations; it stated its unwillingness to settle for some middle ground between independence and 'colonialism', and stressed that the only area for debate concerned the time-frame for transferring specific responsibilities. The FLNKS proposed direct negotiations with the French state – rather than a 'consensual solution' with the RPCR – as the means of progress, and lobbied the UN Special Committee for its further involvement. Wamytan argued in mid-1996: 'If we establish the basis for an Associated State in 1998, with all the attributes of sovereignty, the French state keeping defence, security, etc., but with us having all the rest – we are already, in effect, independent.' The FLNKS was willing to be flexible about the name and the anthem of a sovereign state but was inflexible over the Kanaky flag: 'too many have died for it and, what is more, it's a beautiful flag'.[44] It remained committed to independence, but there were divisions within the coalition over the appropriate strategy for achieving it, the time-period involved, and the form that it would eventually take. After almost two decades of often bitter and violent struggle, the resolution of the issue of independence in New Caledonia was far from being concluded.

Perceptions of Fragility: The Smallest Territories

Concerns over limited economic development and security, often perceived to be the principal constraints to achieving independence in many territories, were overwhelming in the smaller, more isolated ones. In such remote places as Pitcairn, Tokelau and Tristan da Cunha, there could be no consideration of anything other than dependent status. Indeed, when Britain withdrew from its Pacific colonies in the 1970s Pitcairn resisted every effort of the United Kingdom to 'get off the hook', ensuring that it remained a 'captive patron'.[45] The inhabitants of Anguilla and Mayotte actively resisted any move towards independence. Although there are independent states of similar size, few, if any, residents welcomed the prospect of what was perceived as that 'fate' befalling them. In a range of territories – the Isle of Man, Jersey and Guernsey, Ceuta and Melilla, Curaçao and Bonaire, Saint-Pierre-et-Miquelon and Wallis and Futuna, St Eustatius and Saba,[46] the Northern Marianas, American Samoa and elsewhere – the possibility of independence does

not appear to have been used even as a rhetorical device against stub-
born metropolitan states. The Turks and Caicos Islands is the smallest
territory, in population size or land area, where independence has been
seriously contemplated; it is rather larger than some independent states.

Even hints of radical change have usually been short-lived; in
St Helena in 1974 an opposition Labour Party was formed, advocating
private enterprise in response to government control of the economy
and government development aid. In 1976 the party's founder, Tony
Thornton, a South African businessman, was expelled from the island,
and the party failed to win a seat in the Legislative Council elections,
thus demonstrating local 'unwillingness to take steps that could reduce
the flow of British aid'.[47] More than a decade later, not one person in a
large survey sought independence; residents rejected independence on
the grounds of size, isolation and lack of resources, and remained
conscious of the economic benefits of British ties.[48] Indeed in 1996 a
commission set up by the bishop of St Helena recommended closer ties
between the island and Britain. It argued that a royal charter of 1673,
which had stated that St Helena was to be in perpetuity part of England
and its inhabitants citizens, had not been honoured. In particular, the
report said that the British Nationality Act of 1981, which did not give
St Helenians full British citizenship, was a betrayal of islanders' historic
rights. St Helenians, because of the origin of the island as a British
fortress colony, their English language, shared system of values and
loyalty to the monarchy, deserved full citizenship. Arguments about
geographical distance from Britain, racial difference, poverty, or lack of
economic self-sufficiency could not justify continued discrimination.
'Saint Helenians are not trying to become British. They are already, and
always have been British', the report concluded. Comparisons of the full
citizenship rights enjoyed, for instance, by Canary Islanders in Spain, or
residents of Saint-Pierre-et-Miquelon in France, they argued, proved that
integration was possible.

Considering how to redress the islanders' grievances, the bishop's
commission rejected independence – 'it is only feasible if Saint
Helenians as a whole were prepared to accept a devastating increase in
poverty or massive depopulation' – but also considered that the status
quo was not acceptable. Full integration into Britain would be problematic: 'If St. Helena were to become as indistinguishably part of England
as Tunbridge Wells, it could not be accorded full shire-county status, for
it is too small. . . . In theory, St. Helena could become like the Isle of
Wight; in practice, it would be extremely difficult.' Two other alternatives would be easier: either the British government 'could restore a full
British passport to all Saint Helenians who want one, without changing
anything else' or, preferably, the island could become an 'autonomous

United Kingdom overseas territory' with residents 'sharing the full rights of all other British citizens' on the model of the Isle of Man and the Channel Islands.[49]

The discontent of St Helenians was confirmed in April 1997, when a tiny band of islanders, in opposition to cuts in finances, rising unemployment and the perceived 'dictatorial' style of the governor, burned a police van, weather station and bus. A former governor accused London of neglecting the island and, in general, avoiding consideration of the long-term future of British dependencies.[50]

Cocos (Keeling) Islanders were asked in a referendum in 1984 to vote on whether they wished to be a sovereign state, be freely associated with Australia (sharing defence and foreign policy) or be integrated into Australia. Just nine voters (4 per cent of the total) chose independence, and only twenty-one chose free association, despite some encouragement to choose the first option.[51] A decade later a similar referendum on nearby Christmas Island also resulted in just 4 per cent of the electorate voting for full independence, with a minority preferring increased self-government.[52] The vast majority of eligible voters chose a third option, and the islands were integrated into Australia. This almost unanimous opposition to independence is typical of the smallest territories, where the prospect has rarely been considered, even with encouragement from the UN Special Committee on Decolonisation. It is even more typical of outlying islands and regions in many territories, through concern that these areas would be neglected by a new central government if independence occurred. This was apparent in the Azores, and is particularly evident in outlying islands in the French territories, such as the Marquesas and the Australs of French Polynesia.[53]

In somewhat larger territories, the political situation has been more complex. In Anguilla, a quarter of a century after its secession from St Kitts–Nevis in order to remain a British colony, a widespread view held that separation had finalised political status. Underlying secession was the need for security, identity, and local control over economic development. That has substantially been achieved, leading one Anguillan to state: 'All that has happened to Anguilla economically since 1967 and particularly since 1976 is directly related to the creation of formal and stable constitutional arrangements.' The chief minister, Emile Gumbs, has subsequently argued:

> The new Anguilla we set out to build, and to a large extent have built, is now under siege from within, in the form of greed. The drive to immediate riches is threatening our environment, our health and our way of life in Anguilla. If we fall into the clutches of the drug overlords . . . we . . . may stand to lose everything we have fought so hard for – our freedoms: personal, economic and political.

In 1990 the Anguilla government requested the United Kingdom to play a more substantial role in regulating offshore banking. Underlying this perspective is what had become a familiar refrain: the need for stability and 'economic self-reliance to underpin any move to constitutional independence'. Some dissident voices focused on the social consequences of dependence; Victor Ebanks, a member of the House of Assembly, claimed that although Britain proved a stabilising force in earlier years, 'as the need to develop our own institutions and develop a national identity becomes more urgent in the face of an ever-changing world political environment, their tutelage is not being directed to the building of a strong national esteem'.[54] Nevertheless, there is no interest in constitutional change, and 'by general consent, any politician who campaigned for independence in Anguilla would not be elected'.[55]

In Wallis and Futuna, traditional Polynesian leaders (the three kings of Futuna and Wallis) and the Catholic Church have been powerful supporters of the political status quo. During the 1980s less conservative politicians emerged because of the inappropriateness and rigidity with which France provided financial support, rather than in opposition to the political status. Local politics has remained placid in comparison with France's two other Pacific territories. This is partly because, despite French financial assistance, Wallis and Futuna exhibits a 'de facto independence . . . where the customary authorities retain all their prerogatives [and the three kings] are the unchallenged spokesmen with an administration occasionally left powerless'.[56] The Director of Cultural Affairs in the territory, a senior Wallisian bureaucrat, has declared that 'we have independence within the Republic'.[57] Wallis and Futuna achieved a negotiated political dependence, at its own pace and in its own style. The strengthening of the independence movement in New Caledonia caused concern, because it might have destabilised local politics and resulted in unemployment and even return migration. In New Caledonia many Wallisians joined right-wing anti-FLNKS militia, though the 1990s saw some reconciliation between Wallisians and Kanaks.

Mayotte, having voted against independence in 1976, with 99.4 per cent of the electorate choosing France, seems destined to remain a French outpost for the foreseeable future, though the UN General Assembly has twice voted in support of Comorian sovereignty over the island. A referendum should have been held before the end of 1984, but the French government deferred it indefinitely, then said it would be held before the end of the century. Since the Comoros, with a population more than five times that of Mayotte, is one of the poorest states in the world, the prospect of renewed integration is unlikely; indeed, in 1997 a secessionist revolt on the adjoining Comoros island of Anjouan sought to return that island to French rule. More than in most territories, the islanders 'compare the quality of life to that of their former compatriots who chose independence'. As France embarked on an extensive public works programme in Mayotte, these disparities intensified. The present processes of economic integration will forestall demands for independence, or for ties with the Comoros. Most of the population prefer greater political incorporation into France through formal *département* status.[58]

In Niue, independence was sometimes considered, but never seriously discussed. Yet neither the Niuean or New Zealand governments favoured integration with New Zealand. For an island where an increasing proportion of the population had moved to New Zealand, most felt 'that if after 70-odd years New Zealand had not been able to meet their expectations, Niue with her vastly inferior resources could hardly be expected to do so'.[59] There were even fears that New Zealand might thrust independence upon an unwilling territory, but as migration increased such a likelihood diminished. Constitutional changes in Niue have not taken it closer to independence.

Of all the British Caribbean territories, much the most opposed to any movement towards independence has been the Cayman Islands. As in Anguilla, an economic element enters into this stance. When Jamaica gained independence in 1962, the Cayman Islands opted to remain a dependent territory, fearing that independence might prevent special US visa privileges that enabled Caymanian sailors to work on American ships and elsewhere in the United States. Subsequently, a preference for colonial status has never waned. There are no real political parties, though in the 1992 general election a loose grouping called the National Team won twelve of the fifteen seats; it opposed constitutional change and especially the creation of a new post of chief minister. One National Team member observed that such changes would be 'a major step, which leaves only one step before declaring independence. . . . Every move forward relating to the Chief Minister is a move towards independence.'[60] Other candidates were vilified (without apparent justification) as supporters of a chief minister and hence of constitutional change. Discussion of constitutional change had been initiated by Britain in 1990, when the lack of any constitutional provision for a head of government was viewed as an anachronism, leading to undue decision-making by the governor. The constitutional commissioners argued that this structure was 'less advanced – and, we believe, less effective – than those enjoyed by other Caribbean dependent territories for the last 20 or 30 years'.[61] This view was nevertheless rejected in the Cayman Islands, and very few changes of any kind followed a formal constitutional review.

Early in 1993 the UN Special Committee on Decolonisation expressed regret that it was difficult to obtain adequate information on political and social issues in the Cayman Islands, and thus sought to visit the colony. This provoked heated reactions in the Cayman Islands; the Leader of Government Business, Thomas Jefferson, retorted:

> The UN's attitude has always been that the only means of self-determination is independence. Self-determination as far as the Cayman Islands is concerned is being in a position in which we can look after ourselves financially and keep the door open for the UK to represent us around the world and to be a part of the British system, judicially or otherwise. The people of the Cayman Islands do not want a mad rush forward into other forms of constitutional change. I believe they are sufficiently aware of countries, particularly in the Caribbean, that have gone independent and it would appear that they are worse off. We have been able to attract substantial investment into this country. This has to give some type of confidence in our system.[62]

This attitude was expressed even more bluntly by Berna Thompson-Murphy, another member of the National Team:

> The UN has a responsibility to investigate whether colonies would want to become independent. At one time, this was a useful exercise, as there were some colonies which were oppressed by the mother countries; but there are very few, if any, colonies which still fall into this category. In the case of Cayman we are fully committed to remaining a crown colony. . . . Even the discussion of independence is out of the question. . . . If the foreign press headlines say 'UN Commission returns from Cayman following negotiations for independence' you can bet we'll see investors' money leaving Cayman immediately after. We can't allow them any room to suggest that independence can even be discussed.[63]

Indeed the constitutional commissioners had themselves recorded: 'There is no wish whatsoever to alter the present status of the islands as a Dependent Territory on which, it must be said, much of the islands' present prosperity may depend.'[64]

In the British Virgin Islands, there has similarly been minimal interest in independence. The issue did, however, emerge in the 1970s, when discussions were taking place in Bermuda and the Turks and Caicos Islands, and the British government had raised the question of independence for the remaining colonies. Lack of interest did not change as the territory became more reliant on tourism and financial services, avoiding the criticisms and doubt attached to financial services in Montserrat and Anguilla; the combination of 'American money, British security' is perceived as central to future economic and political development. In 1990 the deputy chief minister, Ralph O'Neal, told the UN Special Committee: 'The British Virgin Islands will not be bullied, provoked, coerced or sweetmouthed into independence.'[65] That situation has not subsequently changed.

In some contexts where there was apparent interest in independence, it halted, often quite abruptly, as economic circumstances changed, whilst some territories set clear limits on the degree of decolonisation. Nowhere has the move towards independence been more swiftly re-routed than in Aruba. After discussions with the Netherlands in the early 1980s, Aruba broke away from the other five Netherlands Antilles to achieve a separate status – *status aparte* – comparable to associate statehood. The prime mover in achieving this was the pro-independence party, *Movimento Electoral di Pueblo* (MEP), which argued that other islands were making unjust claims on Aruban resources and revenues. The 1983 discussions resulted in an accord on a ten-year transitional period that would culminate in the independence of Aruba in 1996 (though it would retain a common currency and monetary policy with the Netherlands Antilles). In 1985, however, the island's principal employer, Exxon's Lago oil refinery, closed down, depriving the island of more than one-third of its income. The MEP government immediately introduced an austerity package, and consequently lost its majority in the island council, though it proceeded with plans for autonomy and independence. Continued interest in independence was short-lived, and in 1990 the Aruba government asked the Netherlands to cancel the agreement that would have given it automatic independence in 1996.

In the late 1980s a minority push for independence in Sint-Maarten occurred, as in Aruba, as much in frustration at 'colonialism' from Curaçao as from the Netherlands. Claude Wathey, a senator in the Netherlands Antilles assembly, sought movement towards *status aparte* and on to independence, claiming that economic assistance would be greater after independence; others argued that it was necessary to move away from a 'one-product' tourist economy, that was in effect 'one big slave plantation'.[66] Political support was weak, however; Wathey lost support, and the moment foundered.

Movements towards independence slowed in other territories. After the Cook Islands established 'free association' with New Zealand, it initiated 'the emergence of an embryonic "international personality" of [its] own, and a very careful balancing act [was] required to avoid inadvertent crossing of the boundary into full independence'.[67] Being cast entirely adrift was too much to envisage, and most Cook Islanders perceive their associated status in a positive light. A former cabinet minister has stressed:

Today, we in the Cook Islands take the attitude that we are independent. We have gone as far as we want. Whatever we want we can get. The fact that we don't want full constitutional independence doesn't necessarily mean that we are not independent in practice. If we want tomorrow to be completely independent we have the authority to make that change.[68]

That change would demand renouncing New Zealand citizenship, and – with meagre resources – developing an independent monetary and fiscal policy. The situation was similar in the Northern Marianas, where 79 per cent voted in favour of commonwealth status, as the territory emerged from the Trust Territory of the Pacific Islands in 1976. Subsequently there was no demand for any other political status, despite resentment against Washington for 'insensitivity' to local needs and 'misunder-standing' of the 'internal sovereignty' granted to the Marianas.[69]

Whilst the smallest territories were often wholly opposed to any movement towards independence, opposition was also exceptionally powerful in such large territories as the French Caribbean *départements* (hence the intermittent resort to violence by proponents of independ-ence) and in islands like Guam, where inhabitants sought stronger ties with the metropolitan power. From the 1970s onwards, when many territories were contemplating independence, Guam increasingly sought more substantial ties with the United States. In 1976, in the first of three plebiscites, just 5 per cent voted for independence and 3 per cent for an 'other' unspecified status. Subsequent plebiscites registered declining support for independence. The preferred options were full statehood or commonwealth status, like the neighbouring Northern Marianas.[70] Commonwealth status was perceived as particularly attrac-tive, in terms of growing Chamorro demands for political recognition, emphasised by opposition to US immigration policies, which permitted migrants (then primarily from the Philippines) to enter Guam, and become US citizens, increasing the local population but reducing the proportion of Chamorros in that population. Chamorros resented the loss of local economic control, with much of the tourist industry and other 'modern' activities owned by outsiders, alongside retention by the United States of about one-third of the local land area for military purposes.[71] In 1987 a draft Guam Commonwealth Act, which contained sections on Chamorro self-determination and immigration controls, was prepared by a local Commission on Self-Determination and approved by the electorate; though introduced into both houses of the US Congress, it was never enacted.

Growing political awareness made residents in many overseas terri-tories increasingly conscious of their limited ability to determine their own destiny yet, as often as not, they chose to retain faith in metro-politan states exercising wise judgement on their behalf, intervening in times of crisis and supporting sometimes fragile and minuscule economies. Economic support was widely seen to give residents a stake in a more prosperous economy than would otherwise be possible, and adequate compensation for limited political empowerment. Nevertheless, only in the smallest territories was there real consensus over future political status. Otherwise, even where independence was not an issue, tension and divisions continually surfaced over the nature of the relationship with the metropolitan state. Such divisions were greatest where questions of inequality, ethnicity and national identity were also at stake.

Society, Culture and Nationalism

One of the strongest motivations for seeking independence has been a sense of shared identity which differentiated colonised people from those of the country which ruled over them. The elements of that identity, a crucial aspect of colonial nationalism, included language, ethnicity, religion and culture. The celebrated phrase of one campaigner for Algerian independence – 'Algeria is my country, Islam my religion, Arabic my language'[72] – underlined the differences between a Muslim North African and the French overlords, and implied that he or she was not, and could not be, an imitation French person. Yet relatively few colonies contained anything approaching a culturally homogeneous population, and forging a national identity meant surmounting social cleavages which predated the arrival of colonialists, as well as those produced by colonialism itself. Indeed, the colonial epoch – through such developments as European settlement overseas, the import of slaves and indentured labour, practices of 'divide and rule', the introduction of Christianity, the fostering of new elites, and policies of cultural assimilation – effectively created new societies in domains conquered by expanding powers.

The contemporary overseas territories bear the distinct imprint of the demographic, social and cultural effects of colonialism. They broadly form three groups: those where a population of European descent are a majority (although sometimes with large non-European minorities); those where an indigenous population still predominates or forms a near majority (despite the presence of some residents of European ancestry); and other territories which were uninhabited or where the indigenous population has not survived (such as the Creole territories of the Caribbean) and hence the present-day inhabitants are a product of colonial history.

European populations predominate in a few territories. Among the French outposts, tiny Saint-Pierre-et-Miquelon and Saint-Barthélemy (Guadeloupe) are the only islands where almost all claim European ancestry. Residents of Saint-Pierre descend from fishermen from the Basque region and Normandy who migrated to the North Atlantic, and inhabitants of Saint-Barthélemy also trace their origins to Norman migrants. In the British overseas domains, Falkland Islanders are almost exclusively of British descent. In Gibraltar, the majority of residents are of European though not necessarily British origin; most descend from Spaniards, Genoese or Maltese, but there is a sizeable minority of North Africans. The Isle of Man and the Channel Islands are more exclusively British. Ceuta and Melilla host a large number of North Africans, primarily from Morocco, although the forebears of most residents came from southern Spain. The Canary Islands, Madeira and the Azores have primarily Spanish and Portuguese populations; in the Canary Islands, a few place names, surnames and physical characteristics are all that remain of the Guanches, conquered by the Spanish at the end of the fifteenth century. The majority of Puerto Ricans descend from Spanish settlers, though there are also many Puerto Ricans of African background; hence, despite European ancestral roots, most Puerto Ricans feel themselves a different society from that of the United States. In the northern Atlantic, Faeroe Islanders are all of Scandinavian stock; the Norse settled the islands in the eighth century. Finally, in Oceania, Norfolk Island and Pitcairn have populations of primarily British descent, despite the ideology of Polynesian ancestry.

The population of these territories is not homogeneous; there are, for instance, Indians in Gibraltar and the Spanish enclaves in North Africa. Nevertheless, they are microcosms of European society, itself far from homogeneous. Local folklorists vaunt the particularities of their cultures, such as dress, music and variations in language, but these have tended to disappear in an age of mass consumer culture. In the Faeroes, certain linguistic peculiarities – such as a letter in the Faeroes alphabet which has disappeared from most other Scandinavian languages – are survivals from Old Norse. The Isle of Man has its own language, but few residents can or do speak Manx. Differences between the people of these territories and their compatriots in the 'mother countries' are not strikingly apparent; they share the same ethnic background, language, religion and general culture. (Puerto Rico, where Spanish is the usual language and a Spanish inheritance strongly marks the culture, is something of an exception.) They are also – and it is not inconsequential – of the same physical appearance as the majority of the metropolitan population. The standard of living in these territories is high, relative to most territories, although significantly lower in Puerto Rico than on the mainland of the United States, and lower for Arabs in Ceuta and Melilla than for Spaniards. In Saint-Pierre, French transfers largely account for the reasonably prosperous status of local residents, whilst Saint-

Barthélemy, with a prosperous tourist economy, is better off than most of Guadeloupe. In none of these territories has there emerged a strong independence movement, though Norfolk Islanders, Gibraltarians and Spaniards in the *presidios* have pressed for greater autonomy from their national capital. Britain justified the Falklands War of 1982 partly because of the islanders' wish to remain British. Areas of European demographic domination thus show little inclination to cut links with their metropoles.

A larger group of overseas territories are those where an indigenous population has survived, sometimes flourished, and occasionally constitutes the overwhelming majority. Here differences between the territories and the metropoles are most obvious. Macao, where residents of Chinese ancestry vastly outnumber European or other permanent or short-term residents, is such a case. So is Mayotte, where perhaps 2000 French men and women live among 100,000 Mahorais, almost all of whom are Muslims and only one-third of whom speak French; and Greenland, where a minority of Danes live amidst the indigenous Greenlandic people. All but a handful of residents in Wallis and Futuna are Polynesian, as are some two-thirds of the inhabitants of French Polynesia (although in the latter case much intermarriage between Polynesians and Europeans has occurred). In American Samoa and all New Zealand's territories, the inhabitants are also Polynesian. In Guam and the Northern Marianas, the indigenous population are Chamorros, now a minority in both territories following extensive immigration. In New Caledonia the largest distinct group are indigenous Melanesians, though they too have become a minority. With the exception of the Muslims of various Indian Ocean territories – Mayotte, Christmas Island and the Cocos (Keeling) Islands – and the Buddhists and Confucians in Macao, most of the inhabitants of the territories are Christian. Otherwise, there are significant cultural and social differences between them and their fellow metropolitan citizens.

The situation in Oceania illustrates this cultural diversity. In the territories of France, New Zealand and the United States, a variety of indigenous languages are spoken: Tahitian, Marquesan, Samoan, Wallisian and other Polynesian languages in the southeastern Pacific, almost thirty Melanesian languages in New Caledonia, and Chamorro in the Marianas. Languages such as Samoan and Chamorro were, and are, largely oral, and islanders have long accepted English (or French) as the usual language of education. Although most islanders speak either English or French (depending on the territory), their first language, and the one most often used, is an Oceanic one. Older people sometimes speak only Oceanic languages, and school children, more accustomed to Oceanic languages, face disadvantages in classrooms where a

European language is the medium of instruction. Despite conversions to Christianity, many older values and customs remain strong: ritual exchange of gifts and paying of homage ('custom') in Melanesia, deference to chiefs and elders, ceremonies associated with food and drink (such as the drinking of kava), distinct cuisines, forms of art, music and architecture (for example, the thatched houses of Polynesia), ornamentation (such as Polynesian tattooing), and beliefs in other spirit worlds. Indeed recent years have seen a revival of customs and languages, especially by younger people, in an attempt to reinforce local identities and limit the extent of Westernisation. Such beliefs and practices are indicative of underlying value-systems often at odds with those in metropolitan states.

Cultural differences are not just a matter of ritual and ceremony; they also emphasise profound variations in economic and political principles. For instance, a strong attachment to land, where it is a source of clan identity, communal ownership of property, and allocation of land rights by chiefs – traditional parts of Melanesian culture in New Caledonia – have no counterparts in French law and consequently make land issues a prime point of contention. The role of traditional chiefs, such as the kings of Wallis and Futuna, does not easily blend with the dictates of constitutional authority and representative government; the idea of consensual agreement on major issues differs from the precept of 'one person, one vote' and decisions determined by majority views.

Such differences are evident in New Caledonia. The French, who ruled it from 1853, denigrated what they saw as 'primitive' art and architecture, 'superstitious' beliefs, lawlessness, and general 'savagery'. Missionaries tried to convert the 'heathen' and largely succeeded; adoption of Christianity for Melanesians, however, did not mean wholesale renunciation of traditional society and culture. France saw New Caledonia primarily in terms of its use as a site for a penal colony and a base for settlers. Land alienation reduced Melanesian landholdings to one-tenth of the area of the New Caledonian mainland, generally the least fertile and most mountainous parts of the island, and Melanesians were marginalised socially, economically and geographically. Their population fell sharply from the 1850s until the 1920s, exacerbated by Asian labour migration and subsequently by more diverse migration from Europe, North Africa and Polynesia. The genesis of the independence movement constituted an attempt by indigenous Melanesians to reassert their cultural, social and territorial rights after more than a hundred years of migration and demographic colonisation. Despite associated social and economic change, Melanesians remained culturally distinct and claimed rights based on their status as the first inhabitants of New Caledonia. Ethnicity, and the legitimacy of claims to New

Caledonia, thus became a major, and seemingly irreconcilable, difference between various groups in New Caledonia.

Many territories have witnessed intermarriage between indigenous peoples and migrants. Although ethnic groups are socially distinct and even geographically separate, in several territories and at different scales, as in New Caledonia, Greenland and the Spanish North African *presidios*, social interaction is more common. The fifty inhabitants of Pitcairn Island, for instance, descend from eighteenth-century British sailors on the HMS *Bounty* and Polynesian women with whom they formed liaisons. In French Polynesia, so many residents have both European and Polynesian ancestors that it is unlikely that many 'pure' Polynesians remain. So complete has been ethnic and cultural mixture in French Polynesia that Tahiti has been seen as essentially a 'half-breed' (*métis*) island.[73] However, the socially and politically privileged group in the islands, locally known as *demis* ('halves'), are those with European and Polynesian roots, men and women who are generally fluent in both Polynesian languages and French, and whose culture borrows from the diverse traditions. Here, as elsewhere, culture and ethnicity are partly a matter of choice.

Territories where culture and ethnicity are most intricately interwoven are mainly those where indigenous populations were non-existent, or failed to survive early phases of colonialism. Even then there are exceptions; the migrant populations of both the Cocos (Keeling) Islands and Christmas Island are ethnically Chinese and Malay, and are quite distinct from each other and the smaller European population. Interwoven ethnicities are particularly evident in the various Caribbean territories (including Guyane), Bermuda and St Helena in the Atlantic and Réunion in the Indian Ocean. Most of the populations of the West Indian and Indian Ocean territories are descended from African slaves imported to work on sugar plantations, or, to a lesser extent, from indentured Indian labourers recruited after the abolition of slavery, as well as European settlers. In Martinique the *Békés* are a small group of Europeans descended from the original sugar-planters. Part of the population of Saba is of European descent. Indeed at least fifteen contemporary territories have societies which are a legacy of slavery and the intermarriage of Europeans and Africans.

The predominance of descendants of Africans and *métis* in these Creole populations does not mean that other ethnic groups are excluded. In Guyane an indigenous Indian population is concentrated in the rainforests of the west and south of the country, a population which retains much of its traditional sources of livelihood and customs. In the French West Indies live a number of Syrians and Lebanese who migrated in the late 1800s or early 1900s. There is a significant Indian minority in

Martinique and Guadeloupe, and a much larger Indian population in Réunion. Americans have retired to many Caribbean islands. Even more complicated is the population composition of the Dutch islands in the southern Caribbean. In Aruba, Bonaire and Curaçao, the present-day population descends from Arawak Indians, Spanish and Dutch settlers and African slaves. Dutch is the official language, but many islanders speak Spanish and English, and the lingua franca is Papiamento, which originated with the Portuguese spoken by Jewish emigrants from Portugal, the most numerous settlers in the seventeenth century.

Nevertheless, the Creole islands share various traits. The heritage of slavery weighs heavily, whether or not islands were inhabited before European contact. Uprooted from their native lands, separated from kith and kin, bought and sold as chattels, mixed with slaves from other parts of Africa, reduced to menial farm-hands, African slaves paid the cost of European planters' prosperity. For many, conditions did not immensely improve after emancipation, for there was prejudice and they lacked land, education and capital. The populations of the Creole islands thus remained impoverished, and perennial crises in the sugar market heightened difficulties. Only a small minority managed to escape their condition, although the new African, or more often, *métis* elite of teachers, public servants, and other professional people increasingly gained status, money and power. Particularly in the French Antilles, where freed slaves were given the vote, a small 'coloured' elite largely dominated politics by the beginning of the twentieth century. A distinct Creole culture emerged during the centuries of slavery and persisted after emancipation in the Caribbean and Réunion. Although slaves converted to Christianity, various traditional observances and beliefs – such as those associated with voodoo – survived the crossing from Africa. The effects of slavery created certain social patterns which persist; for instance, the domination of families by mothers and a relatively large number of children born to unmarried couples. African rhythms and musical instruments contributed to Jamaican reggae and Trinidadian calypso, to zouk in Martinique and soka in Guadeloupe, jumbie dances in Montserrat and gombie dances in Bermuda. A Creole cuisine, rich in chilli peppers, blended African, French and Indian flavours; rum became the quintessential drink of the Antilles.[74] Specific languages emerged for communication between various ethnic groups, including Papiamento and Creole. Some in the elite became more Europeanised and, in the French territories at least, colonial assimilationist policies attempted to transform a select group of islanders into black Europeans who repudiated their African inheritance. Intellectual rebels, especially those associated with the Pan-African movement and the literary current of *négritude*, revalued their Africanness or, with *créolité*, celebrated their mixed cultural and ethnic origins. A few rejected mainstream values, drawn by revolutionary Marxism, Rastafarian beliefs or Christian fundamentalism.

These cultural reconstructions provided further indication that residents of the French, British, Dutch and American West Indies, Bermuda and Réunion were different from their compatriots in distant metropoles. Skin colour might be the most evident symbol of difference, and the one which often caused discrimination against migrants from the Caribbean or Indian Ocean to those metropoles. But customs, food, language and music created a social and cultural divide that accentuated the geographical distance between Europe and the island territories. The ethnic and cultural complexion of the territories makes it clear that, except in a very small number of societies dominated by ethnic Europeans, differences between the Europeans, Americans or Australasians, on the one hand, and Pacific islanders, West Indians, Indian Ocean islanders, Inuit and Asians, on the other, are usually great. The residents of St Eustatius, for instance, many descended from African slaves, have very little in common (not even, for most, their language) with the people of Holland; Mayotte and mainland France, or Anguilla and the United Kingdom, inhabit different social, cultural – and economic and geographical – worlds.

These differences did not necessarily create pressure for independence, even though a number of Creole islands did gain independence in the 1960s and 1970s from a Britain anxious to divest itself of colonies. Independence movements in the French Creole islands first emerged in Guadeloupe, but gained little support, much of which was a reaction against traditional French centralisation. In two other Creole island groups where referenda were held on proposed constitutional change, Bermuda and the United States Virgin Islands (as well as in Puerto Rico), pro-independence groups suffered solid defeats. Aruba, which had sought independence in the 1980s, moved away from that option.

Although ethnicity and a shared identity have not created a pro-independence groundswell in most territories (with New Caledonia the principal exception), they have served as a rallying-point for demands for greater autonomy, recognition of local cultures, and frustrations with development. As the economic gains from independence have increasingly been perceived as at best derisory, and more frequently as negative, there has been a distinct shift in arguments for independence away from economics towards culture and identity. Territories where demands for independence have been weakest or non-existent include almost all the European-dominated ones, where there is no distinct cultural identity, other than – often – a pride in maintaining a European heritage in a distant outpost. Frequently that heritage is more antiquated and conservative than in the metropole, a situation that has sometimes produced reactionary local legislation on social issues.[75] Some short-lived small-scale independence movements – as in the Azores or Norfolk Island – have been conservative, in opposition to perceived threats of radical change.

Seemingly paradoxically, other territories where demands for independence have been almost non-existent include those where indigenous populations constitute the bulk of the population, such as Wallis and Futuna, American Samoa, Mayotte and Greenland. Although there is a distinct cultural identity in these territories, it has not been forged in adversity to colonial domination, and there are often important regional divisions. Indeed, national identity has usually incorporated elements of both indigenous and metropolitan cultures. Thus in Wallis and Futuna, where there is ready access to education and medical care and contact with the world through radio and television, islanders have generally been able to reconcile their identity as being both Polynesian and French; perhaps symbolically, many have two houses: a thatched Polynesian *fale* and a more recently constructed concrete house. Although one writer has referred to the paradox of 'the loyalism of a territory where France is kept at a distance',[76] it is precisely through this paradox that the islands maintain a subtle equilibrium between the external institutions of church and state and the kingships that symbolise the Polynesian order. There, as in some other territories which display the greatest ethnic divergence from the metropoles, there has been little hostility to it. The Cook Islands signed a treaty of free association with New Zealand; Cocos (Keeling) Islanders voted overwhelmingly for incorporation into Australia; a large majority of the electorate of Mayotte favoured full integration with France and *département* status. In several territories, a favourable situation prevails: colonialism has not been particularly exploitative (in part because there was little to exploit); the contemporary economy has developed almost entirely through metropolitan involvement, providing some salaried employment; emigration is significant; and political devolution has given, or given back, some power to local elites.

Whilst continued ties with the metropoles may now be widely perceived as positive, ties with distant nations with quite different cultures have not been without tensions. These tensions have often revolved around land tenure (and land alienation) and the role of indigenous languages in education and politics. In Puerto Rico between the world wars, the search for nationhood focused on ethnicity, culture and Catholic religion, and proponents of independence emphasised the manner in which the 'Protestant barbarians' of the United States had sought to crush these distinctive elements of island society.[77] In New

Caledonia nationalism grew in parallel with the attempt to assert Melanesian identity and culture, symbolised in the restoration of the hitherto derogatory word 'Kanak' for militant Melanesians, the pressure for land rights, and the development of 'people's schools' with Melanesian languages the media of instruction. In French Polynesia nationalists reclaimed Tahitian as an official language, but that gain created tensions elsewhere in the territory; in the outlying Marquesan archipelago, islanders refused to study Tahitian rather than Marquesan, and also sought to reassert their own distinct musical tradition.[78] On the other side of the world, in the years before Home Rule, Greenlandic politicians sought to work out and define a Greenlandic national identity. In order to emphasise that Greenland was not part of Europe, geographically, culturally or ethnically (and choosing to ignore not only the mixing of Inuit and Danish heritage, but also blood), a distinctive Inuit identity was specifically nurtured, beyond otherwise highly localised identity and sense of place.[79] Even in unpropitious circumstances, appeals to cultural identity have been voiced.[80] In territories where indigenous populations are diverse, the creation of a national identity has been particularly difficult.[81] In New Caledonia it largely emerged in response to oppressive French policies, but it was weakest in the outlying islands, where land alienation was slight or non-existent and economic benefits more obvious.

Cultural differences, especially those associated with land issues, have been asserted more vigorously. In Guam, for example, the small but well-organised indigenous rights movement worked to increase the Chamorro content of school curricula. Central to the movement for Chamorro self-determination has been indigenous political control – amid substantial immigration – to give the ultimate choice of political status for Guam to those who were residents of the island in 1950 and their descendants, primarily Chamorros. That issue, which became the key theme in the position of the Guam delegation in favour of the 1987 Commonwealth Act, became the stumbling-block for any change in Guam's political status.[82] For many Chamorros, including the Guam Landowners Association (involving families who had lost their land to the federal government), a number of unresolved issues exist, including the return of Chamorro land and resource rights, so 'ending the cultural and economic displacement of the Chamorro people'.[83]

At the very least, indigenous peoples have retained distinctive values and customs that distinguish them from those of the metropoles. Occasionally, such differences led to symbolic confrontations, as in 1972 when the Tahitian nationalist, Pouvana'a, addressed the Territorial Assembly in Tahitian (which the French high commissioner could not understand); symbolic confrontations usually preceded or accompanied demands on the metropole. More frequently, cultural distinctiveness constitutes the stuff of everyday life, rather than being a basis for independence or active dissent; though Tahitians incorporate many elements of French culture into their lives, they also retain numerous Polynesian characteristics, in terms of forms of dress, food consumption, hygiene and medical practice. Thus they draw boundaries between themselves and the French, 'refusing to discard the utilitarian baby with the symbolic bathwater'[84] where the French presence is inequitable but economically valuable. Such forms of resistance and distinctiveness are typical of many territories; they indicate the continuity of cultural differences, which are not necessarily the basis for a sustained challenge to the political system.

A particularly visible symbol of difference is a national flag. Most territories have their own flags (although those of the British outposts include the Union Jack in the canton). The granting of a specific flag to French Polynesia in the 1980s – a representation of outrigger canoes using the traditional colours of the Tahitian monarchy – marked the increasing autonomy of the territory. It is, however, the only one of the DOM-TOMs to have its own flag. The New Caledonian independence movement flies a flag displaying distinctively Melanesian symbols, but it is rejected by opponents of independence and is not recognised by the government. In Puerto Rico the flag that was once the proscribed symbol of independence groups was eventually officially adopted to represent the island; it was then flown at half-mast at the office of the independence movement in opposition to the 'colonial' government which was 'corrupting beloved symbols'.[85] There, as elsewhere, the achievement of symbolic identity – in the form of a flag – emphasised cultural distinctiveness but also countered demands for independence.

The relationship between national identity and demand for independence has been greatest in the mainly Creole territories which were once plantation societies. In the Caribbean most such colonies acceded to independence; those that did not include Guadeloupe, Martinique and Montserrat. By contrast most other Caribbean territories that did not achieve independence – the Dutch Antilles, the other British territories (including Bermuda) and the US territories – either had short-lived plantation economies, terminated by the twentieth century, or were without plantations; they lacked some of the racial frictions that existed elsewhere, even though slavery existed in Bermuda and other territories.[86] Plantations and slavery enhanced the distinct cultural identity of those who had experienced this most avaricious form of colonialism, and of their descendants, often confined to small areas of arable land and with limited access to education and authority.[87] This history influenced and legitimised nationalist movements in the late twentieth century. Where plantations and slavery were weakly developed, so too was cultural identity. In the Cayman Islands, for example, where plantations had never existed and the contemporary economy is dominated by tourism and finance, there is little semblance of national identity. Consequently, those who seek to stimulate Caymanian culture constantly refer to the evolving nature of culture, and the manner in which all cultures are constantly borrowing, incorporating and interpreting; the Director of the National Museum has observed: 'A lot of Caymanians feel threatened, but we take ideas from all these different people and create a new Cayman culture', very different from that forged in more oppressive circumstances.[88]

International migration has brought territories such as the Cayman Islands into a global cultural arena (though several thousand satellite TV dishes are even more effective), and especially into the American world, symbolised by cricket's slow retreat before baseball. Where there has been substantial immigration – as in the three largest Dutch islands (Aruba, Curaçao and Sint-Maarten), the Virgin Islands, the Channel Islands, Guam and the Northern Marianas, Guyane and also Gibraltar – societies have largely failed to develop national identities. Extensive emigration, as in the Azores and Canary Islands, Niue, Pitcairn and the Cook Islands, has also eroded national identities (and sometimes siphoned off the discontented). Despite the cultural resurgence, it has never been more difficult to foster national cultural identities without some reference to the metropole, especially in those Creole societies where the establishment of that identity coincided with the start of colonialism.[89]

The construction of a national identity is thus fraught with difficulty. National identity may be just one discourse of identity among many; hence in many territories the idea of a 'nation-state' appeals to only some of the population. That appeal may be particularly powerful where there is 'alignment of advantage and ethnicity',[90] and consequently social and political tension. It is, however, those tensions that prevent cultural identity becoming national identity. Coherent static cultures do not exist, and some of the more powerful elements that constitute nationalism are absent in many overseas territories, such as a shared belief in a common history, a high regard for fellow nationals (rather than significant social ties elsewhere), a common pride in past and present achievements, and aspirations for the future. Whilst shared attitudes and values are also uncommon in many independent nations, they are more obviously absent in the contemporary territories. Cultural identity is thus only tenuously linked to issues of autonomy and independence.

The United Nations Special Committee on Decolonisation

The process of decolonisation has widely been seen as a matter for negotiation (even violent struggle) between the colonised territory and the metropolitan power. However, decolonisation and its variants were never simply bilateral phenomena that took no account of regional economic and political relationships or of international opinion, most evident in Hong Kong, Macao, East Timor and the Falkland Islands. In the years after the Second World War international support for decolonisation intensified, especially after the earliest phases, and that support was partly directed by the United Nations, often against the will of some metropolitan powers.

The UN Secretary-General had been requested by the General Assembly in 1946 'to include in his annual report . . . a statement summarising such information as may have been transmitted to him by Members of the United Nations . . . relating to economic, social and educational conditions' in the Non-Self-Governing Territories. Eight members of the United Nations voluntarily declared that they were together administering seventy-four non-self-governing territories, and began formally transmitting information on them. These members were Australia, Belgium, Denmark, France, the Netherlands, New Zealand, the United Kingdom (then with forty-three of the seventy-four territories) and the United States (with Alaska, American Samoa, Guam, Hawaii, Puerto Rico, the USVI, and also the Panama Canal Zone, until the Panama government protested that it retained sovereignty over the area). The Soviet Union and India, which also had dependencies, never provided information but escaped strong criticism. Similarly, when Portugal and Spain joined the United Nations in 1955, they declared their dependencies to be integral parts of the state, and thus not subject to the reporting requirement. (Under UN pressure, Spain, in 1960, agreed to provide information, but Portugal never complied.) All the territories for which information was submitted were geographically separate from the metropole, and usually ethnically distinct. (Australia sent information on Papua, but it never reported on the Northern Territory, which was not fully self-governing.) The United Nations thus perpetrated a 'salt-water fallacy', in which colonies were necessarily somewhat distant.[91]

Metropolitan states became increasingly reluctant to submit information. By 1952 reports were no longer submitted on fifteen of the seventy-four territories because, according to the administering nation, they had achieved the 'full measure' of self-government required by the UN Charter. Such claims were rarely subject to scrutiny. The French DOM-TOMs were removed from the list by 1947. Puerto Rico gained self-government in 1953 and the charter of the Kingdom of the Netherlands was adopted for the Netherlands Antilles in 1954, in contrast with the virtually unchanged situation of the territories of the United Kingdom, 'which has never had any qualms about having colonies'.[92] Although France retained its other listed colonies, the difference between the policies of metropolitan powers was very substantial.

The administering states quickly developed the argument that it should be they themselves, rather than the United Nations, which were competent to determine when the territories that they administered had acquired self-government. Hence the United Nations had no authority to overrule national legislation, but should 'take note' of the cessation of reporting. Various non-administering UN members argued, however, that administering states had entered into a bilateral relationship from which they could not free themselves unilaterally, and distrusted the motives of the administering states; this distrust led to general scepticism of any status other than independence or integration.[93] A growing distaste developed for anything less than full independence.

Rather than comply in the face of unilateral decisions taken by administering powers, from 1949 onwards the General Assembly sought to develop a list of factors, centred on political participation, that would assist in the definition of self-government. In 1953 the United Nations reviewed three cases – the Netherlands Antilles, Surinam and Puerto Rico – to examine if it was appropriate for the administering authority to end the transmission of information on these territories. The Netherlands argued that, although neither the political nor constitutional structure of either the Antilles or Surinam was finalised, the Dutch territories had full autonomy in social, economic and educational issues. The United Nations sought further information on political and constitutional evolution, but the Netherlands failed to respond. The General Assembly 'engaged in a face-saving device', expressing the opinion in 1955 that the cessation of transmission of information was now appropriate. In the case of Puerto Rico, the United States argued that the United Nations had no authority to review the situation; it submitted the fact of the establishment of the Commonwealth of Puerto Rico for information only and stated that the territory was now self-governing. Extensive debate followed: a number of member nations focused on educational, social and economic criteria and concurred with the US position, with others arguing that the alternative of independence had never been submitted to the Puerto Rican people and that the United States retained extensive powers (for example, over foreign affairs and defence).[94] By a very narrow vote, the United Nations agreed to the US position. The question of Puerto Rico lingered on, with major debates in the 1970s on whether any effective determination on its future had been made by its people.

Despite the detailed evaluation of these three cases (and of Greenland's situation), the United Nations was never able to influence
substantially the decisions of administering powers, though it continued
to affirm support for self-determination. In 1960, the year that eighteen
colonial territories became sovereign states, the General Assembly
adopted Resolution 1514 (XV) on the Granting of Independence to
Colonial Countries and Peoples. This 'Magna Carta of Decolonisation'
recognised the rights of colonial peoples to accede to independence,
reflecting the prevailing international view that decolonisation via
accession to sovereignty was perceived as necessary and desirable. Article
73 of the UN Charter required colonial powers to report on developments in the non-self-governing territories 'and to develop self-government', though this was nowhere defined. Resolution 1514 listed three
key options for self-determination: independent statehood, free association with an independent state, and integration into an independent
state. Over time the perception has grown (evident in the Cayman
Islands) that the United Nations sought independence as the sole legitimate outcome of decolonisation, but it has considered, and accepted,
other outcomes, such as the forms of free association that developed
between the United States and the Micronesian states. In 1961 the
General Assembly set up a special committee to study the application of
the 1960 declaration and report on progress; it also appointed special
committees on Southwest Africa (Namibia) and the Portuguese territories. Eventually these were combined into the Special Committee on
Decolonisation, most of whose twenty-four members were socialist states
or former colonies, which sought to implement the 1960 resolution.
Yet after the independence of the largest colonies, the process of
decolonisation became more difficult and more complex. In 1965, when
the Cook Islands entered into free association with New Zealand, the
choice of an outcome other than independence, in free and democratic
elections, 'was extremely troubling to many developing nations',[95] in that
full independence, or integration, was no longer the necessary endpoint
of constitutional evolution (though the choice of full independence had
not been offered to the Cook Islanders). Hitherto, the United Nations
had pragmatically acquiesced in the wake of decisions made by administering powers; in the case of the Cook Islanders it accepted a decision
taken by 'colonised peoples'. This demonstrated that the process of
decolonisation could have outcomes other than complete independence, and thus enabled administering powers to attach less significance
to the necessity for independence.

    The authority and significance of the UN Special Committee waned
over time, as many territories gained independence. It was nevertheless regarded as having an important role where the struggle for

independence continued, above all in New Caledonia. New Caledonia was eventually listed again by the United Nations, though the process of inclusion took several years.[96] More tentative efforts to list French Polynesia as recently as 1996 were quite unsuccessful. The year 1990 marked the start of the United Nations International Decade for the Eradication of Colonialism; the Special Committee reviewed the situation, holding regional seminars in both the Caribbean and the Pacific, the two key regions of 'colonial' presence. Ultimately this was 'aimed at ushering in the twenty-first century, a world free of colonialism', though the United Nations recognised the difficulties faced by many of the territories:

> In addition to general problems facing developing countries, the remaining Non-Self-Governing Territories, many of which are small island Territories, also suffer handicaps arising from the interplay of such factors as their size, remoteness, geographical dispersion, vulnerability to natural disasters, the fragility of their ecosystems, constraints in transport and communications, great distances from market centres, a highly limited internal market, lack of natural resources, weak indigenous technological capacity, the acute problem of obtaining freshwater supplies, heavy dependence on imports and a small number of commodities, depletion of non-renewable resources, migration, particularly of personnel with high-level skills, shortage of administrative personnel and heavy financial burdens.

By the mid-1990s, just seventeen territories were still listed by the committee (Table 2). The principal shared characteristic of the listed territories is that the international community does not regard their people as having formally determined their future (though they have participated in free elections). Whilst this distinguishes them from freely associated states (such as Niue, Greenland, and also the Marshall Islands), and from commonwealths and overseas *départements*, and explains the exclusion of most Dutch and Australian territories (and Hong Kong and Macao), it does not distinguish them from such territories as French Polynesia or Wallis and Futuna, or from European territories, such as the Channel Islands or the Azores.

The Special Committee has increasingly been perceived as an anachronism, marked by the reluctance of administering authorities to recognise its role (and the administering authorities are among the largest contributors of UN funds). Those authorities argue that the listed territories are either moving towards or have achieved an appropriate political status, based on the aspirations of their inhabitants, even if these have not been formally ascertained. However, within at least some of these territories (not least East Timor and the Western Sahara), quite different perspectives prevail. The representative of the Guam

Table 2 Territories Recognised by the United Nations Special Committee on Decolonisation

Administering Power	Territory
France	New Caledonia
New Zealand	Tokelau
Portugal	East Timor[1]
Spain	Western Sahara[2]
United Kingdom	Anguilla
	Bermuda
	British Virgin Islands
	Cayman Islands
	Falkland Islands (Malvinas)
	Gibraltar
	Montserrat
	Pitcairn
	St Helena
	Turks and Caicos Islands
United States	American Samoa
	Guam
	United States Virgin Islands

1. On 6 April 1979, Portugal informed the Secretary-General that conditions still prevailing in East Timor had prevented it from assuming its responsibilities for the administration of the territory.
2. On 26 February 1976, Spain informed the Secretary-General that as of that date it had terminated its presence in the Territory of the Sahara and deemed it necessary to place the following on record: Spain considers itself thenceforth exempt from any responsibility of an international nature in connection with the administration of the territory, 'in view of the cessation of its participation in the temporary administration established for the territory'.

Landowners Association, at the 1996 UN Pacific Regional Seminar on Decolonisation, stated:

> We are seeing an increase in political and economic pressure to have Guam de-listed, without a valid act of self-determination. There are arguments being proffered by our administering power to justify this . . . foremost among these arguments are false claims of territorial satisfaction with the economic benefits and stability which can supposedly only occur under the political and economic supervision of the United States. There are, as well, false claims by our administering power that our territory is free to choose otherwise, but that we are actually the ones who desire to maintain the status quo. Worse yet, this purported acquiescence is being presented to the United Nations as a de facto act of self-determination, without the actual exercise ever being conducted. To further substantiate their claims we are being misrepresented and

falsely portrayed as a small island territory with limited resources and little hope for obtaining a sustainable economy, let alone independence.[97]

Representatives from other territories have also opposed the notion that they have already given de facto support to their existing status. Gibraltar has rejected both the British position that the territory's rights to self-determination were curtailed by the provisions of the Treaty of Utrecht in 1713, and the Spanish position that the sovereignty of the territory should be transferred to Spain. Some territories have expressed concern at high rates of immigration that substantially diminished the proportion of indigenous populations, particularly in Guam, New Caledonia, Ceuta and Melilla; elsewhere it has posed problems for the definition of 'the people' of a territory, and thus for referenda on political status.[98] In 1980 a UN resolution (65/118) specifically stated:

> Member states should adopt the necessary measures to discourage or prevent a systematic influx of immigrants or settlers to the territory under colonial domination. This immigration inflow can overturn the demographic composition of the territories and would constitute a major obstacle in the free exercise of the right to self-determination and independence by the inhabitants of these territories.

Nevertheless, the Special Committee is now principally involved with seemingly intractable problems, where its authority is non-existent (as in East Timor), where the majority of local populations see little need for change in the status quo, or where considerable problems are attached to achieving any economic viability.

Most of the territories that are the concern of the UN Special Committee are small, distant from geopolitical areas of global concern and, with only rare exceptions (again, particularly East Timor), are quiescent, especially in comparison with the situation in many world regions. Moreover the United Nations has resolutely insisted on the decolonisation of colonial territories within colonial borders, rather than the emancipation of colonised peoples, though international interest has largely shifted to the fate and future of minorities within independent nations. Consequently the United Nations and the Special Committee now have only the most trivial significance in metropolitan states, though considerable value is attached to the committee's deliberations in some territories as the sole international authority on decolonisation; thus 'the United Nations is not an important lever on US institutions dealing with the territories, but it is a seminal institution for the territories'.[99] The reinstatement of New Caledonia in 1986 had no significance for decolonisation. The committee has become an intermittent forum for debate rather than a stimulus to action.

The Diversity of Decolonisation

The present 'colonial' status of the overseas territories is the outcome of many delicate political compromises, based on the cultural traits of the inhabitants, the social and political strategies of governments, and concerns over security and economic development. Even the smallest territories have not been powerless, and have usually negotiated the form of political dependency that, on balance, has satisfied the majority of the population. No territory has been thrust into independence against its will, and few have failed to achieve significant autonomy (though the United Kingdom has discouraged devolution of authority without political independence). Aruba has been allowed to defer independence; Anguilla managed to stave it off, on disadvantageous terms; Puerto Rico, the USVI, Bermuda, the Cocos (Keeling) Islands and the Netherlands Antilles voted against it; the Northern Marianas chose commonwealth status; and Niue and the Cook Islands settled for a limit of 'free association' with New Zealand. Much earlier the French *vieilles colonies*, in the Caribbean and Indian Ocean, became overseas *départements*, US territories have more recently become commonwealths, and Danish territories negotiated Home Rule. Yet in New Caledonia, a vigorous independence struggle has been fought.

The process of decolonisation is usually assumed to be the transition of a colony into a sovereign state (although the particular moment when this occurs, and the meaning of sovereignty, are open to debate). National liberation and political independence were assumed to coincide, and the more recent disintegration of multi-ethnic states such as the Soviet Union, Yugoslavia and Ethiopia has emphasised this. This was not always so; in many colonies prominent local leaders (such as Marcus Garvey in Jamaica) were torn between seeking more autonomy and eventual independence, and demanding representation in distant parliaments.[100] Underlying all debates on changing political and economic status, and hence relationships with the metropole (and with other regional and metropolitan states), are two conflicting issues, well summarised in the case of Guam:

> There is . . . a fundamental contradiction in what Guam is trying to accomplish. The Chamorro activists belatedly seized upon self-determination as the major principle behind commonwealth. But self-determination marches under the flag of freedom, whereas commonwealth marches under the banner of equality. Although they may seem to go arm in arm, Alexis de Tocqueville noted long ago that freedom and equality will always be at odds with each other.[101]

Political integration, as in the French *départements*, provides little hope of more self-reliant economic development, and limited recognition of local cultural identity. Movement towards more self-reliant economic and political development may reduce external financial support and cause local concern over both the quality of life and security.

It is in the French *départements* that integration is heralded as the means of political evolution; in Réunion, 'integration is a means of decolonisation, just as much as independence for those who have chosen that'.[102] The same argument lies behind Mayotte's campaign for *départementalisation*. The historian Serge Mam-Lam-Fouck has stressed that in Guyane *départementalisation* was decolonisation,[103] and this perspective has shaped much of contemporary French policy towards the DOM-TOMs. Bernard Pons, when minister for DOM-TOMs, stated: 'There are two ways of ending decolonisation: secession or the achievement of full French citizenship.'[104] Less consciously this has been the perspective and practice for Australian, New Zealand, Dutch, Danish, Portuguese and Spanish territories.

In a sense, the French *départements* provided a model for the political evolution of other territories. In rare circumstances, such as the Australian territory of Cocos (Keeling) Islands, the inhabitants voted overwhelmingly to become part of Australia, with all the citizenship and migration rights that this implied.[105] St Helenians have expressed the wish to be full citizens of and fully integrated into the United Kingdom, just like the Channel Islands, whilst Gibraltar has sought to 'move from being a British colony to being a British dependency, in the manner of Guernsey'.[106] Other territories, such as those of Portugal and Spain in the North Atlantic and Mediterranean, never expressed choices other than to be part of the metropolitan state. In Puerto Rico, half the population have voted to become a US state, following the models of Alaska and Hawaii, and both American Samoa and Guam have sought to draw closer to the United States in certain economic and political respects (though neither sought full integration and both stressed cultural distinctiveness). For both these territories, as for Puerto Rico and the USVI, there is reluctance in the United States to countenance more complete integration because of the costs that would be incurred. The nature of that reluctance points to part of the rationale for integration.

One form of political change, intermediate between independence and integration, has largely fallen out of favour. In the 1960s there was widespread support for the notion of regional federations, as intended for the British colonies in East Africa and the eastern Caribbean, but fragmentation was more prevalent than fusion. For some, like the deputy governor of Montserrat, this was a disappointment: 'Ideally Montserrat should have obtained independence by way of integration with neighbouring mini-states, but that option now seems out of the question. It must therefore plan for independence.'[107] Various elements of natural and island identity have discouraged regional integration, though the Federated States of Micronesia reached independence in regional form, and the idea continues to have advocates.[108] Mayotte, Anguilla, Gibraltar, and the Falkland Islands meanwhile 'escaped' what was perceived as unwelcome integration with problematic nearby partners, though Hong Kong and Macao were powerless to resist.

Lack of interest in independence in contemporary territories is not without historical precedent. Many Western Samoans expressed their concern about the wisdom of independence, not through concern over the machinery of government, but over the need for economic development and the question of how this would occur without New Zealand's financial support.[109] Vanuatu gained its independence only after an anti-independence secessionist rebellion was put down. The population of the outlying island of Rodrigues sought to remain a colony, or be integrated with Réunion, rather than become part of independent Mauritius.[110] The British decision to grant independence to the Solomon Islands was met with concern rather than jubilation: 'In contrast with the usual euphoria of people on the verge of independence, many Solomon Islanders faced the prospect of being on their own with trepidation. . . . [Many] still clung to the hope that Britain would have a change of heart about leaving.'[111] More generally, if the inhabitants of several of the small former British colonies had been offered a referendum on their future status, and specifically asked if they wanted to opt for full British citizenship and integration into the United Kingdom, 'there is every chance they would have voted overwhelmingly to do so'.[112] When a similar proposition was put to residents in the various Micronesian territories that formed the United States Trust Territory of the Pacific Islands, the Northern Marianas chose integration as a commonwealth with the United States, and there was very strong support in other territories for a similar status. Moreover, as US aid falls in those territories – the Federated States of Micronesia, Marshall Islands and Palau – that chose independence, many residents have had second thoughts about the wisdom of their choice of free association.

In every contemporary territory, powerful reasons exist for choosing continued political ties with metropolitan powers; they range from concerns over security (from local civil or political unrest rather than external aggression), to dependence on transfer payments (in various forms) and access to migration opportunities. In the latter case, even countries that have achieved independence, such as the Marshall Islands and the Federated States of Micronesia, have retained rights of emigration to the former metropolitan power. Elsewhere, in territories such as Niue and the Cook Islands, the loss of migration rights is the single most important deterrent to the acquisition of full sovereignty. Social ties (through migration, marriage, telecommunications and cultural diffusion) with the metropoles have intensified. As global economic growth rates have slowed, many of the – often neighbouring – states that became independent in the 1960s and 1970s have experienced economic and political problems.

Rather than move towards independence, territories have welcomed, even demanded, the greater involvement of metropolitan states. This has been as true of American Samoa and the Cook Islands, glad of economic 'salvation', as of several Caribbean territories, accepting aid after natural hazards or the regulation of dubious financial and trading affairs by the metropolitan powers (requested in Anguilla, and accepted in Montserrat). In the Netherlands Antilles, the 1990s was a period of 'recolonisation'. There was some reduction of local autonomy in response to Dutch concerns over mismanagement, clientelism and the penetration of international crime; specifically, Sint-Maarten was brought under more direct rule (so by-passing the Netherlands Antilles government). Dutch Caribbean problems have thus become more, rather than less, of a Dutch concern since the illusion of Antillean independence has been abandoned.[113] British involvement in the eastern Caribbean, and French interest in Mayotte, can similarly be perceived as recolonisation. Doubts over economic (and social) development and internal administration have never disappeared, even in the most prosperous territories. The 'models' offered by some neighbouring independent states have deterred support for independence (as Mahorais observe the Comoros); comparisons have been used (as conservatives in New Caledonia have pointed to 'failures' in Vanuatu) to strengthen the case against independence. In the Caribbean, when British territories especially 'look at the post-independence experience of surrounding islands, like Grenada, with its revolutionary violence and Antigua, which is scandal-ridden, they don't like what they see. Seek ye first the political kingdom has become rather passé.'[114] Decolonisation posed certain problems.

Independence may thus constitute threat, rather than promise, and concerns that it may be imposed against the local will. Yet only exceptionally do overseas territories have any significance in the politics of metropolitan states, and most are known there, if at all, primarily as exotic curiosities (or sources of migrants). In the Netherlands, for instance, any further push towards independence is likely to occur only 'if the cost of keeping the islands afloat is set off against cutbacks in the Dutch welfare system'; independence might be used as a threat, even as a punishment, to ensure balanced budgets and more effective economies whilst discouraging secessionist aspirations.[115] Otherwise, the Netherlands is unwilling to be seen as a colonial power. The United

Kingdom has fought a costly war to retain the Falkland Islands, yet other British governments might have different policies. No other metropolitan states are likely to be so forthright as New Zealand in its enthusiasm for decolonisation, to the extent that it 'carefully channelled' the wishes of island people, with 'applause for Islander statements favouring self-government or independence, but stony silence or explicit rejections of statements favouring the status quo or closer integration with New Zealand'.[116] In this sense New Zealand and the United Kingdom have come closest to pressing independence on unwilling populations, yet neither unwillingness to be seen as colonial powers nor financial crises are likely to result in future pressure from the centre.

No territory has had a wholly harmonious relationship with the metropolitan power, although those which have achieved financial independence (such as Bermuda and the Cayman Islands) have approached it.[117] Otherwise intermittent friction has invariably arisen over financial issues, migration, and cultural integrity. Although relationships with the metropolitan powers are usually punctuated by tension and frustration, such problems do not necessarily lead to demands for altered political status (other than constant shifts in the degree of autonomy), and only exceptionally produce demands for unconditional independence. Resolutions of problems are more likely to be sought through greater incorporation. Where such relationships change only slowly, other traces of 'colonial' relationships have been increasingly eroded, leading the Dutch minister responsible for the Netherlands Antilles to refer to a process of 'decolonialisation' as opposed to 'decolonisation'.[118] In these transitions, symbolism is of extraordinary significance. This applies both in terms of material symbols – names, flags, anthems and even postage stamps – and constitutional nomenclature, where the distinction between 'associated state', 'dependent territory' and 'commonwealth', seemingly of little social and economic significance, has produced heated, sustained and emotional arguments.

The critical elements that have fostered independence sentiments have included: the persistence of linguistic and cultural differences; rejection by political leaders of absorption or integration with metropolitan states; long-standing inequalities (especially where those are linked to ethnic divisions, and derive from exploitative economic regimes); and, in some places, the rejection of materialistic Western culture and society. In the territories these have been necessary but insufficient factors in the demand for independence. Charismatic leaders have often been absent (or had economic interests that steered them into other courses); inequalities were seen as inevitable or insubstantial; above all, economic concerns triumphed over fragmented linguistic and cultural differences. The quest for independence thus became more idealistic than pragmatic, and took a more 'cultural' form. This was even evident in political party names, as in Martinique, where MIM became the *Patriotes Martiniquais*, or New Caledonia, where the *Front Uni de Libération Kanake* became, in 1992, the *Congrès Populaire du Peuple Kanak*.

The construction of economic systems that are either exceptionally dependent on metropolitan states or on the fluctuations of the global economy has resulted in close links between economic and political dependence. Moreover, such economic and political dependence may have weakened cultural identity; in France's Caribbean 'love children', the notion of 'killing by kindness' has been evoked.[119] Economic growth in a dependent context has discouraged independence in the Cayman Islands.

As economic growth has been achieved there, the task of developing new forms of cultural or political consciousness has increased. Economic growth, international migration, the spread of consumer society and globalisation have weakened political, social and economic distinctiveness there and elsewhere.

Territories have come closest to independence where economic inequality has been combined with vibrant cultural identity. Such circumstances have also produced what are mainly rhetorical demands:

> Independence was once looked at in a linear way, with the assumption that everyone would seek it. Now, rather than a birthright, people are seeking it as a remedial right used to redress specific grievances like racism or oppression, and clearly not everyone out there wants it.[120]

In many peripheral areas – the Torres Strait in Australia, the Chatham Islands in New Zealand, and even the Isle of Wight in England – demands for independence have been made, primarily to draw attention to specific problems.[121] In several contexts, including French Polynesia, Bermuda and Puerto Rico, independence has been perceived as a virtual panacea for social problems such as drug addiction, alcoholism, broken families and criminality.[122]

Decolonisation was viewed in the territories not as some bureaucratic, procedural change but as a deeply rooted substantial change. Ultimately, as a prominent Aruban advocate of independence observed in response to a question on why that country should become independent, 'that question has been asked by more than 140 countries. You have to fend for yourself, and accept your own responsibility.' Similarly, the Netherlands Antillean premier, Maria Liberia Peters, remarked: 'It's your pride; it's your dignity.'[123] There, and in Puerto Rico, Bermuda and elsewhere, opponents stressed that independence was implausible, anachronistic and lacked popular support, whilst freedom, autonomy, social solidarity and security were already adequate. For some, the local response to perceived problems is increased nationalism; for others, and rather more frequently, it has led to greater demands upon the metropolitan power that fall far short of a new political status.

Alongside those who perceive independence as a panacea are others who recognise its limitations. In French Polynesia, one prominent supporter of independence conceded: 'It would be difficult now as the people aren't ready for independence. The Tahitians live an unnatural life now. They live off imported goods, tinned food and other things. There would be struggles, unemployment, all possible things.'[124] In Guadeloupe, it was similarly stressed, 'We must prefer liberty with its difficulties', or even 'dignity and deprivation'.[125] However, material and ideological austerity has limited popular support. Few independence movements have put forward cogent plans for economic and social development after independence; most suggestions rely either on continued high levels of foreign financial support, or, now less frequently, on some form of 'socialism'.[126] The absence of coherent plans for the post-independence era, and the limited changes that are actually envisaged, paradoxically emphasise both the limited probability of independence and the continuity that would ensue where it was achieved. Where identity is at stake, struggles for independence will continue, but their successful outcome is less likely now than at any time in the past. Only improbable pressure from the metropole would lead to that outcome. Despite intermittent debates over political futures, and regular transitions in political status, the status quo or even integration are likely to prevail over independence.

CHAPTER 5

Military Bases, Geopolitical Concerns

In territories which have remained under their control, metropolitan states have often stationed troops, paramilitary officers, and weapons. Military presence is an affirmation of sovereignty, and troops can ward off real or perceived dangers of foreign attack or irredentist expansion by neighbouring states. They patrol territorial waters and the exclusive economic zones off coasts, and curb contraband, drug-smuggling, illegal immigration and terrorism. These actions have taken on added import-ance in small territories which lie in the vicinity of large and more powerful states and possess permeable land or maritime frontiers. Troops can also be used, if necessary, to quell insurrection and, less dramatically, to provide assistance following natural disasters. Moreover, military forces use overseas territories as training-grounds for war games and combat practice, and certain detachments – the French and Spanish Foreign Legions – have their major bases there.

Portugal, which withdrew its soldiers from Macao in 1975, provides one exception to the general rule of countries maintaining garrisons in dependent territories.[1] The Dutch and British military presence in their West Indian islands is certainly minimal, but a thousand British soldiers are stationed in the Falklands, several thousand Spanish soldiers in Ceuta and Melilla, many thousands of French troops in the DOM-TOMs, and tens of thousands of US service men and women in outposts such as Guam and Vieques (Puerto Rico) and on bases which the United States has leased from Britain.

A wider military rationale, other than territorial defence, governs the operation of bases in these dependencies. The years of European decolonisation after the Second World War largely coincided with the Cold War, when the United States and the Soviet Union competed for allies among nations gaining independence, though many joined the

Non-Aligned Movement. The Americans, however, considering that movement overly sympathetic to the Soviet cause, and fearing 'leftist' uprisings in newly independent states, made the 'containment' of Communism and defeat of 'subversive' movements priorities of their foreign policy. The Soviet Union sought to enlarge its global influence and promoted various Communist parties, 'liberation' movements, independence struggles and 'anti-imperialist' campaigns targeted at the colonial powers and the United States. The colonial world (and the Third World in general) became a symbolic – and, in some cases, real – military battleground for superpower rivalry.

Although the old European colonial powers played a diminished role in international rivalries by comparison with the United States, they generally lined up behind Washington. Britain, France, Denmark, the Netherlands and Portugal were founding members, along with the United States, of the North Atlantic Treaty Organisation (NATO) in 1949; Spain joined in 1982, although Madrid had already made military bases available to the United States. The traditional colonial powers thus formed part of the American camp – a situation which created opportunities for the Soviet Union to win support among nationalist and anti-colonialist groups trying to obtain independence. On the other side of the world, Australia and New Zealand also took the broad American position, though Cold War rivalries were less bitter in the South Pacific region.

Denmark and the Netherlands, like Spain and Portugal, did not aspire to a major role in world affairs. Britain, after a last and unsuccessful attempt to play such a role in 1956, when British, French and Israeli troops invaded Egypt after the Suez Canal was nationalised, gradually retired from the front line of military conflicts. In 1967 the British government declared it would withdraw its military forces from 'east of Suez', allowing the United States to step into its place in the Indian Ocean and consolidate its presence in the Pacific.[2] Nevertheless, Britain, as a permanent member of the UN Security Council, a nuclear power and one of the largest economies in the world, did not disappear entirely from world military affairs. When Argentina attacked the Falkland Islands in 1982, Britain again flexed its military muscle. Though Australia and New Zealand were remote from global strategic shifts, they were not unaffected; Australia acquired the Cocos (Keeling) Islands in 1955 specifically because of its perceived strategic significance, and Christmas Island also became a crucial forward defence position.[3]

By contrast, France, with one of the world's biggest economies and a permanent seat on the Security Council, ardently pursued efforts to maintain its rank as a 'middle-range' world power. Indeed, by developing an independent nuclear force, withdrawing from the military command structure of NATO, and maintaining substantial military bases in both independent states and its territories in Africa, the Caribbean, the Indian Ocean and Pacific (and regularly sending troops to intervene in African affairs), France proved an active and frequent participant in the international arena.[4] Given these international geopolitical strategies, it has been the United States – both on its own and in tandem with, or perhaps as replacement for, Britain – and France which have been most energetic in establishing and preserving a military presence overseas: contingents of soldiers, intelligence facilities, warships, aircraft, missiles, and the testing and stationing of nuclear weapons.

Geopolitics

The United States and, to a lesser extent, France, have remained militarily the most important of the old colonial powers around the globe, although other nations – Spain and Britain in the Straits of Gibraltar, Australia and New Zealand in the southwest Pacific, Denmark in the North Sea – have retained a more localised military presence. US and French actions related not just to issues of sovereignty but to broader geopolitical concerns, which principally involved the US territories in the Caribbean and northwestern Pacific, a US base in the Indian Ocean, Danish–US facilities in Greenland, and French nuclear testing in Polynesia (as well as French bases elsewhere in the DOM-TOMs).

Great claims have been made about the zones where various overseas territories lie. Two Danish geostrategists argued in the early 1980s that

> the technical developments of the last twenty years and the expectation of finding rich resources in the region have made the Arctic Ocean a focus such as it has never been before. Where formerly the Arctic Ocean was looked upon as an icy waste, it has now become a geo-political mediterranean sea. . . . the Arctic Ocean may become the most important area in the region, attracting strategic interest for purposes of controlling not only the air space but also the ocean beneath the ice.

They added that the Arctic 'is central to the industrial countries of the northern hemisphere and very rich in resources, and these facts coupled with the anticipated civilian and military technological developments are likely to play a significant part in global economy, strategy and consequently in security policy'.[5] More recently, Antarctica has become the new global mineral province, more lavishly praised and more eagerly contested.

Many geopolitical experts predicted in the 1980s that the Pacific Ocean was rapidly becoming the new economic, political and strategic 'centre of the world'. Because of the growing might of Japan and the newly industrialising countries of eastern Asia, as well as the strong economies of Australasia and the western coast of North America, the Asia–Pacific zone appeared destined to play a pivotal role in world affairs. The Pacific was the location of an economic boom, but also of political manoeuvring and potential military conflict. Partly for this reason, the superpowers expressed keen interest in making their presence felt; in particular, the Soviet Union was trying to gain trading, diplomatic and political leverage in the Pacific. France, because of its Pacific territories, sought to seize whatever opportunities presented themselves to counter Soviet and US influence.[6] Similar opinions were common in the United States; a senior official of the United States Agency for International Development observed that 'the 21st century may well belong to the Pacific. America, I believe, has a Pacific destiny, yet to be fully realised.'[7] When the Cold War waned, the economic growth of East and Southeast Asia emphasised the value of a regional presence.

Others also stressed the emergence of the Asia–Pacific region and the geopolitical opportunities and dangers this presented. Members of the South Pacific Forum (including Australia and New Zealand) expressed concern about the Soviet Union, but were critical of France's intentions. New Zealand distanced itself from the United States, leaving the Australia–New Zealand–United States (ANZUS) military pact when Washington would not assure Wellington that US warships visiting New Zealand did not carry nuclear weapons. Nations of the South Pacific invited others to join in signing the 1986 Rarotonga Treaty, which mandated the denuclearisation of the South Pacific; France, Britain and the United States, three of the world's declared nuclear powers, declined to subscribe to the convention, though in 1996 France relented.

Some saw the Indian Ocean as a new centre of the world. The Indian Ocean by the 1970s had become the great 'petroleum highway' for the transit of oil from the Middle East to Asia, and the shipping of manufactured goods from Asia to Europe. The greater Indian Ocean region, however, remained unstable, with tensions between India and its South Asian neighbours, the emergence of 'radical' regimes in Southern Yemen, the Sudan and Madagascar, and the rise of Islamic fundamentalism in Iran. Greater numbers of Soviet and US warships patrolled the Indian Ocean, and both countries tried to secure port facilities for their merchant and military fleets. The Indian Ocean, like the Pacific and even the Arctic, seemed an arena for the playing out of economic, political and military rivalries and the clash of ideologies.[8]

Such geopolitical analyses, both warnings about a Soviet 'menace' to the West in various oceans, and predictions of the Pacific or Indian Ocean becoming new centres of the world, were often disputed.

However, arguments about the need to defend the 'West' and to prepare
for millennial changes in the world's economy and society exercised
seductive influence in the 1970s and 1980s, particularly in conservative
political circles in the United States and Britain and among politicians in
France eager for their country to retain its international stature. At least
until the late 1980s, overseas outposts therefore appeared useful – even
essential – bases for military activity.

The United States: A Network of Bases

Greenland and the Arctic

The international court of the League of Nations did not confirm
Danish sovereignty over Greenland until 1933. The value of the cold and
sparsely populated Arctic landmass then seemed limited; fish constituted
Greenland's major natural resource. Within a decade, however, Greenland had become a strategic outpost. In 1940 German armies occupied
Denmark, leaving Greenland in free Danish hands. Danish authorities
in Greenland requested protection against Germany – which maintained meteorological stations there – from the United States, which had
not yet entered the war. The Americans opened a consulate in Greenland's capital, Godthåb (Nuuk), and, in 1941, signed an accord with the
Danes to open temporary air bases in Greenland. Later in the year, with
the accord of the Danes, US forces occupied Greenland; by the end of
the war, thirteen US army bases and four navy bases operated there. The
bases guarded Greenland against possible German moves and safeguarded Greenland's production of cryolite, vital for American manu-
facture of aircraft aluminium. Since aeroplanes could not then fly
between the United States and Europe without refuelling, Greenland
also became a vital transit point.[9]

  The US bases remained after the end of the Second World War,
although some were transferred to Danish control and several were
closed. The US military classified remaining bases as 'essential' and
'required' for the security of the United States and Western countries,
including Denmark and other NATO members. In 1951 Washington
and Copenhagen signed an agreement which permitted the Americans
to retain existing military facilities and establish new ones in Greenland,
to be operated as part of a NATO command under US control, though
with an obligation for US military officials to consult Danish liaison
officers on all matters affecting Denmark or Greenland. The most
important provision of the 1951 accord was US acquisition of the Thule
Air Base in northwest Greenland, and Thule became a major US installation (in strategic terms if not in number of personnel). Money spent
on the construction of the facility over a two-year period equalled total

Danish expenses in Greenland for the twenty-three years from 1950 to 1973.[10]

In the late 1940s American geostrategists, fearing a westward attack by the Soviet Union across Europe, saw Greenland as an eastern frontier for US defence. In the 1950s this changed, as fears grew that Soviet rockets would attack the United States (or its European allies) directly across the North Pole – the shortest route for new strategic bombers.[11] American aeroplanes (including B-52 bombers) were posted to Greenland bases such as Thule. A decade later, strategic reasoning again evolved as the United States decided to place greater emphasis on electronic spying stations, evident in the 1958 decision to build Ballistic Missile Early Warning Systems at bases in Britain, Alaska, and at Thule. The Americans also built four stations in Greenland as part of the Distant Early Warning (DEW) line around the Arctic. Radar devices became the centrepiece of US military activities in Thule and in such other Greenlandic locations as Søndre Strømfjord, Holsteinborg and Kulusuk.

Danish and Greenlandic authorities (both before and after the granting of Home Rule to Greenland in 1979) accepted the US military presence. The head of the Greenland Home Rule government, Jonathan Motzfeldt, explicitly supported the US activities in Greenland while on a visit to the United States in 1980. In any case, the commitment to maintain joint Danish–US bases under NATO command, according to one Danish specialist, 'cannot be altered by the Home Rule authorities and cannot be put to a referendum'.[12] It was, however, suggested that Greenland's Home Rule government could use 'the American base at Thule and its strategic position in NATO as bargaining counters with other North Atlantic states' on issues of resource management, tariffs or defence.[13] In recent years, the US presence in Greenland has been scaled down after some opposition in Greenland. Disputes over the modernisation of the US radar facility at Thule, claimed by the radical *Inuit Ataqatigiit* party to be in breach of the 1972 US–Soviet Anti-Ballistic Missile Treaty, brought down the Greenland coalition government in 1987. In the previous year, the United States had returned half of the land area of the Søndre Strømfjord base (165,000 hectares) to the Inuit and in 1992, it transferred ownership and control of the base to the Greenland government.[14]

Denmark, which retains legal responsibility for Greenland's foreign policy and defence, also maintains military facilities in Greenland, although they are geared to the defence of the island. Roughly ten times as many Danish as US soldiers are stationed there. Danish ships, an air force squadron, a fleet of helicopters and a sledge patrol are all operational and provide logistical services for Inuit communities.[15] Controversy has developed over the relationship between the US and Danish military; a 1983 Danish book charged 'that the Danish and

Greenlandic authorities have had little knowledge, let alone control, of what was happening in the Greenlandic defence areas; that the bases were becoming a part of an American [offensive] "war fighting" strategy; and that Greenland would be a high priority bombing target in any major war'.[16] Authorities in Copenhagen and Nuuk defended the presence of the US bases, claimed that they had full knowledge of American activities and denied that the installations could be used for attacks and that they endangered Greenland. Anti-military and leftist political groups (including some members of Denmark's parliament and Greenland's assembly) nevertheless continued to voice opposition to the bases.

The impact of the US bases on Greenland has been mixed. The United States paid compensation to Inuit for the construction of bases in Søndre Strømfjord and Narsarssuaq during the Second World War, but suspended payments in the early 1950s. Construction of the base at Thule necessitated moving a community of native Inuit; there is some evidence that the Inuit 'were not consulted about the establishment of the base, that – regardless of the question of pressure – the inhabitants were denied any alternative to removal, that the Ministry for Greenland had neglected to look after their interests in the use of their land, and that the state had wrongfully disregarded the inhabitants' wish for compensation'. No compensation was paid to the residents of the Thule area, and an attempt to secure compensation in the early 1960s was stifled.[17]

The United States pays no rent on its bases, although Washington agreed to buy construction materials and supplies from Danish suppliers when feasible. Any revenues accruing to Greenland from the US presence came only from auxiliary expenditure. The Americans also helped with some rescue and medical assistance to the Inuit population. US troops were confined to the bases, and this segregation reduced local expenditure. In any case, bases were largely isolated in remote regions, and American personnel were few. Nevertheless, several hundred Greenlanders work for the Americans, and the Home Rule government has become 'increasingly interested in the economic benefits that the bases may afford Greenland'.[18] The US bases have had less beneficial environmental effects. There have been fears of nuclear contamination and continuing complaints about oil contamination of fishing areas, for instance, after the collision of a US navy tanker with an iceberg in 1977.[19] Nevertheless, no groundswell of opinion is evident in either Greenland or Denmark for the removal of the US bases.

The Caribbean

The political and military leaders of the United States always regarded the Caribbean Sea (and much of Central America) as holding vital strategic importance. The Monroe Doctrine in the early 1800s proclaimed American hegemony over the entire western hemisphere. By the end of the century, with the move of the United States to become an international power, and plans to build a canal through the isthmus of Panama, control of sea lanes and security in waters off the US coast and the necessity of obtaining military bases became new priorities.[20] In particular, political strategists argued that it was essential for the United States to guard the Caribbean and its access to the Panama Canal. One benefit of the Spanish–American War of 1898 was US control of Cuba, Puerto Rico, the Philippines and Guam; added to Hawaii, where Americans established a dominant position at the same time, this provided the United States with the means of creating an arc of strategic bases from the Caribbean to the northwestern Pacific.

The West Indies, adjacent to the United States, held particular importance, and the new US colonies of Cuba and Puerto Rico provided a linchpin for US policy in the region. The United States constructed a major military base at Guantánamo Bay, Cuba (which it retained after Cuba gained independence and even after the revolution of 1959; the base is still a thorn in the side of Fidel Castro's government, which refuses to use the rental money that the Americans pay into a bank account). A member of the US Congress stated in 1909: 'We want Porto [sic] Rico to help us make the Gulf of Mexico an American lake. We want it for purposes of self defence.' That argument, used as justification for continued US control of the island, changed little over time. In 1916, another US Congressman stated that Puerto Rico was 'necessary to the United States as a key to the defense of the whole American continent against aggression from Europe'; in 1943 President Franklin Roosevelt argued that Puerto Rico was the 'centre' of 'an island shield' for the United States, adding: 'Its possession or control by any foreign power – or even the remote threat of such possession – would be repugnant to the most elementary principles of national defense.'[21]

The United States consequently established bases in Puerto Rico which grew in size and importance before and during the Second World War, and the US military presence has subsequently remained strong. In the 1950s and 1960s, it became a crucial base for US troops during the Cold War, especially during the Cuban missile crisis of 1962 and US intervention in the Dominican Republic in 1965. Rapprochement with the Soviet Union (if not with Cuba) reduced the value of the bases by the early 1970s. However, later developments – a 1977 agreement for the hand-over of the US-controlled Panama Canal Zone to Panama, the emergence of 'leftist' forces in parts of Central America (such as the Sandinistas in Nicaragua), American fears of continuing Cuban efforts to export revolution, instability in Haiti, and political turmoil and the ensuing US invasion of Grenada in 1983 – underlined tensions in the

Caribbean and the value of the bases to the United States. The Reagan administration's Caribbean Basin Initiative, aimed at promoting economic development in the West Indies and securing their political alignment with the United States, focused renewed attention on Puerto Rico as a point of departure for American commercial and diplomatic activities in the region. Plans to close or downgrade military installations in Puerto Rico were subsequently rejected, and the United States now stations close to 4000 troops on the island. The economic role of the American presence is substantial. Veterans of the US military make up 4 per cent of Puerto Rico's population, and collect pensions and other social security payments. Puerto Rico receives large payments from the Department of Defense's budget for the operation of the bases and related expenditures. The military has awarded contracts for the supply of various goods (such as fuel and uniforms) to island businesses. In a more general sense, Washington has injected large amounts of money into Puerto Rico to ensure the future of the military bases and to defuse pro-independence sentiment, which has often targeted the US military presence.[22]

Opposition has centred on the 'militarisation' of Puerto Rico and stressed the adverse social and cultural effects which the military presence has wrought. Such reaction has primarily focused on American activities on two offshore islands. US troops had used Culebra (a 28-square-kilometre island with 1200 residents) for navy target practice. Widespread criticism resulted in a presidential order in 1974 for the navy to leave the island, but it postponed the departure for over a year, then transferred most military activity to neighbouring Vieques.[23] In 1941, the US Congress appropriated funds for Vieques to be transformed into a military base, and the US navy acquired 68 per cent of the land area of the island; with a further 12 per cent owned by the Puerto Rican government, only 20 per cent remained for the island's people. Military authorities resettled a number of inhabitants in two villages on Vieques and moved 3000 others to St Croix, in the United States Virgin Islands. Others left voluntarily. The remaining residents often lacked secure title to their lands, as the military preferred to keep land in the public domain (and rent it to tenants) in case it eventually wanted to increase its holdings. Some of the Viequenses found employment at the base but, after associated manufacturing plants closed, unemployment in Vieques reached over 60 per cent in 1988.[24] Residents had to put up with continuous navy exercises. At the beginning of the 1980s, for instance, 3400 bombs (almost 2.5 million kilograms of ordnance) were dropped on the island a year, and there were 158 days a year of naval gunfire, 200 days of air-to-ground combat firing, 228 days of underwater target-practice, and 21 days of marine assaults.[25] Such military activities

created significant environmental degradation, and relations between the Viequenses and navy personnel deteriorated. National military considerations outweighed concerns about the inhabitants of two tiny islands. American interest in maintaining military bases in Puerto Rico was a powerful stimulus to government development plans, tax concessions and financial benefits for the Puerto Rico commonwealth, alongside Washington's opposition to the Puerto Rican independence movement. Strong opposition to 'militarisation' of the island has not won support, because of other benefits from the American presence. The military facilities afforded the United States by continued commonwealth status are a crucial influence on political, economic and social issues on the island and on US policies towards Puerto Rico.

The Indian Ocean and the BIOT

The British Indian Ocean Territory (BIOT) presents the singular case of a British possession excised and created from an existing colony, Mauritius, only to be leased in its entirety to a foreign country, the United States, as a military base. In the mid-1960s Mauritius, a British colony since it was conquered from the French during the Napoleonic Wars, was moving towards independence. The British, having decided to withdraw from most of their remaining overseas possessions, were willing to disengage from the Indian Ocean, but intended to confide guardianship of the West's interests in the region to the United States.

In discussions on the future of Mauritius, British negotiators convinced its leaders to cede the coral atoll of Diego Garcia and other tiny islands of the Chagos archipelago lying 2150 kilometres northeast of the Mauritian mainland. Britain agreed to pay Mauritius £3 million in compensation, to be used for the resettlement in Mauritius of approximately 1300 Chagos islanders (the Ilois). Mauritius's representatives reluctantly agreed to the plan and, with Britain's blessing, Mauritius gained independence in 1968. The Chagos archipelago, meanwhile, had been combined in 1965 with several islands – Aldabra, Desroches and Farquhar – which had formerly been part of the Seychelles, another British possession destined for independence,[26] into the British Indian Ocean Territory. Within weeks, Britain negotiated an agreement (which took effect in 1966) for the lease of the BIOT to the United States for a fifty-year period with provisions for a twenty-year extension of the lease if neither party requested its termination. Britain retains sovereignty over the BIOT, which is nominally administered by a commissioner in the Foreign and Commonwealth Office in London, represented in the islands by a liaison officer from the Royal Navy; but the United States enjoys effective control. Most importantly, through the 1966 agreement,

Washington gained the right to establish a communications base on Diego Garcia. The installation was, in principle, a joint Anglo-American operation, but British presence has been minimal. The United States spent $40 million to set up the base, but does not pay rent on the site. For hand-over of the islands, the US government arranged a $14 million rebate on the price of Polaris missiles being sold to Britain.

The Anglo-American agreement was signed in the midst of the Vietnam War, a time of particular American concern about Communist expansion, perceived worldwide subversion, and instability in the Indian Ocean region. Since the United States claimed no sovereign territory in the area, acquisition of a base seemed essential, and Diego Garcia, easily defensible, equidistant from India and eastern Africa, almost halfway between the Persian Gulf and the Malacca Straits, was ideal. As American concerns about the Indian Ocean heightened, especially after the oil crisis of the early 1970s, the strategic value of the base increased. In 1975 the US president successfully asked London for permission to turn the existing communications operation on Diego Garcia into a 'support facility of the United States Navy'; Diego Garcia became a fully-fledged naval and air base. Subsequently the Iran hostage crisis, the Soviet invasion of Afghanistan, and, rather later, the Iraqi invasion of Kuwait, confirmed the American perception of the base's importance. By the the 1980s, the island was

> a crucial platform for the projection of US military power throughout all sectors of the Indian Ocean, including the Persian Gulf–Arabian Sea. Its docks and berthing facilities offer logistical support to the fleet of American warships patrolling the waters. Its airstrips provide a much needed landing and refueling stop for planes flying from US Pacific bases to various destinations in the ocean and as far away as the Middle East. . . . Tons of military equipment are stored aboard seven prepositioned merchant ships docked in the lagoon and assigned to a US Rapid Deployment Force being created to meet any future crisis in this part of the world.[27]

It was much 'the most sophisticated military base in the Indian Ocean' and 'the pivot of American strategy in the Indian Ocean'.[28] The United States upgraded Diego Garcia in the 1970s, by dredging the lagoon and making other substantial structural changes, and Washington spent more than $300 million on facilities in the early 1980s. Barracks provided permanent accommodation for 600 troops and temporary billets for 1200 others; shops and banks, chapels and bars have made the island a small American town.[29] Visitors, including British citizens and former residents of the Chagos, are barred from entering the territory for any reason.[30] In keeping with its general practice, the US Defense Department has neither confirmed nor denied that it has kept nuclear weapons

stationed on the island or that ships and submarines which use Diego
Garcia as a port have carried nuclear warheads. In short, Diego Garcia
became a US military fortress.

The military presence and the availability of limited information did
not please the BIOT's neighbours. Mauritius, which had not been
informed in 1965 that Britain would lease Diego Garcia to the United
States for military purposes, expressed reservations about its use.[31]
In 1970, both India and Sri Lanka protested at the construction of the
US base. The Non-Aligned Movement had expressed similar views and
in 1971 the UN General Assembly voted in favour of the creation of a
'zone of peace' in the Indian Ocean and the elimination of 'all bases
[and] military installations' in the region.[32] Countries such as Australia,
Malaysia and Indonesia criticised a further agreement between Washington and London concerning Diego Garcia in 1974. The president of the
Seychelles declared in 1979: 'On this question we are categorical: it is
absolutely necessary to dismantle this base. . . . The fact is that the
existence of this American base is a permanent threat to our security and
our independence.'[33] In 1980, a resolution of the Organisation for
African Unity demanded that 'Diego Garcia be unconditionally returned to Mauritius and that its peaceful character be maintained', and
declared that its 'militarisation is a threat to Africa, and to the Indian
Ocean as a zone of peace'. Throughout this opposition, other allies
of Britain and the United States defended the installation, arguing that
the positions of such organisations as the OAU were too radical to be
countenanced.

Mauritius, in particular, was aggrieved at the status of the BIOT.
Although the colonial government of Mauritius had agreed to hand over
the Chagos islands, Mauritian leaders later said that they were given little
choice; as a colony, Mauritius negotiated from a position of weakness.
They implied that London's support for Mauritius's independence was a
quid pro quo of cession of the islands. Sir Seewoosagur Ramgoolam,
then Mauritian prime minister, admitted in 1976: 'We sold Diego Garcia
island to Britain for several million pounds because we doubted whether,
if we had refused, the government in London would give us our
independence. . . . It was a total surprise to us when the British decided
to rent the island to the United States for fifty years.' 'We were forced
into it. We had no choice', added the Mauritian minister for foreign
affairs the following year. Ramgoolam adamantly put forward claims to
the Chagos before the United Nations in 1980; the British ambassador
insisted that 'the United Kingdom has sovereignty over Diego Garcia'.
Mauritius's leaders argued that cession was a violation of the territorial
integrity of the country and the right of self-determination of the
islanders. Jurists state that Mauritius might retroactively challenge the

cession on both these grounds, alongside arguments that Britain obtained transfer of the Chagos and leased Diego Garcia to the United States through fraud, and that Mauritius submitted to British demands under duress.[34]

Britain stressed that it had obtained the Chagos with the full consent of Mauritian leaders; that in 1965 the islands were, in any case, British territory; and that the payment of £3 million constituted appropriate compensation. On Mauritius's contention that Britain had agreed to return the territory to Mauritius when it was no longer needed, London avoided a direct commitment of how or when this might occur. Although Mauritius considered bringing a case on sovereignty over the islands to the International Court of Justice, such an action has not eventuated, and Mauritius and Britain nevertheless retain close ties.

Those who paid the highest price for cession of the Chagos islands were the displaced Ilois, who were moved to Mauritius from the late 1960s to 1973. The British considered that they were only temporary migrant workers employed as labourers on copra plantations and as fishermen, although a number of Ilois families had been in the Chagos for several generations (and their 'temporary' employment now disappeared). Most Ilois were impoverished, lacked formal education, spoke only Creole, and faced many problems in Mauritius. Crowded into the suburbs of Port Louis, they often remained unemployed and lacked esteem in the eyes of Mauritians. The Mauritian government protested to Britain about being saddled with the migrants, and in 1972 London allocated another £650,000 in compensation; these funds, however, were not distributed to the Ilois for six years. Finally, in 1982, the British offered another £4 million to Mauritius for the Ilois; those accepting payments were required to sign papers renouncing further claims and any intention of returning to the Chagos.[35] Mauritius set aside the equivalent of £1 million to provide land for the Ilois, and pronounced itself quit of any further obligations. Many Ilois, however, were discontented and yearned to return to their home islands. Some political groups in Mauritius and overseas sympathisers supported their pleas, though to no avail. There was protest in Britain, especially in the left wing of the the Labour Party, about the excision of the BIOT, the leasing of Diego Garcia to the United States, militarisation of the island, and the treatment of the Ilois. More than one observer remarked on the contrasting attitude of British officials who went to war to defend the right of self-determination of Falkland Islanders yet denied similar rights to the Ilois.[36]

Conflict over the Chagos continues. In 1988, Sir Anerood Jugnauth, Ramgoolam's successor as Mauritian prime minister, reiterated: 'We maintain our claim over Diego Garcia and we will use all diplomatic possibilities to have the island and surrounding archipelago handed over to Mauritius.'[37] The British government refused negotiations, and the United States retained use of Diego Garcia as a major base; in the late 1980s it was a key site for the American Strategic Defense Initiative (Star Wars).[38] In 1990 an American White Paper on defence written by the Secretary of the US Air Force noted that the strategy of US forces was to be able to strike any point in the world from only three bases – one in the United States, another on the Pacific island of Guam, and a third on Diego Garcia; a journalist concluded that this 'puts the Indian Ocean island of Diego Garcia at the epicentre of [Americans'] future worldwide operations'.[39] Indeed, the United States used Diego Garcia as a back-up base during the Gulf War and showed no intention of downgrading it after the end of the Cold War.

The Pacific Ocean

In the eastern Pacific, the United States possesses military bases on the mainland, Alaska and Hawaii. The Japanese attack on Pearl Harbor in December 1941, which brought the United States into the Second World War, highlighted the importance (and vulnerability) of the United States in the Pacific. Not surprisingly, after the war Washington undertook massive efforts to maintain and strengthen its military presence in the region. Through the ANZUS pact and treaties with several Asian countries (such as the now defunct Southeast Asian Treaty Organisation, SEATO), the United States increasingly became a power in the Asia–Pacific region. The wars in Korea in the 1950s and Vietnam in the 1960s and 1970s made the United States a combatant on Asian soil. At least until the 1970s, when the United States granted diplomatic recognition to the People's Republic of China and suffered military defeat in Vietnam, a priority for Washington was to 'contain' communism in Asia and prevent a 'domino' effect from leading to the 'fall' of other countries.

Bases in the central and western Pacific and Asia were vital in this American enterprise. In the 1950s the United States had tested nuclear weapons at Bikini atoll in the Marshall Islands. The United States stationed hundreds of thousands of troops in South Vietnam until the defeat of 1975, maintained tens of thousands of troops in South Korea, and still has large military bases on Okinawa (Japan). In Australia, it maintains smaller intelligence and satellite tracking stations. In the Marshall Islands, Kwajalein atoll was transformed into an American missile tracking facility, becoming the key splashdown site for the Star Wars programme; the indigenous population was removed from the main atoll and relocated on overcrowded Ebeye, and outsiders were discouraged. Continuity of the US military presence was built into the Compact of Free Association when the Marshall Islands became independent. A principal stumbling-block in Palau's movement to independence in free association with the United States was the American desire for land-use rights, and a possible nuclear presence; these were eventually conceded to the United States when Palau, after ten years, finally agreed to the Compact of Free Association in 1993.[40]

Of great importance to the United States in support of these facilities were its bases in Guam, various facilities on the otherwise unpopulated American-owned islands of Johnston, Wake and Midway, and major military installations in Hawaii, providing a *cordon militaire* across the northern Pacific. Guam was particularly important during the Vietnam War, when US aircraft took off from the island on bombing missions in Vietnam, but it maintained its significance as a US base after the end of the war. In 1993, 10,640 active-duty military personnel were stationed in Guam (in a total population of 130,000), and the military payroll included 8970 civilian employees. In that single year the US military contributed $748 million to the territory's economy and paid civilians $180 million in salaries, alongside $53 million in taxes to the local government. (The Guam Department of Education alone received $11.5 million in subsidies from the US Department of Defense in that year.) Nevertheless, after the end of the Cold War, Guam asked Washington to close its naval air station at Agaña, and it did so in April 1995. Furthermore, it released some areas of land that were sought by traditional landowners, though not to the extent or at the rate requested by the islanders. Despite this limited phasing-down of military activity, Guam retained its strategic significance for the United States, especially after its Philippines bases were closed and there emerged increased opposition to the American presence in Okinawa. In 1996, in a second phase of US military intervention in Iraq, Guam was used for the forward deployment of B-52 bombers to carry out strike missions against Iraq. Whilst the route from Guam was circuitous, it entered no foreign air space. Guam was also used as a temporary staging base for Kurdish refugees evacuated from northern Iraq. There was, however, some criticism in Guam that the United States was taking the territory for granted, and concern was voiced over the limited return of land and also over the economic impact of base closures. Guam's Congressman, Robert A. Underwood, observed of Guam's strategic significance that 'I'm hoping that everybody associated with the President's action . . . remembers this when the time comes to negotiate issues for Guam.'[41] On the edge of Asia, Guam's continued strategic significance seems assured.

The Northern Marianas was of great strategic significance during the Second World War, with Saipan a major battlefield and Tinian becoming

the site for the launch of the missions that sent hydrogen bombs to
Hiroshima and Nagasaki, effectively concluding the war. Saipan later
became a CIA training base for Nationalist Chinese agents during the
civil war in China (1949–52). Investment in military infrastructure, and
new employment opportunities, gave local residents a better standard of
development than elsewhere in the Trust Territory of the Pacific Islands,
and contributed to the decision to seek commonwealth status. Subsequently, the package that established the Commonwealth of the Northern Marianas included the right of the US military to use two-thirds of
the island of Tinian as a multi-service military base, Tanapag harbour on
Saipan and the entire island of Farallon de Medinilla (for target
practice) at a price of $19.5 million; some 7463 hectares were leased for
a period of fifty years. Other payments to the commonwealth were
related to the military presence.[42] Despite the agreement to provide
military land, the United States has never exercised this option, preferring to concentrate facilities in nearby Guam, but it has prevented other
forms of development in Tinian. Nevertheless, the continued American
presence in one form or another almost throughout Micronesia, but
above all in Guam, is underpinned by perceptions of the considerable
strategic significance of the Asia–Pacific region.

France: Nuclear Strategy and Geopolitics

Far from withdrawing militarily from its overseas bases, and indeed from
international affairs, as Britain largely did after the mid-1960s, France –
like the United States – has been determined to maintain and exercise
its military power. Although most of France's sub-Saharan African
colonies became independent in 1960, France obtained accords for the
stationing of military advisers and troops in a number of countries. It
kept troops in Côte-d'Ivoire, the Central African Republic, Chad, Gabon
and Djibouti; and it operated a base in Madagascar until the early 1970s.
French soldiers have intervened with military or logistical support in
Congo (Zaire), Chad, Mauritania, the Central African Republic, Togo,
Gabon, the Comoros and Rwanda since the 1960s.[43] France, for instance,
flew 600 soldiers into the Comoros in 1995 to put down a coup (ironically, led by a French mercenary), and sent troops to the Central African
Republic in 1996 to rescue French citizens in the midst of local political
turmoil.

The DOM-TOMs house various military contingents and receive
regular visits from French warships, including vessels powered by
nuclear energy and probably containing nuclear warheads. Ships are
permanently based in several of the DOM-TOMs, and particularly large
numbers of soldiers are stationed in French Polynesia and Guyane;

protection of the space station at Cayenne provides justification for large troop strengths there. In addition to regular forces, including local volunteers and (in the DOMs) conscripts performing compulsory military service, the French Foreign Legion – created as a colonial force in 1830 – has bases in French Polynesia, Guyane and Mayotte. Since the DOM-TOMs have French sovereignty, the military is not obliged to negotiate over the terms on which bases can be used, a signal advantage to France. The various territories provide useful sites for the French military to monitor (and play a role in) world affairs, and the bases represent nodes of French strategic presence around the world. No nation, other than the United States, enjoys such a global chain of bases which allow a military presence, intelligence-gathering and naval patrols in the Caribbean, Atlantic, Pacific and Indian Oceans.[44]

The DOM-TOMs have afforded France the opportunity to test nuclear devices – the most controversial aspect of France's overseas military presence. France developed nuclear weapons in the late 1950s and carried out its first atmospheric test of nuclear devices in southern Algeria, still a French colony, in 1960. The independence of Algeria two years later made it necessary to transfer testing to another site. Several locations were considered, including Kerguelen Island in the far southern Indian Ocean, but the government chose Mururoa atoll in French Polynesia. Mururoa was distant from large population concentrations, it could be easily defended, there were back-up sites at Hao and Fangataufa, and nuclear tests could be carried out in secrecy. In 1963, President de Gaulle announced to a visiting delegation of Polynesian politicians that nuclear testing would begin there, adding that construction and operation of the test site would create new employment and bring substantial French investment into the territory. Neither the Territorial Assembly nor the population of French Polynesia was given an opportunity to vote on whether nuclear testing should be carried out there, and it provoked heated controversy in Tahiti.[45]

Construction of the Pacific testing centre (the Centre d'Expérimentation du Pacifique, or CEP) began in 1963. It brought about an economic revolution in French Polynesia as large numbers of Polynesians obtained salaried employment in jobs connected with the CEP or auxiliary activities, and French monies flowed into the territory.[46] The French exploded their first nuclear device on a barge off Mururoa in 1966, the dramatic mushroom cloud constituting ample evidence of the technological prowess of French nuclear scientists, and the determination of France's political and military leaders to maintain its position in the international 'nuclear club' and in world affairs. Regular atmospheric testing continued, despite protests in Tahiti and internationally. In 1973 Australia and New Zealand brought a case against France before the International

Court of Justice in order to try to stop the testing; France refused to recognise the court's jurisdiction, but nevertheless ceased atmospheric tests after 1974. France moved its testing underground; on Mururoa and nearby Fangataufa atoll, the French drilled deep cavities in which they lodged nuclear devices for explosion. French scientists and military officials argued that underground testing posed no environmental, health or other dangers; many foreign scientists and ecologists (as well as some prominent ones in France) disputed their conclusions, and pointed to the lack of adequate scientific and medical tests. France, however, dismissed allegations of radioactive leaks and radiation diseases, countering that levels of radioactivity were lower in French Polynesia than in France itself and that there was no conclusive evidence connecting French testing with illness or pollution. Opponents of testing added that if the tests were safe, they should be conducted in metropolitan France itself, a position rejected by France because of various geological, strategic and infrastructural considerations. Authorities stressed that French Polynesia was part of France. France resolutely refused to discontinue nuclear testing throughout the 1970s and 1980s, despite mounting criticism from countries in the South Pacific and from opposition groups in French Polynesia. The Communist Party and small ecology parties in the metropole denounced the testing, but otherwise a consensus reigned among mainstream parties that it was necessary to ensure the efficacy of French weapons and to permit the continued modernisation of France's 'deterrent force'. Objections were dismissed as the product of ignorance or Francophobia.

So sensitive was France to criticism and to any possible attempts to interfere with its testing that French secret service agents sank the *Rainbow Warrior*, the flagship of the environmental organisation Greenpeace, in Auckland harbour, in 1985, killing a photographer on board. Greenpeace had been one of the most active organisations protesting against French nuclear testing and was planning to sail the *Rainbow Warrior* to Mururoa as part of an anti-nuclear campaign. Its sinking became a *cause célèbre*. New Zealand police arrested two French agents, who were brought to trial and sentenced to prison. Meanwhile, reports about the incident in France prompted official enquiries, which traced orders for the attack to the highest levels of the French government and led to the resignation of the minister for defence. (It remains uncertain whether the prime minister or even President Mitterrand gave approval for the operation.) Subsequent negotiations between France and New Zealand led to a French apology for the attack, and payment of reparations to New Zealand and to the family of the dead photographer. New Zealand released the two imprisoned French agents and, after a token spell of detention in French Polynesia, they were repatriated to France and decorated with military medals.

Nuclear testing and the *Rainbow Warrior* affair, combined with political upheaval in New Caledonia in the mid-1980s, severely tarnished France's reputation among its neighbours in the South Pacific. Paris tried to rebuild bridges with increased aid to Pacific micro-states, negotiations with the pro-independence movement in New Caledonia, and friendly gestures to Australia and New Zealand. On the issue of nuclear testing, France remained intractable. Nevertheless, in 1992, President Mitterrand, noting that the Soviet Union, the United States and Britain – three of the other declared nuclear powers – had suspended testing, declared an indefinite moratorium on French tests. He reserved France's right to carry out further tests should it need to do so or if the other powers resumed testing. Three years later, the newly elected French president, Jacques Chirac, an avowed disciple of de Gaulle, announced that France would carry out a final set of as many as eight underground tests and then call a permanent halt to testing and sign a comprehensive test-ban treaty. Chirac stated that his decision, which he declared irrevocable, followed recommendations of military experts that further detonations were necessary to ensure the modernisation of French nuclear warheads and enable subsequent computer simulation of explosions.

The decision to renew testing provoked an unparalleled movement of protest. Australia and New Zealand condemned the tests, as did the independent states of Oceania; the South Pacific Forum, the organisation of regional states, broke off contacts with France.[47] The Japanese government was incensed that the French announcement occurred on the fiftieth anniversary of the bombing of Hiroshima. Nine of the fifteen members of the European Union, with varying degrees of vigour, expressed public disapproval of the French tests; several countries rejected Chirac's argument that France's nuclear arsenal provided protection for the whole of the union. Other countries also spoke out against French testing, although the United States, Britain and Russia issued only mildly worded expressions of regret. Large demonstrations, petitions and boycotts of French products were organised in Australasia, the South Pacific and elsewhere, with the largest French demonstrations ever seen against nuclear testing held in Paris. A number of foreign governments sent delegations to Paris to express their opposition, and parliamentarians from several countries journeyed to Tahiti to join protests there. Ecological organisations, including Greenpeace, sent ships to French Polynesia; the French military seized a Greenpeace vessel – on the tenth anniversary of the sinking of the *Rainbow Warrior* – which had trespassed into territorial waters.

Detonation of the first French nuclear device in the new series, in September 1995, brought renewed protests and riots in Papeete. Demonstrators, some of them allied with the major pro-independence party, raged out of control, burning Tahiti's airport and violently attacking many of Papeete's waterfront buildings. The riots – which Paris steadfastly, if implausibly, denied were connected to resumption of the tests – led to a considerable number of injuries and dozens of arrests. They drew unprecedented attention to the pro-independence movement in the French territory; both its leaders and certain outside observers argued that only the withdrawal of France from French Polynesia – the decolonisation of the territory, in their view – could put a stop to testing and French militarisation of Oceania. Government officials in Australia and New Zealand, however, insisted that they did not want France to retire from the Pacific but only to cease nuclear testing. Finally, after six tests, France completed testing in March 1996. The government announced that testing was finally over; France signed the South Pacific Nuclear Non-Proliferation Treaty and lent its support to a comprehensive international test-ban treaty. Workers began dismantling the test site on Mururoa; a small group of scientists remained to monitor the environment. New uses for the atoll – including the rather unlikely possibility of turning it into a tourist resort – were considered.

The most obvious value of French Polynesia for Paris was thus as a site for nuclear testing. Although having such a site at Mururoa and Fangataufa might not have been sufficient reason for France to retain French Polynesia,[48] French sovereignty provided a test site where the French government was not legally accountable for its actions. Moreover, the CEP was the motor of the French Polynesian economy from the mid-1960s to the mid-1990s. The economic health of French Polynesia, heavily dependent on French transfer payments, was closely linked with French possession of a military base and nuclear testing site. Control of New Caledonia, by extension, was useful in order to provide back-up for French Polynesia.

The French are not the only power to have tested nuclear weapons in the Pacific; the United States conducted tests in Micronesia in the 1950s, and Britain carried out tests in Australia and Christmas Island (Kiribati, then the Gilbert Islands) at the same time. These atmospheric tests produced detrimental environmental effects and have been conclusively linked to health problems in populations living near the test sites.[49] Yet the French tests continued for a much longer time, in the face of strident opposition. France placed national concerns – including a perceived need to maintain nuclear weapons – above regional relations in the Asia–Pacific region, and proved willing to brave enormous international opposition and domestic protests.

The Effects of Military Presence

The scale of the metropolitan military presence is remarkable in a number of places: virtually the entire population of the BIOT is composed of US military personnel; Ascension has few activities not connected with military (and telecommunications) installations, and access to other than official personnel is forbidden. The military are a critical symbolic and material presence in Gibraltar. Mururoa and Fangataufa atolls were nuclear bases controlled by the French military, and with a constitutional status different from the rest of French Polynesia. Two-thirds of Vieques Island belongs to the US military, as does one-third of Guam and much of Tinian, and in many territories military establishments occupy significant land areas. On several rocky outcrops – such as the French Iles Eparses in the Mozambique Channel and Kerguelen – a few soldiers and meteorologists are the only residents.

The riots in Tahiti in 1995 underlined not only links between military concerns and continued control over external territories, but also the wide-ranging effects that the establishment and maintenance of military bases produces. French funds connected with the CEP drove the French Polynesian economy, but French testing also stimulated the independence movement. The leader of French Polynesia's major independence party, Oscar Temaru, repeatedly stated that his opposition to nuclear testing and French 'colonialism' went hand in hand. International campaigns for a 'nuclear-free and independent Pacific' similarly joined the two issues of French nuclear testing and the dependent status of France's three Pacific territories. In no more subtle form, such issues have also been raised in Puerto Rico. In most territories, nationalist movements have taken anti-military stances; they reject the benefits which military bases provide, such as civilian employment and relief after disasters, compared with the social costs and the construction of a 'handout mentality'.

A large military presence has been a significant influence on socio-economic change in many territories and particular islands. The Vietnam War brought thousands of GIs to the US base on Vieques; 'truckloads of marines from the base arrived in Isabel Segunda, the main town on Vieques, seeking drink, recreation and women. Violent confrontations often resulted and prostitution grew.'[50] In Spain's North African enclave of Melilla, where one in seven residents is a legionnaire – and members of Spain's Foreign Legion are expected to remain unmarried – prostitution flourishes and use of marijuana and hashish is widespread. One neighbourhood is particularly notorious as a hang-out for off-duty soldiers:

> the barrio is frequently the scene of violent confrontations between legionnaires and the young local men, who are mostly the progeny of Moroccan and ethnically mixed parents (*mulattos*). They consider each other natural enemies in competition for the same spoils, that is, reputations of toughness and womanising. At the same time they are dependent upon each other as the sellers and buyers of drugs.[51]

A seedy nightclub in Dzaoudzi, Mayotte, caters largely for French legionnaires, based only a short distance away, and rumours of prostitution and drugs circulate; waterfront bars in Papeete cater for a similar clientele and have a similar notoriety. 'Squaddies on the piss' characterise Gibraltar, where the military denigrate the civilian population.[52] Sexually transmitted diseases have increased in Guam and elsewhere.

Changes on Ascension Island, which has largely served as a military and telecommunications base since being annexed by Britain at the time of Napoleon's confinement on St Helena, have almost entirely resulted from its military role. It initially became a stopping-off point for Royal Navy ships journeying to West Africa. The United States built Wideawake airport during the Second World War, and used Ascension as a missile tracking station during the Cold War. The airport was later vital to the British during the Falklands War, and flights to the Falklands still transit Ascension. Furthermore, it served as a base for underwater cables – indeed, Cable and Wireless ran the island from 1922 to 1964 – and the BBC maintains a relay station there. At present, the 900 residents (down from 1200 in the late 1980s) are almost all employees of the BBC, Cable and Wireless, the Royal Air Force or the US Air Force. With the population declining because of automation of telecommunications facilities and military cutbacks, the future of the island is uncertain. In the absence of a real private sector, the RAF has begun paying for some of Ascension's central services.[53]

Territories where military bases are located reap benefits from government transfers, investments in infrastructure (especially for transport), local employment, and the spending of military personnel stationed there. They pay the cost in terms of land alienation, uneven development, social problems, environmental pollution, and the dangers of militarisation. The use of the territories as military bases, whatever the arguments advanced in the metropoles that they are vital to national security, is at best a mixed blessing for the local populations.

After the Cold War

Not all metropolitan powers, however, perceived their overseas territories as critical geopolitical outposts of empire, though few were devoid of strategic value at some time. In the eighteenth century the Falkland Islands were the key to the Pacific, and St Helena was also a strategic outpost in the nineteenth century, before the construction of the Suez and Panama Canals. Norfolk Island was prominent a little before that,[54] and Gibraltar and Ceuta represented crucial military posts even earlier. At various times in earlier centuries, most Caribbean territories were of strategic importance, though the numerous forts and cannon have long been only tourist attractions. Several territories were of interest during the major wars of the twentieth century, but at other times were of no military significance. Nevertheless, many were often seen to have potential value; in the 1960s one observer claimed, 'The Falkland Islands, valuable in two World Wars, may become supremely important if the Panama Canal is destroyed by a nuclear attack.'[55] Neither Britain, the Netherlands nor other metropolitan powers sought a global strategic presence, withdrawing from distant dominions rather than consolidating, as did France and the United States. But, just as the end of eighteenth- and nineteenth-century wars brought reconsideration of the value of some territories, so the end of the Cold War brought new considerations of the global role of metropolitan powers.

The end of the Cold War in the early 1990s – the break-up of the Soviet Union, the disavowal of Marxism by Russia, the uneasy rapprochement between Russia and the United States, destruction of part of the old Soviet arsenal, and moves to greater disarmament – has brought a major change to international military considerations and strategy. The long-term effects on the military uses of overseas bases remain to be seen. Even before the end of the Cold War, the United States reduced its military presence and troop strength both at home and overseas, but US forces are unlikely to withdraw completely from most present bases. Indeed any attempts by Asian governments (notably, that of Japan) to obtain US withdrawal might lead to greater reliance on bases in US 'flag territories', such as Guam and the Northern Marianas, or in nations linked to the United States by treaties of free association, such as Palau. The weakness of the independence movement in Puerto Rico enables the United States to retain this strategic outpost in its 'front yard'; the USVI provides a back-up, if need be. If Washington wants to keep a military presence in the Indian Ocean – which it still regards as vital – the BIOT will remain an ideal site unless the British government demands American evacuation, an unlikely eventuality.

The French are not likely to remove troops and military installations from their overseas territories, despite the end of nuclear testing in French Polynesia. Various arguments that the DOM-TOMs provide France with an unequalled position in different parts of the world hold great influence with mainstream political parties, and France has always viewed a military presence in its outposts as both a right and a responsibility. A military presence affirms France's sovereignty, and the territories can provide bases for rapid-deployment forces. Even if Britain and Spain do not aspire to play a large and independent role in world affairs, it is unlikely that London or Madrid will remove troops from their respective territories on either side of the Straits of Gibraltar. So long as Argentina is considered even a remote threat to the Falklands, Britain will keep a substantial military force in the South Atlantic. There is no plan for Danish troops to quit Greenland. In short, demilitarisation of overseas territories is not likely to occur so long as the administering powers perceive a need to defend their sovereign rights and make a show of their international strength.

Military activities have been scaled down throughout the territories – the United States (and also Britain and Canada) have closed bases in Bermuda, and the United States returned part of the Søndre Strømfjord base to the Greenland government; France has ceased nuclear testing in French Polynesia. Yet the territories still have both a real and a potential military role, evident in American use of the BIOT and Guam for bombing flights during the Gulf War. In at least some cases, the territories are still seen as the forward line and outmost reaches of national defence and security planning.[56]

The new geopolitics of the territories, however, is less a question of defending sovereign rights, building up large military bases and deploying troops as part of a global stand-off between the superpowers and their allies, than it is of regional concerns and issues outside the strict calculations of military value. The French space station in Guyane is a case in point. Only the French, Russians, Chinese and Americans currently have facilities from which military and commercial satellites can be launched, and Paris has championed the value of its base in Kourou not only for France but for the whole European Union. Indeed, the Ariane launching programme is officially a joint venture of several members of the union. France argues that Guyane has advantages in terms of geographical location and security which could not be replicated inside Europe. The space station thus represents substantial economic and strategic stakes for France and the European Union, and its telecommunications and intelligence-gathering form a counterbalance to the aerospace activities of other countries. Several other territories, such as Ascension, host telecommunications stations which are significant in satellite-tracking, whilst in the Cayman Islands, the United States can monitor both drug-trafficking in the region and events in Cuba.

Meteorological studies and other scientific work in the territories hold increasing importance with continuing concerns about global warming, ozone depletion and other long-term environmental changes. Even the smallest outposts, including the Iles Eparses in the Mozambique Channel and Tristan da Cunha, accommodate weather stations. A number of marine studies centres (such as the French IFREMER organisation, which carries out work in several of the DOM-TOMs) provide invaluable information on depletion of fishing stocks, pollution and erosion, and the possibilities of extracting natural resources from the ocean environment. Although such work does not necessitate the continued 'dependency' of territories, it does give them added value in national and international affairs.

International political, domestic and even military affairs are often intertwined. Use of maritime resources, including fishing rights, in exclusive economic zones depends on the maintenance of claims to sovereignty and its defence when necessary. In rare cases, as with Port-aux-Français, Kerguelen, a territory without a permanent population can be used as a flag-of-convenience registry for ships, allowing circumvention of labour legislation in the metropole. Part of the reason for the Anglo-Argentine dispute over the Falkland Islands relates to the likelihood of profiting from substantial petroleum reserves in the area surrounding the islands.[57] Grand plans have been mooted for earning profits from Antarctica, especially if it becomes possible to extract mineral resources from under the ice. Claims by Britain, France, Australia and other nations to sections of Antarctica could potentially provide substantial, if not unchallenged, rights to whatever commercial benefits might be procured.[58]

Yet another dimension to the international role of the territories is of a darker nature: drug-trafficking, contraband trade, shady financial dealings and illegal migration. These are sometimes linked. In 1993 an offshore bank in Anguilla was used to trap Colombian-based drug-traffickers. 'Operation Dinero', involving the US Drug Enforcement Agency, led to the arrest of 100 people in the United States, Italy and Spain, and the seizure of assets worth $50 million, nine tonnes of cocaine and a shipment of arms destined for Croatia. Many of the islands of the Caribbean, including several territories, are known to be sites for the transit of illegal drugs from South America to North America and Europe. Such problems are less frequent in other regions, though finance, politics and crime are intertwined in Guam and the Marianas, which are to some extent the interface between organised crime in East Asia (especially Japan) and the United States.[59] Dubious financial transactions – money-laundering, illegal speculation, business practices which would not be allowed in metropoles – are not uncommon; Russian 'mafia money' has reached the Caribbean. Allegations that the local government turned a blind eye to shady financial activities played a role in bringing down the long-serving chief minister of Gibraltar in 1996, and caused the Dutch to impose 'higher supervision' on administrative and business activities in Sint-Maarten in the early 1990s. The territories also attract illegal migrants and clandestine refugees who hope to use them as transit points to metropolitan states; the Australian government, for instance, in 1996 faced the problem of whether to grant refugee status and residency, or expel, several hundred Chinese who arrived in four boats on Christmas Island in the Indian Ocean. Although metropolitan authorities, in principle, keep a watchful eye over law codes and business practices, and exercise the legal, police and customs authority to regulate local affairs, this is not always possible. Borders between a number of territories – for instance, between the Dutch and French sides of St Martin and between the British and United States Virgin Islands – are porous, providing opportunities for irregular movements of people, money and goods. Such illegal economic activities are of greater strategic and security concern than military incursions; hence the territories have increasingly seen less of a military presence, and more of a paramilitary and police presence.

Drug-dealing is a particularly troubling issue, primarily in the Caribbean, though Gibraltar, Ceuta and Melilla have been implicated in drug-smuggling between Spain and Morocco. In 1996, American authorities estimated that 154 tonnes of cocaine arrive in the United States each year from the eastern Caribbean, and an even larger quantity transits through the islands on the way to Europe. The Cayman Islands and the Turks and Caicos are gateways to Florida, and the BVI is a link to the USVI and Puerto Rico. Aruba, St Martin and Puerto Rico have been identified by Washington as sites of drug-running: 'Today, Puerto Rico is an island under siege by the increasing problems of drug trafficking. Puerto Rico is the epicentre of the Caribbean drugs *en route* to the US mainland, Europe and Canada.' Puerto Rico's status complicates the problem; once drugs have managed to penetrate police barriers and enter Puerto Rico, they can then be shipped to the US mainland without going through customs. Drugs have contributed to many of the problems, such as crime, which beset Puerto Rico; the island has the highest per capita murder rate in the United States, and two-thirds of murders in 1995 were drug-related.[60] Fortunately, no other territory confronts drug problems of that magnitude.

The old era of geopolitics and superpower rivalry has ended; the post-war period where Greenland, the Azores and the BIOT were more important for the United States than for the metropolitan power, or, in some respects, the local inhabitants, is winding down. That period brought economic gain to many territories but often at considerable social cost, not least for the Ilois of the BIOT. Superpower adherence to the concept of the 'domino effect' and the uncertainties of geopolitics were good reason to retain most territories. Despite the decline in size of public purses, the pursuit of economic rationalism, the abandonment of grand visions of a place in the oceans of the future, and the demise of the 'domino effect', a small number of territories have found that inertia and geographical significance have given them a continued, if minor, strategic role. At the same time, the rise in significance of other security concerns has given metropolitan strategic intervention a new form. The issue of drug-smuggling from territorial bases shows that the 'confetti of empire' cannot be eliminated from geopolitical equations or ignored in international affairs. However, as drug-smuggling and other illegal activities must be policed, and illegal migrants transit (or stay), so the territories have steadily become a strategic disadvantage rather than an advantage. The enormous costs of anti-drug surveillance are a source of tension between territories, metropoles and neighbouring govern-ments.[61] Even after the ending of the Cold War, islands and enclaves can provide strategic benefits for military bases, intelligence-gathering, scientific work and, in general, showcasing of national might. At the very least they are a form of strategic denial to other nations. Yet they can also create international difficulties because of illegal or irregular activities which take place there. On balance, however, the international liabilities have not led to metropolitan powers abandoning sovereignty over their distant domains.

CHAPTER 6

Disputed Territories, 'Colonial' Conflicts

Colonial boundaries were often arbitrarily fixed, as great powers claimed territories, conquered new possessions from old claimants, traded or sold outposts, and drew lines across maps of distant domains from the security of European capitals. In some cases, they disputed territories; sovereignty over uninhabited Clipperton in the eastern Pacific, to which both France and Mexico claimed rights, was not decided until the early 1930s. Similarly, not until the early twentieth century was Denmark's sovereignty confirmed over a portion of Greenland claimed by Norway. Even at the time of decolonisation, many frontiers remained so arbitrary that the United Nations, fearing chaos if attempts were made to redraw maps, stated that the borders of newly independent states should conform to old colonial boundaries. That principle did not stop numerous secession movements, civil wars and military conflicts between nations trying to gain or regain territories they considered rightfully their own. The United Nations also asserted that the interests of local populations should be taken into account and rights to self-determination recognised in decolonisation or cession, principles which sometimes clashed with that of territorial integrity.

Contemporary overseas territories have not been immune to disputes between rival claimants. In the Indian Ocean, for instance, the Comoros claims the French-administered island of Mayotte; France, the Comoros and Madagascar all claim the Iles Eparses in the Mozambique Channel; Mauritius disputes France's claim to the Tromelin reef and claims the British Indian Ocean Territory. In the South Pacific, France and Vanuatu quietly dispute Matthew and Hunter islands east of New Caledonia, and Tokelau and American Samoa intermittently disagree over Swain's Island (Olosega). Rival claims create international tension, even when contested areas, usually islands, have no permanent population. Substantial exclusive economic zones and hopes for dis-covering and developing undersea resources give potential economic value to such outposts, and strategic location provides another rationale for affirming claims. In populated territories, calls for the protection of the safety, citizenship rights and lifestyles of residents create another powerful argument for sovereignty. Failure to defend claims, or will-ingness to relinquish possessions, suggests lack of national honour and loss of face, yet the need to do so burdens budgets and challenges military capacities. Claims and counter-claims form powerful pillars of national myths.

Although relatively few overseas territories are the object of heated disputes, there are notable exceptions. With the fate of Hong Kong resolved, Macao, which, barring unforeseen circumstances, will have become part of the People's Republic of China by the end of the century, has been the prime example of irredentist claims resolved by outright cession (and largely over the heads of the local population). Spain and Britain have argued for centuries, sometimes virulently, about Gibraltar; Morocco regularly reasserts its claim over Spanish Ceuta and Melilla. In the most dramatic confrontation concerning overseas terri-tories, Britain and Argentina went to war over the Falkland Islands and its dependencies in 1982. These conflicts illustrate the complex grounds on which rival claims are advanced and the way in which disputes can poison international relations.

Macao

China regained control of the most populous and wealthiest British colony, Hong Kong, in 1997. The retrocession, after 186 years of British rule, created grave concern about the territory's economy and the human rights of its population as a 'Special Administrative Region' of China. Yet the British government in the 1980s agreed to relinquish control of the colony in the hope that Beijing would adhere to its promise to maintain capitalism and allow some measure of autonomy to Hong Kong for at least a fifty-year period. Similar arrangements were designed for Macao, to be retroceded to China in 1999.[1]

Portuguese traders first arrived in Macao in 1507, and a permanent Portuguese settlement dates from 1557. Colonists founded the city on a small peninsula with few inhabitants, and took over two neighbouring islands – a total area of 15.5 square kilometres. The lands were leased by China to Portugal, which paid taxes and duties to Chinese authorities; Portugal did not claim sovereignty over the territories until 1783. Macao became the main port for Western trade with China in the early modern age, colonial authorities claiming in the 1600s that Macao was the world's wealthiest port. China kept a watchful eye over the foreigners' activities and occasionally, to Portuguese annoyance, interfered in Macao's affairs.[2] Macao's importance as a trading-centre declined in the 1700s and early 1800s, and British acquisition of a superior port in Hong Kong dealt a great blow to the city.[3] Macao's star fell, and even its legal status seemed uncertain when China failed to ratify a treaty negotiated in 1862 which recognised Portugal's sovereignty. Not until 1887 did Lisbon manage to secure a treaty which recognised 'the perpetual occupation and government of Macao and its dependencies by Portugal'. The constitutional designation for Macao changed over time – Lisbon made it an 'overseas territory' in 1933, an 'overseas province' in 1951, and an 'autonomous region' in 1971 – but, in general, a Portuguese governor ruled the territory, whilst a locally elected body held restricted powers.[4]

After the revolution China officially claimed Macao, as it did Hong Kong and Taiwan, but made no efforts to obtain control. Riots by Chinese residents of Macao sympathetic to Mao's Cultural Revolution occurred in 1966 and 1967, after a dispute with the colonial government on the setting-up of a Chinese school. Portuguese police killed eight protesters, and China reputedly massed troops near the colony's border. In 1967 the governor reportedly offered to cede the territory immediately to China, but Beijing declined, fearing destabilisation of Hong Kong.[5] Portugal's stakes in Macao were meagre. Most of the small number of Portuguese in the territory hold jobs in the administration or the army. At least 97 per cent of population are ethnic Chinese, almost none of whom speak Portuguese; a substantial number have migrated, some illegally, from China. The remainder are of mixed Portuguese and Asian ancestry and are Portuguese-speaking and Catholic. Portuguese economic interests are minor and Macao is much less prosperous than Hong Kong. If Portugal clung to Macao (and indeed most of its other possessions) in the 1960s and early 1970s, this was largely because of inertia and the unwillingness of the authoritarian government which had ruled Portugal since the 1920s to give up these vestiges of the country's once great place in world affairs.

The 'revolution of the carnations' in 1974, sparked by a colonial war in Angola, brought down the Portuguese dictatorship. The new government moved rapidly to divest itself of its colonies, and by 1975 Macao remained the only distant Portuguese territory. Rumours circulated that Lisbon had unsuccessfully tried to return it to China. In 1976, the Portuguese parliament adopted an Organic Law, which declared Macao to be Chinese territory under Portuguese administration. Portugal thus renounced claims to sovereignty over Macao. Although Portugal and China did not establish diplomatic relations until 1979, Lisbon made no moves in Macao which would anger Beijing and China's influence in Macao's affairs continually strengthened. China was more eager to regain control of Hong Kong, and settlement of the Anglo-Chinese dispute was more urgent. Only after the 1984 signature of the accords between Beijing and London for retrocession of Hong Kong did China turn its attention to Macao. In 1986, Beijing and Lisbon began nine months of negotiations which culminated in an agreement for Portugal to withdraw and China to take over Macao on 20 December 1999. The Hong Kong accord provided a precedent, and renunciation of Portuguese sovereignty in 1976 made the outcome certain. The main subjects for negotiation were the timing of Portuguese withdrawal, the fate of Portuguese nationals, and the legal and institutional status of Macao after 1999. The date of Chinese takeover provided a niggling point of contention. China insisted that Macao be returned before 2000, but Chinese authorities had sometimes said that Macao and Hong Kong should be handed back on the same date.[6] Portugal argued that a longer transition period was needed because of lack of a trained administrative elite to take the reins of government. Macao's laws were written in Portuguese and needed translation into Chinese; in the mid-1980s, not a single lawyer or judge was Chinese – all were Portuguese expatriates, as were all senior bureaucrats.

The fate of Portuguese nationals in Macao's population was more tendentious. According to Portuguese law, any person born in Macao before 1982 could claim full Portuguese citizenship, which (unlike the status of the Chinese in Hong Kong) included right of abode in Portugal (and, by extension, other states of the European Union). This was particularly important for the 8000 to 10,000 mixed-blood Macanese, many of whom considered themselves more Portuguese than Chinese and staffed the middle and lower ranks of Macao's administration. Portuguese law also held out the possibility of passports (and citizenship) to some 100,000 residents of Macao, almost a quarter of the territory's total population. Beijing feared an exodus in 1999 but remained unwilling to recognise dual citizenship. After much discussion, China agreed to protect the culture of the Macanese, to allow nationals of either China or Portugal to work in Macao's administration after 1999, and permit any residents of Macao who held Portuguese passports at that date to continue to use them as 'travel documents' after the handover. This decision stopped short of recognising dual citizenship, but satisfied both Lisbon and many of Macao's inhabitants.

Portugal and China agreed on a Basic Law, which spelled out the situation Macao would enjoy as a Special Administrative Region after 1999. The arrangements were somewhat more generous than those agreed for Hong Kong. Portuguese will continue to be (along with

Chinese) the official language, and most Portuguese laws remain in force, even though there is uncertainty about exact provisions.[7] Macao will have its own flag and emblem, and may enter into international agreements and join international organisations as 'Macao, China' (provided that such agreements do not contravene Chinese national policy). There will be a substantial degree of self-government under a local assembly. The Macao currency, the *pincata*, will continue to be legal tender, and the city will be a free port. Gambling (which provides one-third of the territory's revenues) will be permitted, although it is currently illegal in China. The Basic Law states that 'the previous capitalist system and way of life are to remain unchanged for fifty years'. Freedom of the press, of speech, of assembly and of religion are guaranteed.[8]

Since China and Portugal signed the accord on retrocession in 1987, despite occasional minor disputes, the process for hand-over has moved steadily ahead. Portugal's government and Macao's authorities take no major decision without the prior counsel and consent of China. Portuguese domestic opposition to the hand-over of Macao is non-existent. Few of Macao's residents have any ties with Portugal, and even many of the Lusophone Macanese have never set foot there. The arrangements for the Special Administrative Region claim to safeguard the political system, economic structures and culture of Macao. In the lead-up to 1999, Macao's economy boomed, despite rising crime rates, gambling violence and scandals involving government corruption. New construction included an airport, a new harbour, and a larger bridge between the mainland and Taipa Island. A railway link between Macao and Guangdong has been planned. Gambling and tourism flourish.[9] Generous provisions for residents to obtain and keep Portuguese citizenship provide insurance against any change in Chinese policy, and the two years between the retrocession of Hong Kong and that of Macao will provide a brief period in which to judge Beijing's attitudes.

Britain versus Argentina: The Falklands

Though Britain peacefully and almost willingly relinquished Hong Kong to China (just as Portugal is giving up Macao), London's response to irredentist claims and a military effort to take over another territory could not have been more different. Indeed just as Margaret Thatcher's government was beginning talks with China on Hong Kong, it was fighting a war in the South Atlantic to retain control of the Falkland Islands. The Falklands (Malvinas) group (including two major islands, East Falkland or Soledad, and West Falkland or Grande Malvina) are 400 kilometres east of Argentina and 8000 kilometres from Britain. The

12,000 square kilometres of the islands are home to 2000 Falklanders – most of whom live in the capital, Port Stanley – plus a large contingent of British soldiers.

Discovered in the 1500s – although whether by a Briton, Portuguese or Spaniard is uncertain – the Falklands remained uninhabited until the 1760s. Spain claimed overlordship, based on a papal bull and the Treaty of Tordesillas which, in the late 1400s, divided the 'new worlds' between Spain and Portugal. In the early 1700s foreign explorers and traders occasionally called at the islands; seamen from the French city of Saint-Malo named the islands the Malouines (which became Malvinas in Spanish). In 1764 Louis de Bougainville, under the banner of the French king, established the settlement of Port-Louis on East Falkland. Unaware of the French establishment, a British commander set up a settlement on Saunders Island, off West Falkland, the following year. Both powers considered the Falklands a useful port on the long route from Europe to the Pacific.

Spain protested about both the French and British settlements. In 1767 Bougainville evacuated his settlement, and France ceded its rights to the islands to Spain. In 1774 the British, also under Spanish pressure, abandoned their settlement, leaving behind a plaque which stated London's claims to 'Falkland's Island' [sic]. Two years later, the Spanish government placed the islands under the administration of the governor of Buenos Aires. Argentina gained independence in 1810; the new government claimed the Falklands, although Buenos Aires took official possession only in 1820. In 1829 Argentina named a governor, set up a small settlement, introduced sheep-raising, and tried to control American whaling in the waters off the islands; when Argentina seized three American whaling ships, a US warship destroyed the Argentinian settlement. Argentina protested, reaffirmed its rights and rebuilt the tiny colony. However, the garrison revolted and killed the new governor in 1832; an Argentinian ship arrived to restore order just before a British ship sailed into the Falklands. The British commander raised the Union Jack, claimed possession of the islands and expelled the Argentinians. The Falklands officially became a Crown colony in 1840; a governor and a few Scotsmen arrived to establish a British pastoral settlement.

Argentina hotly disputed the British takeover, and Buenos Aires made continual diplomatic representations over the next 150 years to recover the islands, though to no avail. Britain indeed extended its regional sphere of influence, formally claiming South Georgia and South Sandwich (the Falkland Island Dependencies) in 1908, as well as a slice of Antarctica and other sub-Antarctic islands. Wrangling continued by diplomatic means, with occasional military incidents. In 1948, for example, when the Peronist government in Buenos Aires became more strident in its claims, Britain sent warships to the South Atlantic. Argentina and Chile mobilised forces, but the US government intervened to defuse the situation.

The question of ownership of the Falklands is a matter of arcane disagreement among legal experts.[10] Whether discovery or settlement provides the basis for possession is part of the dispute; if it is settlement, there exist different views as to whether settlement must be symbolic or effective and, if effective, for how long it must last. There is also disagreement on whether claims can be nullified (or simply expire) by lack of real signs of possession (such as trade, administration or settlement), and whether one government can legally usurp the claims of another. Claims based on discovery are not proved, although both Argentina and Britain have produced maps as evidence of Spanish or British discovery. Argentina claims its rights on the basis of *uti possidetis*, succession to the Spanish claim on the islands – itself based on treaties of the 1400s, as confirmed by French withdrawal and recognition of Spanish overlordship in the 1760s – and to their own activities in the islands from 1810 to 1833. The British have traditionally argued that Spanish claims did not include the islands, that Argentina would not have inherited Spanish rights even if they had existed, and that Argentinian actions in the 1820s, including appointments of non-resident governors, did not constitute effective possession. The British base their claims on the 1833 takeover in the legal principle of 'acquisitive prescription'. Confidential legal studies by the British Foreign Office in 1910, 1928 and 1946 cast some doubt over the legitimacy of British title to the Falklands on the basis of British discovery or legitimate settlement in 1765: hence the British reliance on the 1833 takeover to substantiate their claims. According to London, Argentina was not then in effective possession of the islands, and so they were *terra nullius*; Britain was perfectly within its rights in raising the flag. Argentina has countered that the British action was nothing more than 'gunboat diplomacy', as the British navy wrested the islands away from a weaker country. British authorities deny this interpretation and insist that the continuous presence of British settlers on the islands since 1833 reinforces its claims and, furthermore, obliges Britain to protect its subjects and take their interests into consideration. Argentina considers that British subjects live illegally on the islands, and thus have no right to self-determination.

Argentina became more adamant in advancing its counter-claims in the years after the Second World War. Indeed, in a country troubled by dramatic swings between prosperity and need, battered by frequent changes of government and often under the control of populist or authoritarian rulers, the idea of regaining the Falklands took on overweening importance. One British writer sums up the role played by the

Malvinas in Argentinian life: 'Argentina's claim to the Islands was not an instance of political opportunism. It was an important and integral part of Argentina's national myth.'[11] Its claims on the Falklands have never wavered. In the 1960s Britain seemed prepared to discuss the future of the islands with Argentina; though Britain had not refuted claims on sovereignty, it was in the process of decolonising elsewhere. With a small and declining population, a desolate landscape and a harsh climate, an economy comprised solely of sheep-raising, without evident resources and with no apparent strategic value, the Falklands hardly appeared an essential British outpost.

Indeed, the islands held interest primarily for the residents and those with economic interests there. The main economic activity of the islands was the production of wool for European markets. The largest company, the Falkland Islands Company, owned 46 per cent of the total area of the islands and accounted for 44 per cent of total wool production; most of the rest of the land was owned by absentee proprietors.[12] The Falkland Islands Company was the islands' major shipper and banker. So powerful was it that a journalist wrote in 1978 about the inhabitants of rural areas (the 'camp') outside Port Stanley, that:

> The men of the Camp . . . live in Company houses on Company land. They shop in the Company store for goods delivered by Company ships, and have bills deducted from Company wages. Many of them use the Company as a bank, the wool they shear from the Company sheep goes to Tilbury, again by Company ship, where it is unloaded at the Company wharf, stored in the Company warehouse and sold on the Company wool exchange in Bradford. . . . For better or worse the Falklands are Company islands.[13]

Some Falklanders resented 'colonial' domination by the company, but relied on it for their livelihoods; during the Falklands War, they also relied on it to lobby for British intervention.

In the 1960s Argentina displayed renewed interest in winning sovereignty over the Falklands, and brought the issue to the United Nations, which in 1965 passed a resolution calling on London and Buenos Aires to discuss the archipelago. Britain proposed a thirty-year moratorium on discussions of sovereignty, a suggestion Argentina rejected. By 1967, according to then secret Foreign Office papers, British negotiators had accepted the principle of British renunciation of sovereignty subject to certain conditions and a transition period before withdrawal. The Falkland Islanders, fearful of this and aided by an active press campaign and support from a number of members of parliament, demanded that Britain not 'give away' the islands. This lobbying effectively ended the vague British plan to transfer sovereignty to Argentina. Buenos Aires, predictably, felt frustrated, but lobbying efforts indicated that the

Falklands were not just an international issue but could become a delicate point in British domestic politics. A new element complicated the dispute when oil companies expressed interest in 1969 in prospecting for petroleum in the waters around the Falklands; a few years later the area was estimated to contain four or five times as much oil as the rich North Sea reserves.[14]

Anglo-Argentine negotiations recommenced in the early 1970s at a time when the islands were becoming more dependent on Argentina for trade and an air service. Another UN resolution regretted lack of progress in the talks, but Buenos Aires stepped up demands for a solution, and the British Labour government, elected in 1974, declared its intention to deal with the question. Two years later, when a British ship, the *Shackleton*, sailed to the South Atlantic to study the region's natural resources, Argentina demanded more serious negotiations, and fired warning shots over the bow. Britain and Argentina recalled their respective ambassadors. Further action was diverted by a military coup in Argentina in 1976. The military regime embarked on a 'dirty war' against dissidents, radicals and others, and there was an enormous death toll from government persecutions. The generals also faced international tensions with Chile, the two countries coming to the brink of war in 1978 over three small islands in the Straits of Magellan. American intervention and Vatican mediation averted armed conflict, although Buenos Aires was upset with the Vatican's decision in Chile's favour. The generals meanwhile established close relations with the United States.

Throughout the 1970s, London and Buenos Aires discussed possible solutions to the Falklands problem. Various incidents nevertheless created regular conflicts: one example was the discovery in mid-1977 that a contingent of Argentinians – members, Buenos Aires claimed, of a scientific expedition – had been stationed in the South Sandwich Islands for over a year. After the return of the Conservatives to power in Britain in 1979, under Margaret Thatcher – for whom the generals felt ideological sympathy – Argentina held renewed hopes for an accord. Early in Thatcher's administration, London and Buenos Aires again appointed ambassadors, restoring full diplomatic representation.

Argentina pressed its case for outright recognition of its sovereignty and transfer of the islands. British negotiators suggested a number of alternatives, including the setting-up of a 'condominium' which would allow joint Anglo-Argentine rule of the islands. A variant on the plan would give Argentina sovereignty over the land, whilst Britain retained sovereignty over the islands' inhabitants, and a proposed 'Andorra solution' would vest co-sovereignty in the two powers but leave islanders free to run their own affairs. A more promising solution was for British cession of sovereignty to Argentina with immediate leaseback of the islands to Britain;[15] the suggested length of the lease varied from only a few years to 999 years. Another scenario envisaged the separation of the islands, with the two main ones divided between Britain and Argentina; yet another possibility was transfer of sovereignty over the Falklands to Argentina, while Britain would retain the Falkland Island Dependencies. Argentina, not surprisingly, favoured complete relinquishment of British sovereignty; the preferred solution of the British was leaseback. By 1981 talks had stalemated. An increasingly impatient Argentinian government again rejected British proposals for a moratorium on the sovereignty issue; the Foreign Office still accepted the idea of cession with a lease-back, but the islanders were decidedly hostile. Rumours spread of a possible military move by Argentina's leaders; General Leopoldo Galtieri, who took power in 1981, eager for a foreign policy success, said that gaining control of the Falklands was a major priority before the rapidly approaching 150th anniversary of British takeover on 3 January 1983.[16]

Action seemed timely, especially since Argentina knew of a British 1981 Defence White Paper which recommended that London abandon its naval presence in the South Atlantic and Antarctic; the government had also announced its intention (despite opposition in parliament and the Falklands) to withdraw the only British vessel, the *Endurance*, from the region, leaving fewer than a hundred military personnel to defend the Falklands. Late in 1981 an Argentinian scrap-metal dealer, Constantino Davidoff, who in 1978 had won a British contract to dismantle a whaling factory in the South Georgia Islands, visited the remote archipelago aboard an Argentine navy vessel; although there were questions about his having followed the right procedures, London did not protest. In January 1982 the junta met in Buenos Aires and formulated more strongly worded demands for British negotiations and contingency plans for military action. In March, Davidoff returned to the South Georgia Islands, where he landed several dozen men, again breaching protocol by not informing the Falklands authorities before disembarkation. Reports denied by Argentina said that the men were armed and uniformed, and that they had raised the Argentine flag. The British dispatched the *Endurance* with twenty marines to dislodge the Argentinians; Buenos Aires reacted by sending a ship to protect the workers. Argentina and Britain warily faced each other in South Georgia.

In London, members of parliament attacked Thatcher for lack of more decisive action and demanded that negotiations on the Falklands be frozen. British ships, perhaps including nuclear submarines, were dispatched to the South Atlantic, and military manoeuvres began at British bases in Gibraltar and Belize. The Argentinian junta, determined to seize the opportunity to stake its claims before the arrival of British reinforcements, launched an invasion of the Falklands during the night of 1–2 April 1982. Within hours, several thousand troops had defeated the handful of British soldiers on the islands, taken Port Stanley and forced the governor, Rex Hunt, to surrender. Argentina raised its flag over the renamed Puerto Argentino, and crowds in Buenos Aires celebrated the takeover of the Islas Malvinas. Westminster MPs accused Thatcher and the foreign minister, Lord Carrington, of incompetence, and lobbied for swift and definitive military action to liberate the Falklands. The United Nations passed a resolution calling for cessation of hostilities. The US Secretary of State, Alexander Haig, offered his services as mediator and shuttled between London and Buenos Aires.

Haig advanced proposals for a ceasefire, the withdrawal of Argentinian and British forces, and the setting-up of an interim UN administration over the islands whilst the belligerents negotiated. Mediation foundered on Argentinian demands that its 'territorial integrity' be acknowledged and British demands that the islanders' right of self-determination be recognised; Haig, in particular, was unable to produce wording about respect for the 'will and wishes', the 'interests', the 'aspirations', or simply the 'points of view' of the Falklanders which satisfied both London and Buenos Aires. Argentina took comfort from Haig's argument that the British were willing to negotiate – he told them that the British 'don't care about the sovereignty of the islands' – but also knew that the United States was supplying military intelligence and logistical support to Britain.

As mediation failed, Argentina sought support from its South American allies. Panama, Peru and Venezuela sent aeroplanes and ammunition to Argentina, and Cuba and Nicaragua – whose leftist leaders made odd partners for Argentina's generals – even offered soldiers. The British government decided to retake the Falklands by force; Admiral Sir John Fieldhouse, commander-in-chief of the British fleet, stated that this was 'the most difficult thing we have attempted since the Second World War'.[17] British military actions soon got under way, as troops rushed from the United Kingdom via the Atlantic island territory of Ascension. Royal Marines retook South Georgia on 25 April, then bombarded Argentinian positions in Port Stanley on 1 May. The following day, a British torpedo sank the *General Belgrano*, killing more than 300 men. Since the ship had been sailing outside a British-proclaimed 200-mile exclusion zone around the occupied Falklands, questions were raised about the legitimacy of the attack. The sinking of the *General Belgrano* hardened Argentinian resolve. Two days later Argentinian Exocet missiles hit the *Sheffield*, also with loss of life. Observers feared an escalation of the conflict, including possible Soviet support for Argentina to counter increased US support for the British.

On 21 May, British troops landed on the western side of East Falkland, and fighting on land complemented naval skirmishes. After taking the strategic point of Goose Green, British troops launched an offensive on Port Stanley. Argentinian forces – composed largely of young, untrained soldiers who were now cold, demoralised and undernourished – proved no match for the British, and on 14 June the Argentinians surrendered and evacuated the Falklands. In Britain, crowds celebrated the British victory and Thatcher basked in triumph; successful leadership during the war was subsequently of immense aid to her in domestic politics. In Argentina, angry crowds branded Galtieri a coward; the defeat and popular protest led to his resignation and the fall of the junta within months of the war's end. The war left 750 Argentinians, 255 Britons and three Falkland Islanders dead. The British lost four warships, a requisitioned civilian ship and twenty-five aircraft; Argentina lost several ships and forty-five aircraft. The cost of the war has been estimated at £700 million for the British and a similarly high sum for Argentina. Parts of the Falklands were left devastated by the fighting; many of the 18,000 landmines placed by the Argentinians have yet to be disarmed.

Participants, politicians and academics have analysed the Falklands War.[18] For many Britons, London's response to the invasion represented a legitimate reaction to an unprovoked act of aggression, and defence of British subjects in a territory over which Britain held sovereignty; it was a defence, as well, of British values and the British way of life against the dictatorship in Argentina. Others, such as the Labour MP Tam Dalyell – forced off his party's front bench for failure to support the military campaign – argued that Thatcher over-reacted to the invasion to buttress her domestic standing; that the way in which she prosecuted the war, especially the sinking of the *General Belgrano*, intentionally thwarted possibilities for a peaceful settlement;[19] and that Thatcher needed a clear military victory to secure her political fortunes. British interests in the South Atlantic, whether actual or potential, may also have played a role. The potential for oil held out possibilities for economic gain, and Thatcher's comment that the Falklands were the 'gateway' to the Antarctic revealed that the islands were not without some strategic interest.[20] Indeed, Britain has shown greater concern for its South Atlantic possessions since Argentina established a claim in Antarctica in 1943 which overlapped the Falkland Island Dependencies, and subsequent British interest in South Georgia and the South Sandwich Islands was largely because of their relative proximity to Antarctica.[21] Port Stanley is 'the only major ice-free port in reasonable striking distance of Antarctica. . . . And that continent is the world's last major untapped source of mineral wealth.'[22]

Argentinians later admitted that the war was a military blunder. Argentina's president, Carlos Menem, stated that 'from a strategic point of view, it was a bad decision',[23] though the campaign was a justified effort to secure Argentinian rights in the face of British 'occupation' of the islands, procrastination in negotiations, and unwillingness to relinquish sovereignty. Five years after he oversaw Argentina's war efforts, former foreign minister Nicanor Costa Méndez stated: 'There was no other way out in order to preserve Argentine rights.' Others have claimed that Buenos Aires planned only a temporary occupation of the Falklands, and Costa Méndez stated that the invasion took place 'with the objective of asking, and compelling more than asking, the United Nations, through the Security Council, to intervene' in the dispute.[24] Many Argentinians hoped, however, that the occupation would last, despite international condemnation of the use of force. Using the parallel of another capture of a disputed colonial territory, the Indian military takeover of the Portuguese outpost of Goa in 1961, Costa Méndez stated: 'India occupied Goa, there were criticisms but, at the end of the day, it was accepted.'[25] The domestic situation in Argentina played a large role in the timing of the invasion. Galtieri's recent appointment and uncertain hold on power, mounting opposition to the military regime and its human rights abuses, and economic chaos made an attack on the Falklands a useful diversion.

The rest of the world did not sit idle while Britain and Argentina fought, and the reaction of various countries to the war indicated how such a small territory could become a flashpoint in international relations.[26] The solidarity with which Latin American countries supported Argentina surprised Britain and the United States; more predictably, Argentina won support from Third World countries which saw the British response as old-fashioned gunboat diplomacy.[27] Other than Spain, which had strong historical and cultural connections with South America, the states of the Commonwealth and 'Western' countries spoke in favour of Britain. The potential of the Falklands to involve other belligerents was never great, nor did the war become an East–West confrontation, though one Argentinian commentator interpreted the clash as the first war between the North and the South and a precedent for big-power intervention in Grenada, Somalia and the Persian Gulf.[28]

At the time of the war, Argentinian opinion seemed firmly behind Galtieri's action. The British largely supported Thatcher's response, and there was an outpouring of popular nationalist fervour throughout the United Kingdom. The leader of the Labour opposition, Michael Foot, summed up the view of many Britons: 'There is no question in the Falkland Islands of any colonial dependence or anything of the sort. It is a question of people who wish to be associated with this country and who have built their whole lives on the basis of association with this country.' However, even the US ambassador to the United Nations, Jeanne Kirkpatrick, remarking on the question of sovereignty, suggested that 'if the Argentines own the islands, then moving troops into them is not armed aggression'. Still others wondered why there was so much fuss about what Ronald Reagan casually termed 'that little ice-cold bunch of land down there'.[29]

Opinion similarly divided about the significance of the British ousting of the Argentines from the Falklands. For Thatcher, the victory solved the sovereignty issue once and for all. The British government extended full citizenship rights to Falklanders, a measure designed to cement their ties to the United Kingdom; only residents of the Falklands and Gibraltar, of all Britain's dependent territories, have such full citizenship. Argentina denied that British victory solved the sovereignty question, and since the British recapture of the Falklands, the Anglo-Argentine controversy has continued. Renewed tensions occurred in 1986 when Britain declared an exclusive 150-nautical-mile fishing zone around the islands.[30] The British foreign secretary accused Argentina of 'indifference to Falklands conservation needs', 'aggressive patrolling' of waters near the Falklands, and procrastination on talks over natural resource management in the South Atlantic. But the signing of fishing agreements between Argentina and the Soviet Union and Bulgaria had also provoked Britain into establishing the fishing zone, offering the Falklands' economy diversity and a firmer footing by selling licences for squid-fishing.

Following the British proclamation on the fishing zone, Buenos Aires made symbolic moves towards greater military preparedness. It accused Britain of extending colonial hegemony in the South Atlantic, and renewed claims on the Falklands and its dependencies. The Organisation of American States unanimously voted against the fishing zone, though the US representative toned down the resolution. In Britain, the shadow minister responsible for dependent territories accused the Thatcher government of dragging Britain 'still deeper in the quagmire of the Falkland commitment'.[31] Nevertheless, over one single weekend, the Falklands government earned £1.5 million from fishing licence fees sold largely to Japanese, Spanish and Polish vessels; in the first five months of the zone's operation, new revenues from licensing were put at £12.5 million. The territory, according to the head of the Falkland Islands Corporation, 'emerged as probably the richest fishery in the world'.[32]

Five years after the war, according to a British newspaper, 'the Falkland Islands have become . . . a problem no less intractable than that of Northern Ireland. . . . The deadlock seems absolute, if absurd.'

Argentina continued to demand cession of the islands, though renouncing the use of force to obtain them and promising to recognise the islanders' right to stay there. Islanders, however, remained totally opposed to eventual Argentinian administration and sceptical about such promises; one commented that in 1982, 'they told us that there would be no threat to our way of life. But what did they do when they arrived? They changed the names of the settlements and told us we must drive on the right. How are they to be trusted?' Conservatives in Britain steadfastly defended the islanders' right to self-determination and British rights to the archipelago.[33]

Meanwhile, Britain spent considerable funds creating 'Fortress Falklands'. In the five years after the war, London spent £1860 million on the islands' defence and, although the exact level of British military strength was a carefully guarded secret, British soldiers outnumbered the 2000 islanders. Construction of a £300 million airport provided improved defence possibilities. Projects funded by a five-year £31 million development grant included new roads, extended electrification, improved radio and telecommunications links, a hydroponic garden designed to supply fresh fruit and vegetables, oil-prospecting, promotion of tourism, land reform which allowed islanders to acquire properties previously held by absentee landlords, and a scheme to attract migrants. This not only improved the standard of living in the Falklands, but further entrenched the British presence.[34] Likelihood of British relinquishment of the islands seemed more remote than before the 1982 invasion.

Despite UN resolutions asking for Anglo-Argentine negotiations, Britain and Argentina remained at loggerheads. Carlos Menem, elected president in 1989, proclaimed: 'We will acknowledge no sovereignty other than Argentina's [over the Falklands] and to attain that, we will pursue it through all diplomatic channels. I do not know how many generations it will take, but we will recover what is ours.'[35] Yet Menem ended the trade boycott of Britain, consular ties and air links were restored, and various concessions were made on fishing and navigation. Buenos Aires and London restored diplomatic relations in 1990, and reciprocal visits by ministers, sports teams, cultural groups and tourists became common. Argentinian naval vessels joined British ships in the Gulf War. Anglo-Argentine trade increased steadily. An Argentinian minister pointed out that forty times as many Britons live in Argentina as in the Falklands. Officials generally evaded talk of sovereignty, although Buenos Aires protested strongly at any assertion of British sovereignty, as when London announced plans to authorise oil exploration off the Falklands in 1991. The Argentine foreign minister, Guido di Tella, called for amicable cooperation and neatly summed up the state of play on the sovereignty dispute: 'We do not recognise British rights over the islands and they do not recognise ours.'[36] Direct contact between the islands and Argentina, however, has remained stalled; the only way to travel from the Falklands to Argentina remains via either Britain or Chile.

The tenth anniversary of the Falklands War provided an opportunity for each side to reaffirm its claims, though now in diplomatic language. Thatcher celebrated the anniversary of the victory with promises to defend the islands. The Falklanders, basking in new-found prosperity, swore their determination to remain British. President Menem floated a proposal to submit the dispute over the islands to international arbitration, pledged 'never again war', and predicted that Argentina would recover the Falklands 'before the year 2000'. In 1993 an English-language newspaper in Buenos Aires reported that Argentina was considering trying to buy the islands, a suggestion scorned by Britain.[37] A new 1994 constitution tied Argentina to obtaining complete sovereignty over the Falklands, and President Menem argued in 1995 that the 'solution which best suits us is sharing the government under two flags', alongside an offer of $800,000 per Falkland Islander. Both notions were rejected by Falkland Islanders then and again in 1997.[38]

The Falklands sovereignty issue is unsolved. However, in the eyes of many Britons and almost all Falklanders, there is no 'problem': the Falklands are British. With infrastructural developments completed, substantial revenues pouring in from fishing licences and, perhaps soon, from oil, the financial burdens of British control have considerably diminished. Any effort to 'give in' to Argentinian demands would be dangerous for British politicians. It would certainly incite the ire of islanders and provoke a significant lobby in the United Kingdom ready to argue not only the islanders' right to self-determination but also the economic and strategic advantages – including proximity to the Antarctic – that the islands represent. The islands, for many, have become a symbol of British resolve, the efficacy of the British military, and Britain's continued international role. Nevertheless, the Falklands remains a sore point in Anglo-Argentine relations and represents a very significant British commitment far from 'home'.

For Argentina, the Falklands loom infinitely larger than for the British. More than a decade after the war, visitors to Buenos Aires could still see banners and T-shirts bearing the slogan '*Las Malvinas son Argentinas*'. Maps must include the Malvinas as part of Argentine national territory, and the daily newspapers faithfully provide weather forecasts for 'Puerto Argentino'. Politicians proclaim their fervent intention to 'recover' the islands, and the newly developed wealth of the archipelago provides a fresh incentive for renewed diplomatic efforts. Now a democratic society, Argentina also enjoys a booming economy.

The situation is radically different from that of 1982, yet changed conditions have not lessened Argentinian determination, through peaceful and diplomatic means, to gain control of islands it has never ceased to regard as part of the nation.

Gibraltar

The case of Gibraltar has similarities to that of the Falkland Islands: a small territory, lying close to another state, is claimed by one country on the basis of historic rights and the principle of self-determination by the local population, whilst the neighbouring state demands cession of the territory. Significant differences exist between the Falklands and Gibraltar: Spain, for example, has never contested the rights of Britain to legal control (though not sovereignty) over 'the Rock'. But the disputes have brought Britain into conflict with countries with which it has traditionally enjoyed important ties. Britain and Spain have not gone to war over Gibraltar, but latent tension and, sometimes, open hostility have marred relations between the two countries.[39]

Lying on the southern tip of the Iberian peninsula, Gibraltar measures less than 6 square kilometres, most of which is covered by the mountain which forms the territory's most prominent feature. At its base, 31,000 people live in the town of Gibraltar, a British possession since 1704, when a combined Anglo-Dutch force captured the fortress during the War of Spanish Succession. The Treaty of Utrecht, which formally ended the war in 1713, ceded 'to the Crown of Great Britain, full and entire propriety of the Town and Castle of Gibraltar, together with the port, fortifications and forts thereunto belonging'; however, the territory was 'yielded to Great Britain without any territorial jurisdiction, and without any open communication by land with the country round about'. Although Spain, in several subsequent treaties, acknowledged British territorial authority over the peninsula, it maintains that it never relinquished sovereignty. The Utrecht treaty also stated that, should Britain decide to renounce its rights to Gibraltar, Spain would resume control.[40]

Gibraltar occupies one of the most historically significant strategic positions in Europe, guarding the narrow strait which separates the Mediterranean Sea from the Atlantic Ocean. Already in antiquity the Pillars of Hercules – Gibraltar on the north of the strait and Monte Hacho on the south, now in a Spanish enclave – were vital outposts for defence and trade. In 711 Arabs conquered Gibraltar, their leader Tariq giving his name to the Djabal-al-Tariq (Tariq's Mountain), which became Gibraltar in English and Spanish. The Spanish recaptured Gibraltar in 1309, only to see it fall to the sultan of Fez a quarter of a century later. In

1462 the Spanish, pursuing the 'reconquest' of the Iberian peninsula, again secured Gibraltar and held it until the British takeover. The British made Gibraltar a Crown colony in 1830, turning it into a fortress under military administration. It became the most westerly of a chain of possessions which included Malta, Cyprus (and, later, Palestine). British interests in the Mediterranean, especially in Egypt, were crucial through-out the colonial period, and the opening of the Suez Canal in 1869 heightened the role of Mediterranean sea routes. In the world wars, Gibraltar was a valuable supply and repair base, convoy centre and anti-submarine station for the navies of Britain and its allies.

During the Second World War, the British evacuated almost the entire population of Gibraltar, 16,700 people, to Northern Ireland, Madeira and Jamaica; only several thousand Spaniards remained. The war had great effects on the Gibraltarian population, most of whom were of Genoese descent, although some claimed Maltese, Portuguese or other ancestry:

> The evacuation . . . had the effect of knitting the Gibraltarians into a closer community than ever before. Be they in London, Jamaica or Madeira, they were made much more aware of the fact that they were 'different', a community, indeed almost a nation! . . . The desire to return to 'El Peñon' [the peninsula], the 'fatherland', became an obsession with many. The Gibraltarian identity had undoubtedly been strengthened. Linguistically, although Spanish was to continue as the language of most homes, the greater contact with the English language during these years was to have a profound effect, particularly upon the younger generation.[41]

In 1942 Gibraltarians established an Association for the Advancement of Civil Rights (AACR), which aided in the repatriation of Gibraltarians; the AACR also promoted greater self-government for the colony. In 1921 Britain had established a City Council to which Gibraltarians elected representatives, although an appointed governor ruled the territory, and appointed members dominated the council. In 1945, for the first time, the majority of the members of the council were elected. The leader of the AACR, Sir Joshua Hassan, emerged as the dominant politician. Five years later Gibraltar was given its own constitution, as well as Executive and Legislative Councils; in 1964, a Council of Ministers was created with Hassan as chief minister. The City Council and Legislative Council merged into a House of Assembly in 1969, when a new constitution was adopted. Its preamble stated that 'Her Majesty's government will never enter into arrangements under which the people of Gibraltar would pass under the sovereignty of another state against their freely and democratically expressed wishes' – legal enshrinement of the principle of self-determination. The constitution changed the official name of the peninsula from the 'Colony of Gibraltar' to the 'City of Gibraltar'.

Spain's refusal to accept British sovereignty over Gibraltar was seldom expressed in other than symbolic terms until 1964, when Franco's government approached the UN Special Committee on Decolonisation about Gibraltar. South American and Third World representatives lent support to Spain, whilst members of the Commonwealth supported Britain. Hassan, addressing the committee, affirmed that the territory's continued association with the United Kingdom was 'the free choice of the people of Gibraltar'. The Spanish representative replied that Gibraltar represented a colonial anachronism and denied the right of Gibraltarians to self-determination under provisions of the UN Charter because they did not form a real 'people' but only an artificial population created through British imperialism; the Spanish brought to New York a descendant of the original population of Gibraltar, who argued that 'indigenous' Gibraltarians had been displaced by British conquest. Hassan denied the claim and won considerable support for Gibraltarians' right to have a say in the future of the city. Madrid, however, won sympathy for its position that continued British rule of Gibraltar constituted a violation of Spain's territorial integrity. At the conclusion of the debates, the Special Committee adopted a motion which simply recognised the existence of the dispute, and invited Spain and Britain to negotiate further on the 'interests' of Gibraltarians.[42]

The resolution, seen to favour Spain by implicitly bringing into question British sovereignty, produced a large demonstration of support for Britain on Hassan's return to Gibraltar. The Franco government then closed the Spanish consulate in Gibraltar and began to restrict free passage between Spain and Gibraltar, allowing only a restricted number of Spanish citizens to work or travel there. Two years later, in 1966, Madrid proposed that Gibraltar be returned to Spain in return for the right of Gibraltarians to retain British nationality and have self-government within Spain. Britain rejected this, but suggested that the issue be submitted to the International Court of Justice; Spain refused. In 1967, stepping up the confrontation, Madrid closed the narrow Spanish–Gibraltarian border to traffic and closed nearby Spanish airspace to British aeroplanes.

Britain countered with a referendum on the future of Gibraltar; 12,138 voters cast ballots in favour of continued ties with London, and just 44 voted against. (The United Nations ignored the results, reaffirming its commitment to safeguarding the 'national integrity' of member states.) The following year, Madrid totally closed the frontier (except to a few Spanish workers and humanitarian cases); later it forbade all Spaniards from working in Gibraltar, prohibited even pedestrians from crossing the border, ended a ferry link with Algeciras, and cut Spanish telephone lines to the British colony. Gibraltar was thus completely isolated from Spain, a tiny enclave dependent on British ships and aeroplanes for supplies and connections with the outside world. Britain remained unmoved and disinclined to discuss Gibraltar with Franco's government. Use of Gibraltar as a NATO navy base, and an important site for British ship-building, underlined the territory's importance to Britain, and Gibraltarians stood firm in their loyalty to London. Spain remained intransigent, but unwilling to use force, and the stalemate lasted for over a decade. The confrontation stiffened Gibraltarians' resolve. According to Hassan, the 'coercive campaign by General Franco's authoritarian regime, designed to make the people of Gibraltar sue for a settlement on sovereignty, had the opposite effect: the Gibraltarians were alienated from Spain and their many links with Britain, formed and developed over very many years, were reinforced'.[43]

The end of authoritarian government in Spain, with Franco's death in 1975, did not immediately affect the dispute, although telephone links between Spain and Gibraltar were restored two years later and, in 1980, the Spanish and British agreed 'to restart negotiations'. Little eventuated over the next couple of years. Spanish attempts to join both NATO and the European Community gradually tempered its attitude to Britain, though Spain joined NATO in 1982, hoping that the move might help secure recognition for its claim, or at least allow internationalisation of Gibraltar. The Falklands War, however, postponed further negotiations and indicated that Britain might be even less willing to relinquish sovereignty; tacit Spanish support for Argentina further dampened British enthusiasm for talks.

Nevertheless, the Socialist government which came to power in Madrid in 1982, anxious to improve relations and win London's approval for its application to the European Community, partially opened the border.[44] In 1984 the border was completely opened, and Britain and Spain again agreed to reopen bilateral discussions on Gibraltar, including consideration of 'questions of sovereignty'. Spain did not renounce its claims to sovereignty, but offered to give Gibraltar an autonomous status (similar to that of Catalonia or the Basque country) if it became part of the Spanish kingdom. Spanish officials admitted that any change needed the consent of Gibraltar's population. Yet an opinion poll in the mid-1980s revealed that 94 per cent of Gibraltarians opposed any British negotiations with Spain on the issue of sovereignty. Gibraltarians had by this time acquired full British citizenship rights under the British Nationality Act of 1981, strengthening their bargaining position. Subsequent incidents irritated Anglo-Spanish relations. In 1987, European Community discussions on the deregulation of air travel were hampered by a dispute on the status of the Gibraltar airport. Spain objected to the airport, which Madrid says lies in a no man's land under the terms of the Utrecht treaty, being considered a regional British facility accommodating cheap flights from the United Kingdom to the Continent. London offered Spanish flights the right to land on the Gibraltar runway, and agreed to consider Madrid's request that a Spanish air terminal be constructed adjacent to the airport. However, the Gibraltar government vetoed the arrangement; Spanish aeroplanes still do not use Gibraltar's air facilities.

Elections in Gibraltar in 1988 brought to power the Socialist Labour Party under Joe Bossano. The new chief minister argued that Britain had made unnecessary concessions to Spain, and contended that Gibraltar's status should be a matter for discussion only between Gibraltar and London; this position partially contributed to his victory over Hassan's AACR, which had ruled Gibraltar for forty years but had adopted an increasingly conciliatory approach towards the Spanish. Bossano's programme said that Gibraltarians were 'determined to survive as a People, to resist "osmosis" and to prevent the absorption of Gibraltar by Spain'; his government promised to develop 'the necessary economic self-sufficiency' for survival. Bossano hinted that such self-sufficiency might allow Gibraltar to become independent (or perhaps quasi-independent through a treaty of 'free association' with Britain).[45] In the same year, fears arose that Gibraltar might become a centre of international terrorism after British military police shot dead three members of the Provisional Irish Republican Army in the city. The incident also provoked an outcry against the tactics of the British police, but an inquest determined that the killings were lawful. In 1989 the British government nevertheless decided to remove 600 soldiers (plus 100 civilian support staff), roughly half of its infantry battalion in Gibraltar, despite Bossano's reservations. The British foreign secretary promised that the move did not signify a change of heart about the status of 'the Rock'.[46]

Underlying the recurrent arguments between Britain and Spain were various socio-economic changes, including substantial economic development. Traditionally, British military expenditures provided much of the financial wherewithal for the colony, yet such expenditures declined dramatically from 65 per cent of Gibraltar's gross domestic product in 1965 to just 9 per cent in the mid-1990s. Britain has now withdrawn most of its military forces, leaving only 300 soldiers (and 200 reservists) in 1994.[47] Furthermore, in 1984, the Royal Navy ceased using the naval shipyards for construction and repairs. Such disengagement might well have spelled economic crisis. The Gibraltar government made a concerted effort at stimulating new development. Bossano stated:

> We believe that it is essential that we give priority to Gibraltar's economic development because our development as a people and our political develop-ment . . . cannot in fact proceed without achieving economic viability and without being able to demonstrate to the rest of the world that we are entitled to be respected as a people in our own right because we are able to earn a living as a people in our own right.[48]

The government undertook measures to transform Gibraltar into a financial centre, tax haven and tourist destination. Gibraltar's status in the European Union provided an advantage for attracting business, and the government's tax policy further helped to favour offshore business: there is no value-added tax, corporate taxes are low, the business with-holding rate is the lowest in Europe, and there are no taxes on offshore bank accounts. Some three dozen banks now operate in Gibraltar (including several Spanish institutions), and the number of companies registered there exceeds the number of residents. The government has attempted to recruit even more companies, with a project to reclaim 300,000 square metres of land from the sea as a site for office-space,[49] and it has actively promoted tourism to those visitors with an interest in military history or wanting an overseas holiday in an English environ-ment. European visitors, and Moroccans who take the ferry from Tangier, profit from duty-free shopping, tours of 'the Rock', and the 'Old England' atmosphere of pubs and restaurants, as well as the possi-bility of excursions to Spain.

Economic growth has made Gibraltar far less dependent than at any time in the past on British largesse; British aid dropped from £4.9 million in 1980 to only £700,000 in 1988, and continued to decline. Economic success allowed the government to strive for greater political autonomy, and Bossano's supporters hope that Gibraltar will become a financial haven like the Channel Islands, a Mediterranean Hong Kong, or a self-governing or independent micro-state like Liechtenstein or Monaco. The Spanish hinterland of Gibraltar has also profited from the boom, and several thousand Spaniards commute to Gibraltar,[50] though Madrid fears that prosperity and rapidly declining reliance on Britain might further harden Gibraltarian opposition to integration with Spain.

A new problem which has surfaced in the 1990s, creating problems for Gibraltar and tension with Spain, is tobacco and drug-smuggling. Spanish officials say that drug-running, mainly of hashish, from Morocco to Europe via Gibraltar has risen from 8 tons in 1992 to an estimated 50 tons in 1995. An estimated 1.5 billion cigarettes – 50,000 for each Gibraltarian – are smuggled into Spain from the colony yearly, according to the Spanish. Between eight and thirty boats leave Gibraltar for the Spanish coast each night on smuggling missions. Spain argues that it lost the equivalent of £420 million in customs revenues from 1989 to 1994 because of smuggling. It accuses British and Gibraltarian authorities of laxity in controlling illicit trade, and alleges that Gibraltar's financial institutions are involved in money-laundering of the profits of the tobacco and drug trade. Authorities in London and Gibraltar have denied the accusations, stating that Spanish complaints are only a 'convenient smokescreen' behind which the Spanish can harass Gibraltar. Go-slow actions at the Spanish–Gibraltar border, where Spanish authorities make punctilious passport and customs checks, are also employed to make life difficult for the territory.[51]

The Gibraltar government thus maintained a strong stand against Spain's claim to sovereignty and Madrid's charges that Gibraltar turns a blind eye to smuggling and money-laundering. The re-election of Bossano as chief minister in 1992, with 73 per cent of all votes, seemed recognition of the success of his economic programmes, despite an 11-per-cent unemployment rate, as well as validation of his refusal to consider cession of Gibraltar to Spain. Four years later, in the next general election, Bossano was defeated, prey to charges of authoritarian rule, complicity with contraband traders, and a confrontational stance against both Britain and Spain. Voters were not swayed by Bossano's announcement during the campaign that he would request the British government to transform Gibraltar's status from that of a colony to one of free association with Britain. The victor, the leader of the Social Democratic Party, Peter Caruana, said that his new government would give 'priority to economic prosperity rather than to confrontation and struggle against Britain', and would pursue a more flexible approach to Spain.[52]

Spain meanwhile continued to press its case, in 1991 advancing a plan for co-sovereignty in which Queen Elizabeth and King Juan Carlos would be joint heads of state of Gibraltar. The Spanish king, in a speech at the United Nations, referred to the 'persistence of colonialism' in this 'historical residue', which, he argued, formed an obstacle to better Anglo-Spanish relations; a Spanish foreign minister referred to Gibraltar as a 'cancerous tumour' on Spain.[53] (The former prime minister of Spain, Felipe González, referred to Gibraltar somewhat more delicately as the 'pebble on the bottom of Spain's shoe'.) Symbolic deeds sometimes matched polemical words: Madrid delayed the signing of the Schengen Agreement to open borders between eight countries in the then European Community in 1991, arguing that settlement of the 'colonial problem' first needed to be agreed. Early in 1997 Spain made a fresh proposal for shared sovereignty. The proposal envisaged joint control for a period of fifty to sixty years, with Britain controlling most of Gibraltar's affairs, including foreign relations; Spain would play a role 'gradually commensurate with the new arrangements'. Britain rejected this, since it took no account of the feelings of Gibraltarians, whilst Gibraltar's chief minister, Peter Caruana, described the proposals as absurd. Caruana asked the European Union for assistance with Gibraltar's grievances against Spain, including the ban on maritime air links with Spain, restrictions imposed on planes approaching Gibraltar, and Spain's refusal to recognise Gibraltarian identity cards or the territory's international telephone code. The Spanish press denounced the visit to the European Union as unnecessary, since Britain dealt with foreign affairs, and the European Union did not receive the delegation. Britain insisted that Spain recognise all Gibraltarian passports, as a dependent territory within the European Union, but the lack of response led to a march and demonstrations in Gibraltar demanding Spanish recognition for their EU rights.

Even with the partnership of Britain and Spain in NATO and the European Union, the status of Gibraltar remains a problem. Spain's claim to sovereignty is evident in such issues as the operation of Gibraltar's airport, the status of the border, and concern about migration and smuggling. The British government is bound by a constitutional obligation to honour the wishes of the Gibraltarians. The Gibraltar government increasingly seems to have the economic security, popular support and political will to keep the Spanish at bay and, if desired, keep a distance from the British too. Suggestions of resolving the dispute by some compromise between Madrid and London have rested increasingly on the willingness of Gibraltarians to accept any settlement.

Several solutions, similar to those proposed for the Falklands, have been envisaged for Gibraltar. Britain could transfer sovereignty to Spain but lease back the territory for a number of years,[54] a solution which would come close to satisfying Madrid but is not acceptable in Gibraltar and unpopular in Britain. Integration of Gibraltar into the United Kingdom, once considered when Bossano headed a party advocating 'statehood', no longer seems attractive to any of the parties. Outright independence or independence-in-association with Britain is financially feasible. Gibraltar could join other independent European micro-states, such as Monaco and San Marino, although delegating part of its sovereignty (for example, in foreign policy) to another country. Yet Spain would be unlikely to accept such an arrangement, and British Prime Minister John Major stated in 1991 that 'independence is not an option for Gibraltar'. Gibraltar could become a condominium under joint Spanish and British rule, or an area of temporary or permanent co-sovereignty (like Andorra).[55] Other suggestions, for instance that Gibraltar become a 'colony' of the European Union or that it be placed under the suzerainty of the United Nations, have won little support.

Ceuta and Melilla

Less than 20 kilometres across the Straits of Gibraltar from the British colony lies the city of Ceuta (or Sebta, in Arabic), where Monte Hacho faces the Rock of Gibraltar as the southern Pillar of Hercules. Ceuta and Melilla, further east on the coast, together with several tiny offshore islands, form the 'lands of Spanish sovereignty in North Africa', Spanish enclaves in Morocco. Morocco claims Ceuta and Melilla as integral parts of its national territory, while Spain claims them through conquest, historic rights, effective occupation, the wishes of a majority of the local population, and strategic necessity.[56] Europeans have ruled Ceuta since 1415, when Portuguese armies conquered the city, from which Moors had set out to take over the Iberian peninsula in 711; the battle for Ceuta was seen as a long-delayed counter-attack. In 1580 Spain inherited control of Ceuta after the union of the Spanish and Portuguese crowns. Melilla fell into Spanish hands, through conquest, in 1497. The cities can claim to be two of the oldest surviving colonies in the world.[57]

The enclaves were important ports in the early modern age, but by the beginning of the 1800s neither their fortunes nor those of Spain prospered. In 1822 the Cortes, the Spanish parliament, authorised the government to abandon the outposts, and some politicians later suggested that Spain withdraw from North Africa. Nevertheless, trade continued, and migration from the poor Andalusia and Murcia provinces of Spain increased the population. War between Spain and Morocco in 1859–60 led to a slight expansion of the territory of Melilla.[58] The two cities became free ports in 1863, leading to some economic development. The emergence of greater Spanish interest in Africa in the 1890s provided new justification for retaining the territories. The *presidios* then served primarily as penal colonies and garrisons, although the penitentiary was closed in 1906. With Gibraltar under British rule, control of the southern straits held great value for the Spanish.

In 1912 France and Spain established a protectorate over Morocco.[59] Although France's protectorate covered most of the country, Spain won a deep band of the coast from the Atlantic almost to the border between Morocco and (French) Algeria, including the hinterland of Ceuta and Melilla and the Rif mountains. Spain also received the area on the Atlantic coast between Morocco and Mauritania, the Rio de Oro or Western Sahara, as well as two other enclaves on the Atlantic, Ifni and Tarfaya. The carving-up of Morocco took place even while Spain faced a rebellion in the Rif region. From 1909 to 1927, Abd el-Krim led a campaign against the Europeans, dealing Spanish forces a signal defeat in 1921. French intervention reinforced Spanish commitment to North Africa and deepened the special relationship between the Spanish domains and the military. The Spanish Foreign Legion was founded in the protectorate in 1920. General Franco, who took part in the fateful battle of 1921 as a young officer, rose to prominence in the legion; he led his forces from Melilla to the Spanish peninsula in 1936 to combat the Spanish Republic.

In the early twentieth century, 'Spain, itself a poor country ravaged by political turmoil, used the Protectorate principally for a training ground for its army, and secondarily for the extraction of iron ore.' In 1925, at the height of militarisation of the *presidios*, Melilla contained 41,110 soldiers and 52,000 civilians. Iron exports formed the major economic resource of Spanish Morocco, and some kaolin and clay were also mined. Fishing and shipping (because of the free-port status) made the cities busy commercial centres; in the mid-1930s, Ceuta was said to be the busiest port in Spain. Nevertheless, Ceuta and Melilla were frontier outposts, populated by soldiers, Christian migrants from southern Spain, Muslims from the Rif mountains, and Jews from around North Africa. Poverty, violence, ethnic tensions, lawlessness, alcoholism and prostitution marked the cities. The Spanish colonial masters lorded it over Muslims: 'Spain despised everything Rifian, probably because it uncomfortably reminded them of the rural Andalusian society which the majority of the colonists had come from.'[60]

The years immediately after the Second World War brought little change to the *presidios*, although migration of Muslims and Jews increased. Jews flocked to Melilla, particularly after the independence of Morocco in 1956 and Algeria in 1962, to become the backbone of the city's trade; less than 2 per cent of the population, they comprised one-fifth of all wholesalers by the 1980s. Several hundred Hindus arrived from India to become successful merchants, and gypsies established a camp on the outskirts of Melilla.[61] Ceuta and Melilla entered a phase of economic transformation. Fishing experienced a terminal decline, and farming and grazing practically disappeared from the cities' small hinterlands. Exports from Morocco fell, but Ceuta became a major port for the transit of petroleum to Morocco (and elsewhere in Africa).

More than ever before, the cities live off trade connected with their status as duty-free ports. Ceuta, only half an hour by hydrofoil and a little more by ferry from Algeciras in southern Spain, attracts many duty-free shoppers. (Melilla, an overnight trip by boat from Málaga, has much less shopping trade.) Much of the economy revolves around business with Morocco; Moroccans travel to Ceuta from Tetuan and Tangier, and to Melilla from Nador, to purchase goods which are more expensive or unavailable in Morocco. Algerians shop in Melilla for the same reason. Consumer trade with North African countries is in only one direction, at least in the case of Ceuta; the mayor has stated: 'We buy hardly anything from Morocco. Perhaps a few vegetables, that's all.' Even sand is imported from Spain.[62] Some of the trans-border trade is legitimate, but much of the economy rests on contraband movement of goods smuggled from Ceuta and Melilla into Morocco. By 1970 Ceuta had been labelled 'the smugglers' paradise'.[63] In the mid-1980s, Morocco estimated that contraband trade represented one-sixth of the annual budget of Morocco and equalled a quarter of the value of its exports.[64] Although both Moroccan and Spanish authorities occasionally promise to crack down, contraband trade has continued to flourish.

Illicit trade, in principle, is a major sticking point in relations between Morocco and Spain, whose views on sovereignty over the territories completely differ. When Morocco gained independence, Spain relinquished all of its territory on the Mediterranean coast of North Africa, except for the *presidios*; it also retained the Western Sahara, Tarfaya and Ifni. Morocco regained Tarfaya in 1958, and Spain withdrew from Ifni in 1969. King Hassan's formal demands for cession of the Spanish *presidios* encountered outright Spanish refusal. In 1974 King Hassan stepped up calls for return of the Western Sahara, and the next year, after Franco's death, 350,000 Moroccan volunteers undertook a peaceful 'Green March' to the region in a dramatic demonstration of Moroccan claims on 'Spanish Sahara'. Spain, unwilling to fight for a sparsely populated desert territory, agreed at the end of 1975 to withdraw from the Western Sahara and allow its division between Morocco and Mauritania, pending a UN-supervised referendum to determine its fate. In 1979 Mauritania withdrew from its zone, which Morocco then occupied. Rabat claims the entire Western Sahara as the 'southern provinces' of the Kingdom of Morocco. Neither Spain nor the United Nations recognises Moroccan control; an indigenous political movement, the Polisario Front, has unsuccessfully pushed for international recognition and independence, and Morocco stalled a referendum mandated by the United Nations in 1988.

The year of the 'Green March' into the Western Sahara saw renewed Moroccan efforts to gain control of Ceuta and Melilla. The Moroccan ambassador to the United Nations raised the question before the General Assembly, linking it to Spanish claims on Gibraltar: 'Spain cannot refuse a dialogue [on the issue] because this is the same process which it is proposing in order to solve the question of Gibraltar.' The Spanish representative denied any connection between the three territories. King Hassan nevertheless insisted: 'I suppose that one day in the future, England logically must restore Gibraltar to Spain. . . . The day that Spain has Gibraltar, Morocco must necessarily get Sebta and Melilla.'[65]

Morocco tabled a memorandum on Ceuta and Melilla before the UN Special Committee on Decolonisation, calling the *presidios* 'the last vestiges of colonialist occupation' on the Mediterranean coast of Africa: 'Throughout its history and to the present day, Morocco has never abandoned its major concern of recovering these enclaves in order to achieve its territorial integrity.'[66] Morocco received a sympathetic hearing and successfully pressed for support from the Non-Aligned Movement and the Organisation of African Unity, demanding, in the words of a resolution by African foreign ministers, the 'liberation of its territories occupied by Spain'. Spain, nonetheless, continued to reject cession or even negotiation.

Maintaining substantial military detachments in the enclaves and paying inflated salaries to public servants there undoubtedly create burdens on the Spanish budget. Episodic violence has also been a problem. In 1975 several bombs exploded in Ceuta; authorities detained 400 Moroccan citizens for questioning, then expelled a number of them. Rabat protested, and called for its nationals and other Muslims (who made up one-third of the *presidio* population) to remain calm. A special national lottery was organised for aid to the 'Sebta refugees'. When a young Moroccan was killed by a Spanish policeman in Ceuta, tensions heightened and Morocco denounced 'human rights violations'. Demonstrations by several hundred Moroccans just outside the Ceuta frontier led to unfounded fears that Rabat might attempt a 'Green March' on the *presidio*. Three years later, three bomb attacks rocked Ceuta within a six-month period, the last leaving seventeen people injured.[67]

In 1983 Muslims inside Melilla held their first public demonstrations in fifty years to complain about poor living conditions.[68] Two years later, Muslim discontent was aggravated over the issue of citizenship rights. Only 3000 of the Muslims in the city held Spanish citizenship, although many others had been born in Melilla or were long-term residents; those born in Melilla lacked Moroccan citizenship and, unless they could prove their birth in the Spanish enclave, were stateless. Most of the Muslims, poor and illiterate, lived in precarious conditions and worked for modest wages, though life in Melilla was nevertheless preferred to Morocco, where one-third of the workforce was unemployed. In 1985, the Cortes passed an Alien Act which instituted stricter requirements for residence and citizenship and permitted expulsion of illegal migrants. Muslims protested, demonstrating for the right to remain legally. Their leader, an economist named Aomar Mohammedi Dudú (himself a Spanish citizen), charged that the law 'intended to legalise slavery in Melilla' and that Spain 'wanted to make us eternal foreigners in our own city'.[69] The Spanish government partially relented by agreeing to issue residence permits to many Muslims. It appointed Dudú as adviser on minority affairs to the minister of the interior, and promised to improve infrastructure and social conditions. The moves did not quieten disturbances and, in 1987, clashes between Muslims and Spanish police left forty persons wounded. Dudú resigned his post and, fearing for his safety, fled to Morocco; Melilla's authorities issued a warrant for his arrest (and indicted him for corruption). His followers, previously intent on gaining the right to Spanish citizenship for Muslims, now changed sides; Dudú's supporters passed a resolution calling Melilla an 'Arab and Muslim city of the Maghreb'. A Coordinating Committee of Moroccans in Melilla demanded cession of the city to Morocco, and gained support from a Moroccan nationalist party. A group calling itself the Moroccan Movement for the Liberation of Sebta and Melilla took out an advertisement in the French newspaper Le Monde, proclaiming: 'The Moroccan people and their active forces will have the honour of liberating the territories occupied by Spain.'[70] Because of lack of Moroccan government support, disunity among Muslims, the waning influence of Dudú, and the strength of the Spanish military presence, the movement soon petered out. The European population remained firmly opposed to cession, wary about granting citizenship to large numbers of Muslims, and fearful that Muslim activists were Morocco's Trojan horse in the territories. They particularly felt that more generous concessions of citizenship would open the door to greater Moroccan migration, the 'Moroccanisation' of the enclave and increased competition from Muslim businessmen.[71]

Growing migration and high birth-rates increased the Muslim population of the enclaves, and ethnic inequalities became more evident. Racial segregation exists in both cities, despite official efforts to calm tensions. Christian Spaniards, Muslims and the small communities of Hindus and Jews coexist in relative peace, but mix only on formal occasions and in specific areas; different rituals and ceremonies reinforce communal identity and solidarity. Tensions ignited on further occasions, as in 1991 when a group of masked legionnaires attacked a Muslim neighbourhood in Melilla, breaking windows, destroying cars, injuring several people and spreading terror, after Muslims had been involved in a fistfight with soldiers. Officials blamed the conflict on drugs (said to be widespread in the legion) and warned that such clashes could escalate into wider ethnic confrontation.[72] Comments made by one observer on the 1986 disturbances – that Melilla had a 'situation potentially not unlike that of Algeria before independence from France, or Northern Ireland today' – then seemed pertinent.[73] At least one other political problem has faced Spain because of the presidios. In 1990 the Socialist government of Felipe González held a one-seat majority in the Cortes. When Melilla's voters chose a non-Socialist candidate for their single seat in the parliament, González was forced to form a coalition. The incident highlighted the exaggerated importance that 'colonial' outposts could have for states in difficult political situations.

Spanish policy maintains that the territories are not colonies but true parts of the Spanish nation; the enclaves were Spanish territories before the Moroccan state came into existence and, therefore, Morocco has no rights even to advance claims. In the early 1980s, Spanish conservatives accused Socialists of willingness to 'give up' the territories, although the Socialist government, in power from 1982 to 1996, showed no intention of doing so; nonetheless, 'many politicians in Madrid consider Melilla a colony which should be abandoned'.[74] Yet withdrawal from territories where some 145,000 inhabitants live under the Spanish flag would be unlikely to gain support. A move to give up Ceuta and Melilla in return for hand-over of Gibraltar – in both cases, moves which local populations would oppose – would be implausible and ill-fated.

Spanish inhabitants of the North African cities loudly proclaim their 'Spanishness', and argue that the situation of Ceuta and Melilla has nothing to do with colonialism and offers no parallel with Gibraltar. The official historian of Ceuta states that 'the situation of Gibraltar and that of Ceuta has no connection whatever. The Calpe of Antiquity [Gibraltar] was taken by force from Spain, which could not or did not know how to recover it. Old Abyla [Ceuta] never belonged to Morocco. . . . The people of Ceuta and the Spaniards must be clear about our indestructible *españolidad*.'[75] (Nevertheless, some 40 per cent of inhabitants of Melilla own property on the Spanish mainland.) Inhabitants proudly speak of links with the Spanish army: 'One could say that Ceuta is a living military museum. Among no other people does one so sense this vital spirit. . . . It is not a question of military life dominating civil life, but rather that the two are joined, and all of the *Ceutís* can repeat a famous saying – that they are half-peasants and half-soldiers.'[76] In the 1980s, Spain stationed 10,000 troops in Ceuta and Melilla, and at the beginning of the 1990s, there were 7500 soldiers and 1500 officers and non-commissioned officers in Melilla alone – one man to every seven civilians.[77] *Ceutís* and *Melillenses* also champion their Catholicism. The citizens of Ceuta in 1954 proclaimed the Virgin Mary permanent mayoress of their city; this prompted the burghers of Melilla to try to proclaim Jesus Christ their mayor, an initiative which the Vatican vetoed. Public ceremonies reinforce the alliance between Spanish citizenship, the military and Catholicism.[78] The citizens of Ceuta and Melilla form a vocal lobby for the continuation of Spanish sovereignty. The Spanish military, too, ardently defends Spanish control of the enclaves; inspired by memories of overseas glory and the exploits of the legion, 'their attachment to Ceuta and Melilla is visceral', explains a senior official, and 'they cannot conceive [of] Spain without them'.[79] (Given the importance of the military in the enclaves, the reverse may also be true.) The extreme right, because of the connections between Spanish North Africa and Franco, is also a strong promoter of Spanish sovereignty.

Moroccans accuse Spain of historical and obsessive fear of the Moors, and lambast Ceuta and Melilla as 'museums of colonialism'.[80] King Hassan's statements in the 1970s linked the cases of vestigial 'colonialism' on either side of the strait, and put Madrid on notice that Morocco would not abide Spain's recovery of Gibraltar without its withdrawal from the enclaves. In the 1960s the Spanish government indicated to King Hassan that some prospect of ceding the two enclaves to Morocco existed, once Gibraltar was returned to Spain.[81] However, Rabat has made no military attempts to take over the Spanish enclaves. Ceuta is dependent on Morocco for water supplies, and Melilla receives almost all its fruits and vegetables from Morocco. Melilla's airport is located on land which Spain rents from Morocco. Rabat could exercise coercive tactics to try to force Spanish negotiations, but, as the Spanish blockade of Gibraltar from 1969 to 1984 showed, such strategies do not always work. Morocco's pressure on Spain has been muted. In attempting to negotiate closer economic and political ties with the European Community, King Hassan did not want to risk offending Spain or Britain, because of the Gibraltar question, by loudly demanding an end to the status quo. Moreover a 'gentleman's agreement' enabling Moroccan takeover of the Western Sahara after the 'Green March' may have reduced Moroccan demands on Ceuta and Melilla.[82]

By the mid-1980s, Morocco's approach to the enclaves had shifted slightly, unlinking the issues of the *presidios* and Gibraltar. In 1987 King Hassan stated: 'My attitude towards Ceuta and Melilla is that this is a question of an anachronistic situation which cannot be compared to that of Gibraltar, given that Gibraltar is in Europe. Gibraltar is under the control of a European power, allied through the EC and NATO to Spain.'[83] The *presidios* were a colonial question, whilst Gibraltar might not be. In the same year, in the wake of civil disturbances in Melilla, the Moroccan government suggested that Madrid and Rabat set up a working party, noting that 'the solution to Ceuta and Melilla must take into account the imprescriptible rights of Morocco [and] the vital interests of Spain in the region'. The wording was not unlike Spanish statements on Gibraltar, yet nothing came of the proposal. Moroccan calls for return of the enclaves regularly recurred. In 1990, on the occasion of Namibia's accession to independence, Moroccan journalists remarked that the Spanish enclaves were now the last colonies in Africa, and a minister of state wrote: 'Let us hope that these cities are not going to become museums of colonialism and that Madrid will not persist in maintaining a [colonial] attitude which international morality has universally condemned.'[84] In 1991 Spain and Morocco signed a treaty of friendship, and two Moroccan ministers met a Spanish minister at the Ceuta border. Unexpectedly (at least to the public), the Moroccans accepted a Spanish invitation to cross the border and visited Ceuta for several hours, the first time Moroccan ministers had officially set foot in the enclaves. The main Moroccan political parties, however, soon repeated the country's claims on the *presidios*. The visit evidently did not symbolise renunciation of Moroccan territorial rights. In 1994 authorities in the enclaves began a campaign to get the Spanish government to grant statutes of autonomy to Ceuta and Melilla. Perhaps in response, King Hassan reiterated suggestions for a joint Spanish–Moroccan working party and reaffirmed that Morocco intended to gain control of the enclaves by 'the peaceful process of negotiation'.[85] Spanish ratification of the autonomy statutes in 1995 was denounced by the Moroccan government, which, on taking office in that year, declared the recovery of Ceuta and Melilla to be one of its major objectives. At much the same time, responsibility for two explosions in Ceuta was claimed by the *Organización 21 de Agosto para la Liberación de los Territorios Marroquíes Usurpados*. This group had apparently been inactive since 1975, and the Spanish government suspected that it was now receiving covert assistance from Morocco. Hundreds of Spanish fishing vessels, including some from Ceuta, were obliged to withdraw from Moroccan waters, following the European Union's failure to renegotiate the agreement with Morocco, and there were violent scenes when Spanish fishermen and farmers sought to obstruct the entry of Moroccan produce into the ports of southern Spain.

Gaining sovereignty over the Spanish territories would represent a major political and emotional victory for Morocco, and the country would acquire valuable ports. Unless the cities became special administrative districts of Morocco and maintained their free-port status, trade would be severely affected; Morocco, experiencing problems of unemployment and economic difficulty, would face a new challenge to revive the cities' economies. Spanish withdrawal would almost certainly lead to large-scale emigration of Spanish citizens. Winning control over the cities, therefore, might be a pyrrhic victory.

A further consideration in Moroccan policy is the status of the Western Sahara. Linking the return of Ceuta and Melilla with sovereignty over the Western Sahara (or even a larger area of 'Greater Morocco', including parts of Mauritania and Algeria) places Moroccan demands in the context of efforts to secure its 'natural' territorial integrity. However, allegations of Spanish colonialism ring hollow in some quarters, given what is regarded as Moroccan expansionism in the Western Sahara and strong-arm efforts – for instance, the construction of militarised walls between the region's southern border and Mauritania – to protect its claims. The Saharawi independence movement, Polisario, has won recognition by several dozen nations. The unwillingness of Morocco (and, to some extent, of Polisario) to organise

a referendum on self-determination seems to violate the will of international organisations. For Morocco, there is no contradiction in claims
on the former and present Spanish 'colonies', but not all in the world
community see the situation in the same light.[86]

Through Spanish unwillingness to give up the cities and Moroccan
unwillingness or inability to seize control of them, a transfer of sovereignty over Ceuta and Melilla appears as unlikely as British withdrawal
from Gibraltar. Various alternatives proposed for the British colony – co-
sovereignty, leaseback, a condominium status – seem never to have been
discussed by Moroccan or Spanish authorities in the case of Ceuta and
Melilla. A loosening of ties between the Spanish central government and
the cities through the granting of more autonomy might be regarded as
provocation by increasing the power of a population even more likely to
resist incorporation into the Moroccan kingdom than are the authorities
in Madrid. Despite various resolutions by several international bodies,
such as the Organisation of African Unity, there is little world pressure
on Spain to withdraw from the enclaves. As long as a majority of Ceuta's
and Melilla's population wish to keep (or obtain) Spanish citizenship,
there is little pressure from within the territories for Spanish withdrawal.
The pro-Moroccan movement, which briefly burgeoned in the 1980s –
but only after an initial pro-Spanish outburst – has withered. A radical
change in status, and indeed any dramatic move to effect such a change,
would risk upsetting the delicate social balance in the cities and trouble
the cordial relations between Madrid and Rabat (and by extension
between the European Union and Morocco). The status quo seems
likely to endure.

Mayotte

Far away from the Straits of Gibraltar another disputed territory, Mayotte
(Maoré) is one of four islands which make up the Comoros archipelago
between Madagascar and the east African coast. France took over
Mayotte in 1843 under terms of a treaty negotiated with its sultan
(himself a political refugee from Madagascar who had imposed his rule
on the island). At a time when France was seeking to establish toeholds
in the Indian and Pacific Oceans, it afforded France a base to comple-
ment Réunion. Mayotte is a small island of 376 square kilometres with
scant natural resources. French settlers remained few in number, and
efforts to develop sugar plantations met with only modest success. The
indigenous Islamic people, of mixed African, Malagasy, Arabic and
Persian ancestry, accepted French overlordship, partly because of their
historic fear of raids from Madagascar and expansion by sultans in
neighbouring islands of the Comoros chain.

In 1886 France took over Grand Comoro, Anjouan and Mohéli, the other Comoros islands, largely to preclude their takeover by rival imperial powers; the protectorate subsequently changed into annexation. The Comoros were a poor backwater of the French empire, attracting few settlers, steadfastly resisting Christian evangelisation, earning meagre profits, and largely forgotten.[87] France did not decolonise the Comoros at the beginning of the 1960s, when other African outposts gained independence. There was little nationalist pressure for French withdrawal, and the Comoros seemed too small and poor to sustain sovereignty. France extended increasing autonomy to the Comoros as an 'overseas territory' with representation in the French parliament and an elected local assembly. Comorians were French citizens, with right of abode in the metropole – an opportunity which few could or wanted to accept. In 1962 the capital of the territory was transferred from Mayotte to Grand Comoro, so alienating a number of the residents of Mayotte, who considered their island worthy of special regard because of the length of its attachment to France; they felt threatened by the political domination of leaders from the other islands.

A nationalist movement had emerged in the Comoros by the early 1970s, although Mahorais expressed little enthusiasm for it. In late 1974 Valéry Giscard d'Estaing's government, which was willing to divest France of several remaining overseas outposts, organised a referendum on independence. Fully 94.6 per cent of the votes cast in the four islands of the territory favoured independence, while 5.4 per cent of the electors voted against separation from France. However, on Mayotte, voting was dramatically different from that of the territory as a whole: only 36.2 per cent of Mahorais voted for independence versus 63.8 per cent who voted against it. Since France had not announced beforehand whether independence would require a favourable vote from all four islands or a simple majority of all votes, and given the obvious disinclination of Mayotte to be decolonised, Paris was in a quandary. Whilst officials muddled over what course of action to take, the leader of the Comoros government, Ahmed Abdallah, issued a unilateral declaration of independence in mid-1975; he sent a delegation to rally Mayotte to the newly independent country, but it was soundly rebuffed by Mahorais. Faced with the *fait accompli* of Comorian independence, Paris recognised the Federal Islamic Republic of the Comoros and organised two new rounds of voting in Mayotte. In early 1976 over 99 per cent of electors voted in favour of Mayotte remaining part of the French Republic, and a few months later, four-fifths asked for it to be fully integrated into France as a *département.*

Although a small group of French politicians welcomed the desire of the Mahorais to 'stay French', most were less than overjoyed with the results of referenda in which a colony manifestly refused to be decolonised. Given the glaring lack of economic development on the island, and a society and culture which differed greatly from that of France, authorities rejected *départementalisation*, instead announcing that yet another referendum would be held some time in the future to determine Mayotte's permanent status. Meanwhile, the island became a 'territorial collectivity' of France, a constitutionally hybrid status, and Paris reluctantly began to design development plans for the island.

The Comoros government attacked France for failure to take into consideration overall vote totals in 1975, for not withdrawing from the island, and for maintaining its 'colonial' status. Abdallah's government argued that separation of the islands constituted a violation of the UN principle of safeguarding the territorial integrity of colonies which accede to independence. After overtures by the Comorian government, the United Nations and the Organisation of African Unity condemned French colonialism in Mayotte and demanded cession of the island to the new state.[88]

The population of Mayotte, supported by a small but vocal lobby in France, protested that they had no wish to join the Comoros state. They argued that Mahorais were ethnically and culturally different from inhabitants of the neighbouring islands; they insisted that Mayotte had joined with the other islands into one colonial territory for purely administrative convenience, and that France could not legally or morally reject the results of the referenda, which represented the democratic expression of the will of the population. Arguments based on self-determination, advanced by Mahorais, thus clashed with arguments based on territorial integrity, stressed in the independent Comoros.[89]

The Mahorais were concerned for their future if they joined the Comoros, not only because of long-standing antagonism with nearby islands but also because of the trend of Comorian politics. Indeed, the Comoros fared badly after independence. A band of foreign (largely French) mercenaries deposed Abdallah at the end of 1975 and installed in power a young revolutionary, Ali Soilih. Soilih abolished the central government, burned the national archives, criticised the place of Islam in the state, attacked the sultans who comprised the traditional elite, promoted adolescent commandos to positions of authority, and undertook a programme of Marxist-inspired economic restructuring. The Comorian economy, already in severe straits, plunged into crisis, and Soilih's opponents said that he had installed a reign of terror. In 1978 the same mercenaries who had put Soilih in power returned to overthrow him; Soilih was shot, allegedly trying to escape. Abdallah returned from exile as president. The political situation stabilised over the next few years, although with little improvement of the economy. Opposition gradually mounted to Abdallah, who had become increasingly authoritarian under the influence of mercenaries who remained in charge of his presidential guard. Charges of massive corruption, trafficking in arms to Iran and shady deals with South African investors further compromised the government. France, despite its quarrels with Abdallah, had remained the major source of aid and trade for the Comoros. It became increasingly dissatisfied. In 1989, perhaps after Paris had issued an ultimatum to Abdallah to rein in the mercenaries and undertake reforms, the mercenaries themselves acted. Abdallah was assassinated in mysterious circumstances. A new government, with French backing, forced the mercenaries to leave the Comoros. However, the country's political situation has remained troubled – with several failed coups since 1989 – and the Comoros is one of the poorest of the world's independent nations.[90]

In view of this situation, the reluctance of Mahorais to join the Comoros is not surprising. Moreover, Mayotte has profited from increased French largesse. The island has almost no natural resources: *ylang-ylang*, a flower essence used in perfume, is the only appreciable export, and most commodities (even food) are imported. There is no real industrial sector, and tourism is undeveloped: there are fewer than a hundred hotel rooms in Mayotte. The public service provides the largest number of salaried jobs. France, particularly since the late 1980s, has poured considerable money into Mayotte for infrastructure, subsidised housing, and the social security benefits that are received by most of the population. Because of French transfers, most Mahorais enjoy a markedly higher standard of living than the citizens of the Comoros, encouraging substantial legal and illegal immigration from the other three islands. The Mahorais gain certain advantages from 'colonial' status, although there are conflicts between their traditional culture and French culture; polygamy, for example, is legal in Mayotte. The benefits accruing to France from Mayotte are few. The population numbers 100,000 people, but only one-third speak French.[91] Paris spends far more on the island than it recoups in profits. Two thousand metropolitan French men and women live there, almost all of whom are public servants. The strategic importance of Mayotte, despite a detachment of the Foreign Legion, remains minimal.

Tensions between Mayotte and the independent Comoros are evident, whilst an attempt by Anjouan in 1997 to secede complicates the situation even further. In early 1995, in an effort to curb the flow of illegal migrants who form one-fifth of Mayotte's population, Paris imposed a visa requirement for all citizens of the Comoros who wished to visit metropolitan France or Mayotte. The Comorian government angrily suspended air links between Mayotte and the other islands, the nearest of which is only twenty minutes away. The Comoros continues to claim Mayotte as part of its sovereign territory, and various international organisations regularly press France to withdraw from Mayotte. The vast majority of the Mahorais population nevertheless rejects union with the Comoros and favours *départementalisation*. The promised referendum on the 'final' status for Mayotte, regularly postponed, is now scheduled to be held before the end of the century.

The Comoros would certainly score a symbolic victory by recovering Mayotte, and would be a substantially larger nation for doing so.[92] It would gain the economic infrastructure which France has been constructing on Mayotte, and which (though modest by French metropolitan standards) is superior to that of the other islands. However, as Mayotte becomes better endowed with schools, hospitals, highways, salaried jobs, government transfers and imported commodities, disparities between it and the other islands increase and the likelihood of Mahorais willingly accepting incorporation into the Comoros diminishes still further.[93] The firm stance of the Mahorais would make it extremely difficult for the French government to accede to the wishes of the Comoros to gain control of Mayotte, even if Paris wholeheartedly embraced such a proposition.

Settling 'Colonial' Conflicts

Even though all are vestiges of European imperialism, the cases of Macao, the Falkland Islands, Gibraltar, Ceuta and Melilla, and Mayotte differ considerably because of geographical location, size, resources and the geopolitical context. It is unlikely that the model of integration of Macao and Hong Kong into a state which has long claimed them will provide a precedent for cession of the other outposts. Portugal has seemed anxious to disengage from its Asian colony since the 1960s and willingly renounced sovereignty over Macao in 1976. Although Britain appeared ready to withdraw from the Falklands in the 1960s and 1970s, that attitude reversed sharply during the 1982 war; neither Britain nor Spain seems willing to relinquish its enclaves on the Straits of Gibraltar. France would find it difficult to transfer Mayotte without the consent of its population.

Macao's population has been less reluctant about the return of the city to China only because Portugal's colonial rule had produced relatively little impact on the territory, and because Lisbon extended rights of citizenship to many Macanese who might wish to settle in Portugal. Gibraltar's population, however, is absolutely opposed to incorporation into Spain, although some prefer the prospect of becoming a (semi-)independent city-state rather than continued dependent status.

Falkland Islanders and the Spaniards in Ceuta and Melilla may appreciate increased autonomy, but they adamantly refuse union with the neighbouring claimant states; the Mahorais campaign for full integration into the French Republic. In both Mayotte and the Falkland Islands, substantial economic investment in the 1980s increased the islanders' attachment to the metropole. Historical, ethnic, political and economic ties with the metropolitan powers remain strong in the British and Spanish territories, and are growing in Mayotte.

Inhabitants of these outposts fear the prospect of incorporation into much larger and sometimes rather different states. In Macao there is some concern about their future in the People's Republic of China. The agreements for hand-over, in theory, guarantee basic rights, economic structures and lifestyles (at least for fifty years), but many doubt that China will honour its commitments. Although Gibraltarians might have fewer fears about living under the Spanish flag, Falkland Islanders would not be confident about life in Argentina, and *Ceutís* and *Melillenses* would need to adapt to a markedly different system under the rule of an Islamic state. The Mahorais have vivid memories of traditional rivalries inside the archipelago, and they fear dictatorship and greater impoverishment if incorporated into the independent Comoros. It is unlikely that the hopes of Argentina, Spain, Morocco or the Comoros will soon be fulfilled. Yet claims will continue because they are potent platforms in domestic politics, rallying-points for national identity, and affluent outposts.

Somewhat ironically, these claims provided an imperative for continued interest by 'colonial' rulers in these small territories. Attempts by claimant states to assert their rights – as occurred with the closing of Spain's borders with Gibraltar in 1969 and, more dramatically, with Argentina's attack on the Falklands in 1982 – and social unrest inside the territories centred on questions of sovereignty and citizenship – as occurred in Ceuta and Melilla in the 1980s – have jolted administering states into taking greater notice of their outposts. After Portugal agreed to return Macao to China, that enclave witnessed an economic boom. The effects of fifteen years of isolation after Franco's closure of the Spanish border with Gibraltar forced that city to develop a diversified and self-sufficient economy based on offshore banking, finance and tourism. Since 1975, and the independence of the Comoros, France has pumped money into Mayotte in a belated effort at development. The Falklands has accumulated far more British money (and garnered more support) since the 1982 war than ever before, and is less obviously a 'company colony'. The events in the Spanish enclaves in the mid-1980s also forced Madrid to inject greater development funds into its African outposts.

Various factors work against efforts to 'regain' claimed territory by force. They include harmonious relations between Britain and Spain in the European Union and NATO; democratisation and economic development in Argentina; and the sensitivity of Morocco to alienating friendly neighbours (partly because of the Western Sahara issue, partly because of the need for good economic and political links to pursue its own development and staunch nascent Islamic fundamentalism). However, the same factors augur well for cooperation among claimant states, 'colonial' powers and the contested territories. Some mutually acceptable arrangement – co-sovereignty, leaseback, establishment of a condominum – may eventually emerge, but the status quo is likely to endure for the immediate future.

Macao, the Falkland Islands, Gibraltar, Ceuta and Melilla and Mayotte are all exceptional; no other territories are claimed by different powers (other than a Brazilian claim on Guyane and a Venezuelan claim on neighbouring Aruba, Bonaire and Curaçao),[94] nor have the other territories experienced the tensions (and, in the case of the Falklands, warfare) produced in these outposts. Western Samoa, for instance, does not claim American Samoa, nor does Indonesia claim Christmas Island. When Canada and France came into dispute in the North Atlantic, the 'cod war' concerned fishing rights in the area between Saint-Pierre-et-Miquelon and Newfoundland, not sovereignty over the French islands.[95] There have, however, been disagreements between Britain and France over the Minquiers, the southernmost Channel islands.[96] All these cases illustrate the way in which small and distant outposts in which status is ambiguous or contested can become flashpoints. They highlight unresolved issues of nationalism and irredentism; territorial integrity and the historical boundaries of states; self-determination and the rights of local residents; and questions of human rights centred on citizenship, migration and rights of residency. There are also a number of immediate problems affecting the territories, particularly control of exclusive economic zones for trade and for maritime and submarine resources, including oil; contraband and unlawful trade, especially in drugs; and illegal migration. All these are capable of provoking controversy, conflict and even violence.

CHAPTER 7

The End of Empire?

Fundamental changes in the global political order in the past decade have thrown open complex issues of sovereignty, territoriality and nationhood. Questions of what constitutes nation-states, relations between nation-states and their constituent peoples and territories, and the nature of national sovereignty are no longer so clear-cut as they once seemed. In many places nationalists press for smaller states, which might not be fundamentally different from those whose dominance their advocates resist so passionately. Tensions between indigenous peoples, ethnic minorities, and modern nation-states take many forms, though most are concerned with some combination of issues concerning cultural identity and resource sovereignty.[1] Vague attempts to construct from above a 'New World Order' have been met by a myriad of efforts to construct another new world order, rather closer to the 'bottom', that have challenged the centralised power of major nation-states and global institutions. These efforts have transformed global cartography, especially in the post-socialist states, and within nation-states have produced legislative changes aimed at granting increased sovereignty to indigenous people. Thus in Canada, for example, the Nunavut nation now has special status, and in Australia Aboriginal nations, such as the Jawoyn,[2] are moving to a form of national statehood within a nation-state. Established federal states – from the Federated States of Micronesia to the United States – provide further complexities of scale, legitimacy and competing constitutional regimes.

In what is widely perceived as the post-colonial period, decolonisation has occurred not in 'the last colonies', but within the existing nation-states (notably Yugoslavia and the Soviet Union), and wherever indigenous peoples have been able to stake out new claims, and thus challenge myths of unproblematic and uncontested national identities. There have been other largely unsuccessful, nationalist and separatist claims in parts of many developing countries, such as in Sri Lanka, Irian Jaya (Indonesia) and Bougainville (Papua New Guinea); of these, only the struggle for Eritrea has succeeded in recent decades.[3] In many cases, such challenges to nation-states have occurred in conditions where political hegemony has been repressive, resources alienated or extracted without adequate payment, and cultural identities have been denied. They have been challenges to a form of internal colonialism, with widespread support at the local level.[4] In the overseas territories, the situation is invariably quite different.

The Overseas Territories

The dependent overseas territories present a world of anomalies. Language, ethnicity, religion, and culture typify some of the distinctiveness of far-flung outposts attached to metropolitan states. In American Samoa, the indigenous population speak a Polynesian language, whilst in the northern islands of the Netherlands Antilles, English is the most common language. Few people in Mayotte speak French, and even fewer speak Portuguese in Macao. In the Dutch islands of Aruba, Bonaire and Curaçao, the everyday language is Portuguese-based Papiamento. In many other territories, even dialects rarely distinguish the language from that of the metropolitan state. Ethnicity and demographic mixture have been complicated by colonial heritage. Inhabitants of Bermuda, the West Indies, Réunion and St Helena have both African and European ancestors, just as Tahitians have both Polynesian and European forebears, and Guamanians descend from indigenous Micronesians, Spaniards and Americans. Falkland and Norfolk Islanders are predominantly of European origin; their forebears were Christians. Expatriation, transportation, slavery and indentured labour created new population structures in outposts ruled by Europeans, Americans, Australians and New Zealanders. There are substantial numbers of Indians, descendants of indentured labourers or migrant traders, in territories as varied as Guadeloupe, Ceuta and Réunion. Muslims and Jews live together in Ceuta and Melilla. One of the oldest synagogues in the Americas is in Curaçao; there is a Jewish community in Gibraltar and a synagogue in Tahiti. Trances and spirit possession are not unusual in Mayotte, and animism is common in Guyane, despite cultural shifts. Such particularities testify to the facts of historical conquest, cosmopolitan influences and cultural diversity in each territory.

Territorial economies are even more diverse than their populations. Many no longer produce such 'traditional' exports as agriculture and fisheries products – though the Faeroes, and especially Saint-Pierre-et-

Miquelon, are critically dependent on fishing. Some smaller territories, such as Wallis and Futuna, Tokelau and Mayotte, remain dominated by traditional subsistence food production, though a more bureaucratic sector has been grafted on. By contrast, a much larger number – from the Isle of Man to Christmas Island – are bastions of such tertiary-sector activities as tax havens and casinos. Less frequently, economic development has been so limited that, as in Montserrat, Niue and the Cook Islands, the bulk of the island-born population now lives overseas, and many islanders depend on remittances. Only Puerto Rico and Macao have successful manufacturing sectors. In most cases, financial support from metropolitan states has propped up ailing economies, to the extent that aid-dependency is normal. The government sector dominates employment, whilst policy-makers yearn for the perceived economic panacea of tourism. If metropolitan control has scarcely impoverished overseas territories, few ever being profitable producers, neither has it enabled them to develop vibrant and diversified economies.

The duration of foreign control in the territories is remarkable. The Channel Islands have been administered – often lightly – by Britain more or less since 1066; the Isle of Man was ceded to the Scots by Norway in 1266, leading to a century of conflict between Scotland and England, after which England effectively took control. Greenland and the Faeroes were Danish possessions by the late 1300s; Spain acquired the Canary Islands in the 1400s and took Melilla at the end of the century. In short, the possession of many outposts has a long history. By contrast, France and the United States did not acquire their South Pacific territories until the second half of the nineteenth century. Britain officially annexed Ascension in the 1920s. South Georgia was not 'created' until 1985. Length of colonisation does not predetermine independent or dependent status.

The ways in which colonies were acquired emphasise the vagaries of colonial history. In Réunion and St Helena, Europeans took possession of unoccupied islands simply by raising the flag. Many indigenous inhabitants of Caribbean islands had been exterminated by the time the present metropolitan powers established control. However, the controversy over the Falkland Islands centres largely on whether Spain (or Argentina, once it had gained independence from Spain) or Britain got to the islands and settled them first. The United States purchased the Virgin Islands from Denmark. Denmark gained control of the Faeroes and Greenland after the Norwegian and Danish crowns were united, and Spain inherited Ceuta after the union of the Spanish and Portuguese kingdoms. Britain fought Spain to obtain Gibraltar; the United States got Guam and Puerto Rico after defeating Spain. The United States took control of American Samoa after a 'gentlemanly' agreement to divide the islands of the Samoan archipelago among several competing powers. Britain transferred Niue, Tokelau and the Cook Islands to New Zealand, and the Cocos (Keeling) Islands and Christmas Island to Australia. Sweden ceded Saint-Barthélemy to France, and Portugal will retrocede Macao to China. Meanwhile, Britain has leased the British Indian Ocean Territory to the United States. Conquest, occupation, inheritance, purchase and cession all played roles in forming present-day 'colonial' portfolios.

Several territories are pieces of larger colonies which gained independence. The BIOT was, until 1965, part of the British colony of Mauritius. The independence of Jamaica and the Bahamas meant that the Cayman Islands and the Turks and Caicos Islands, respectively, became separate British colonies. Anguilla fought strenuously to remain British after the independence of St Kitts–Nevis. Similarly, Mayotte stayed French after the independence of the other Comoros islands. Ceuta and Melilla in the early twentieth century were part of more extensive Spanish claims in North Africa. South Georgia and the South Sandwich Islands were separated from the Falklands, and Aruba broke away from the other Netherlands Antilles.

The diversity of the territories is further indicated by the constitutional nomenclature applied to them and their administrative arrangements. The British have Crown colonies and dependencies; the French have overseas departments, territories and territorial collectivities; the Americans have commonwealths, and incorporated and unincorporated territories. The Kingdom of Denmark consists of three parts, as does the Kingdom of the Netherlands. Macao is a 'special territory' of Portugal; Ceuta, Melilla and the Canary Islands are autonomous communities of Spain, and the Azores and Madeira autonomous regions of Portugal; whilst the Australian outposts are external territories of that country. New Zealand and the United States maintain special relationships through free association with nominally sovereign nations. The differences are more than semantic, for they imply varying theories and practices of governance. The French, Spanish and Dutch territories elect voting representatives to national assemblies; the US commonwealths and unincorporated territories have only non-voting delegates in the lower house of the Congress. The British territories do not elect members of parliament at Westminster, and those registered on electoral rolls in Australia's Indian Ocean territories vote in mainland seats.

Such diversity means that it is difficult to make generalisations about contemporary overseas territories, but also suggests that the reasons 'colonial' powers acquired and retained such outposts, and the ways in which they administer them, adhere to few general processes of history or politics. No single reason neatly explains why 'confetti of empire' continue to exist; neither in the present, nor indeed in the colonial past, is it possible to find a grand design to explain the extent and survival of 'the last colonies'.

Nationalism and Internationalism

Nationalist sentiment has been most vibrant where assimilation has most obviously failed; it occurs primarily where 'peoples' sense of self remains bound up in the gross actualities of blood, race, language, locality, religion or tradition'.[5] The demand for independence has consequently been associated with such themes as cultural and ethnic identity, uniqueness, minority status, the desire for freedom, and a perceived right to independence. Nationalism gains greatest legitimacy where ethnic boundaries do not cut across political ones.[6] Still, despite its apparent orientation to local personalities and local goals, nationalism is often a colonial (or quasi-colonial) construction and, beyond that, 'a mechanism of adjustment and compensation, a way of living with the reality of [uneven] historical development'.[7] Colonial rule emphasised – or, in some cases, created – ethnic nationalism by strengthening and enlarging cultural allegiances, centralising administration, bringing ethnic groups into wider fields of interaction and exposing them to the various facets and resources of modernisation. In some respects, ethnic nationalism was ascribed rather than achieved. Nationalism emerged in opposition to the incursion of colonialism and was its inevitable outcome, determined by its past rather than its present or future. In the territories, however, ethnicity is not always different from that of the metropolitan power. Other local markers – such as particular languages, religions and customs – are not always evident; many are shared, and increasingly so, with the metropole.

In contemporary territories, the degree of violence and mistrust, racism and deceit, as elaborated upon by anti-colonialists, and evident within some nation-states, is rarely apparent. In Namibia, two decades ago, 'South Africa, as the last colonial power with a will to hold, is necessarily more committed to using force to do so':[8] virtually the last vestiges of an old colonial order. Whilst there have been critical problems in New Caledonia and French Polynesia (where France also displays a 'will to hold'), and numerous incidents elsewhere, often where distinctive ethnicity and socio-economic inequality coincide, such problems pale into insignificance in comparison with everyday life in the recent history of the Balkans. It is there, and probably in other 'internal colonies' such as Tibet or Kurdistan, that contemporary colonialism – in its most negative sense, in terms of ethnic conflicts and the domination of one people by another – is primarily evident. In this sense, these peripheral regions rather than the overseas territories have become the last colonies.

The revival of nationalism has been accompanied by a decline in adherence to the notion that political borders are immutable. Iraq sought to breach Kuwait's border, and was repelled only by key metropolitan states upholding the principle of territorial integrity in a region of unusual strategic and economic interest. In Africa, with much less global geopolitical significance, concern for territorial integrity is more limited. Morocco had surprisingly little difficulty in incorporating the Western Sahara (despite UN protests); Ethiopia came apart (enabling the emergence of Eritrea); Somalia imploded; and much of Liberia was effectively ruled by neighbouring states.[9] Other continents have experienced territorial expansion and contraction, signs of the fluidity that remains a trait of the international political system.

Nation-states have become weaker and less well-defined as economic, political and cultural life is increasingly global; 'the 1990s promises to be the decade when almost the whole world is finally incorporated into the modern world economy'.[10] Not only are there internal pressures related to regionalism, representation and self-determination, but there are external demands of world markets and supra-national institutions. Transnational corporations and trade-related organisations, such as the European Union, the International Monetary Fund, and the World Trade Organisation, alongside the United Nations and similar regional bodies, exert powerful influence. The process of globalisation accelerated as primary production gave way to tertiary economic activity and the collapse of the Bretton Woods system of fixed exchange rates ended the domination of the international economy by nation-states. Technology has changed the economics of competition and cooperation. Nation-states have responded by adjusting their international structures 'upwards' in attempts to regain control of economic space (thus following the strategies of transnational corporations which have increasingly gone beyond national boundaries, made more porous through deregulation). Thus regional economies and 'growth triangles', both cutting through and linking nations, have in places gained greater economic significance than national economies.[11] The world economy has become even more global, in two senses: almost all nations have disavowed socialist ideology and welcomed overseas capitalist investment (and thus international ties); and major economic events in particular places, such as the Mexican financial crisis of the early 1990s, have widespread ramifications.

Not only is there a hierarchy of states[12] – in which such places as the United States and Tonga are evidently in very different positions – but it is increasingly apparent that countries are marked by a considerable extent of uneven development. Moreover, they are challenged by other economic and political institutions.[13] Uneven development is as marked within nations as between them, with marginalisation the converse of globalisation. Most nation-states are far from homogeneous; many are fragmented, notably various island states, or contain vastly different geographical regions. Religious, cultural, linguistic or ethnic minorities, as in the cases of France and Spain, are often located in the periphery. Much the same is true of the United Kingdom, where the seemingly unexpected persistence of ethnicity, even in a modern era of commercial and industrial development, led to a resurgence of separatist sentiments in the 1960s, with a particularly violent outcome in Northern Ireland, and drew attention to the phenomenon of internal colonialism.[14] In certain circumstances, the core of a nation dominates the periphery and exploits it materially, as modernisation emphasises rather than reduces regional differences; that situation is likely to be more common where minorities occupy fragmented peripheries.[15] Within most nations, at least intermittent tensions occur between centres and peripheries that have threatened the viability or effectiveness of national development, to the extent that the permanence of nation-states is a relatively recent concept. At a larger scale, as in the European Union, national divisions such as border controls, trade barriers – and perhaps eventually currencies – are being subsumed, at exactly the same time that provincial separatism has grown. Some effective loss of sovereignty has been imposed on all states through globalising processes, but especially on weak or 'quasi-states'. In them, external intervention (for example, in the official guise of World Bank and IMF 'structural adjustment programs') has been considerable,[16] and so challenged most notions of national sovereignty. In the era of decolonisation, metropolitan states were both divesting themselves of colonies, and freely giving away some of the prerogatives of the nation-state, as regional groupings and international institutions gained importance.

In a variety of ways national sovereignty is limited. In Europe most nations willingly ceded significant power to the European Union (at the cost of some degree of national identity, symbolically apparent in the loss of distinctive national passports), and in many other regions supranational trading blocs have emerged. Small independent nations especially have not always taken up supposed critical elements of national identity: in the Caribbean, several island states (Antigua, Dominica and St Kitts) share the same currency, and Jamaica (among others) turns to the British Privy Council for critical legal decisions. Australia (and other former British colonies) have governors-general – the queen's representatives – who on occasion have made decisions of grave national significance. The government of the Republic of Ireland has a critical

role in resolving the political evolution of Northern Ireland. Such
instances are interminable, emphasising that nations are neither absolutely autarchic, nor do they necessarily seek to be so. Sovereignty is both
transferred upwards to supra-national institutions (such as the European
Union or NAFTA) and devolved downwards to regional entities closer to
'the people' (the situation sought in Scotland and Corsica). The usual
criteria of sovereignty – absolute internal supremacy and external
independence – are both subject to limitations. No nation claims total
sovereignty over foreign nationals in its midst; more dramatically, such
activities as genocide and apartheid are seen as too important to be left
to domestic rule, no matter how powerful the national government
might claim to be. At the very least there is a difference between *de facto*
and *de jure* sovereignty, and one does not necessarily guarantee the
other.[17] Moreover, in the contemporary world, independence and
dependency have rather different meanings than they did to proponents
of European nationalism in the nineteenth century or to leaders of
independence movements in the colonial world in the decades after the
Second World War. But even in Europe, the birthplace of nationalism,
anomalies persist, especially for the smallest states: the heads of state of
Andorra are the French president and a Spanish bishop; Switzerland
takes charge of Liechtenstein's foreign and monetary policy; France has
treaty rights to intervene in Monaco. Such anomalies emphasise the
great diversity of sovereignty in theory and in practice.

Globalisation is multi-dimensional. It is primarily economic, reflected
in trade, aid and investment. It is manifest in American efforts to impose
upon large (and competing) nations, such as Japan, rates of exchange
and trade practices, whilst threatening isolation and sanctions. In part it
is strategic, in overseas military adventures, apparent in the French
presence in sub-Saharan Africa and in the Pentagon's empire of distant
military bases and the willingness to intervene in regional conflicts (as in
Kuwait), or national conflicts (as in Grenada and Somalia). It is
obviously technological and cultural, visibly evident in the global role of
computers, television, jeans and the omnipresent dollar.[18] Environmental problems, such as acid rain, global warming or nuclear melt-
down, are increasingly international. Finally, attempts have been made
to develop international norms on human rights standards. In a sense,
the converse of this centrifugal globalisation is renewed international
migration, despite attempts to strengthen political borders. Whilst
changes in small states are not mere reflections of, or responses to,
changes in metropolitan states, exogenous forces have acquired overwhelming significance.

With the virtual demise of the Second World of orthodox Marxist
socialism, resistance to globalisation has been less evident, despite

concern over the activities of transnational corporations, uneven development, and the resurgence of Islam. In another sense, this pervasive global reach is resented as neo-colonialism: a colonisation that no longer conquers land, transports settlers or seeks political and cultural change, but thoroughly transforms distant places at the behest of metropolitan nations, international organisations and transnational corporations – despite local attempts to achieve control over national economies and cultural identity. To a very considerable extent, 'the more people are bound together economically, the more they want to be independent politically and culturally. In other words, the more people integrate, the more they feel the need to differentiate and to claim the freedom to assert their own distinctiveness.'[19] Globalisation and localism proceed simultaneously. Questions of identity – issues often linked to land and language – have become as important as economic issues in the quest for development. The assertion of ethnicity is combined with economic integration, but interdependence highlights cultural difference and emphasises histories, cultures and heritages that may be under threat: 'freedom depends on identity, and destiny on shared memory'.[20] Identities and memories, however transformed, remain powerful emotional stimuli for political change and stability.

It is evident that globalisation, in various forms, has reduced the weight of the nation-state. Still, the 'forces of late modernity' have certainly not diminished – and have even underlined – the extent of ethnic nationalism (as in much of the post-socialist world or Canada). Historically, nationalism presupposed a nation that had an economic threshold which could be the basis of a modern capitalist economy, with a population and a land area sufficient for economic viability and political independence. Economic criteria apparently ruled out micro-states as effective political units.[21] In the contemporary post-industrial era, information technology, flexible specialisation and decentralised production have rendered these criteria largely obsolete. Size has become less important, but political independence 'has remained an important intrinsic value and goal of ethnic communities in every continent'.[22] Consequently, the demand for political independence is now much more powerful within nations where ethnic (and religious) communities have been marginalised than it is in the overseas territories.

Pluralism and Diversity

Nation-states have become more flexible and diverse over time, most obviously so as decolonisation rapidly increased the number of nations and as a world political and economic system emerged. Moreover, the establishment of autonomous territories for distinct peoples within states represents a move to a pluralist structure that explicitly recognises social divisions and the decentralisation of political power, not merely of administrative responsibilities. Both elements are combined in the emergence of regional government. A strong state underwrites the autonomous regions in Spain and Portugal and the Home Rule governments in the Faeroes and Greenland, and provides a secure arena in which they can operate.[23] Within the territories too, administrative arrangements have diversified. No metropolitan power has the same structure or extent of authority in its different territories as in the colonial era. Constitutional and legal arrangements in the territories vary extensively, but almost all have a substantial degree of administrative autonomy and responsible government. Most have negotiated the constitutional structure with which the majority of inhabitants are comfortable.

The overseas territories have not sought independence – and only exceptionally considered that possibility – for a number of reasons. Many are simply too small to contemplate any kind of existence without a powerful international protector and benefactor, which does not only provide for defence, but is a source of aid, transport infrastructure (and access) and welfare provision. Some are fearful of problems that have occurred in nearby independent states. In New Caledonia, supporters of the status quo direct the gaze of pro-independence supporters towards neighbouring Vanuatu and point to evidence of corruption, violence, poverty and uncertainty. Bloodshed in Grenada, and the consequent US invasion, did not go unnoticed elsewhere in the Caribbean. Furthermore, colonialism has only exceptionally been rapacious in the territories in alienating land or destroying cultural integrity, although in some places, such as Guam, that destruction has been so thorough as to seriously impede efforts to revive languages and customs.[24] Rather, colonialism has enabled particular kinds of development, in tourism and the finance sector, which might be more difficult to achieve in an independent state. Some forms of development, such as manufacturing industry in the Northern Marianas, have only been contingent on special metropolitan legislation. The more consequential elements of territorial economies are so linked to the world system that political stability and security are constantly lauded as crucial to their survival.

Nationals of overseas territories, other than most British dependencies, have considerable access to migration and employment opportunities in the metropole. Migration is a safety-valve, even to the extent that more than half the nationals of Tokelau and American Samoa live in the metropole. Territories moving towards greater autonomy have never wished to relinquish these ties. Especially where migrant populations are more numerous than those at 'home', multiple identities have been developed; circulation becomes so frequent that Puerto Rico, at least, has been cast as a 'commuter nation'.[25] Migration, invariably selective, may even have led to the loss of those best able to stimulate local development. Communications have accelerated the rise of globalisation; in Guam television 'makes us homesick for places we have never been',[26] and few territories lack the blandishments of new goods and places that television presents. Even remote St Helena, one of the few places in the world so neglected,[27] received television in 1995. Information technology has created a new globalism in a way unimaginable in the era of colonial conquest. Pitcairn and Tokelau have no ports, but have almost instantaneous links with the rest of the world through radios or telephones; indeed in April 1997 Tokelau became the last part of the world to receive a telephone service. Outposts thousands of kilometres away from the metropoles of which they form a part are only hours away by jet and moments away on the information superhighway. Proximity and distance are less traits of integration or isolation than at any time in history. New linkages have been perceived as new opportunities to interact in a wider world of greater homogeneity, where cultural distinctiveness is no longer so important or so evident.

Ultimately, the residents of many territories are concerned about an unknown future. For decades Bermudians argued that they were poorly informed over possible consequences of independence and thus not ready to take that step; in Aruba, the real possibility of independence made residents reconsider. In some contexts 'not ready' actually implied that it might already have been too late; in French Polynesia, where many feared impoverishment, the moment appears to have passed. Independence had become a difficult, perhaps unpalatable choice, where rights such as mobility and welfare payments might end. It is difficult to see, for example, what real benefits the Faeroes or Greenland would obtain by separating from Denmark, one of the more generous of 'colonial' powers. The ideological and cultural elements of independence have proved inadequate motivation in the context of potential economic and material austerity. In many small territories, 'the real enemy is not present exploitation. It is future neglect,'[28] where viability through self-reliance is inherently implausible. Even some of those who seek independence see it as a long-term goal rather than an immediate prospect.[29]

Identity is the crux of contemporary nationalism, yet in many territories the notion of identity is problematic. In some cases it is fragmented, with few common elements, infrequently forged in the adversity of colonialism (though evident in New Caledonia or French Polynesia or, in a different way, in former plantation colonies). In other cases, identity is not greatly dissimilar to that of the metropolitan state. In

Bermuda, for example, supporters of decolonisation have emphasised both the psychological and cultural gains from independence and, where possible, the demeaning nature of colonialism. One supporter of independence has argued that 'to black Bermudians colonialism means chains, and puts them at a racial disadvantage'. In the 'richest colony in the world', though, such sentiments are rare; they are equally unusual elsewhere. Otherwise, as in Guam, there have been conscious revivals of 'tradition' but, perhaps too often, as empty practice[30] rather than cohesive cultural movements. In places ranging from Mayotte to Greenland, indigenous cultures have flourished, whereas local identities in the Azores and Madeira scarcely differ from those of mainland Portugal. Over time, educational transformations and population mobility have weakened cultural identity and nascent social movements. Even the geography of small size and isolation (and, often, 'island-ness') has not been enough to create or emphasise markedly different identities.

In this reluctance to seek independence, the territories are effectively continuing a process that began a quarter of a century earlier in various parts of the world, as several states – particularly small island states – hesitantly acceded to independence. 'Decolonization in its final stages was separated not only from considerations of development and leadership but from almost any empirical considerations whatsoever.'[31] The extraordinary rush to independence in the 1960s and 1970s, and its lack of historical precedent, was quite striking:

> It is ironical in a post-colonial age – which has in effect virtually elevated the state into being the only widely accepted political standard – to recall that great empires in the past, the British not least, recognized, even encouraged, political diversity – so that within its capacious and variegated jurisdictions were not only colonies but suzerains, tributaries, condominia, protectorates, protected states, etc.[32]

Although it has been argued that, especially in the British case, precipitous decolonisation was a result of 'every remaining dependency . . . impatiently demanding equal independence and receiving it in very short order',[33] in fact, the converse was often true, and not only in the smallest colonies. The Australian desire to grant independence to Papua New Guinea was much greater than local demand; the Solomon Islands, Vanuatu and Mauritius went to independence as much with trepidation as jubilation. These island states were not isolated exceptions,[34] but were representative of the end of one era and the dawn of another.

Reluctance to accede to independence was, in some respects, legitimised by social, political and economic problems in the states that emerged in the last phase of decolonisation. Though new states officially sought greater self-reliance and regional economic cooperation, in the

post-colonial era they became more closely integrated into the economies of distant metropolitan states. Indeed, for Tuvalu,

> where the British and the local elite together managed to push through a
> transition to formal independence, the key role of the new state will now be
> to recruit a new patron and to seek out new opportunities for Tuvaluan
> labour and capital to penetrate the rest of the world. Closed-country models,
> whether in the political or economic realms, simply do not fit . . . the 1980s.[35]

As the apparent close of the era of formal decolonisation indicates,
micro-states (and territories) which have a 'special relationship' with
a metropolitan power may be better off than those which do not.
All remain dependent on multilateral and bilateral aid. It has been
bluntly stated that 'the particularly poor island countries are those
which have failed to establish sufficiently intimate relations with a
prosperous protector',[36] just as the remaining British territories might
be better off through strengthening their ties with the United Kingdom
in the manner that some French 'colonies' became DOM-TOMs.[37]
As one Australian minister for Pacific Island affairs has pointed out,
although it is 'an unfortunate fact for those who believe in independence and freedom of determination', that standards of living,
including health levels, are higher in associated territories, 'perhaps
the best thing that countries like Australia should be doing in the South
Pacific is encouraging moves towards closer satrapy – towards closer
association and, indeed, even eventual incorporation of these polities
into the major powers such as Australia'.[38] The smallest states are steadily
moving towards a situation of constrained autonomy, yet none appears
likely to relinquish what was sometimes a hard-won independent
political status.

In no territory has a majority of the electorate cast its vote for parties
or politicians who unequivocally demand independence; only in
New Caledonia has a majority of the indigenous population – itself a
demographic minority – overwhelmingly supported an independence
movement. Pro-independence parties, though well-organised, vocal and
influential, have not won territorial elections. In most places their
support is declining. In the Turks and Caicos Islands, the withering of
the independence movement was matched by a rise in sentiment for
colonial ties to Canada if the United Kingdom sought to impose
independence.[39] Self-determination increasingly favours constitutional
dependency rather than sovereign independence. The movement away
from a once seemingly inexorable trend towards independence has
emphasised the diversity of political status and the uncertainties of
contemporary political transactions:

The path to independence for colonial peoples used to be seen as the march of history, temporarily delayed in some territories but ultimately inevitable. From the perspective of the 1990s, this particular march of history begins to look like an artefact of a period and set of circumstances, and decolonisation has lost its simple teleology. While the rhetoric of decolonisation expands and diversifies the reality of decolonisation diminishes.[40]

There is now greater flexibility of response to the complex and competing challenges of achieving economic growth, retaining cultural identity and strengthening autonomy.

If the bulk of residents in overseas territories now perceive that their interests are best served by retention of dependent status (though often with greater autonomy and more generous aid), the benefits are less evident in the metropolitan states, where increased immigration and aid are perceived as costs. In a global economy now dominated by the tertiary sector, even the raw materials available in a few territories (including the nickel of New Caledonia and the timber of Guyane) are of no great value, and the gains from enlarged EEZs are hypothetical rather than real. Equally, in a post-Cold War world, their strategic significance has also declined, whilst the cost of overseas military deployment and the maintenance of security have escalated; several military bases have closed and France has ended nuclear testing in French Polynesia. Some territories – Gibraltar, Ceuta, Norfolk Island, St Helena and Macao – are residuals of much earlier strategic and economic situations. Though metropolitan states may not wish to lose these 'windows on the world', they have become increasingly anachronistic, even embarrassing, when violence, irregular financial activities or drug-running attracts world attention.

Otherwise they are almost entirely unknown, and lie beyond the bounds of national imagination. Critical events in New Caledonia and the Falklands took the metropolitan states by surprise, and forced awareness of overseas territories on oblivious nations. Their few representatives are generally ignored in national parliaments and their concerns rarely if ever debated. Indeed, the United Kingdom, Denmark and the Netherlands would be willing to withdraw, if withdrawal were sought by territorial residents; the Netherlands perceives itself as 'trapped in the [Caribbean] region'.[41] Even France, in New Caledonia, and the United States have permitted referenda that might have resulted in independence. Territories are an administrative inconvenience and an economic liability, and their rights (such as those of migration) a threat rather than a promise for metropolitan states. Economic and social problems which beset the territories are now more pressing problems for the metropoles than challenges from independence movements. Yet metropolitan powers have little choice but to remain. Whilst it may be curious that metropolitan powers seek to retain distant places, at considerable cost to the national economy, there is international moral and political pressure on them to mitigate the effects of decolonisation, and not merely to depart when strategic or other interests are no longer important.[42] There are also local pressures. In Aruba, politicians resisting independence argued that its imposition would constitute a violation of their rights of self-determination; in Mayotte and St Helena, residents insist that it is their right to become a fully incorporated element of the national polity. Most territories are burdens – whether light or heavier – which metropolitan countries have resigned themselves to bear.

Just as old notions of exploitative colonialism scarcely hold true in most territories, so external pressures in support of decolonisation have weakened. At a global level the UN Special Committee on Decolonisation has lost significance as it retains its focus on territorial decolonisation.[43] Such non-government organisations as the Unrepresented Peoples Organisation are primarily concerned with indigenous minorities, rather than decolonisation in the more traditional sense. On a regional scale, there have been calls for independence, particularly in the French Pacific territories, from non-government organisations such as the Nuclear-Free and Independent Pacific Movement, and from some regional governments, but these have rarely been concerted or influential. More frequently, other states – often despite their own histories – fear the potential for regional destabilisation posed by the emergence of small, new states. A prominent Australian public servant has argued that 'sentimental notions of self-determination for the East Timorese and Bougainvilleans, among others, threaten our national security';[44] similarly Spain opposes independence in Gibraltar, just as the United States does in Puerto Rico. Small states are vulnerable and problematic. Moreover, most metropolitan states have some, at least intermittently, troublesome peripheral regions or 'colonised' minorities, whose aspirations they are not anxious to encourage by supporting similar regions or groups elsewhere. Notions of a 'domino effect' survive in a different form. There is little to be gained by antagonising other 'colonial' powers.

In almost half a century, the greatest global phase of decolonisation coincided with the emergence of the so-called Third World, but optimism, even euphoria, about post-colonial futures has often been overwhelmed by disappointment and frustration. Many newly independent states have found the challenge of achieving development and democracy exceptionally difficult or, in the latter case, to be avoided. Most have sought renewed aid relationships with colonial powers and concessions of various kinds, particularly in the areas of trade and migration, effectively reconstructing key elements of the colonial order through negotiated neo-colonialism.[45] Surinam, for example, has not only sought renewed Dutch aid but even the return of a Dutch military presence, from a 'reluctant patron', to discourage dissidents and secessionists.[46] On Anjouan secessionists have sought to leave the Comoros Islands and reclaim French sovereignty. However, widespread 'aid fatigue', alongside concern over accountability, and aid delivery to regimes whose interest in human rights and equitable development has been slight, have led donor nations to focus on fewer recipients. Viability, whether economic, social or political, cannot necessarily be equated with independence. Increasingly, the extent of disillusionment with the (New) World Order among less developed countries triggers uncertainty within the overseas territories about embarking on a more independent form of development. Consequently, the idea that, in the words of a Réunion senator, Albert Ramassamy, 'for the old colonies that have become *départements*, integration is a means of decolonisation just as much as independence'[47] is no longer a troubling one for many people and places. This was the view of Cocos (Keeling) Islanders and is essentially the argument of those in Mayotte and St Helena who seek full integration into the metropole, and those in Puerto Rico who promote 'statehood as equality'; the PNP leader, Carlos Romero Barcelo, saw 'statehood as the only dignified way for the US to eliminate Puerto Rico's second-class citizenship and to end Puerto Rico's colonial status'.[48] Integration enables the three principal benefits of 'colonial' status to be safeguarded in perpetuity. These benefits are aid, migration, and security (for defence, political propriety and economic growth).

As one ideological world becomes dominant, and even nationalism is constructed in European terms, the 'retreat to self-reliance' has become less and less palatable. Overseas territories have sought to construct, and be involved in, a world of choices. By freely choosing development strategies that allow some manipulation of metropolitan state policies, the territories will continue to 'live with some degree of uncertainty, but with insurance provided by the realities of geopolitics'.[49] In this they are no less viable or anomalous than many micro-states – such as Barbados or Malta – but they have a structure of dependence, and interdependence, that is very similar. Even so, several dependent territories – in various ways, not least financial – have a much greater international role than many states.

A range of institutions now transcend the nation, as the nation-state increasingly appears to be just one scale of governance. But it has been, like nationalism, a necessary creation, albeit an imaginary community – an artificial product of symbols and histories.[50] So too are colonies, the product of a dualism that distinguished the world core from its periphery; the contemporary overseas territories demonstrate the extent of this fiction. The word 'colony' will remain an emotive one, at the very least a mark of dependence and indeterminacy, and overseas territories will survive; but the link between the two concepts has already dwindled in these places, as sovereignty has been untied from territory. Pragmatism has triumphed over emotion in a world of interdependence, not independence. The great issues of justice, equality, freedom and human rights remain paramount, especially for indigenous peoples, but, again, in contexts where classical issues of decolonisation are scarcely valid. In various circumstances – as in New Caledonia, where the late pro-independence leader, Jean-Marie Tjibaou, legitimately claimed 'so long as one Kanak survives, a problem for France remains'[51] – people will protest against the iniquities of a perceived colonial presence. But in many territories, similar declarations will be more evidently rhetorical devices, designed to achieve less unbalanced links with the global economy, greater degrees of sovereignty, autonomy and cultural identity, but not political independence. Formal political independence now means little. The 'last colonies' have become the avatars of the post-modern future.

APPENDIX

Profiles of Overseas Territories

This appendix provides summary information and a few key references on the specific territories covered in this book. They are listed under the names of the administering powers in alphabetical order. The information has been compiled from a variety of sources, including the works listed here and in the endnotes, as well as *The Europa World Year Book 1996* (London, 1996) and *The Statesman's Year-Book* (London, 1996). Also of use are the various annual reports issued by territorial governments and other official publications.

Bibliographical Note

On the British overseas territories, the only comprehensive academic account is George Drower, *Britain's Dependent Territories: A Fistful of Islands* (Aldershot, 1992); a very readable account of 'journeys to the surviving relics of the British Empire' by a journalist is Simon Winchester, *Outposts* (London, 1985). A more impressionistic account of six Atlantic and Caribbean territories is Harry Ritchie, *The Last Pink Bits* (London, 1997). On the French possessions, Robert Aldrich and John Connell, *France's Overseas Frontier: Départements et Territoires d'Outre-Mer* (Cambridge, 1992), is the most comprehensive volume in English; Helen M. Hintjens, *Alternatives to Independence* (Aldershot, 1995), concentrates on the four overseas *départements* and places them in a wider context. There are several studies in French. Recent ones include Gérard Belorgey and Geneviève Bertrand, *Les DOM-TOM* (Paris, 1994); Jean-Luc Mathieu, *Les DOM-TOM* (Paris, 1988); and Dominique Ghisoni, Wassissi Iopué and Camille Rabin (eds), *Ces Iles que l'on dit françaises* (Paris, 1988); older, but still important, is J.-C. Guillebaud, *Les Confettis de l'empire* (Paris, 1976). A series of books has marked half a century of France's overseas *départements*: Paulin Bruné, *Mon Dieu, que vous êtes français: Essai sur la décolonisation par assimilation* (Paris, 1996); Fred Constant and Justin Daniel (eds), *1946–1996: Cinquante Ans de départementalisation outre-mer* (Paris, 1997); Robert Deville and Nicolas Georges, *Les Départements d'Outre-Mer: L'autre décolonisation* (Paris, 1996); and F. Federini, *La France d'Outre-Mer: Critique d'une volonté française* (Paris, 1997).On the Dutch West Indian islands, there is no single book of any great merit, though there are several useful articles. There are no comparable works on the overseas outposts of other European nations, although the small number of their territories partly accounts for the lack of such studies.

The most comprehensive study of US dependencies is Arnold Leibowitz, *Defining Status: A Comprehensive Analysis of United States Territorial Relations* (Dordrecht, 1989), although it confines itself largely to discussion of legal and constitutional issues. Australian territories are discussed in the report of the House of Representatives Standing Committee on Legal and Constitutional Affairs, *Islands in the Sun: The Legal Regimes of Australia's External Territories and the Jervis Bay Territory* (Canberra, 1991).

Several studies of islands contain useful chapters on various overseas territories. Helen M. Hintjens and Malyn D. D. Newitt (eds), *The Political Economy of Small Tropical Islands: The Importance of Being Small* (Exeter, 1992), includes chapters on Europe's overseas territories, non-sovereign states in the eastern Caribbean and the western Indian Ocean, Montserrat, the Federated States of Micronesia, and the Cook Islands. J.-P. Doumenge *et al.* (eds), *Iles Tropicales: Insularité, 'Insularisme'* (Bordeaux, 1987), has specific papers on Saint-Martin, Réunion and New Caledonia, as well as general pieces on the Caribbean, Pacific and Indian Oceans.

The largest number of territories are located in the Caribbean. General historical overviews of the region include Franklin W. Knight, *The Caribbean: The Genesis of a Fragmented Nationalism* (Oxford, 1990), and J. H. Parry, Philip Sherlock and Anthony Maingot, *A Short History of the West Indies* (London, fourth edition, 1987). Paul Sutton (ed.), *Europe and the Caribbean* (London, 1991), has chapters on the links of Britain, France and the Netherlands with the West Indies. Richard D. E. Burton and Fred Reno (eds), *French and West Indian: Martinique, Guadeloupe and French Guiana Today* (London, 1995), examines the French outposts in the region.

Many dependent territories also lie in the Pacific Ocean. D. Denoon *et al.*, *The Cambridge History of the Pacific Islanders* (Cambridge, 1997), is a comprehensive work. I. C. Campbell, *A History of the Pacific Islands* (St Lucia, Queensland, 1989), provides a good introduction to Oceania, and the various chapters in K. R. Howe *et al.* (eds), *Tides of History: The*

Pacific Islands in the Twentieth Century (Sydney, 1994), examine particular cases and themes. On the French South Pacific territories, see Robert Aldrich, *France and the South Pacific since 1940* (London, 1993), and Stephen Henningham, *France and the South Pacific: A Contemporary History* (Sydney, 1992).

For a discussion of independent island micro-states, many of which have economies and social structures similar to those of the dependent territories, see John Connell, *Sovereignty and Survival: Island Microstates in the Third World* (Sydney, 1988).

Australia

Ashmore and Cartier Islands
Area: 5 sq. km.   Population: no permanent population.

These small and uninhabited islands in the Timor Sea north of the Australian mainland are deemed to form part of the Northern Territory of Australia, and are administered by a parliamentary secretary.

Australian Antarctic Territory
Area: 5,896,500 sq. km.   Population: no permanent population.

The Australian zone of Antarctica – 42 per cent of the total area of the continent – is administered by the Antarctic Division of the Department of Environment, from headquarters in Hobart, Tasmania. Since 1954 Australia has maintained a research programme at Casey, Mawson and Davis bases.

Senate Standing Committee on National Resources, Australian Parliament. *The Natural Resources of the Australian Antarctic Territory* (Canberra, 1985).

Murray-Smith, Stephen. *Sitting on Penguins: Australia and the Antarctic* (Port Melbourne, 1991).

Wilder, Martijn. *Antarctica: An Economic History of the Last Continent* (Sydney, 1992).

Christmas Island
Area: 135 sq. km.   Population: 3000 (1995 estimate).   Chief centre: Flying Fish Cove.

Christmas Island lies in the Indian Ocean, 1400 kilometres west of the Australian continent. Annexed by Britain in 1888, its administration was transferred to Australia in 1958. At a 1994 referendum, islanders voted overwhelmingly against independence. Three-quarters of the population are of Chinese origin, although there are ethnically Malay and mainland Australian residents. The major resource has traditionally been phosphate, but recent efforts have aimed at developing casino tourism. The Australian government is represented by a resident Administrator, and there is an elected Shire Council. The laws of the state of Western Australia apply.

Neale, Mary. *We Were the Christmas Islanders* (Chapman, 1988).

Cocos (Keeling) Islands
Area: 14 sq. km.   Population: 593 (1992).   Chief centre: West Island.

The twenty-seven islands of the Cocos (Keeling) chain in the eastern Indian Ocean were annexed by Britain in 1857. In 1886 London granted all land on the islands to John Clunies-Ross, and the islands remained the preserve of his family, although official administration was vested in the British colony of Singapore. In 1955 administration was transferred to Australia, and in 1977 the Australian government purchased almost all of the interests of the Clunies-Ross family. In 1984 a large majority of the islands' residents voted to remain part of Australia. There is an Administrator appointed by Canberra, as well as an elected Island (or Shire) Council.

Ackrill, Margaret. *British Imperialism in Microcosm: The Annexation of the Cocos (Keeling) Islands* (London, 1994).
Bunce, Pauline. *The Cocos (Keeling) Islands: Australian Atolls in the Indian Ocean* (Milton, Queensland, 1988).

Coral Sea Islands Territory
Area: 8 sq. km.   Population: no permanent population.

The territory consists of a number of coral reefs and low-lying atolls spread over a maritime area of 780,000 square kilometres east of Queensland. Other than a small meteorological station on one island, the area is uninhabited. The governor-general of Australia has statutory rights to issue ordinances for the territory, the laws of the Australian Capital Territory can be nominally extended to the islands, and the Norfolk Island court has jurisdiction over the territory. The Administrator is a parliamentary secretary.

Burmester, Henry. 'Outposts of Australia in the Pacific Ocean'. *Australian Journal of Politics and History*, 29 (1983), pp. 14–25.

Heard Island and the McDonald Islands
Area: 369 sq. km.   Population: no permanent population.

Four thousand kilometres southwest of Perth in the southern Indian Ocean, the uninhabited islands have been part of Australia since 1947. They are administered by the Antarctic Division of the Australian government.

Norfolk Island
Area: 35 sq. km.   Population: 2285 (1991).   Chief centre: Kingston.

Fourteen hundred kilometres east of Brisbane, Norfolk Island was discovered by Captain Cook in 1774 and used by the British as a penal colony until the mid-nineteenth century, when Pitcairn Islanders were resettled there. Britain transferred control to the Australian government in 1913. An Administrator is appointed by Canberra, but the island's Legislative Assembly of nine members enjoys considerable self-government. Agriculture has declined as the major economic activity, largely replaced by tourism.

Hoare, Merval. *The Winds of Change: Norfolk Island* (Suva, 1983).
Treadgold, M. L. *Bounteous Bestowal: The Economic History of Norfolk Island* (Canberra, 1988).

Denmark

Faeroe Islands
Area: 1399 sq. km.   Population: 43,719 (1994).   Chief centre: Tórshavn.

Made up of eighteen islands midway between Iceland, Norway and Scotland, the Faeroes or Faroes (Føroyar) were settled by Vikings in the ninth century. They became part of Norway in 1035 and passed to Denmark in 1380. In 1948, a Home Rule bill passed by the Danish parliament made the Faeroes a 'self-governing community within the Kingdom of Denmark'. The national government retains responsibility for external relations and defence, constitutional matters, justice, and insurance and banking; a high commissioner represents Copenhagen in the Faeroes. The island has the oldest parliament in the world that is still functioning, the Løgting, founded over a thousand years ago. Islanders also select two members of the Danish national parliament. Fish make up more than 90 per cent of exports; sheep-farming and tourism are other economic activities. Danish government subsidies provide supplementary revenue. Standards of living are high, and unemployment low.

West, John F. *Faroe: The Emergence of a Nation* (London, 1972).
Wylie, Jonathan. *The Faroe Islands: Interpretations of History* (Louisville, Kentucky, 1987).

Greenland
Area: 2,175,600 sq. km.   Population: 55,117 (1993).   Chief centre: Nuuk (Godthåb).

Greenland (Kalaallit Nunaat) is the world's largest island. The indigenous Inuit, or Eskimos, are related to the native peoples of Alaska, northern Canada and Siberia. Norway annexed Greenland in 1261, but attempts at settlement failed. In 1380 Denmark nominally took control but did not officially claim the island until 1605. In 1721 the Danish government supported the establishment of a trading post and Lutheran mission; in 1776 the government declared a Danish monopoly on trade and shipping which lasted until 1950. Norway contested Denmark's control of Greenland, but the International Court of Justice ruled in Denmark's favour in the 1930s. Since the Second World War, Greenland has hosted US air bases.

In 1953 Greenland became a Danish county and its inhabitants gained full Danish citizenship. In 1979 a Home Rule government was set up with a prime minister and parliament (Landsting). Greenland elects two members to the Danish national parliament. The Danish government, represented by a high commissioner, looks after defence and foreign relations, the judicial system, and public health, but the Home Rule government is responsible for other areas.

The economy is based on fishing; in northern Greenland whaling and sealing remain important. Some cryolite, lead, zinc and silver are mined. Nevertheless, Greenland relies on large subsidies from Denmark. In 1985 Greenland withdrew from the European Community because of disputes on fishing policies. Eighty per cent of the population is of Inuit or mixed European and Inuit descent; many inhabitants live in isolated villages, where much Inuit culture survives. The main language is Inuit, although Danish is widely used. Some 6000–7000 Greenlanders live in mainland Denmark.

Bach, H. C., and Taagholt, Jørgen. *Greenland and the Arctic Region: Resources and Security Policy* (Copenhagen, 1982).
Nuttall, Mark. *Arctic Homeland: Kinship, Community and Development in Northwest Greenland* (London, 1992).
Vieter, Theodor. *Die Autonomie Grönlands: Das Autonome Nordland* (Vienna, 1990).

France

Austral and Antarctic Territories
Area: Kerguelen Islands: 7215 sq. km; Crozet Islands: 515 sq. km; Amsterdam Island: 85 sq. km; St Paul Island: 7 sq. km; Terre Adélie (Antarctica): 432,000 sq. km.   Population: No permanent population; approximately 145 seasonal inhabitants.   Chief centre: Port-aux-Français, Kerguelen; administrative centre: Saint-Denis, Réunion.

The Austral and Antarctic Territories (TAAF) consist of the large French claim in Antarctica (Terre Adélie) and several sub-Antarctic island groups (Crozet, Kerguelen, Saint-Paul and Amsterdam) over which France established control in the late nineteenth and early twentieth centuries. Nevertheless, the French claim in Antarctica, like those of other nations, is not universally recognised. Teams of French scientists work in Antarctica, and scientific expeditions and the French navy regularly visit the islands. The TAAF is administered by a French official (the *Administrateur Supérieur*), whose headquarters was moved from Paris to Réunion in 1996, and by appointed executive and scientific councils. Past attempts to develop the sub-Antarctic islands for sealing, fishing or pastoralism enjoyed little success. The territorial waters around the TAAF remain largely unexploited. The main base in Kerguelen, Port-aux-Français, is used as a nominal registry port for some French merchant ships.

Delépine, Gracie. *Les Iles australes françaises* (Paris, 1995).
Institut du Pacifique. *L'Antarctique* (Paris, 1985).
Kauffman, Jean-Paul. *L'Arche des Kerguelen. Voyages aux îles de la Désolation* (Paris, 1993).
Robert, Jean. *L'Antarctique et la Terre Adélie* (Aix-en-Provence, 1990).

French Polynesia
Area: 4167 sq. km.   Population: 219,520 (1996).   Chief centre: Papeete, Tahiti.

French Polynesia covers a maritime area the size of Western Europe in the eastern part of the South Pacific. The territory consists of five archipelagos (the Society, Marquesas, Tuamotu, Gambier and Austral Islands); the major island is Tahiti, where more than half of French Polynesia's population live. France took over the Society and Marquesas Islands in 1842 and gained control of the other islands by the end of the 1800s.

French Polynesia is a *territoire d'outre-mer* which elects members of the French parliament in Paris and a Territorial Assembly in Papeete; the assembly chooses a president of the government and ministers. Since 1984, the local government has exercised considerable autonomy in local matters. Paris, represented by a high commissioner, retains control of the crucial areas of immigration, international relations, defence, monetary policy, constitutional issues, and police.

Fish, vanilla and phosphate were traditional exports but now provide little revenue. The main export is pearls, but total exports cover less than one-fifth of imports. Tourism plays a large role in the economy. The French government remains the largest employer; the public service is generally considered to be inflated, and its employees receive wages sometimes double those of bureaucrats in the metropole.

Nuclear testing in French Polynesia – the testing sites at Mururoa and Fangataufa atolls, back-up bases at Hao, and support and administrative establishments in Tahiti – provided the engine of Tahiti's economy from the early 1960s until cessation of testing in 1996. Although highly controversial both in French Polynesia and internationally, nuclear testing provided substantial employment for local workers and metropolitan expatriates, and attracted massive government investment and transfers. An independence movement emerged in French Polynesia in the 1950s but was effectively suppressed by Paris. In the 1970s it resurfaced and adopted an anti-nuclear stance. Major riots occurred in Papeete in 1987 and 1995, partly linked to labour unrest but, particularly in the latter case, tied to opposition to a resumption of nuclear testing after a two-year moratorium.

Clipperton Island, an uninhabited rocky outcrop of 21 square kilometres located 6500 kilometres east of Tahiti and 1300 kilometres west of Mexico, has been recognised as a French possession since the 1930s. The island contained some deposits of guano but now has no appreciable economic value; however, the exclusive economic zone of waters around Clipperton covers 425,000 square kilometres. The island is administered by the French high commissioner in Papeete, although technically it is not part of French Polynesia.

Chesneaux, Jean (ed.). *Tahiti après la bombe. Quel avenir pour la Polynésie?* (Paris, 1995).

Poirine, Bernard. *Tahiti: La fin du paradis?* (Paris, 1994).

Pollock, Nancy J., and Crocombe, Ron (eds). *French Polynesia: A Book of Selected Readings* (Suva, 1988).

Regnault, Jean-Marc. *Des Partis et des hommes en Polynésie française* (Papeete, 1995).

Skaggs, J. M. *Clipperton: A History of the Island the World Forgot* (New York, 1989).

Guadeloupe and Dependencies

Area: 1780 sq. km.   Population: 387,034 (1990).   Chief centre: Pointe-à-Pitre; administrative centre: Basse-Terre.

Acquired by France in the 1630s, Guadeloupe was developed, as were many Caribbean islands, for sugar plantations owned by French settlers and worked by African slaves. Most of the planters were expelled during the French Revolution. Competition from beet sugar production and the abolition of slavery, in 1848, brought on an economic crisis, although indentured Indian labourers supplied a new workforce. Some sugar and rum production continues, whilst cultivation of bananas and other tropical fruits has diversified the agricultural economy. Because of competition from other producers, the French government (and the European Union) provide price support. Government employment, social welfare payments and government transfers are key features of the economy. In recent years, tourism has grown in importance.

A large number of Guadeloupeans have migrated to metropolitan France, initially recruited in the 1950s for employment in postal and hospital services. As French citizens Guadeloupeans enjoy unrestricted right of abode in the metropole. Guadeloupe (along with the small neighbouring islands of La Désirade, Les Saintes, Marie-Galante, Saint-Barthélemy and the French part of St Martin) forms a *département d'outre-mer* with elected departmental and regional councils and mayors, as well as representation in the French parliament.

The 1970s saw the growth of a vocal and sometimes violent independence movement; although it never managed to gain control of local assemblies, as an extra-parliamentary force, the independence movement wielded much influence. Paris reacted strongly against pro-independence violence and outlawed one major pro-independence group. Since the early 1980s, the independence campaign has waned.

Saint-Martin, 13 by 15 kilometres, was divided in the 1600s between France and the Netherlands. The French section of the island forms a municipality within the *département* of Guadeloupe. It is highly developed as a tourist resort, as is nearby **Saint-Barthélemy**. Unlike the rest of the French West Indies, the population of Saint-Barts, as it is commonly known, are almost all of European ancestry.

Bangou, Henri. *Les Voies de la souveraineté. Peuplement et institutions à la Guadeloupe* (Paris, 1988).
Bebel-Gisler, Dany. *Le Défi culturel guadeloupéen* (Paris, 1989).
Monnier, Yves. *L'Immuable et le changeant: étude de la partie française de l'île de Saint-Martin* (Bordeaux, 1983).

Guyane
Area: 91,000 sq. km. Population: 114,808 (1990). Chief centre: Cayenne.

A vast equatorial area on the northern coast of South America, Guyane (or French Guiana) attracted French interest from the 1600s onwards, although the tropical climate dissuaded large-scale settlement. The mid-1800s saw a relatively short-lived gold rush. France then established an infamous prison colony at Devil's Island, near Cayenne, which operated until the Second World War; the 'green hell' of the penal establishment – and such famous prisoners as Captain Alfred Dreyfus – brought notoriety to the colony.

In the 1960s, France established a space station at Kourou; it represents the major economic activity, employing local workers and metropolitan scientists and technicians. The public service is another major employer. The population is largely of African descent, although there are metropolitan French residents, Hmong from Laos (settled there in the 1970s), Amerindians in the dense southern jungles (the Inini) and refugees from neighbouring Surinam (the former Dutch Guyana). Guyane, like Guadeloupe, is a *département d'outre-mer*. There has been support for independence from a few individuals and groups, but the independence movement is not a major actor in local politics.

Mam-Lam-Fouck, Serge. *Histoire de la Guyane française. Les grands problèmes guyanais: permanence et évolution* (Paris, 1997).
Miles, Alexander. *Devil's Island: Colony of the Damned* (Berkeley, 1988).

Martinique
Area: 1128 sq. km.   Population: 368,400 (1991 estimate).   Chief centre: Fort-de-France.

Like Guadeloupe, a West Indian colony acquired in the 1630s, Martinique owed its prosperity to sugar and rum produced on the estates of European settlers (the *Békés*) using a labour force of African slaves. After the emancipation of slaves in 1848, sugar production declined markedly. Sugar, and particularly rum, are nevertheless still important products, along with tropical fruits. Martinique has a prosperous tourism industry, which attracts clients from Europe and North America. As in the other French outposts, the public service is a key employer; government transfers and social welfare payments represent important economic assets. Many Martinicans moved to metropolitan France in the 1950s and 1960s. *Béké* families still own many plantations, but political life (and much of economic life) is controlled by local Creoles of African (or Afro-European) descent. Martinique remains a *département d'outre-mer* with, since the early 1980s, an increased though limited amount of autonomy. A small independence movement has retained its vitality in the 1990s.

Burton, Richard D. E. *La Famille coloniale: La Martinique et la mère patrie, 1789–1992* (Paris, 1994).
Constant, Fred. *La Retraite aux flambeaux: Société et politique en Martinique* (Paris, 1988).
Miles, William. *Elections and Ethnicity in French Martinique: A Paradox in Paradise* (New York, 1986).

Mayotte
Area: 375 sq. km. Population: 94,410 (1991). Chief centre:
Mamoudzou.

Mayotte forms part of the Comoros archipelago off the east coast of
Africa. In a 1974 referendum, the inhabitants of three of the islands
opted for independence, whilst those of Mayotte voted against it.
Subsequent ballots reaffirmed Mayotte's desire to remain part of France
(and indeed have complete integration through *départementalisation*).
Mahorais are almost all Muslim; few speak French. Most live in villages,
and Mayotte's economy is based largely on subsistence agriculture and,
increasingly, on French government transfers and public welfare
payments. The oil of the *ylang-ylang* flower, used as a perfume essence, is
the only export, although it contributes only a tiny proportion of the
island's revenues. Tourism is little developed. There is a population of
some 2000 technicians, white-collar professionals and bureaucrats
from the metropole. There are also a number of migrants, legal or
clandestine, from the Federal Islamic Republic of the Comoros.

Aldrich, Robert. 'France in the Indian Ocean: Declining Independence
   in Mayotte', in Robert Aldrich and Isabelle Merle (eds), *France Abroad:
   Indochina, New Caledonia, Wallis and Futuna, Mayotte* (Sydney, 1997),
   pp. 99–168.
Blanchy-Daurel, Sophie. *La Vie Quotidienne à Mayotte* (Paris, 1990).
Pujo, Pierre. *Mayotte la française* (Paris, 1993).
Salesse, Yves. *Mayotte. L'Illusion de la France. Propositions pour une
   décolonisation* (Paris, 1995).

New Caledonia
Area: 19,103 sq. km. Population: 196,800 (1996). Chief centre:
Noumea.

Composed of the Grande Terre, Loyalty Islands, Isle of Pines and several
smaller islands, New Caledonia has been a French possession since the
mid-nineteenth century. The indigenous population are Melanesians
(Kanaks); a subsistence economy and decentralised social and political
structures characterised the country before European takeover. From
1863 to 1897, France transported thousands of convicts and political
prisoners to New Caledonia, tried to attract free settlers, and recruited
indentured labour from the New Hebrides, Japan, Indonesia and
Vietnam. New Caledonia was promoted as the only real French settler
colony other than Algeria. Its major economic resource, nickel, was first
developed in the late 1800s; New Caledonia has the world's second
largest reserves of nickel ore. A nickel boom in the 1960s attracted
further migrants, including many from metropolitan France and from

French Polynesia and Wallis and Futuna; Melanesians were thus reduced to a demographic minority.

Modern Melanesian political activism began in the 1940s, but not until the 1970s did it give birth to a pro-independence movement. Long-term French settlers (the *Caldoches*), who controlled economic and political power, and recent migrants strongly opposed independence. Opinions polarised, and considerable violence, including assassinations, hostage-taking, disruption of elections and strong-arm response by French police and army units followed in the mid-1980s. In 1988, the two main political parties and the government signed an agreement for division of New Caledonia into three 'provinces', each with its own administration under the authority of the French high commissioner. The plan, the Matignon Accord, foreshadowed a supposedly definitive referendum on the future of the territory in 1998.

Bensa, Alban. *Nouvelle-Calédonie, un paradis dans la tourmente* (Paris, 1990).

Connell, John. *New Caledonia or Kanaky? The Political History of a French Colony* (Canberra, 1987).

Faberon, J.-Y. *L'avenir statutaire de la Nouvelle Caledonie* (Paris, 1996).

Spencer, Michael; Ward, Alan; and Connell, John (eds). *New Caledonia: Essays in Nationalism and Dependency* (St Lucia, Queensland, 1988).

Réunion

Area: 2512 sq. km.   Population: 630,700 (1993 estimate).   Chief centre: Saint-Denis.

France took over the uninhabited Indian Ocean island of Réunion in the 1630s; settlers established a plantation economy based on production of sugar and other agricultural products, and imported slaves from Africa. The abolition of slavery in 1848 created labour problems for Réunion and led to recruitment of contract workers from India. By the early twentieth century, sugar production had dropped and the colony was somnolent. In 1946, Réunion (like the French West Indian colonies) became a *département d'outre-mer* with representation in the French parliament and a locally elected assembly. Despite some agricultural production, the economy has become increasingly dependent on government transfers. Emigration to France was important from the 1950s to the 1970s. The population of the major centres now has a high standard of living, but poverty remains (notably in the highlands).

The **Iles Eparses** include the Glorieuses group, Juan de Nova, Europa and Bassas da India in the Mozambique Channel, and the Tromelin reef east of Madagascar. They are administered by the prefect of Réunion. There is no permanent population, although small detachments of military personnel and scientists are based on several of the islands. Madagascar, the Comoros and Mauritius claim several of the islands.

Institut d'Emission d'Outre-Mer. *La Réunion* (Paris, 1994).
Hoarau, Alain. *Les Îles éparses* (Saint-Denis, 1994).
Leguen, Marcel. *Histoire de l'Île de La Réunion* (Paris, 1979).
Weber, Albert. *L'Emigration réunionnaise en France* (Paris 1994).

Saint-Pierre-et-Miquelon
Area: 242 sq. km.   Population: 6392 (1990).   Chief centre: Saint-Pierre.

Left to France as a consolation prize for its loss of a North American empire to Britain in 1763, Saint-Pierre, Miquelon and Langlade lie off the southern coast of Newfoundland. Sparsely populated by French metropolitan settlers but often used as a base for fishermen in the North Atlantic, the islands' main resource was cod, exported to France's Caribbean colonies in the nineteenth century. Fishing remains the major productive activity, although it has given rise to conflict between France and Canada about fishing rights in territorial waters. The islands attract a small amount of tourism from France and Canada, and receive significant government transfers from France. The islands are a *collectivité territoriale* (similar to a *département d'outre-mer*) of France.

Guyotjeannin, Charles. *Saint-Pierre et Miquelon* (Paris, 1986).

Wallis and Futuna
Area: 274 sq. km.   Population: 13,705 (1990).   Chief centre: Mata-Utu, Wallis Island.

Wallis and Futuna (and uninhabited Alofi) are Polynesian islands situated between French Polynesia and New Caledonia. They became a French colony in the 1880s; in 1962 they became a *territoire d'outre-mer*. A prefect represents the French state, there is an elected Territorial Assembly, and the islands elect representatives to the French parliament. The Catholic Church is of considerable importance, and the traditional king of Wallis and two kings of Futuna continue to play an important role in local life, especially in questions relating to Polynesian customs and land matters. Wallis and Futuna have only a trivial amount of exports (primarily handicrafts and postage stamps). The two main sources of revenue are government transfers and migrant remittances from Wallisians and Futunans in New Caledonia. The nickel boom and rapidly developing economy in New Caledonia attracted many islanders in the 1960s; more Wallisians and Futunans live in New Caledonia than in their home islands. There is virtually no tourism.

Connell, John. 'Wallis and Futuna: Stability and Change at the Ends of Empire', in Robert Aldrich (ed.), *France, Oceania and Australia: Past and Present* (Sydney, 1991), pp. 91–116.
Poncet, Alexandre. *Histoire de l'île Wallis* (Paris, 1972).

Netherlands

Aruba
Area: 193 sq. km.   Population: 77,898 (1993 estimate).   Chief centre: Oranjestad.

Lying in the Caribbean north of Venezuela, Aruba has been a Dutch possession since the 1600s. Aruba was one of six islands in the Netherlands Antilles until 1986, when it obtained separate status (*status aparte*) as one of three autonomous entities in the Kingdom of the Netherlands. The Dutch monarch appoints a governor. There is an elected legislature (Staten), a prime minister and other ministers. The Staten has the right to be consulted on national legislation which concerns the island; a minister plenipotentiary appointed by the Aruban government represents the island in The Hague. The Dutch government had agreed to *status aparte* on condition that Aruba accede to independence in 1996; however, enthusiasm for separation waned, and Dutch and Aruban authorities in 1994 agreed to cancel plans for independence. Aruba's economy in the 1970s and early 1980s was based on processing petroleum from Venezuela, but most of the refineries were closed by 1985. Financial services remain important, but Aruba's main source of income is now tourism. Dutch government transfers are significant. The Aruban population counts Dutch, African and South American ancestry; the common language is the Creole Papiamento.

Hartog, J. *Short History of Aruba* (Aruba, 1975).

Netherlands Antilles
Area: 800 sq. km (Bonaire: 288 sq. km; Curaçao: 444 sq. km; Saba: 13 sq. km; St Eustatius: 21 sq. km; Sint-Maarten (Dutch side): 34 sq. km). Population: 189,474 (1993). (Bonaire: 10,187; Curaçao: 144,097; Saba: 1130; St Eustatius: 1839; Sint-Maarten: 32,221.) Chief centre: Willemstad, Curaçao.

The Netherland Antilles consists of **Bonaire** and **Curaçao** in the southern Caribbean off the coast of Venezuela, and, in the Leeward Islands further north, **Saba**, **St Eustatius** and the Dutch sector of **Sint-Maarten**. The Dutch acquired the Leeward Islands in the 1630s, the French and Dutch dividing St Martin between them; the Netherlands took possession of the southern islands in the seventeenth century. In 1954 a Dutch royal charter granted autonomy in domestic afffairs to a newly constituted federation of the six islands, the Netherlands Antilles, from which Aruba withdrew in 1986. The monarch appoints a governor for the Netherlands Antilles, and resident lieutenant-governors for each island. A legislature, the Staten, comprises members from each island of the 'Antilles of Five'. A prime minister presides over a Council of Ministers. Each of the islands has an elected Island Council. There has been considerable dispute about division of powers between the Dutch government, the government of the Netherlands Antilles and the Island Councils. Some parties in Sint-Maarten (and, to a lesser extent, in Bonaire and Curaçao) occasionally pressed for a separate relationship with The Hague, a proposal to which Dutch authorities have responded unfavourably. In 1993 a referendum on Curaçao rejected calls for withdrawal from the Dutch Antillean federation; in 1994, Bonaire, St Eustatius and Saba voted overwhelmingly for continued membership, as did (with a smaller proportion of the vote) Sint-Maarten. Accusations of widespread corruption, drug-trafficking and organised crime in Sint-Maarten prompted the Dutch government to place the island under 'higher supervision' and institute tighter financial regulations in 1992.

The islands differ substantially among themselves, although international tourism now plays a large role in the economy of each, offshore economic activities are important in the larger islands, and English is a common language. Government subsidies and public employment are vital to economic welfare. Curaçao, the largest and most populous of the islands, has specialised in oil refining, petroleum transhipment and ship-repairing. Bonaire has some manufacturing and financial activities. Sint-Maarten is a major holiday destination, with a rapidly growing population and substantial migration from elsewhere in the Caribbean. The two smallest islands, Saba and St Eustatius (Statia), have a number of small-scale tourist activities. The population of Saba is divided among those of European and African (or mixed descent), while that of the other islands is primarily African in ancestry.

Ayisi, Eric O. *St Eustatius: The Treasure Island of the Caribbean* (Trenton, New Jersey, 1992).

Klomp, Ank. *Politics on Bonaire* (Maastricht, 1986).

Koot, Willem; Tempel-Schoorl, Corrie; and Marcha, Valdemar. *Apart or Together* (Utrecht, 1990).

Sekou, Lasana M. *The Independence Papers: Readings on a New Political Status for St. Maarten/St. Martin* (Sint-Maarten, 1990).

Van den Bor, Wout. *Island Adrift: The Social Organization of a Small Caribbean Community: The Case of St. Eustatius* (The Hague, 1981).

New Zealand

Cook Islands

Area: 237 sq. km.   Population: 18,500 (1994 estimate).   Chief centre: Avarua, Rarotonga.

The Cook Islands, composed of fifteen Polynesian islands (of which thirteen are inhabited) in the south central Pacific, became a British colony in 1888, but administration was transferred to New Zealand in 1901. In 1965 the Cook Islands became a self-governing territory; its residents are New Zealand citizens with the right of abode. More than half of all Cook Islanders live in New Zealand. The islands also have the constitutional right to independence. The head of state is the British queen, represented by a governor-general in New Zealand, who appoints a high commissioner to the Cook Islands, takes charge of the Cook Islands' external affairs and defence, and provides the bulk of aid. The leader of the parliamentary majority becomes prime minister. Agriculture, tourism and offshore business form the major economic activities, mainly in the southern 'high' islands, but there has been corruption and various financial scandals came to light in 1996.

Crocombe, Ron (ed.). *Cook Island Politics: The Inside Story* (Auckland, 1979).
Gilson, Richard. *The Cook Islands, 1820–1950* (Wellington, 1980).

Niue

Area: 263 sq. km.   Population: 2321 (1994).   Chief centre: Alofi.

Niue, located 930 kilometres west of the Cook Islands, was part of the Cook Islands colony until 1904. It was granted self-government in 1974. The Polynesian inhabitants are New Zealand citizens, and many more Niueans now live in New Zealand than on the island. The major export of the island until the 1980s was coconut cream; some coconuts, honey and handicrafts are still exported. There is little tourism. Government transfers from New Zealand and migrant remittances provide most of the islanders' income. There is a New Zealand high commissioner in the territory, as well as a premier and an elected assembly.

Chapman, Terry M. *The Decolonisation of Niue* (Wellington, 1976).
Fisk, E. K. *The Island of Niue: Development or Dependence for a Very Small Nation* (Canberra, 1978).

Ross Dependency
Area: 450,000 sq. km.   Population: no permanent population.

Ross Dependency of Antarctica was placed under the jurisdiction of New Zealand in 1923. New Zealand carries out scientific research at Scott Base under the aegis of the Ministry of Research, Science and Technology.

Quartermain, L. B. *New Zealand and the Antarctic* (Wellington, 1971).

Tokelau
Area: 10 sq. km.   Population: 1507 (1996).   Chief centre: Atafu Island.

Three isolated and quite distinct Polynesian atolls in the central Pacific make up the territory of Tokelau, which became a British possession in 1877 and was transferred to New Zealand in 1926. The Tokelau Islands Act of 1948 vested all executive functions in the Administrator, appointed by the New Zealand government. Inhabitants elect a council for each of the atolls and a legislative assembly with limited functions. Subsistence agriculture is the basis of the economy; the public service is the largest employer, and government transfers and remittances are large.

Hooper, A. and Huntsman, J. *Tokelau: A Historical Ethnography* (Auckland, 1996).
Wessen, Albert F. (ed.). *Migration and Health in a Small Society: The Case of Tokelau* (Oxford, 1992).

Portugal

Azores Islands
Area: 2330 sq. km.   Population: 237,800 (1991).   Chief Centre: Ponta Delgada, São Miguel.

The Azores (Açôres) consist of three widely separated island groups in the eastern Atlantic Ocean. The nearest group lies 1450 kilometres west of Lisbon. The uninhabited islands were first settled by Portugal in the mid-fifteenth century and became a major way-station on the route from Europe to the Americas. There was significant migration to the New England region of the United States, Hawaii and other destinations in the 1800s and 1900s. Poor and largely neglected by Portugal, the islands were ruled by officials directly appointed by Lisbon until the Portuguese revolution of 1974. The Azores became an autonomous region in 1976 and has a significant degree of self-government. Residents, who are Portuguese citizens, elect representatives to a Regional Legislative

Assembly and to the Portuguese parliament. There is a regional government, and a minister of the republic represents Lisbon in the islands. A
small independence movement was active in the mid-1970s. Farming,
pastoralism and fish-canning are the major economic activities.

Rogers, Francis M. *Atlantic Islanders of the Azores and Madeiras* (North
  Quincy, Massachusetts, 1979).

Macao
Area: 19 sq. km.   Population: 395,304 (1993 estimate).

The Portuguese first arrived in Macao (Macau) on the south coast of
China, west of Hong Kong, in 1507, and established a settlement there
fifty years later; not until 1783, however, did Portugal claim sovereignty
over Macao. In 1971 Macao was proclaimed an 'autonomous region' of
Portugal. China nevertheless demanded retrocession of Macao, just as it
demanded return of Hong Kong. In 1986 Beijing and Lisbon recognised
Macao officially as a territory of Chinese sovereignty under Portuguese
administration; Macao will be ceded to China in 1999. The foreign
affairs of Macao are the responsibility of the president of Portugal, while
executive power lies with the governor appointed by Lisbon after consultation with the Legislative Assembly of Macau, which has both
appointed and elected members. There is also a Superior Council of
Security and a Consultative Council. Most higher-level public servants
and members are Portuguese. In practice, the Chinese government has
great influence in Macao's affairs. Tourism (including legalised gambling), trade and public works projects comprise the territory's economy; the opening of an airport and a major construction programme
are designed to boost Macao's fortunes. Most of the population is
Chinese, though with a number of Eurasians and a small community of
Portuguese officials; few residents speak Portuguese. Portugal has
promised generous concessions of passports and residence permits to
Macao residents after its withdrawal from the territory.

Coates, Austin. *A Macao Narrative* (Hong Kong, 1987).
Cremer, R. D. (ed.). *Macau: City of Commerce and Culture* (Hong Kong,
  1987).
Lo Shiu Hing. *Political Development in Macau* (Hong Kong, 1995).
Porter, Jonathan. *Macau: The Imaginary City* (London, 1996).

Madeira Islands
Area: 794 sq. km.   Population: 253,400 (1991).   Chief centre: Funchal,
Madeira.

Composed of seven islands, much the largest of which is Madeira, the
archipelago lies 980 kilometres southwest of Lisbon in the Atlantic; its

centre, Funchal, it the third-largest city in Portugal. The previously uninhabited islands were settled by Portuguese in the mid-fifteenth century, and Madeira became famous for its fortified wine. The islands remained poor, however, and there has been much emigration; one million Madeirans now live overseas. Ruled directly by Lisbon until 1974, Madeira subsequently became an autonomous region with its own Legislative Assembly and government. Residents also elect delegates to Portugal's parliament, and a minister represents Lisbon in Madeira. The major economic activity is tourism, which attracts almost 500,000 visitors annually. In addition to wine, Madeira also produces sugar and other agricultural products, fish and handicrafts.

Spain

Canary Islands
Area: 7273 sq. km.   Population: 1,493,784 (1991).   Chief centres: Las Palmas and Santa Cruz de Tenerife.

One hundred kilometres west of the African coast, the Canary Islands consist of Tenerife, Gomera, La Palma, Hierro, Lanzarote, Fuerteventura and Gran Canaria, as well as several smaller islands. They were colonised by Spain from the 1470s. The original Guanches, probably of Berber stock, were wholly absorbed by intermarriage with settlers. The islands were important stopping-off points for ships, and later aeroplanes, travelling to Africa, the Americas or beyond. Spain ruled the islands directly, and autonomy was severely curtailed under the Francoist regime. The Canaries, under terms of the 1978 constitution, forms an 'autonomous community' divided into two provinces. There is an elected legislature, and residents also choose deputies to the Spanish parliament. Several independence groups have very limited influence. Tourism is the major economic activity, but there is also export agriculture, fishing and some manufacturing.

Martin, Raul Hernandez; Godenau, Dirk; Mesa, Antonio Vera; and Fuentes, Carlos Rodriguez. *L'Economie des Iles Canaries* (Paris, 1997).

Ceuta
Area: 18 sq. km.   Population: 71,926 (1994).

Less than 20 kilometres across the Straits of Gibraltar from Algeciras, Ceuta (or Sebta in Arabic) is a Spanish enclave surrounded by Morocco. The Portuguese conquered Ceuta in 1415 and, after the union of the Spanish and Portuguese crowns in 1580, Spain gained control of the city. In the late 1800s the city was an important Mediterranean port, and was used for a penitentiary and garrison. With the British entrenched in

Gibraltar, Spain also retained Ceuta for its strategic position. In the early 1900s Ceuta served as a base for Spain's expanding activities in North Africa. When Morocco gained independence in 1956, Spain continued to hold Ceuta (and Melilla), despite Moroccan claims.

The city contains a major Spanish military base. It is a duty-free port which attracts shoppers from both the Spanish mainland and Morocco; there is much contraband trade across the Moroccan border. In addition to permanent residents (*Ceutís*), there is a large Moroccan population (relatively few of whom are Spanish citizens or have legal right of abode in Ceuta) and small Jewish and Indian communities. Periodic clashes between Christians and Muslims have occurred. In 1995 Ceuta became an autonomous region of Spain (much like Catalonia or the Basque country) and a local assembly was established; the head of the local government carries the title of president. A government delegate (*delegado del gobierno*) represents Madrid, and the national government controls such areas as defence and foreign relations. The population elects representatives to the Spanish parliament.

Carr, Matthew, 'Policing the Frontier: Ceuta and Melilla'. *Race and Class*, 39 (1977), pp. 61–66.

Naciri, Mohamed. 'Les Villes méditerranéennes du Maroc: entre frontières et périphéries'. *Hérodote*, 45 (1987), pp. 212–244.

Péroncel-Hugoz, Jean-Pierre. 'Ceuta et Melilla', in *Villes du Sud* (Paris, 1990), pp. 95–102.

Rézette, Robert. *Les Enclaves espagnoles au Maroc* (Paris, 1976).

Melilla
Area: 14 sq. km.   Population: 62,569 (1991).

East of Ceuta, close to the Moroccan–Algerian border, lies the Spanish enclave of Melilla, which Spain conquered in 1497. Like Ceuta, Melilla has been a free port since the late 1800s and formed part of a larger Spanish sphere of influence in North Africa in the early twentieth century. In the 1930s General Franco led troops from Melilla to the Spanish mainland in the war against the Spanish Republic. Despite Moroccan opposition, Spain retained control of Melilla after 1956. The city became an autonomous region of Spain in 1995; it has a president and elected assembly, as well as representation in the Spanish parliament. Trade is an important economic activity, involving visitors from the Spanish mainland, Morocco and Algeria. Finance from the Spanish government for public works projects, administration and defence is important in both Melilla and Ceuta.

The **Peñon de Velez de la Gomera, Peñon de Alhucemas** and **Chafarinas Islands**, tiny offshore islands, are administered as part of Melilla. There are small military detachments on each.

Driessen, Henk. *On the Spanish–Moroccan Frontier: A Study in Ritual, Power and Ethnicity* (Oxford, 1992).

United Kingdom

Anguilla
Area: 96 sq. km.   Population: 8960 (1992).   Chief centre: The Valley.

The most northerly of the Caribbean Leeward Islands, Anguilla has been a British possession since 1650. An arid climate made it unsuitable for plantations, and droughts and cyclones hampered development; cotton and salt provided the basis of the economy. Anguilla was formerly part of the St Kitts–Nevis colony, but in the 1960s its population reacted strongly against plans for St Kitts–Nevis to become independent in 1967. It became a totally separate dependency in 1980, and is administered under a constitution adopted by the British parliament in 1982. The British appoint a governor, and there is an elected House of Assembly and a chief minister. There was substantial emigration to Britain and the United States after 1945. British government transfers were vital to the small population which remained. Anguilla possesses no major natural resources other than its climate and beaches, but the local government opposed the development of tourism throughout the 1970s. In more recent years, a small and prosperous tourism industry has emerged, aimed at the higher end of the market. Tourism has brought nearly full employment and led to the virtual demise of agriculture and salt production. Political life concentrates on local issues, and there is no independence movement.

Brisk, Colin J. *The Dilemma of a Ministate: Anguilla* (Columbia, South Carolina, 1967).
Petty, Colville L., and Hodge, Nat. *Anguilla's Battle for Freedom, 1967* (Anguilla, 1987).
Petty, C. L. *A Handbook History of Anguilla* (Anguilla, 1991).

Bermuda
Area: 53 sq. km.   Population: 59,549 (1993 estimate).   Chief centre: Hamilton.

Bermuda, settled by the British from 1612, officially became a Crown colony in 1684; it is Britain's oldest remaining non-European outpost. Located in the western Atlantic 900 kilometres east of the American state of North Carolina, Bermuda is composed of twenty inhabited islands, most of which are linked by causeways. Bermuda historically served Britain as a trading post, naval station and penal colony. Most

Bermudians descend from British settlers and African slaves. Bermuda has had a representative assembly since 1620, but was given self-government only under a new constitution in 1968. There is a British-appointed governor, an appointed Senate and an elected House of Assembly. The premier and ministers are selected from members of the legislature. The major economic activity is tourism, complemented by an offshore insurance and finance industry. The United States and Canada maintained military bases in Bermuda until 1995. Bermuda is one of the few overseas territories which receives no budgetary aid from the administering power. There was some pro-independence pressure in the 1970s and 1980s, but support dwindled in the 1990s. A referendum on independence, held in 1995, was clearly won by opponents of independence.

Ahiakpor, James C. W. *The Economic Consequences of Political Independence: The Case of Bermuda* (Vancouver, 1990).

Davies, Elizabeth W. *The Legal Status of British Dependent Territories: The West Indies and North Atlantic Region* (Cambridge, 1995).

Zuill, W. S. *The Story of Bermuda and Her People* (London, 1973).

British Antarctic Territory
Area: 1,710,000 sq. km.   Population: no permanent population.

The British Antarctic Territory became a separate colony in 1962 and is administered by a commissioner in the South Atlantic and Antarctic Department of the Foreign and Commonwealth Office. The British Antarctic Survey carries out research at six stations.

British Indian Ocean Territory
Area: 60 sq. km.   Population: no permanent population.   Chief centre: Diego Garcia.

The British Indian Ocean Territory (BIOT) consists of the Chagos archipelago (the main island of which is Diego Garcia), which, until 1965, was part of the British colony of Mauritius. Copra production was the main economic activity of some two thousand Ilois, a Catholic Creole population. In 1966 the British government agreed to rent the islands to the United States for an indefinite period for use as a military base. The British transferred the entire Ilois population to Mauritius, despite protests by the Ilois and the Mauritian government and some compensation; Mauritius still claims the BIOT as part of its national territory. The United States currently uses Diego Garcia as its main military installation in the Indian Ocean region. There is a British commissioner and an Administrator for the BIOT, both located at the Foreign and

Commonwealth Office in London. A Royal Navy commander represents London in the BIOT, but supervision of the US forces (and an expatriate workforce) lies largely with US military officials.

Edis, Richard. *Peak of Limuria: The Story of Diego Garcia* (London, 1993).
Jawatkar, K. W. *Diego Garcia in International Diplomacy* (London, 1982).
Madeley, John. *Diego Garcia: A Contrast to the Falklands* (London, 1985).
Walker, Iain. *Zaffer Pe Sanze: Ethnic Identity and Social Change among the Ilois in Mauritius* (Vacoas, Mauritius, 1986).

British Virgin Islands

Area: 153 sq. km.   Population: 16,749 (1991).   Chief centre: Road Town, Tortola.

The British Virgin Islands (BVI) comprise more than forty small islands, of which some fifteen are inhabited, in the Caribbean; the main island is Tortola. The islands were used as trading outposts from the 1600s onwards. The constitution, most recently amended in 1977, gives the local government considerable autonomy. A governor is appointed from London and a Legislative Council is locally elected; one member serves as chief minister. There is no move for independence, and the BVI government defends the constitutional status quo of the islands. Only 'belongers', those with long-standing links to the islands, usually established by birth or family connections, are allowed to own land and vote. There has been considerable emigration, and BVI residents move relatively freely to the neighbouring United States Virgin Islands. The BVI exports some fish and agricultural products, but the basis of the economy is tourism; there is also offshore banking and finance. The official currency is the US dollar. Cruise ships call at the islands, there are a number of tourist hotels, and several small islands have been turned into reserves for holiday houses.

Cohen, Colleen Ballerino, and Mascia-Lees, Frances E. 'The British Virgin Islands as Nation and Desti-Nation: Representing and Siting Identity in a Post-colonial Caribbean'. *Social Analysis*, 33 (1993), pp. 130–151.
Kersell, John E. 'Developing the British Virgin Islands: The First Crown Colony'. *Public Administration and Development*, 9 (1989), pp. 97–109.

Cayman Islands

Area: 259 sq. km.   Population: 31,930 (1994 estimate).   Chief centre: George Town, Grand Cayman.

Britain took possession of the Cayman Islands in the early 1600s, and settlers from Jamaica arrived by 1670. The Caymans remained a dependency of the colony of Jamaica until 1959, when it became a separate Crown colony. The British-appointed governor is responsible for external affairs and defence, internal security, and the public service. There is a Legislative Assembly of elected and ex-officio members, headed by a speaker. However, there is no premier or chief minister in the Cayman Islands, one outcome of implacable opposition to independence. Tourism, international finance and property development are the main economic activities. All have prospered in recent decades, as the colony became an internationally renowned tax haven, and the population has grown very rapidly.

Connell, John. 'The Cayman Islands: Economic Growth and Immigration in a British Colony'. *Caribbean Geography*, 5 (1994), pp. 51–56.

Channel Islands
Area: 194 sq. km.   Population: 144,369 (1993).   Chief centres: St Helier (Jersey), St Peter Port (Guernsey).

The Channel Islands, lying in the English Channel off the French coast, are the remaining portions of the Duchy of Normandy, the domain of William the Conqueror in the eleventh century. They form two separate dependencies of the British Crown, though not part of the United Kingdom, being Crown fiefdoms under the jurisdiction of the sovereign rather than the state. An Anglo-French dialect was the common language until recent times, and French was used for official purposes. The main islands are Jersey and Guernsey, each of which forms a Bailiwick, over which the monarch appoints a lieutenant-governor. Several smaller islands (Alderney, Sark, Herm and others) form part of the Bailiwick of Guernsey, although there are administrative anomalies; there is, for instance, a hereditary Seigneur of Sark. Each Bailiwick has an appointed bailiff, who is president of the Assembly of the States, the local assembly composed of appointed and elected members. Offshore finance and banking and similar business concerns form the main economic activities, encouraged by low income tax and favourable business regulations. There is significant tourism from both Britain and France, as well as some agriculture (notably horticulture and the raising of Jersey and Guernsey cattle).

Jamieson, A. G. *A People of the Sea: The Maritime History of the Channel Islands* (London, 1986).
Lempriere, Raoul. *The Channel Islands* (London, 1990).

Falkland Islands
Area: 12,173 sq. km.   Population: 2704 (1996).   Chief centre: Stanley.

In the southwestern Atlantic, the unoccupied Falkland Islands were discovered in 1592. France established a settlement in 1764, but subsequently withdrew in favour of Spain. Since 1833 the islands have been continuously occupied by British settlers; only two of the two hundred islands have a permanent population.

The Falklands War of 1982 dramatically showed the conflict between Britain and Argentina over possession of the Falkland (Malvinas) Islands. Argentinian claims are based on inclusion of the islands in Spanish colonial territory before Argentinian independence and later claims advanced by Buenos Aires. Britain's claims rest largely on discovery and effective occupation. Most of the islanders are of British ancestry. In the 1970s, as the Falklands suffered economic difficulties and Britain sought to disengage itself from several remaining colonies, London reportedly considered ceding the territory to Argentina. Invasion of the islands, however, brought a quick response. The war initially galvanised public opinion in Britain and Argentina, although defeat contributed to the overthrow of the dictatorship in Buenos Aires.

Britain has since poured substantial funds into the islands to stimulate the economy and provide for a much strengthened defence presence. A new constitution, adopted in 1985, guarantees the right of the islands to remain a British territory so long as their inhabitants wish. Falkland Islanders enjoy an unrestricted right of abode in the United Kingdom and other privileges of British citizenship. A governor represents the monarch; a Legislative Council is composed of the Governor and ex-officio (non-voting) and elected members. Pastoralism remains a major economic activity, although there is some fishing and offshore oil has been discovered.

Beck, Peter. *The Falkland Islands as an International Problem* (London, 1988).
Costa Méndez, Nicanor. *Malvinas: Esta es la historia* (Buenos Aires, 1993).
Freedman, Lawrence, and Gamba-Stonehouse, Virginia. *Signals of War: The Falklands Conflict of 1982* (Princeton, 1991).
Gough, B. *The Falkland Islands/Malvinas: The Contest for Empire in the South Atlantic* (London, 1992).

Gibraltar
Area: 6 sq. km.   Population: 28,051 (1993).

At the southern tip of the Iberian peninsula, Gibraltar has been a British possession since 1704. It occupies one of the most strategic positions in Europe and was an important staging-post for British activities in the Mediterranean and a supply and repair base for naval vessels. Spain has regularly demanded British cession of Gibraltar. From the mid-1960s until the mid-1970s, Spanish authorities kept the land border between Spain and Gibraltar closed; the colony relied on ships and aeroplanes for provisions. The British, Spanish and Gibraltarian governments have since generally maintained cordial relations, though without giving way on the issue of sovereignty. A governor-general represents the British Crown; most administration is the responsibility of the chief minister, an elected House of Assembly and an appointed speaker. Gibraltar is governed under a constitution adopted in 1969, which contains assurances that Gibraltar will remain attached to Britain unless the population freely and expressly decides otherwise.

Recent years have seen great economic development despite the withdrawal of British military bases and closing of dry-docks. The development of offshore financial services, tax havens and tourism has brought renewed prosperity. There are, however, allegations of smuggling off the Gibraltar coast. The population of Gibraltar is of mixed British and southern European descent, and there are a significant number of North Africans. Thousands of Spaniards commute to Gibraltar for work. Holders of a Gibraltarian British dependent territory passport are the only residents of Britain's overseas territories (other than Falkland Islanders) with unrestricted right of abode in the United Kingdom.

Dennis, Philip. *Gibraltar and its People* (Newton Abbot, 1990).
Levie, Howard S. *The Status of Gibraltar* (Boulder, Colorado, 1983).
Morris, D. S., and Haigh, R. H. *Britain, Spain and Gibraltar, 1945–90: The Eternal Triangle* (London, 1992).

Isle of Man
Area: 572 sq. km.   Population: 69,788 (1991).   Chief centre: Douglas.

The Isle of Man lies in the Irish Sea between England and Ireland. Variously ruled by Welsh, Scandinavian, Scots and English overlords, it was gradually purchased by the British government from 1765 to 1828. It is not, however, part of the United Kingdom but a dependency of the Crown, like the Channel Islands. The monarch appoints a lieutenant-governor, and the British government takes charge of the island's external affairs and defence. Acts of the British parliament do not automatically apply in the Isle of Man, which has its own parliament, the Tynwald, composed of an appointed Legislative Council and an elected House of Keys. There is an independent judiciary and legal system, although laws are similar to those of Britain. The island is a tax haven; several hundred finance and insurance companies are nominally domiciled there or maintain offices. The only other significant economic activity is tourism. The Manx have the right of abode in Britain.

Kermode, D. G. *Devolution at Work: A Case Study of the Isle of Man* (Farnborough, 1979).

Robinson, Vaughan, and McCarroll, Denny. *The Isle of Man: Celebrating a Sense of Place* (Liverpool, 1990).

Solly, M. *Government and Law in the Isle of Man* (London, 1994).

Montserrat

Area: 102 sq. km.   Population: 10,639 (1992 estimate).   Chief centre: Plymouth.

Montserrat, settled by the Irish in 1632, is a small West Indian island of volcanic origin. Montserrat historically was a plantation colony, but from the mid-1800s, limes and cotton replaced sugar cane as the major exports. The 1960s saw a crisis in the agricultural economy, and from the late 1950s to the early 1970s one-third of the population emigrated, mostly to Britain.

The island has since developed as a tourist and second-home destination. A private school of medicine attracts students primarily from the United States. A number of offshore banks operate, although accusations of corruption in connection with offshore finance arose in the 1980s. Such charges caused the British parliament to adopt a new constitution for Montserrat in 1989; it transferred authority over financial activities from the elected Legislative Assembly and chief minister to the British-appointed governor. Interest in independence in the early 1980s has waned. Montserrat is especially prone to natural disasters. Hurricane Hugo in 1989 destroyed many buildings; British aid financed reconstruction. Since 1995 the eruption of Mt Soufrière has devastated Plymouth, forced the evacuation of half of the population, and caused severe problems that threatened abandonment of the island.

Fergus, Howard A. *Montserrat: History of a Caribbean Colony* (London, 1994).

Fergus, Howard A. *Rule Britannia: Politics in British Montserrat* (Montserrat, 1985).

Philpott, Stuart B. *West Indian Migration: The Montserrat Case* (London, 1973).

Pitcairn Islands

Area: 5 sq. km.   Population: 54 (1995).   Chief centre: Adamstown.

More than 2000 kilometres southeast of Tahiti, the Pitcairn Islands – Henderson, Ducie and Oeno, as well as Pitcairn Island proper, the only inhabited island – form one of the most isolated and smallest areas of human habitation in the world. Settled by Polynesians, Pitcairn was discovered by Europeans in 1767. In 1799, seven survivors of the mutiny on the *Bounty*, accompanied by a handful of Tahitians, took refuge there. In 1838 Pitcairn officially became a British colony. The island has its own system of law, dating from the 1820s, and elects a magistrate; the Crown is represented by a British governor, a post held by London's high commissioner in New Zealand. The inhabitants are of mixed European and Polynesian ancestry and speak a Tahitian-influenced English. The main revenue comes from government transfers, the sale of postage stamps and small-scale agricultural and artisanal activities. Since the islands do not have an airstrip, provisions (and a few visitors) arrive only episodically by ship. Pitcairn is Britain's only remaining sovereign outpost in the Pacific Ocean.

Birkett, Dea. *Serpent in Paradise* (London, 1997).
Christian, Glyn. *Fragile Paradise* (London, 1982).

St Helena and Dependencies
Area: St Helena 122 sq. km; Ascension, 88 sq. km; Tristan da Cunha, 98 sq. km.   Population: St Helena, 5,700 (1992); Ascension, 900 (1996 estimate); Tristan da Cunha, 300 (1993).   Chief centre: Jamestown.

Lying in the southeastern Atlantic, discovered by the Portuguese in 1502, annexed by the Netherlands in 1633, and later ceded to Britain, St Helena gained fame as the island to which Napoleon was exiled in 1815 and where he died in 1821. Ships regularly called at the island on the voyage from Europe to the Indian Ocean and the Orient, but the opening of the Suez Canal allowed most vessels to bypass it. The only appreciable economic activity of the rugged volcanic island was then the production of hemp, sold to the Royal Navy for making ropes; the industry ended when the Royal Navy switched to synthetic rope in the 1960s. St Helena has since lived on small-scale agricultural and artisanal activities, some trade with Britain and South Africa, and subsidies and public welfare payments from Britain. Much of the population, largely of mixed European and African ancestry, remains relatively poor. There have been attempts to develop tourism, but there is no airport, the journey by sea is time-consuming and costly, and ships seldom head to St Helena. There is a British governor, and a Legislative Council of elected members and ex-officio members.

Two small islands are dependencies of the Crown colony of St Helena. **Ascension Island** is an arid, volcanic island 1130 kilometres northwest of St Helena. It was uninhabited until the arrival of Napoleon in St Helena in 1815, when a small British naval garrison was stationed on the island. For more than a century the island was referred to as HMS *Ascension*. The major activity is telecommunications. Access to the island is discouraged. Formally annexed by Britain in 1922, Ascension is governed by a British Administrator in the major settlement, Georgetown. **Tristan da Cunha** was also discovered by the Portuguese, and officially annexed by Britain in 1938. Historically it was a sealing station. The entire population was evacuated to Britain in 1961 after a major volcanic eruption, but returned to the island two years later. It is the most remote populated island in the world. The economy is linked to a fishing company. A British Administrator lives on the island, and since 1969 has been advised by an elected Island Council. Nightingale and Gough Islands, which are inaccessible and uninhabited, lie off Tristan da Cunha.

Bishop of St Helena's Commission on Citizenship. *St Helena: The Lost County of England* (St Helena, 1996).
Castell, Robin. *St Helena, Island Fortress* (Uxbridge, 1977).
Cross, Tony. *St Helena, including Ascension Island and Tristan da Cunha* (London, 1980).

South Georgia and South Sandwich Islands
Area: South Georgia: 3592 sq. km; South Sandwich Islands: 311 sq. km. Population: no permanent population.

South Georgia lies 1300 kilometres east of the Falklands, and the South Sandwich Islands are 350 kilometres further east. Britain annexed the islands in 1775, and they were administered as part of the Falkland Islands dependency until 1985. They now form a separate dependency, although the governor of the Falkland Islands is, ex officio, commissioner for the islands. A group of Argentinians (claiming to be scientists) occupied the South Sandwich Islands from 1976 to 1982, and the Argentine invasion of South Georgia in 1982 touched off a war between Britain and Argentina.

Headland, Robert. *The Island of South Georgia* (Cambridge, 1985).
Venables, Stephen. *Island at the Edge of the World: A South Georgia Odyssey* (London, 1991).

Turks and Caicos Islands
Area: 430 sq. km.   Population: 12,350 (1990).   Chief centre: Grand Turk.

The Turks and Caicos consists of over thirty small islands, eight of them inhabited, southeast of the Bahamas. The islands were administratively linked to the Bahamas in 1765, transferred to Jamaica in 1848, and became a separate British dependency in 1962. They gained internal self-government in 1976. There is a governor, and a Legislative Council of thirteen elected and three ex-officio members; a chief minister heads the government. From the mid- to late 1980s, financial scandals in the Turks and Caicos involved charges of financial impropriety, drug-smuggling, arson, and administrative malpractice by government officials; the constitution was temporarily suspended. Prior to that there was significant interest in independence. Fishing is an important activity, and lobster and conch the main exports. Tourism and second homes now constitute the most important economic activity, and the finance sector has revived.

Connell, John. 'The Turks and Caicos Islands: Beyond the Quest for Independence'. *Caribbean Geography*, 3 (1991), pp. 33-42.

United States

American Samoa
Area: 195 sq. km.   Population: 53,000 (1993 estimate).   Chief centre: Pago Pago, Tutuila Island.

In 1899 the United States acquired title to the five principal islands and two atolls of eastern Samoa which subsequently became American Samoa. The colony was administered by the Department of the Navy until 1951, then passed under the authority of the Department of the Interior. American Samoa is now officially an 'unincorporated territory' of the United States. A bicameral legislature (*Fono*) was established in 1948; the members of the Senate are chosen by county councils following traditional Samoan procedures, while twenty members of the House of Representatives are elected by popular ballot. A governor, formerly appointed by American authorities, has been elected since 1978. A delegate with restricted voting powers is elected to the lower house of the US Congress, but Samoans do not vote in US presidential elections. Samoans are nationals of the United States, to which they have free entry, and can become US citizens with little difficulty; the majority of American Samoans live in the United States. Many residents of America Samoa are migrants from other nearby Polynesian states. The main commercial activity is the canning of tuna, and fish products represent the major export, but most American Samoans are employed by the government. American Samoa is a duty-free port, and businesses enjoy various tax incentives.

Gray, J. A. C. *Amerika Samoa* (Annapolis, 1960).
Holmes, Lowell Don. *Samoan Village* (New York, 1974).
Michal, Edward J. 'American Samoa or Eastern Samoa? The Potential for American Samoa to Become Freely Associated with the United States'. *The Contemporary Pacific*, 4 (1992), pp. 137–160.

Guam
Area: 549 sq. km.   Population: 152,695 (1995).   Chief centre: Agaña.

Spanish missionaries and soldiers first arrived on Guam, located in northwestern Oceania, in 1699, and the island remained in Spanish hands until it was lost to the United States in the Spanish–American War of 1898. Since 1950 Guamanians have been citizens of the United States, and the island is an 'unincorporated' US territory. There is a governor (popularly elected since 1970) and a unicameral elected legislature. The territory has a delegate in the US House of Representatives, although he cannot vote in plenary sessions. Almost half of Guamanians trace their ancestry to the indigenous Chamorro population, and Chamorro (along with English) remains an official language; one-fifth of the population are of Filipino origin. The main source of revenue is government expenditure, largely connected with military installations. Military bases, primarily operated by the US Navy, cover over one-third of the area of Guam, and US military personnel and their dependants number over 23,000 inhabitants. The second most important economic activity is tourism, largely drawing on visitors from Japan.

Rogers, Robert F. *Destiny's Landfall: A History of Guam* (Honolulu, 1995). Souder-Jaffery, Laura, and Underwood, Robert A. (eds). *Chamorro Self-Determination* (Mangilao, Guam, 1987).

Johnston Atoll
Area: 2.6 sq. km.   Population: no permanent population.

Johnston Atoll, 1130 kilometres southwest of Hawaii, was acquired by the United States in 1856. It served as a submarine base during the Second World War and then was used for atmospheric nuclear testing in the 1950s and 1960s. The government announced plans in 1983 to construct a facility for the disposal of chemical weapons on Johnston Atoll. Six years later, it moved 400,000 artillery shells containing deadly nerve gas to the atoll. The announcement of the stock-piling of nerve gas provoked loud protests from environmental groups and the South Pacfic Forum. The US government said in response that it would destroy the weapons by 1995. Meanwhile, a major hurricane forced the evacuation of over 1000 military personnel and civilians and created widespread damage to the island in 1994. The atoll is closed to the public.

The US government has proposed incorporating **Wake Island**, an atoll of 8 square kilometres and a population of 2000 (1988), located 2060 kilometres east of Guam, into that territory. However, the Republic of the Marshall Islands has claimed Wake Island (Enenkio) on the basis of traditional Micronesian links. It is currently administered by the Department of the Air Force, which operates a military air base there.

The United States claims several other small and isolated islands in the Pacific; they are not formally attached to any other US territory. **Baker and Howland Islands** are uninhabited atolls, now wildlife refuges, 2575 kilometres west of Hawaii. **Jarvis Island** lies 2090 kilometres south of Hawaii and is also an uninhabited wildlife refuge. Both are administered by the US Fish and Wildlife Service. Three low-lying coral island groups without permanent populations are administered by the Department of the Navy. **Klingman Reef**, 1500 kilometres southwest of Hawaii, and **Midway Island**, 1850 kilometres northwest of Hawaii, are naval defence areas. **Palmyra** comprises a chain of islets lying 1600 kilometres south of Hawaii.

Northern Mariana Islands
Area: 464 sq. km.   Population: 59,000 (1994 estimate).   Chief centre: Saipan.

The Northern Marianas is an archipelago of sixteen islands (of which Saipan is the most important) in the northwestern Pacific. The islands were a Spanish possession from 1565 until 1899, when they were sold to Germany. At the end of the First World War, Japan took over the islands and administered them until 1944. Then, under a United Nations trusteeship, they passed under US control. In 1975 three-quarters of the islands' population voted to become a commonwealth of the United States. Three years later, an elected bicameral legislature was set up; the island also elects a governor. The United Nations trusteeship officially ended in 1986. US government transfers play a significant role in economic life. Also important are tourism (with most tourists coming from Japan) and a protected manufacturing sector (that mainly employs migrants from Asia), which have resulted in recent rapid population growth.

McPhetres, Agnes. 'Northern Mariana Islands: US Commonwealth', in
    R. Crocombe and A. Ali (eds), *Politics in Micronesia* (Suva, 1983),
    pp. 146–160.

Puerto Rico
Area: 8959 sq. km.   Population: 3,685,000 (1994 estimate).   Chief centre: San Juan.

Christopher Columbus first visited Puerto Rico, then inhabited by Taino Indians, in 1493, and Spaniards settled the Caribbean island in 1508. It remained a Spanish plantation and trading colony until 1898, when it became a US territory. Puerto Rico was made a commonwealth of the United States in 1952 and is administered by an elected governor and legislature. Puerto Ricans also elect a representative to the House of Representatives in Washington (who, however, has a limited vote). In the late 1940s, the US government launched a programme of economic development for Puerto Rico, which suffered from widespread poverty, stagnant agriculture and lack of industrialisation. 'Operation Bootstrap' provided various tax and employment incentives for American companies to establish factories, and Puerto Rico industrialised rapidly. Pharmaceuticals, textiles and other manufactured products became major exports. Tourism also developed, and there is some commercial agriculture. US military expenditure, especially on the offshore island of Vieques (most of which is a military base), is substantial. Puerto Rico nevertheless has remained one of the poorest regions of the United States, a fact contributing to massive migration of islanders to the mainland (especially New York and Florida). American authorities were ambivalent about integration of Puerto Rico into the United States as a fully-fledged state, although a pro-statehood political party had strong advocates in Puerto Rico. The pro-independence movement attracted a number of intellectuals and other supporters, and extremists occasionally engaged in violence. In a 1994 referendum the pro-independence party gained 5 per cent of the vote; an option for retention of commonwealth status outpolled a statehood option.

Carr, Raymond. *Puerto Rico: A Colonial Experiment* (New York, 1984).

Dietz, James L. *Economic History of Puerto Rico: Institutional Change and Capitalist Development* (Princeton, 1986).

Falk, Pamela S. (ed.). *The Political Status of Puerto Rico* (Lexington, Massachusetts, 1986).

Fernandez, Ronald. *The Disenchanted Island: Puerto Rico and the United States in the Twentieth Century* (New York, 1992).

Meléndez, Edwin, and Meléndez, Edgardo. *Colonial Dilemma: Critical Perspectives on Contemporary Puerto Rico* (Boston, 1993).

Peruse, Roland I. *The United States and Puerto Rico: Decolonization Options and Prospects* (Lanham, Maryland, 1987).

United States Virgin Islands
Area: 347 sq. km. Population: 101,809 (1990). Chief centre: Charlotte Amalie, St Thomas Island.

The islands which now form the unincorporated territory of the Virgin Islands of the United States (USVI) were historically controlled by the Spanish, British, French and Dutch before Denmark took over St Thomas and St John in 1670 and purchased the third major island, St Croix, from the French in 1733. The islands remained a Danish possession, a plantation colony largely peopled by descendants of

Africans, until 1917, when they were sold to the United States. The US Congress passed an Organic Act for the islands in 1954 which created an elected Senate; since 1970 the governor has also been elected by the population. The 1980s saw much discussion about the future status of the island, and a referendum on the issue scheduled for 1989 was postponed because of Hurricane Hugo. When the referendum was held in 1993, 80 per cent of votes were in favour of retaining the islands' current status, 14 per cent opted for full integration into the United States, and 5 per cent preferred independence. Virgin Islanders are US citizens with right of abode on the the mainland (where a significant number have migrated), but they do not vote in US presidential elections and their delegate to Congress does not have full voting rights. The 'unincorporated' status provides tax privileges, and the USVI is a free port. Tourism is the major economic activity.

Bough, James A., and Macridis, Roy C. (eds). *Virgin Islands: America's Caribbean Outpost* (Wakefield, Massachusetts, 1970).
Leary, Paul M. *United States Virgin Islands: Major Political Documents, 1671–1991* (Charlotte Amalie, 1992).

Notes

1 The Legacy of Empire

1   David Wainhouse, *Remnants of Empire: The United Nations and the End of Colonialism* (New York, 1964), p. 1.
2   The decolonisation of Namibia was similarly described in a book entitled *Namibia: The Last Colony*, by R. Green, M. Kiljunen and K. Kiljunen (eds) (Harlow, 1981), though, in the text, this is qualified as 'the last major colony'.
3   H. A. Turner, *The Last Colony: But Whose?* (Cambridge, 1980), p. ix. A 1995 article on Hong Kong was entitled 'The Last Vestige of British Colonialism' (*Sydney Morning Herald*, 11 July 1995). Immediately prior to reintegration, China banned descriptions of Hong Kong as a British colony, demanding that it be described as a place where the British 'carried out colonial rule', reflecting Beijing's view that sovereignty over the territory was never lost, but what had been lost was the power of administration.
4   Barrie Macdonald, *Cinderellas of the Empire* (Canberra, 1982).
5   F. Elliott and M. Summerskill, *A Dictionary of Politics* (Harmondsworth, 1957), p. 67.
6   Robert Aldrich and John Connell, *France's Overseas Frontier: Départements et Territoires d'Outre-Mer* (Cambridge, 1992); Jean-Claude Guillebaud, *Les Confettis de l'empire* (Paris, 1976).
7   George Drower, *Britain's Dependent Territories: A Fistful of Islands* (Aldershot, 1992), and Simon Winchester, *Outposts* (London, 1985). Britain refers to the overseas territories as 'dependent territories', nomenclature intended to suggest a less one-directional relationship than 'colony'.
8   In the case of the United States, 'At least until recent times, the collective consciousness of most Americans, influenced by textbook accounts of their own war of independence, held that their nation had only fought in defence of freedom and democracy. Colonialism is an evil committed by others, and the notion that America also has a colonial record is met with strong denial.' This denial, a myth 'ingrained in the psyche of the American people', has proved of considerable significance for understanding America's approach to decolonisation: R. Kiste, 'United States', in K. Howe, R. Kiste and B. Lal (eds), *Tides of History* (London, 1994), pp. 228–229; see also Martin Glassner, *Political Geography* (New York, 1996), p. 255.

9   Also excluded are enclaves under foreign military rule, such as the US military base at Guantánamo in Cuba and the British bases in Cyprus.

10 The French overseas *départements*, Guadeloupe, Martinique, Guyane and Réunion, are only constitutionally distinct to a limited extent (see Aldrich and Connell, *France's Overseas Frontier*), though the existence of a Ministry of the DOM-TOMs has effectively emphasised this separate status.

11 Also excluded are such unusual entities as Kaliningrad, separated from Russia by Lithuania, and other similar but much tinier outliers, like Pantelleria (Italy) and Bornholm (Denmark). See G. W. S. Robinson, 'Exclaves', *Annals of the Association of American Geographers*, 49 (1959), pp. 283–295; and Honoré M. Catudal, *The Enclave Problem in Europe* (Birmingham, Alabama, 1979).

12 In the post-war years both the Ukraine and Byelorussia were members of the United Nations, though within the Soviet Union, they had minimal political independence. Conversely, some small states, such as San Marino and Nauru, have chosen to remain outside the United Nations.

13 J. Crawford, *The Creation of States in International Law* (Oxford, 1979), pp. 133–139. There is no criterion for statehood that relates to population size.

14 This too may seemingly be arbitrary. Such entities as the Republic of China (Taiwan) and the Turkish Republic of Northern Cyprus are not widely recognised, whereas the Sovereign Military Order of Malta (the Knights of Malta), which occupies just three acres in Rome, issues its own coinage and is recognised as a sovereign entity by forty countries. See Peter Freedman, 'What Makes Countries Count?', *Geographical Magazine*, 63 (March 1993), pp. 10–13.

15 The implementation of the first stage of the peace agreement between Israel and the Palestine Liberation Organisation generated a movement towards the creation of an independent Palestinian state in Gaza and the West Bank; the implications of this for decolonisation are discussed elsewhere. See Ghazi Falah and David Newman, 'State Formation and the Geography of Palestinian Self-Determination', *Tijdschrift voor Economische en Sociale Geografie*, 87 (1996), pp. 60–72.

16 Crawford, *The Creation of States*, p. 360.

17 *Ibid.*, p. 367. The United Nations provides for integration 'on the basis of complete equality' with an independent state as a method of self-government. Crawford (p. 370) states that this has occurred with UN approval in the cases of Greenland (1953), Surinam (1954), the Netherlands Antilles (1954), Alaska and Hawaii (1959), and without express UN approval in the cases of French Polynesia, New Caledonia, Guyane and Réunion (1947). Elsewhere Crawford regards Réunion's relationship with France and that of the Cocos (Keeling) Islands with Australia as examples of 'wholesale integration': J. Crawford, 'Islands and Sovereign Nations', in R. Chapman (ed.), *Islands '88* (Hobart, 1988), p. 4.

18 This arbitrariness is greatest for a small number of entities for which classification proved particularly difficult. Thus East Timor has been excluded, though the United Nations continues to recognise Portugal as the administering authority, on the grounds that Indonesia has become the de facto government. Alaska and Hawaii were considered to be fully integrated into the United States, although they obviously differ from the US mainland in various ways: their geographical separation; their link to the United States by purchase and thus recent occupation and conquest,

respectively; and their distinctive indigenous populations. It would be appropriate to include, for Norway, the sub-Antarctic territories and Jan Mayen; because neither has a significant population, they are reluctantly excluded from this study. The Åland Islands, something of a case study in international law (see Crawford, *The Creation of States*), are here regarded as part of Finland, whereas the Azores, Madeira and the Canary Islands, the latter two relatively close to the Moroccan coast, are all included here as territories. Clearly, any definition which demands an exceptionally rigorous examination of a host of criteria is akin to estimating the number of angels that might balance on a pin-head or measuring the length of a piece of string; in a book that seeks to examine some broad social, economic and political issues that link dependent territories, this is inappropriate for the continuum is complex.

19   In the 1996 Olympic Games, Bermuda, the Netherlands Antilles, Aruba, American Samoa, the Cayman Islands, Cook Islands, Guam, the British Virgin Islands, the United States Virgin Islands, Puerto Rico (and also Hong Kong) all sent teams.

20   Two such examples are United States Department of State, 'Status of the World's Nations', special issue of *Geographic Notes*, 2 (1992), pp. 16–21; and Glassner, *Political Geography*, p. 273. Neither of these includes the Azores, Canary Islands, Madeira, Ceuta or Melilla; otherwise they are similar to the classification used here.

21   Maria Mies, *Women: The Last Colony* (London, 1988).

22   Frantz Fanon, *The Wretched of the Earth* (London, 1965), p. 48.

23   Green *et al.*, *Namibia*, p. 2.

24   Macdonald, *Cinderellas of the Empire*.

25   Bruce Knapman, 'Capitalism's Economic Impact in Colonial Fiji, 1874–1939: Development or Underdevelopment?', *Journal of Pacific History*, 20 (1985), p. 83.

26   Grant Simpson, 'Wallerstein's World Systems Theory and the Cook Islands: A Critical Examination', *Pacific Studies*, 14 (1990), pp. 73–94.

27   Linda Latham, *La Révolte de 1878* (Noumea, 1978); and R. Dousset-Leenhardt, *Colonialisme et contradictions: Nouvelle-Calédonie 1878–1978. Les causes de l'insurrection de 1878* (Paris, 1978).

28   D. Strang, 'Global Patterns of Decolonisation, 1500–1987', *International Studies Quarterly*, 35 (1991), pp. 429–454.

29   See, for example, Victor Prescott, 'The Spratly Islands', *Quadrant*, 39 (October 1995), pp. 58–63.

30   Francis Fukuyama's *The End of History and the Last Man* (New York, 1992) initiated much discussion of this.

31   General views of 'colonialism' and 'decolonisation' are somewhat narrow in that decolonisation, seemingly, has not ended, and probably never will. The demands of people in Chechnya, Abkhazia, Nagorno-Karabakh and other enclaves of Eastern Europe, alongside such regions as Aceh (Indonesia) or Kurdistan, where disputes have been longstanding, have not only created flashpoints in contemporary international political developments but suggested that any national, ethnic or territorial group which feels aggrieved may adopt the tactic of attacking the 'colonial' rule of an overlord and demanding, sometimes with weapons in hand, self-rule, autonomy or outright independence.

32   *Sydney Morning Herald*, 16 November 1996, 25 August 1997.

2 Constitutional Issues

1   These options are discussed by Paul Leary in two unpublished papers, 'The Virgin Islands of the United States and the Principle of Self-Determination' (Regional Seminar of the United Nations Special Committee on Decolonisation, Bridgetown, Barbados, June 1991), and 'The Political Status of the United States Virgin Islands' (University of Sint-Maarten, Philipsburg, February 1992).

2   See Marilyn F. Krigger, 'The Implications of the 1993 Status Plebiscite in the United States Virgin Islands', unpublished paper to the conference 'Looking to the Future: Relations between the United States and American Samoa, Guam, the Northern Marianas, Puerto Rico and the United States Virgin Islands' (Washington, 1994).

3   Thus, for instance, the electorate of metropolitan France (and France's other overseas outposts) was asked to approve a new plan for New Caledonia in 1988 but did not vote in an independence referendum in 1986.

4   For example, most jurists agree that the granting of self-government to the Canadian federation in 1867 or the union of the Australian colonies into a commonwealth in 1901 did not constitute 'independence'. The 'Balfour definition' of 1926, confirmed by the Westminster Conference of 1931, in which London recognised the (British) Commonwealth of Nations as a community of independent and equal partners, are more plausible dates of independence. See James Crawford, *The Creation of States in International Law* (Oxford, 1979).

5   As for representation in the overseas territories by national governments, only Washington does not appoint an official who singly exercises all the powers of the national government in external territories. The other metropoles are represented by officials bearing the title of governor, or lieutenant-governor, high commissioner, prefect, administrator, government delegate, or minister of the republic.

6   Albert P. Blaustein and Phyllis M. Blaustein (eds), *Constitutions of Dependencies and Special Sovereignties*, 8 vols (Dobbs Ferry, New York, 1975–), is an indispensable and regularly updated compendium.

7   Bishop of St Helena's Commission on Citizenship, *St Helena: The Lost County of England* (St Helena, 1996); see also Harry Ritchie, *The Last Pink Bits* (London, 1997), pp. 229–230. After the volcanic eruptions in Montserrat in 1995, the British government allowed Montserratians residency and the right to work in Britain for up to two years.

8   Clipperton Island in the eastern Pacific is the administrative responsibility of the high commissioner of French Polynesia. The Iles Eparses in the Indian Ocean are administered by the prefect of Réunion. Neither, however, is technically part of those territories. Mururoa and Fangataufa atolls were ceded by French Polynesia to the French metropolitan government for nuclear testing purposes and are under the control of military authorities.

9   See Robert Aldrich and John Connell, *France's Overseas Frontier: Départements et Territoires d'Outre-Mer* (Cambridge, 1992), chapter 3 for a detailed discussion.

10   *Ibid.*

11   The Pacific TOMs also use a separate currency, the CFP (Cours du Franc du Pacifique) franc, although it is automatically convertible to French francs at a fixed rate.

12   See Robert Aldrich, *France and the South Pacific Since 1940* (London, 1993), especially chapters 5 and 8, for further discussion of the TOMs.

13   Aldrich and Connell, *France's Overseas Frontier.*

14   John Connell, 'New Caledonia: The Matignon Accord and the Colonial Future', Research Institute for Asia and the Pacific, University of Sydney, Occasional Paper no. 5 (1988).

15   Robert Aldrich, 'France in the Indian Ocean: Declining Independence in Mayotte', in Robert Aldrich and Isabelle Merle (eds), *France Abroad* (Sydney, 1997), pp. 99–168; A. L. Sanguin, 'Saint-Pierre et Miquelon, département français d'Amérique du Nord', *Norois*, 28 (1981), pp. 133–234.

16   George Drower, *Britain's Dependent Territories* (Aldershot, 1992), pp. 20–26. For a more detailed study of constitutional and administrative issues in Bermuda and Britain's Caribbean outposts, see Elizabeth W. Davies, *The Legal Status of British Dependent Territories: The West Indies and North Atlantic Region* (Cambridge, 1995).

17   Quoted in Davies, *Legal Status of British Dependent Territories*, p. 4.

18   *The Europa World Year Book 1996*, vol. II (London, 1996).

19   Not only Jersey and Guernsey, but the three smaller islands of Alderney, Sark and Herm have separate constitutional arrangements. Jersey and Guernsey each have a lieutenant-governor and commander-in-chief, who represents the sovereign. The senior appointed local official is a bailiff. The Assembly of the States of the Bailiwick of Jersey consists of twelve senators, twelve constables and twenty-nine deputies, all of whom are elected, though for different terms of office; the Church of England Dean of Jersey, as well as the attorney-general and the solicitor-general, may address the Assembly of the States and attend its sessions but have no voting rights. The States of Deliberation include a bailiff, twelve popularly elected conseillers, the procureur (attorney-general) and comptroller (solicitor-general) (although the latter two cannot vote in the assembly), thirty-three People's Deputies chosen by popular election, ten Douzaine Representatives elected by parishes, and two representatives of the island of Alderney. There is also a States of Election, composed of the bailiff, twelve jurats, twelve conseillers, ten parish rectors, the procureur and comptroller, thirty-three People's Deputies and thirty-four Douzaine Representatives; it elects the jurats and conseillers. In Alderney (part of the Bailiwick of Guernsey), there is an elected States of Alderney, the chief officer of which is a president. The senior officials of Sark, another dependency of Jersey, are a hereditary Seigneur of Sark, a seneschal and greffier. Bermuda's Green Paper on *The Implications of Independence for Bermuda* (Bermuda, 1995) briefly reviewed the constitutional situation of the Isle of Man and the Channel Islands: 'That system, as we have said, is unique and not capable of description by any of the usual categories of political science. It is full of anomalies, peculiarities and anachronisms which even those who work the system find hard to define precisely' (p. 16).

20   For instance, in the British Virgin Islands, 'civil aviation' is part of the portfolio of a local government minister, but issues concerning international aviation – and almost all aviation issues fall into this category, given the Virgin Islands' geography – come under the purview of the governor: Davies, *Legal Status of British Dependent Territories*, p. 182.

21   *Ibid.*, p. 338.

22   *Ibid.*, pp. 175, 37.

23   By 1997 the combination of neglect, isolation and autonomy posed
      problems: firearms laws were regularly broken, and a series of other crimes
      resulted in a British government decision to post a police officer there, for
      six to eight weeks a year, the first ever external administration official of any
      kind: *Independent on Sunday*, 1 June 1997.
24   West Indies and Atlantic; South Atlantic and Antarctica: Hong Kong;
      Southern Europe; East Africa; South Pacific.
25   The United States shows other variants of incorporation and affiliation.
      Alaska and Hawaii were 'territories' before they became states in 1960. The
      Federated States of Micronesia, the Republic of the Marshall Islands and
      the Republic of Palau, formerly a part of the US-administered UN Trust
      Territory of the Pacific Islands, are sovereign and independent nations
      bound to the United States by treaties of 'free association' through which
      the United States has taken over responsibility for their defence and
      security. All are members of the United Nations. Washington allows free
      access to the United States for citizens of these countries, grants them large
      amounts of aid and permits their exports to enter the United States duty-
      free. In return, the United States gains use of port and land facilities for its
      navy. See Roy H. Smith and Michael C. Pugh, 'Micronesian Trust Terri-
      tories: Imperialism Continues?', *Pacific Review*, 4 (1991), pp. 36–44; Ellen
      Bonepath and M. James Wilkinson, 'Terminating Trusteeship for the
      Federated States of Micronesia and the Republic of the Marshall Islands:
      Independence and Self-Sufficiency in the Post-Cold War World', *Pacific
      Studies*, 18 (1995), pp. 61–77; and Donald R. Shuster, 'Palau's Compact:
      Controversy, Conflict and Compromise', *ISLA*, 2 (1994), pp. 207–236.
      Several tiny Pacific Ocean atolls – including Johnston and Midway – are
      directly administered by the US Navy or the Department of the Interior;
      without a permanent population, they are used for military and meteoro-
      logical purposes.
26   The authoritative work on legal issues is Arnold H. Leibowitz, *Defining
      Status: A Comprehensive Analysis of United States Territorial Relations*
      (Dordrecht, 1989). See also various papers in George Boughton and Paul
      Leary (eds), *A Time of Change: Relations Between the United States and American
      Samoa, Guam, the Northern Marianas, Puerto Rico and the United States Virgin
      Islands* (n.p., 1994).
27   Quoted in Raymond Carr, *Puerto Rico: A Colonial Experiment* (New York,
      1984).
28   See Ronald Fernandez, *The Disenchanted Island: Puerto Rico and the United
      States in the Twentieth Century* (New York, 1992).
29   For an overview, see James A. Bough and Roy C. Macridis (eds), *Virgin
      Islands, America's Caribbean Outpost: The Evolution of Self Government*
      (Wakefield, Mass., 1970).
30   Edward J. Michal, 'American Samoa or Eastern Samoa? The Potential for
      American Samoa to Become Freely Associated with the United States', *The
      Contemporary Pacific*, 4 (1992), pp. 139–41.
31   Anne Perez Hattori, 'Righting Civil Wrongs: The Guam Congress Walkout
      of 1949', *ISLA*, 3 (1995), pp. 1–27.
32   Joseph F. Ada, 'Time for Change', *ISLA*, 3 (1995), pp. 129–137. See also in
      the same issue, Wilfred P. Leon Guerrero and John C. Salas, 'Issues for the
      United States Pacific Insular Areas: The Case of Guam', pp. 139–145.
      Similarly Guam's senator, Robert Underwood, has concluded: 'Guam is a
      colony. The Chamorro people have been victimised. We, as a unique island

society, continue to suffer from the excesses of the past and the cavalier treatment of our grievances in the present': R. A. Underwood, 'The State of Guam's Agenda in Washington', *ISLA*, 4 (1996), p. 129. At the UN Fourth World Conference on Women in 1995 the lieutenant-governor of Guam expressed her support for full autonomy and the Chamorro people's desire for decolonisation.

33 In a referendum on the constitution in 1996, some nineteen questions were raised but all were so complex that they were rejected, leaving in place the original constitution, last amended in 1986: Samuel McPhetres, 'Common-wealth of the Northern Mariana Islands', *The Contemporary Pacific*, 9 (1997), pp. 198–202.

34 Nevertheless, there have been increased tensions between the US government and the Northern Marianas on questions concerning tax rebates, labour conditions, immigration, land sales and minimum wages. See the chronicles in *The Contemporary Pacific*, 7 (1995), p. 130, and chapter 3.

35 The other part of the island of Sint-Maarten is Saint-Martin, constitutionally a commune of the French DOM of Guadeloupe.

36 On constitutional questions, see Willem Koot, Corrie Tempel-Schoorl and Valdemar Marcha, *Apart or Together?* (Utrecht, 1990); and Rosemarijn Hoefte, 'Thrust Together: The Netherlands Relationship with Its Caribbean Partners', *Journal of Interamerican Studies and World Affairs*, 38 (1996), pp. 35–54.

37 On 'arrested decolonisation' in the Netherlands Antilles, see Gert Ooostindie, 'The Dutch Caribbean in the 1990s: Decolonization, Recolonization?', *Caribbean Affairs*, 5 (1992), pp. 103–119, and his 'Ethnicity, Nationalism and the Exodus: The Dutch Caribbean Predicament', in G. Oostindie (ed.), *Ethnicity in the Caribbean* (London, 1996), pp. 206–231; Leo J. De Haan, 'Small Islands in the Caribbean, the Last Remains of the Tropical Netherlands: The Netherlands Antilles and Aruba', *Tijdschrift voor Economische en Sociale Geografie*, 84 (1993), pp. 378–85; and Hoefte, 'Thrust Together'.

38 *Factsheet Denmark: The Faeroe Islands* (Copenhagen, 1983); Home Rule Act of the Faeroe Islands, No. 137 of 23 March 1948.

39 Greenland Home Rule Act, No. 577 of 29 November 1978; *Factsheet Denmark: Greenland* (Copenhagen, 1983). There has been significant discussion – and some criticism – of the Home Rule arrangements. See Isi Foighel, 'A Framework for Local Autonomy: The Greenland Case', in Yoram Dinstein, *Models of Autonomy* (London, 1981), pp. 31–52; Godmundur Alfredsson, 'Greenland and the Law of Political Decolonization', *Jahrbuch für internationales Recht*, 25 (1982), pp. 290–308; Nils Oervik, 'Greenland: The Politics of a New Northern Nation', *International Journal*, 39 (1984), pp. 932–961; Alvin Kienetz, 'Ethnonationalism and Decolonialization in Greenland and Northern Eurasia', *Canadian Review of Studies in Nationalism* 14 (1987), pp. 247–259; Stanley C. Ing, 'Greenland Home Rule and Canada', *International Perspectives*, 22 (January–February 1984), pp. 24–26; and Tom Høyen, 'Greenland: A Country in Transition', *Polar Record*, 24 (1988), pp. 9–14.

40 Gervase Clarence-Smith, *The Third Portuguese Empire, 1825–1975: A Study in Economic Imperialism* (Manchester, 1985). On 'insular' Portugal, see Francis M. Rogers, *Atlantic Islanders of the Azores and Madeiras* (North Quincy, Mass., 1979).

41 Jacqueline M. Ross, 'Portugal', in Blaustein and Blaustein, *Constitutions of Dependencies* (1989).

42 R. Alonso and F. G. Pereira, 'The Constitution and Legal System', in R. D. Cremer (ed.), *Macau: City of Commerce and Culture* (Hong Kong, 1987), pp. 185–198; Lo Shiu Hing, *Political Development in Macau* (Hong Kong, 1995).
43 See chapter 6 for a discussion of the negotiations and agreement.
44 See chapter 6 for a discussion of the conflict over the Spanish enclaves.
45 *Europa World Year Book 1995*, vol. I (London, 1996), pp. 2825–2830; personal communication from Javier Hernandez, First Secretary, Spanish Embassy in Australia, 25 October 1995.
46 *Islands in the Sun: The Legal Regimes of Australia's External Territories and the Jervis Bay Territory*, Report of the House of Representatives Standing Committee on Legal and Constitutional Affairs (Canberra, 1991), and information kindly supplied by the Department of the Arts, Sport, the Environment, Tourism and Territories, Canberra. See also Merval Hoare, *The Winds of Change: Norfolk Island, 1950–1982* (Suva, 1983), chapters 3–4.
47 Stephen Levine, 'Tokelau', *The Contemporary Pacific*, 7 (1995), pp. 159–164; David Barber, 'Tokelau to Stand Alone', *Pacific Islands Monthly*, 66 (August 1996), p. 11. See also Stephen Levine, 'Tokelau', *The Contemporary Pacific*, 8 (1996), pp. 197–202.
48 John Henderson, 'Micro-states and the Politics of Association: The Future of New Zealand's Constitutional Links with the Cook Islands and Tokelau', in W. von Busch *et al.* (eds), *New Politics in the South Pacific* (Suva, 1994), pp. 99–112.
49 Terry M. Chapman, *The Decolonisation of Niue* (Wellington, 1976); Stephen Levine, 'Niue', *The Contemporary Pacific*, 8 (1996), pp. 191–197.
50 Henderson, 'Micro-states and the Politics of Association', p. 103.
51 *Annual Report to the States by the Chief Adviser* (St Helier, 1992), p. 24.

3 The Economic Transition

1 John Connell, *New Caledonia or Kanaky? The Political History of a French Colony* (Canberra, 1987), pp. 36–37.
2 J. E. Kersell, 'Government Administration in a Small Microstate: Developing the Cayman Islands', *Public Administration and Development*, 7 (1987), pp. 95–107. See also Eric Ayisi, *St Eustatius: The Treasure Island of the Caribbean* (Trenton, 1992), p. 86.
3 See, for example, Stephen Royle, 'Health in Small Island Communities: The UK's South Atlantic Colonies', *Health and Place*, 1 (1995), pp. 257–264.
4 John Connell, *Sovereignty and Survival* (Sydney, 1988), pp. 2–8; Carmelo Leon and Matias Gonzalez, 'Managing the Environment in Tourism Regions: The Case of the Canary Islands', *European Environment*, 5 (1995), p. 173; Kenneth Moore, 'Modernization in a Canary Island Village', in Joseph Aceves and W. Douglas (eds), *The Changing Face of Rural Spain* (New York, 1976), p. 18.
5 M. F. Drucker, 'The Changed World Economy', *Foreign Affairs*, 20 (1986), pp. 781–782.
6 John Connell, 'Wallis and Futuna: Stability and Change at the Ends of Empire', in Robert Aldrich (ed.), *France, Oceania and Australia: Past and Present* (Sydney, 1991), p. 92.
7 Mark Nuttall, 'Sharing and the Ideology of Subsistence in a Greenlandic Sealing Community', *Polar Record*, 27 (1991), pp. 217–222. See also Hanne Sandell and Birger Sandell, 'Kaphope: A Settlement and its Resources', *Arctic Anthropology*, 23 (1986), pp. 281–298, and 'Polar Bear Hunting and

Hunters in Ittoqqortoormiit/Scoresbysund, NE Greenland', *Arctic Anthropology*, 33 (1996), pp. 77–93; and Ole Marquardt and Richard Caulfield, 'Development of West Greenlandic Markets for Country Foods Since the 18th Century', *Arctic*, 49 (1996), pp. 107–119.

8   Robert Kauders, 'A Tristan Year', *Geographical Magazine*, 59 (February, 1987), pp. 68–72.

9   David A. Thomasson, 'Montserrat Kitchen Gardens: Social Functions and Development Potential', *Caribbean Geography*, 5 (1994), pp. 20–31.

10 Wout van den Bor, *Island Adrift: The Social Organization of a Small Caribbean Community: The Case of St Eustatius* (The Hague, 1981), pp. 41–56, 57–58, 65–67.

11 Klaus de Albuquerque and Jerome McElroy, 'Agricultural Resurgence in the United States Virgin Islands', *Caribbean Geography*, 1 (1983), pp. 121–132.

12 Robert Aldrich and John Connell, *France's Overseas Frontier* (Cambridge, 1992), pp. 21–22, 133–137.

13 Kelvin Santiago-Valles, *'Subject People' and Colonial Discourses: Economic Transformation and Social Disorder in Puerto Rico, 1898–1947* (Albany, 1994); James L. Dietz, *Economic History of Puerto Rico: Institutional Change and Capitalist Development* (Princeton, 1986), pp. 24–52; Peter Jackson, 'Migration and Social Change in Puerto Rico', in C. Clarke, D. Ley and C. Peach (eds), *Geography and Ethnic Pluralism* (London, 1984), p. 197.

14 Aldrich and Connell, *France's Overseas Frontier*, pp. 33, 135; Pierre Maurice, 'Structural Characteristics of the Economy of La Réunion', in R. Appleyard and R. Ghosh (eds), *Economic Planning and Performance in Indian Ocean Island States* (Canberra, 1990), p. 79.

15 Stuart Philpott, *West Indian Migration: The Montserrat Case* (London, 1973), pp. 19, 29–32; D. Lowenthal and G. Comitas, 'Emigration and Depopulation: Some Neglected Aspects of Population Geography', *Geographical Review*, 52 (1962), pp. 205–207.

16 Aldrich and Connell, *France's Overseas Frontier*, p. 135.

17 Margaret Ackrill, 'The Cocos (Keeling) Islands', in Appleyard and Ghosh (eds), *Economic Planning and Performance*, pp. 134–5.

18 Connell, 'Wallis and Futuna', p. 93.

19 John Connell, 'The Islands of Micronesia: The Challenges to Economic Development', in *ESCAP, Pacific Island Countries* (New York, 1995), pp. 50–79.

20 Francis M. Rogers, *Atlantic Islanders of the Azores and Madeiras* (North Quincy, Mass., 1979), pp. 239–248.

21 Miguel Sanchez-Padron, 'Interpreting Dependency in the Canary Islands', in Robin Cohen (ed.), *African Islands and Enclaves* (Beverly Hills, 1983), pp. 26–27.

22 Aldrich and Connell, *France's Overseas Frontier*, pp. 135–137.

23 Lord Shackleton, *Falkland Islands Economic Study, 1982* (London, 1982); Stephen Royle, 'Changes in the Falkland Islands since the Conflict of 1982', *Geography*, 79 (1994), pp. 19–24; A. McNaught, 'Farming on the World's Edge', *Geographical Magazine*, 65 (August 1993), pp. 47–51; Stephen Fidler, 'Sheep are Not Paying Their Way', *Financial Times*, 1 April 1997, p. 15.

24 George Drower, *Britain's Dependent Territories* (Aldershot, 1992), p. 65.

25 Foreign policy was then the prerogative of Denmark. The principal country that took advantage of the rich fishing grounds off the Faeroes was the United Kingdom. The most important Danish export to Britain was bacon, hence Denmark was uninterested in any extension of Faeroese territorial

waters. Radicals accused Denmark of selling the Faeroese fishing grounds
for Danish bacon. See Rolf Guttesen, 'How Did the Faeroese Fishing
Industry Cope with the New Conditions Imposed by the 200 km EEZ?',
Ocean and Coastal Management, 18 (1992), pp. 339–340. Subsequently the
Faeroes gained the 200-nautical-mile territorial limit, but did not join the
European Union, as Denmark did, because the common fisheries policy
would effectively destroy the fisheries economy.

26   For more than twenty years there was a fishing dispute between Saint-
Pierre-et-Miquelon, France and Canada over the territorial waters of
Canada and Saint-Pierre. During the dispute fishing boats were im-
pounded, Canadian ports closed to French ships and violence flared. In
1989 an international tribunal awarded France a quarter of the 14,500
square nautical miles it claimed seaward of Saint-Pierre, but gave the
French fleets an exclusive ten-mile-wide corridor running seaward for
200 miles. See Douglas Day, 'The Saint Pierre and Miquelon Dispute:
Towards a Further Redefinition of French Fishing Rights in the Northwest
Atlantic', *Ocean and Coastal Management*, 18 (1992), pp. 371–403. In 1989
and 1990 the situation in Saint-Pierre was complicated further when
French factory ships based at Saint Malo sailed into the area and, after
protests by islanders, were withdrawn by the French government. The 1989
agreement expired in 1992, further disputes ensued, there was a temporary
halt to industrial fishing in a wide area, and Saint-Pierre-et-Miquelon
continued to protest against its eroded marine sovereignty.

27   Stephen Royle, 'Economic and Political Prospects for the British Atlantic
Dependent Territories', *Geographical Journal*, 161 (1995), p. 310.

28   In early 1996 there were disputes between Britain and Argentina concerning fishing off South Georgia in territorial waters that Argentina does not
recognise. Britain arrested fishing boats and Argentina notified Britain of
its intention to seek an international legal settlement: *Sydney Morning
Herald*, 8 May 1996; see chapter six.

29   Mark Nuttall, 'Greenland: Emergence of an Inuit Homeland', in Minority
Rights Group (ed.), *Polar Peoples* (London, 1994), p. 12; G. Poole, 'Fishery
Policy and Economic Development in Greenland in the 1980s', *Polar Record*,
25 (1990), pp. 109–118; Brit Floistad, 'Greenland's International Fisheries
Relations: A Coastal State in the "North" with Problems of the "South"',
Cooperation and Conflict, 24 (1989), pp. 35–48.

30   J. Lewis and A. Williams, 'Regional Autonomy and the European Communities: The View from Portugal's Atlantic Territories', *Regional Politics
and Policy*, 4 (1994), pp. 67–85; Carlos Labajos, Beatriz Rojo and Rafael
Arranz, 'The Canary Islands Fishing Policy', *Marine Policy*, 20 (1996),
pp. 463–474.

31   Aldrich and Connell, *France's Overseas Frontier*, pp. 140–141.

32   David North, 'Seven Strategies for Success', *Pacific Islands Monthly*, 65
(February 1995), pp. 15–17; Eni Faleomavaega, *Navigating the Future:
A Samoan Perspective on US–Pacific Relations* (Honolulu, 1995), pp. 43–44;
Michael P. Hamnett and William Pintz, *The Contribution of Tuna Fishing and
Transhipment to the Economies of American Samoa, the Commonwealth of the
Northern Mariana Islands, and Guam* (Honolulu, 1996).

33   Maurice, 'Structural Characteristics of the Economy of La Réunion', p. 79.

34   Connell, 'Wallis and Futuna', p. 93.

35   See also G. Barrett, 'The Fish Pot Ban: Reef Overfishing and State Management in Bermuda', *Maritime Anthropological Studies*, 4 (1991), pp. 17–39.

36 J.-M. Kohler, *Pour ou contre le pinus: Les Mélanésiens face aux projets de développement* (Noumea, 1984).

37 Aldrich and Connell, *France's Overseas Frontier*, pp. 139–140; Connell, *New Caledonia or Kanaky?*, pp. 124–133; Stephen Henningham, 'Nickel and Politics in New Caledonia', in S. Henningham and R. May (eds), *Resources, Development and Politics in the Pacific Islands* (Canberra, 1992), pp. 64–78.

38 Robert Aldrich, *France and the South Pacific since 1940* (London, 1993), pp. 81–83.

39 Knud Sinding and Graham Poole, 'A Multi-Billion Dollar Gold Deposit in Greenland?', *Polar Record*, 27 (1991), pp. 139–140; Graham Poole, Michael Pretes and Knud Sinding, 'Managing Greenland's Mineral Revenues', *Resources Policy*, 18 (1992), pp. 191–204; Knud Sinding, 'At the Crossroads: Mining Policy in Greenland', *Arctic*, 45 (1992), pp. 226–232.

40 Royle, 'Economic and Political Prospects', p. 317; Stephen Fidler, 'Daunting Prospects of Untamed Riches', *Financial Times*, 1 April 1997, p. 13.

41 Sam Cole, 'Paradise Lost? Rediscovering Tradition in Aruba', *Caribbean Review*, 14 (Summer 1985), pp. 22–23, 43; Jaap van Soest, 'Organizations for Economic Development in the Netherlands Antilles, 1937–1953', *Caribbean Studies*, 19 (1980), pp. 69–86; Leo de Haan, 'Small Islands in the Caribbean, the Last Remains of the Tropical Netherlands: The Netherlands Antilles and Aruba', *Tijdschrift voor Economische en Sociale Geografie*, 84 (1993), pp. 378–385.

42 José Villamil, 'Puerto Rico, 1948–1976: The Limits of Dependent Growth', in José Villamil (ed.), *Transnational Capitalism and National Development* (Atlantic Highlands, 1979), pp. 241–260; Robert Tata, 'The Relationship Between Puerto Rico's Economic Structure and Development', *Singapore Journal of Tropical Geography*, 2 (1981), pp. 129–135; Dietz, *Economic History of Puerto Rico*, pp. 182–310.

43 Norman Long, 'The Puerto Rico Model of Industrialisation: New Dimensions in the 1980s', *Development Policy Review*, 6 (1988), pp. 311–322.

44 Eliezer Curet, *Puerto Rico: Development by Integration to the US* (Rio Piedras, 1986); James Dietz and Emilio Pantojas-Garcia, 'Puerto Rico's New Role in the Caribbean: The High Finance/*Maquiladora* Strategy', in Edwin Meléndez and Edgardo Meléndez (eds), *Colonial Dilemma: Critical Perspectives on Contemporary Puerto Rico* (Boston, 1993), pp. 103–115.

45 Various territories, such as the Spanish and Portuguese territories (other than Macao), the French departments (including Mayotte, Saint-Pierre-et-Miquelon and the Austral and Antarctic Territories) and the US territories, use the same stamps as the metropolitan state, though most have had their own stamps at some time in the past. Aruba, the other Antilles (collectively), Greenland and the Faeroes all have their own stamps, as do Tokelau, Niue and the Cook Islands. In 1969 both the Channel Islands and the Isle of Man gained authority to issue their own stamps and, soon afterwards, the Channel Islands split into three stamp-issuing entities – Guernsey, Jersey and Alderney. All the British territories (except BIOT) have their own stamps. Each of the Australian territories (including the Antarctic Territory) issues its own stamps; all but those of Norfolk Island can also be used within Australia.

46 Malcolm Treadgold, *Bounteous Bestowal: The Economic History of Norfolk Island* (Canberra, 1988).

47 David North, 'The Sovereignty Business', *Pacific Islands Monthly*, 64 (July 1994), pp. 8–15.

48 Stephen Royle, 'The Economics of Dependency in St Helena', in D. Lockhart and D. Drakakis-Smith (eds), *Environmental and Economic Issues in Small Island Development* (London, 1991), p. 68.

49 Van den Bor, *Island Adrift*, p. 361.

50 Richard Prentice, 'Tourism', in V. Robinson and D. McCarroll, *The Isle of Man* (Liverpool, 1990), pp. 248–267.

51 Rogers, *Atlantic Islanders*, pp. 257–258; James J. Parsons, 'The Canary Islands Search for Stability', *Focus*, 35 (1985), pp. 22–29.

52 De Haan, 'Small Islands in the Caribbean', p. 383; John Kersell, 'Small-scale Administration in St Martin: Two Governments of One People', *Public Administration and Development*, 13 (1993), p. 56.

53 John Connell, 'The Cayman Islands: Economic Growth and Immigration in a British Colony', *Caribbean Geography*, 5 (1994), pp. 54–55; David Weaver, 'Grand Cayman Island and the Resort Cycle Concept', *Journal of Travel Research*, 29 (1990), pp. 9–15. Almost all the physical infrastructure of tourism has been concentrated at Seven Mile Beach, north of the capital; by 1990 the government had to set a three-year moratorium on hotel construction there to encourage decentralisation and ease congestion.

54 John Connell, 'Anguilla: The Tourist Trajectory in an Island Microstate', *Caribbean Geography*, 4 (1993), pp. 131–138.

55 Tourism developed more slowly in Curaçao than Aruba, because of inconsistent government policy, the less 'welcoming attitude' of the people, and riots in 1969, when angry oil workers set fire to the centre of Willemstad: de Haan, 'Small Islands in the Caribbean', p. 382; Eddy Baetens, 'Curaçao: Restructuring in the 1980s and 1990s', *Caribbean Geography*, 3 (1991), p. 128. See also Ronnie Pieters and Diana Gevers, 'A Framework for Tourism Development on Fragile Island Destinations: The Case of Bonaire', in M. Conlin and T. Baum (eds), *Island Tourism* (Chichester, 1995), pp. 123–132.

56 André-Louis Sanguin, 'Saint-Barthélemy, île normande des Antilles françaises', *Etudes normandes*, 30 (1981), p. 64; Yves Monnier, *L'Immuable et le Changeant* (Bordeaux, 1983).

57 Victor Teye, 'Land Transportation and Tourism in Bermuda', *Tourism Management*, 13 (1992), pp. 395–405.

58 Brian Archer, 'Importance of Tourism for the Economy of Bermuda', *Annals of Tourism Research*, 22 (1995), pp. 918–930; Michael Conlin, 'Rejuvenation Planning for Island Tourism: The Bermuda Example', in Conlin and Baum (eds), *Island Tourism*, pp. 181–202.

59 Treadgold, *Bounteous Bestowal*, pp. 210–215.

60 Connell, 'The Islands of Micronesia', p. 73.

61 John Connell, ' "Trouble in Paradise": The Perception of New Caledonia in the Australian Press', *Australian Geographical Studies*, 25 (1987), pp. 54–65.

62 Leonard Rayner, 'Macao', *The Round Table*, 303 (1987), pp. 199–206.

63 John Seekings, 'Developing Tourism in a Political Impasse', *Tourism Management*, 14 (1993), pp. 61–67.

64 Manuel Valenzuela, 'Spain: The Phenomenon of Mass Tourism', in A. M. Williams and G. Shaw (eds), *Tourism and Economic Development: Western European Experiences* (London, 1988), pp. 40–60; Leon and Gonzalez, 'Managing the Environment'.

65 J. Lewis and A. Williams, 'Portugal: Market Segmentation and Regional Specialisations', in Williams and Shaw (eds), *Tourism and Economic Development*, pp. 107–129.

66 Lewis and Williams, 'Regional Autonomy and the European Communities', p. 72.

67 Chris Cooper, 'Strategic Planning for Sustainable Tourism: The Case of the Offshore Islands of the UK', *Journal of Sustainable Tourism*, 3 (1995), pp. 193–209.

68 Torben Christensen, 'Greenland Wants Tourism', *Polar Record* (1992), pp. 62–63.

69 Simon Milne, 'Tourism Development in Niue', *Annals of Tourism Research*, 19 (1992), pp. 565–569.

70 David Weaver, 'Alternative Tourism in Montserrat', *Tourism Management*, 16 (1995), pp. 593–604.

71 Royle, 'Economic and Political Prospects', pp. 315–317; see also Stephen Royle, 'Tourism to the South Atlantic Islands', in D. Lockhart and D. Drakakis-Smith (eds), *Island Tourism* (London, 1997), pp. 323–344.

72 Susan Roberts, 'Fictitious Capital, Fictitious Spaces: The Geography of Offshore Financial Flows', in S. Corbridge, R. Martin and N. Thrift (eds), *Money, Power and Space* (Oxford, 1994), p. 92.

73 E. C. Dommen and P. Hein, 'Foreign Trade in Goods and Services', in E. Dommen and P. Hein (eds), *States, Microstates and Islands* (London, 1985), p. 166.

74 Roberts, 'Fictitious Capital, Fictitious Spaces', p. 98.

75 Stephen Royle, 'Off-shore Finance and Tourism as Development Strategies: Bermuda and the British West Indies', in D. Barker, S. Lloyd-Evans and D. McGregor (eds), *Sustainability and Development in the Caribbean* (Mona, 1997). See also Harry Ritchie, *The Last Pink Bits* (London, 1997), p. 44.

76 Dommen and Hein, 'Foreign Trade in Goods and Services', pp. 167–168; Roberts, 'Fictitious Capital, Fictitious Spaces', p. 103; Mina Caulfield, 'Taxes, Tourists and Turtlemen: Island Dependency and the Tax-haven Business', in A. Idris-Soven, E. Idris-Soven and M. Vaughan (eds), *The World as a Company Town: Multinational Corporations and Social Change* (The Hague, 1978), pp. 345–374; Susan Roberts, 'Small Place, Big Money: The Cayman Islands and the International System', *Economic Geography*, 71 (1995), pp. 237–256.

77 *Independent*, 3 June 1997. A number of other territories also have flag-of-convenience registries. See Anthony van Fossen, *The International Political Economy of Pacific Islands Flags of Convenience* (Brisbane, 1992).

78 De Haan, 'Small Islands in the Caribbean', p. 383.

79 David Devoss, 'The Empire Cashes In', *Asia Inc*, 5 (July 1996), p. 30; Jerome L. McElroy and Klaus de Albuquerque, 'The Social and Economic Propensity for Political Dependence in the Insular Caribbean', *Social and Economic Studies*, 44 (1995), p. 174.

80 *Financial Times*, 29 June 1990.

81 Within the Channel Islands, there are organisational and operational distinctions between the islands. Sark and Alderney have separate parliaments and different financial regimes from the two larger islands. In the 1990s Alderney sought to develop a distinct financial centre, independent from Guernsey.

82 Richard Evans, 'Banking on the Black Economy', *Geographical Magazine*, 65 (September, 1993), p. 40; Paul Sutton and Anthony Payne, 'The Off-Limits Caribbean: The United States and the European Dependent Territories', *Annals of the American Academy of Political and Social Science*, 535/538 (1994), pp. 87–95.

83 Ron and Marjorie Crocombe, 'The Cook Islands', *The Contemporary Pacific*, 8 (1996), pp. 174–182.

84 Roberts, 'Fictitious Capital, Fictitious Spaces', p. 106. In 1995 most Asian businesses transferring out of Hong Kong went to the Cayman Islands rather than Bermuda because of concern over possible independence: *South China Morning Post*, 28 May 1995.

85 Devoss, 'The Empire Cashes In', p. 24.

86 Roberts, 'Fictitious Capital, Fictitious Spaces', p. 108. The Cayman Islands governor commented in 1996: 'These islands have a history of profiting from the misguided nationalism of their neighbours' (quoted in Devoss, 'The Empire Cashes In', p. 27). John Grisham's novel *The Firm* (New York, 1991) and the subsequent film, which dealt with illegal money-laundering in the Cayman Islands, were much disliked in the Cayman Islands. However the Cayman Islands has not escaped criticism: see A. P. Maingot, 'Offshore Secrecy Centers and the Necessary Role of States: Bucking the Trend', *Journal of Interamerican Studies and World Affairs*, 37 (1995), pp. 1–24.

87 Lo Shiu Hing, *Political Development in Macau* (Hong Kong, 1995), pp. 171–196, 233–235. At the end of 1996 Portuguese police were struggling to control Chinese gangsters who attempted to assassinate the government official responsible for controlling casinos, in a battle for profits, whilst triads were also engaged in smuggling: *Sunday Times*, 9 February 1997; *Guardian*, 2 May 1997.

88 These include reports of American and Italian Mafia involvement in Sint-Maarten, drug-smuggling from Curaçao and Aruba (see de Haan, 'Small Islands in the Caribbean', p. 380), the use of the Virgin Islands for the transhipment of narcotics from South to North America (*Financial Times*, 29 June 1990), and cigarette-smuggling from Gibraltar to Spain and elsewhere (*Guardian Weekly*, 24 December 1995). Drug-trafficking through the BVI, the Turks and Caicos Islands and Aruba and Sint-Maarten has been well documented (Sutton and Payne, 'The Off-Limits Caribbean'); see chapters 5 and 6.

89 Aldrich and Connell, *France's Overseas Frontier*, pp. 153–155.

90 M. Dodge, 'Military Disaster Relief in Micronesia', in D. Rubinstein and V. L. Dames (eds), *Uncle Sam in Micronesia: Social Benefits, Social Costs* (Guam, 1991), pp. 33–36.

91 Archer, 'Importance of Tourism', p. 921. It was argued, by some, that this significant loss of income stimulated the resurgence of demands for Bermudian independence. After the closure of the base, Bermuda became one of the few places in the world without a McDonald's outlet. In 1997 disputes over an attempt by the former premier, Sir John Swan, to introduce a chain of McDonald's restaurants caused the premier, David Saul, to resign, and led the governor to sign a Prohibited Restaurants Bill, after much debate over its constitutional validity.

92 Gilles Blanchet, 'Quel avenir pour la Polynésie Française?', *Journal de la Société des Océanistes*, 102 (1996), pp. 31–46.

93 John Connell, 'The End Ever Nigh: Contemporary Population Change on Pitcairn Island', *Geo Journal*, 16 (1988), p. 194; Dea Birkett, *Serpent in Paradise* (London, 1997), p. 153.

94 Kauders, 'A Tristan Year', p. 70; Harry Ritchie, *The Last Pink Bits* (London, 1997), p. 211.

95 Van den Bor, *Island Adrift*, pp. 85, 86. Until the expansion of tourism in Saba in the 1970s, almost all employment was with the government and was

rotated to give more people a chance of scarce wage employment. See Julia Crane, *Educated to Emigrate: The Social Organisation of Saba* (Assen, 1971), pp. 101–102.

96 Lise Lyck and Jørgen Taagholt, 'Greenland: Its Economy and Resources', *Arctic*, 40 (1987), p. 57.

97 Connell, 'Wallis and Futuna', p. 95.

98 David Nevin, *The American Touch in Micronesia* (New York, 1977), p. 32.

99 Lo Shiu Hing, *Political Development in Macau*, p. 129.

100 In some places the discrepancies are enormous; in Guam government salaries are generally considerably higher than in the private sector, whilst politicians' salaries were higher than in every US state except one.

101 Ayisi, *St Eustatius*, pp. 40–41.

102 L. C. Brown, *The Land Resources and Agro-Forestal Development of St Helena* (Surbiton, 1991), p. 50; Simon Gillett, 'Developing St Helena', *Public Administration and Development*, 3 (1983), pp. 151–160.

103 Ank Klomp, 'Bonaire Within the Dutch Antilles', in Betty Sedoc-Dahlberg, *The Dutch Caribbean: Prospects for Democracy* (New York, 1990), p. 107.

104 *Islands Business*, 19 (May 1993), p. 49.

105 J. O. Domingo, 'Employment, Income and Economic Identity in the United States Virgin Islands', *The Review of Black Political Economy*, 18 (1989), p. 50; on St Eustatius, see Van den Bor, *Island Adrift*, p. 16.

106 Antony Hooper, 'The MIRAB Transition in Fakaofo, Tokelau', *Pacific Viewpoint*, 34 (1993), p. 258; see also Antony Hooper, 'Aid and Dependency in a Small Pacific Territory', Department of Anthropology, University of Auckland, Working Paper No. 62 (1982).

107 David Marlow, 'Constitutional Change, External Assistance and Economic Development in Small Islands: The Case of Montserrat', in Helen Hintjens and Malyn Newitt (eds), *The Political Economy of Small Tropical Islands* (Exeter, 1992), pp. 45–46.

108 Van den Bor, *Island Adrift*, p. 78.

109 E. A. Markham and H. Fergus, *Hugo versus Montserrat* (London, 1989); Carol Harden and Lydia Pulsipher, 'Come a Nasty Gale: The Response to Hurricane Hugo on the Island of Montserrat, West Indies', *Focus*, 42 (Summer 1992), pp. 9–13. The government postponed a planned referendum on independence and concentrated on reconstruction of the island economy.

110 Van den Bor, *Island Adrift*, p. 60.

111 Dietz, *Economic History of Puerto Rico*, pp. 146–158, 397.

112 Nancy Pollock, Takapoto, 'La Prosperité, retour aux îles', *Journal de la Société des Océanistes*, 34 (1978), pp. 133–135; Victoria Lockwood, 'Development and Return Migration to Rural French Polynesia', *International Migration Review*, 24 (1990), pp. 347–371.

113 Lockwood, 'Development and Return Migration', pp. 89–90; see also Victoria S. Lockwood, *Tahitian Transformation: Gender and Capitalist Development in a Rural Society* (Boulder, 1993).

114 De Haan, 'Small Islands in the Caribbean', pp. 383–384; Ayisi, *St Eustatius*, pp. 87–93.

115 Van den Bor, *Island Adrift*, p. 99; Ackrill, 'The Cocos (Keeling) Islands', p. 128.

116 Hooper, 'The MIRAB Transition', pp. 241–264. This was true even earlier in the Cook Islands: see Grant Simpson, 'Wallerstein's World Systems Theory and the Cook Islands: A Critical Examination', *Pacific Studies*, 4 (1990), pp. 73–94.

117 Kent Brooks, 'Nationalism in Greenland', in G. Trompf (ed.), *Islands and Enclaves* (New Delhi, 1993), p. 108; see Lawrence Millman, *Last Places* (New York, 1990), pp. 169–172.

118 Van den Bor, *Island Adrift*, p. 71.

119 Ayisi, *St Eustatius*, pp. xiv, 89.

120 To a substantial extent, this is a result of a combination of aid-dependency and few realistic economic opportunities, a situation that may have changed following the growth of tourism. In the Falkland Islands, for example, where islanders were regarded as lacking in entrepreneurial spirit in the 1970s, the situation changed quite sharply with new opportunities following the breakdown of the old landholding system. See Stephen Royle, 'Health in Small Island Communities', p. 263.

121 Gillett, 'Developing St Helena', pp. 152–153. In Niue, where aid was extensive, aid policies endangered the very attributes that policy-makers were seeking to foster: egalitarianism, income equality, homogeneity and self-reliance. See Trevor Matheson, 'Aid in an Island Micro-State: The Case of Niue', unpublished PhD thesis, ANU, Canberra, 1986.

122 I. G. Bertram and R. Watters, 'The MIRAB Economy in South Pacific Microstates', *Pacific Viewpoint*, 26 (1985), pp. 497–519.

123 Migration (and remittances) are not necessarily central to this process of evolution, as long as there is a substantial external source of rentier income. Bernard Poirine has characterised French Polynesia's economy as a 'close cousin' of MIRAB economies, through the acronym ARAB: Atomic Rent, Aid and Bureaucracy: 'Rent, Emigration and Unemployment in Small Islands: The MIRAB Model and the French Overseas Departments and Territories', *World Development*, 22 (1994), p. 1998.

124 Barbara Dreaver, 'Good Night, Cook Islands', *Islands Business*, 74 (May 1996), p. 21; see also Crocombe and Crocombe, 'The Cook Islands', *The Contemporary Pacific*, 8, (1996), pp. 174–182, and 9 (1997), pp. 218–227.

125 De Haan, 'Small Islands in the Caribbean', p. 384. Much the same is true in Guam, where the government 'is influenced heavily by patronage, nepotism and by rich Chamorro business families. It routinely over-spends, kept hiring more friends for government jobs until it was forced to freeze hiring last year, and borrows to pay for daily running costs. Last year it ran itself into a financial crisis. It had debts of over US$600 million and couldn't pay some bills': Robert Keith-Reid, 'A Little Bit of America', *Islands Business*, 22 (December 1996), p. 27. Similarly, in Réunion several business-men and politicians were gaoled in 1994 and 1995, because of diverse financial scandals, and Guyane politicians have faced charges of extensive corruption: *Le Monde*, 15 May 1997. In 1996 the governor of the Turks and Caicos Islands accused the local police of 'incompetence, sloth and corruption' provoking much resentment and demands that he be recalled to Britain; a decade earlier two members of parliament had been jailed in the United States for cocaine-trafficking: Ritchie, *The Last Pink Bits*, pp. 164–165.

126 Marie-Louise Petersen, 'The Impact of Public Planning on Ethnic Culture: Aspects of Danish Resettlement Policies in Greenland after World War II', *Arctic Anthropology*, 23 (1986), pp. 271–280; Nuttall, 'Greenland', pp. 17–20; Millman, *Last Places*, pp. 169–172.

127 Luz-Marina Garcia-Herrera, 'Economic Development and Spatial Con-figuration in the Canary Islands', *Antipode* 19 (1987), pp. 37–38; Aldrich and Connell, *France's Overseas Frontier*, pp. 115–122; Gerard Baudchon,

'Movement in the French Pacific: Recent Situation and Prospects', *Asian and Pacific Migration Journal*, 1 (1992), pp. 333–349.

128 Katherine E. Browne, 'The Informal Economy in Martinique: Insights from the Field, Implications for Development Policy', *Human Organization*, 55 (1996), pp. 225–234.

129 Vaughan Robinson, 'Social Demography', in Robinson and McCarroll, *The Isle of Man*, pp. 146–147; Orlando Ribeiro, *L'Ile de Madère: étude géographique* (Lisbon, 1949), pp. 145–147; Lewis and Williams, 'Regional Autonomy and the European Communities', p. 68; Parsons, 'The Canary Islands Search for Stability'.

130 Van den Bor, *Island Adrift*, pp. 56–57. Much the same was true in Saint-Barthélemy; see Julianne Maher, 'Fishermen, Farmers, Traders: Language and Economic History on St Barthélemy, French West Indies', *Language in Society*, 25 (1996), pp. 392–394.

131 Van den Bor, *Island Adrift*, p. 60.

132 Crane, *Educated to Emigrate*, pp. 6, 77–80, 158–163. By the late 1930s St Eustatius was also described as having a 'remittance society': Van den Bor, *Island Adrift*, p. 61.

133 Jean Glasscock, *The Making of an Island: Sint-Maarten, Saint-Martin* (Wellesley, 1985), p. 51; John P. Augelli, 'The British Virgin Islands: A West Indian Anomaly', *Geographical Review*, 46 (1956), pp. 51–52.

134 Jerome McElroy and Klaus de Albuquerque, 'Migration Transition in Small Northern and Eastern Caribbean States', *International Migration Review*, 22 (1988), pp. 30–58.

135 Villamil, 'Puerto Rico, 1948–1976', p. 249; Joseph P. Fitzpatrick, *Puerto Rican Americans* (Englewood Cliffs, 1971); Adrian Bailey and Mark Ellis, 'Going Home: The Migration of Puerto Rican-Born Women from the United States to Puerto Rico', *Professional Geographer*, 45 (1993), pp. 148–158; Marta Tienda, 'Puerto Ricans and the Underclass Debate', *Annals of the American Academy of Political and Social Science*, 501 (1989), pp. 105–119.

136 Frank Bovenkerk, 'Caribbean Migration to the Netherlands', *Caribbean Review*, 10 (1981), pp. 34–37; de Haan, 'Small Islands in the Caribbean', p. 384; Willem Koot, 'Les Antillais au Pays-Bas: perspectives de retour', *Revue Européenne des Migrations Internationales*, 3 (1987), p. 117; Gert Ooostindie, 'Caribbean Migration to the Netherlands: A Journey to Disappointment?', in M. Cross and H. Entzinger (eds), *Lost Illusions: Caribbean Minorities in Britain and the Netherlands* (London, 1988), pp. 54–72.

137 Aldrich and Connell, *France's Overseas Frontier*, pp. 109–112; Stephanie Condon and Philip Ogden, 'Afro-Caribbean Migrants in France: Employment, State Policy and the Migration Process', *Transactions of the Institute of British Geographers*, 16 (1991), pp. 440–457; Stephanie Condon and Philip Ogden, 'Emigration from the French Caribbean: The Origins of an Organised Migration', *International Journal of Urban and Regional Research*, 15 (1991), pp. 505–523; Fred Constant, 'La Politique française de l'immigration antillaise de 1946 à 1987', *Revue Européenne des Migrations Internationales*, 3 (1987), pp. 9–30; Albert Weber, *L'Emigration réunionnaise en France* (Paris, 1994).

138 Ackrill, 'The Cocos (Keeling) Islands', p. 226.

139 Tokelau had however been very badly affected by the Peruvian labour trade in the 1860s, when there was catastrophic depopulation: see H. E. Maude, *Slavers in Paradise: The Peruvian Labour Trade in Polynesia, 1862–1864* (Canberra, 1981).

140 Antony Hooper and Judith Huntsman, 'A Demographic History of the Tokelau Islands', *Journal of the Polynesian Society*, 82 (1973), p. 392; Albert Wessen, Antony Hooper, Judith Huntsman, Ian Prior and Clare Salmond, *Migration and Health in a Small Society: The Case of Tokelau* (Oxford, 1992).

141 Jean-Claude Roux, 'Migration and Change in Wallisian Society', in R. T. Shand (ed.), *The Island States of the Pacific and Indian Oceans* (Canberra, 1980), pp. 167–176; John Connell, 'Wallis and Futuna Workers in New Caledonia and the New Hebrides', in C. Moore, J. Leckie and D. Munro (eds), *Labour in the South Pacific* (Townsville, 1991), pp. 133–139.

142 Jean Chesneaux, 'Can Two Opposite Views of the Past be Turned into One of the Future?', *Pacific Islands Monthly*, 52 (December 1981), p. 27.

143 Connell, *New Caledonia or Kanaky?*, pp. 223–225. To some extent the process of 'demographic colonisation' continues; between 1989 and 1996 the Melanesian proportion of the population fell (to 44 per cent of the total) following migration from France and the European Union.

144 John Connell, 'Paradise Left? Pacific Island Voyagers in the Modern World', in J. Fawcett and B. Carino (eds), *Pacific Bridges* (New York, 1987), pp. 375–404. As early as the 1950s the BVI, even though its economy was in recession, was a target for migrants from other British Caribbean islands (and beyond) seeking to migrate into the USVI and onwards to the United States: Augelli, 'The British Virgin Islands', p. 57. On migration into Puerto Rico, see Maria del Carmen Baerga, 'Migration in a Small Semiperiphery: The Movement of Puerto Ricans and Dominicans', *International Migration Review*, 24 (1990), pp. 656–683.

145 Philpott, *West Indian Migration*, pp. 111–112; Lowenthal and Comitas, 'Emigration and Depopulation', pp. 217–218.

146 Matthew Carr, 'Policing the Frontier: Ceuta and Melilla', *Race and Class*, 39 (1977), pp. 61–66; Aldrich and Connell, *France's Overseas Frontier*, pp. 105–108.

147 Macao was also seeking to increase its population to as much as one million, before the enclave rejoined China in 1999, by granting residency permits to any Chinese investors who purchased a $250,000 piece of real estate: Uli Schmetzer, 'Macao: A Colonial Outpost in the Making', *Chicago Tribune*, 1 June 1995.

148 Connell, 'The Islands of Micronesia', pp. 50–79.

149 Lawrence Hamilton, Rasmus Ole Rasmussen, Nicholas Flanders and Carole Seyfrit, 'Outmigration and Gender Balance in Greenland', *Arctic Anthropology*, 33 (1996), p. 93.

150 Centraal Bureau voor de Statistiek, *Volks en Woningtelling Nederlands Antillen* (Willemstad, 1993).

151 In 1992 those who sought to migrate to Sint-Maarten (or elsewhere in the Dutch Antilles) had to buy a home for a minimum of $135,000 and employ an Antillean for at least 30 hours per week, at a salary of about $350 per month. In 1996 the Dutch government was reviewing the situation because of the massive loss in revenue to the Dutch economy.

152 Klaus de Albuquerque and Jerome McElroy, 'West Indian Migration to the United States Virgin Islands: Demographic Impacts and Socioeconomic Consequences', *International Migration Review*, 16 (1982), p. 90; Domingo, 'Employment, Income and Economic Identity', pp. 37–57; Mark J. Miller and William Boyer, 'Foreign Workers in the USVI: History of a Dilemma', *Caribbean Review*, 11 (1982), pp. 48–51.

153 Connell, 'The Cayman Islands', pp. 56–60.

154 *Les Nouvelles Hebdo* (Noumea), 91 (16 November 1989), pp. 8–10.

155 Jerome McElroy and Klaus de Albuquerque, 'The Economic Impact of Retirement Tourism in Montserrat: Some Provisional Evidence', *Social and Economic Studies*, 41 (1992), pp. 127–152.

156 Robinson, 'Social Demography', pp. 147–149; Richard Prentice, 'The "Manxness of Man": Renewed Immigration to the Isle of Man and the Nationalist Response', *Scottish Geographic Magazine*, 106 (1990), pp. 77–78; K. Atkinson, 'A Study of Post-war Immigration to the Isle of Man, Local Objections to the Issue and Limited Government Response', unpublished BA Honours thesis, University of Leeds, 1995.

157 In the 1990s the European Union was examining the island's immigration laws because of concern over their treatment of EU citizens: *Guernsey Evening Press*, 8 May, 1 June 1993.

158 *Bermuda Sun*, 23 June 1995.

159 Domingo, 'Employment, Income and Economic Identity', p. 50.

160 Petersen, 'The Impact of Public Planning', p. 227; Lyck and Taagholt, 'Greenland', p. 57; Mark Nuttall, *Arctic Homeland: Kinship, Community and Development in Northwest Greenland* (London, 1992), pp. 102–104.

161 Treadgold, *Bounteous Bestowal*, pp. 265–266. At the time of the 1991 census, some 434 of the permanently resident population of 1912 were migrant workers, on the island for periods of up to six months, whilst other residents had been there for quite short periods. Similar resentment of newcomers has occurred in Gibraltar (see chapter 6).

162 Connell, 'The Islands of Micronesia', p. 60. As in the United States Virgin Islands, foreign migrant workers in the Northern Marianas cannot become permanent residents (much less citizens) so the citizen minority continue to dominate business and political life and migration is more easily able to be regulated in accordance with the demands of the labour market. By contrast, Guam is subject to US migration laws, hence foreign workers are more easily able to remain. In the Northern Marianas, there was also resentment over the migration of nationals, mainly from Asia, coming to Saipan to give birth to children who would then automatically become US citizens. See Samuel F. McPhetres, 'Challenges to Democracy in the Commonwealth of the Northern Mariana Islands', in R. Crocombe (ed.), *Culture and Democracy in the South Pacific* (Suva, 1992), p. 223.

163 In extreme form it has been argued, 'The prosperity of the Cayman Islands is a magnet now for the poor, unskilled and illiterate from Jamaica, and illegal immigrants are already burdening the economy – burdening the school and medical systems and bringing with them drugs that they sell to keep themselves in food and lodging': Peter Benchley, 'Fair Skies for the Cayman Islands', *National Geographic*, 167 (1985), p. 815. There is no doubt that the crime rate and the extent of drug abuse have risen substantially in the past two decades, with the Cayman Islands having the highest prison population per capita outside Russia. Similar situations occur elsewhere in the Caribbean, and are not a function of migration alone.

164 Colleen Ballerino Cohen and Frances E. Mascia-Lees, 'The British Virgin Islands as Nation and Desti-nation: Representing and Siting Identity in a Post-colonial Caribbean', *Social Analysis*, 33 (1993), pp. 130–151; Betsy Oakes, 'Workers in the British Virgin Islands: The Complexities of Residence and Migration', *Social and Economic Studies*, 41 (1992), pp. 67–87; Bill Maurer, 'Orderly Families for the New Economic Order', *Identities*, 2 (1995), pp. 149–171.

165 A. J. Jowett, A. Findlay, F. Li and R. Skeldon, 'The British Who Are Not British and the Immigration Policies That Are Not: The Case of Hong Kong', *Applied Geography*, 15 (1995), pp. 245–265.

166 Kauders, 'A Tristan Year', p. 72; see also Bishop of St Helena's Commission on Citizenship, *St Helena: The Lost County of England* (St Helena, 1996); and Kenneth Bain, *St Helena: The Island, Her People and Their Ship* (York, 1993), pp. 16–20.

167 Jackson, 'Migration and Social Change in Puerto Rico', p. 200.

168 Dietz, *Economic History of Puerto Rico*, p. 228.

169 Ayisi, *St Eustatius*, p. 163.

170 Fred Constant, 'The French Antilles in the 1990s: Between European Unification and Political Territorialization', *Caribbean Studies*, 26 (1993), p. 304.

171 Bertram and Watters, 'The MIRAB Economy'; see also Victoria Lockwood, 'Welfare State Colonialism in Rural French Polynesia', in V. Lockwood, T. Harding and B. Wallace (eds), *Contemporary Pacific Societies* (Englewood Cliffs, 1993), pp. 81–97.

172 Karl Theodore, 'The Adjustment and the Promise: A Suggestive Sketch of the Aruba Economy', *Social and Economic Studies*, 40 (1991), p. 158.

173 *Ibid.*

174 Deborah Berman Santana, *Kicking Off the Bootstraps: Environment, Development and Community Power in Puerto Rico* (Tucson, 1996).

175 Ayisi, *St Eustatius*, p. 164.

176 Connell, 'The Cayman Islands', p. 55.

177 If all vehicles in Macao were arranged end to end they would exceed the length of roads by at least 50 per cent: see Jonathan Porter, 'The Transformation of Macao', *Pacific Affairs*, 66 (1993), p. 11.

178 David Lowenthal and Lambros Comitas, 'Emigration and Depopulation: Some Neglected Aspects of Population Geography', *Geographical Review*, 52 (1962), p. 207. After particularly violent volcanic eruptions in mid-1997, the British government organised a referendum to determine if the remaining five thousand islanders, and those who had left the island, wished to be rehoused on the island or resettled in other Caribbean states or in Britain.

179 John E. Kersell, 'Developing the British Virgin Islands: The First Crown Colony', *Public Administration and Development*, 9 (1989), p. 106.

180 Crane, *Educated to Emigrate*, p. 242.

181 However, there were calculations of the relative costs of fighting the war and resettlement of the entire population in the United Kingdom, which indicated that the latter was by far the cheapest 'option'.

4 The Quest for Independence?

1 John Crawford, *The Creation of States in International Law* (Oxford, 1979); Sheila Harden, *Small is Dangerous: Micro States in a Macro World* (London, 1985).

2 D. Fieldhouse, *The Colonial Empire* (London, 1982, 2nd edn), p. 411. The UN position, however, was that decolonisation should eventually extend even to Pitcairn: Stanley de Smith, *Microstates and Micronesia* (New York, 1970), p. 45.

3 D. P. J. Wood, 'The Smaller Territories: Some Political Considerations', in B. Benedict (ed.), *Problems of Smaller Territories* (London, 1967), p. 24.

4   De Smith, *Microstates and Micronesia*, pp. 12–14; David Wainhouse, *Remnants of Empire* (New York, 1964).
5   John Connell, 'Tuvalu: Independence or Dependence?', *Current Affairs Bulletin*, 56 (February 1980), pp. 27–31.
6   Barrie Macdonald, 'Secession in Defence of Identity: The Making of Tuvalu', *Pacific Viewpoint*, 16 (1975), pp. 26–43.
7   Robert Aldrich and John Connell, *France's Overseas Frontier* (Cambridge, 1992), pp. 209–210.
8   See Wood, 'The Smaller Territories', p. 34.
9   Geoff Bertram, 'The Political Economy of Decolonisation and Nationhood in Small Pacific Societies', in A. Hooper *et al.* (eds), *Class and Culture in the South Pacific* (Suva, 1987), p. 25.
10 Angel I. Rivera and Aaron Ramos, 'The Quest for a New Political Arrangement in Puerto Rico: Issues and Challenges', *Caribbean Studies*, 26 (1993), pp. 267–268.
11 Fernando Martin, 'Independence: The Only Permanent Solution', in R. J. Bloomfield (ed.), *Puerto Rico: The Search for a National Policy* (Boulder, 1985), p. 177; see also Juan Manuel Carión, 'The National Question in Puerto Rico', in Edwin Meléndez and Edgardo Meléndez (eds), *Colonial Dilemma: Critical Perspectives on Contemporary Puerto Rico* (Boston, 1993), pp. 67–75.
12 Juan M. Garcia-Passalacqua, 'The 1993 Plebiscite in Puerto Rico: A First Step to Decolonization?', *Current History*, 93 (1994), pp. 103–107.
13 Raymond Carr, *Puerto Rico: A Colonial Experiment* (New York, 1984), p. 117.
14 R. W. Anderson, 'Political Parties and Politics of Status', *Caribbean Studies*, 21 (1988), p. 29.
15 It has been argued that if Puerto Rico became a US state, a new wave of clandestine violence would be launched on the island and in the United States, to the extent that Puerto Rico could even become America's Northern Ireland. See Ronald Fernandez, *Los Macheteros: The Wells Fargo Robbery and the Violent Struggle for Puerto Rican Independence* (New York, 1987).
16 Marilyn F. Krigger, 'The Implications of the 1993 Status Plebiscite in the United States Virgin Islands', unpublished paper to the conference, 'Looking to the Future: Relations between the United States and American Samoa, Guam, the Northern Marianas, Puerto Rico and the United States Virgin Islands' (Washington, 1994); see chapter 2.
17 Francis M. Rogers, *Atlantic Islanders of the Azores and Madeiras* (North Quincy, Mass., 1979), pp. 12–15; C. M. Maddocks, 'The Azores: A Representative Case of a Micro-Region', unpublished MA thesis, Eastern Kentucky University, 1978; Tom Gallagher, 'Portugal's Atlantic Territories: The Separatist Challenge', *The World Today* (September 1979), pp. 353–359; Don Moser, 'The Azores: Nine Islands in Search of a Future', *National Geographic*, 149 (1976), pp. 261–288.
18 Domingo Garí Hayek, *Historia del Nacionalismo Canario* (Las Palmas, 1992); M. Eddy, 'Influences and Independence', in A. Eames (ed.), *Gran Canaria* (London, 1995), pp. 89–93.
19 Malcolm Treadgold, *Bounteous Bestowal: The Economic History of Norfolk Island* (Canberra, 1988), pp. 287–288; Stephanie Bunbury, 'Norfolk Islanders Cling to the Spirit of Mutiny', *Modern Times*, 4 (June 1992), pp. 12–14; *Sydney Morning Herald*, 12 February 1994. In 1995 conservative support for a more independent status increased as Australia seemed to be moving towards becoming a republic: *Sunday Telegraph*, 10 December 1995.

20   The only other European-dominated overseas territory where there has been any semblance of an independence movement is Gibraltar (see chapter 6) and, to a much lesser extent, the Isle of Man, where *Mec Vannin* (Manx Nationalist Party) was committed to full independence, but had minimal support, as did more militant elements. See Richard Prentice, 'The "Manxness of Man": Renewed Immigration to the Isle of Man and the Nationalist Response', *Scottish Geographical Magazine*, 106 (1990), pp. 79–80.

21   Aldrich and Connell, *France's Overseas Frontier*, pp. 210–213.

22   S. B. MacDonald and A. G. Gastmann, 'Mitterrand's Headache: The French Antilles in the 1980s', *Caribbean Review*, 16 (1984), p. 20.

23   Aldrich and Connell, *France's Overseas Frontier*, pp. 239–240; Richard Burton, 'The French West Indies à l'heure de l'Europe: An Overview', in Richard Burton and Fred Reno (eds), *French and West Indian: Martinique, Guadeloupe and French Guiana Today* (London, 1995), pp. 16–17; William F. S. Miles, 'Déjà Vu with a Difference: End of the Mitterrand Era and the McDonaldization of Martinique', *Caribbean Studies*, 28 (1995), pp. 339–368.

24   *Antilla*, 228 (May 1988), p. 27.

25   Greg Chamberlain, 'French Guiana', *Latin American and Caribbean Review* (London, 1985), p. 99.

26   Bridget Jones and Elie Stephenson, 'Society, Culture and Politics in French Guiana', in Richard Burton and Fred Reno (eds), *French and West Indian* p. 57.

27   *Le Monde*, 3 April 1997.

28   John Connell, 'Britain's Caribbean Colonies: The End of the Era of Decolonisation', *Journal of Commonwealth and Comparative Politics*, 32 (1994), p. 94; Jerome L. McElroy and Klaus de Albuquerque, 'The Social and Economic Propensity for Political Dependence in the Insular Caribbean', *Social and Economic Studies*, 44 (1995), pp. 170, 171.

29   Howard Fergus, 'The Montserrat Independence Issue: Will Conservatism Continue to Prevail?', *Caribbean Affairs*, 2 (July 1989), p. 147.

30   *Ibid.*, p. 151.

31   *Montserrat Reporter*, 3 July 1992.

32   *Montserrat News*, 22 August 1992.

33   Tony Thorndike, 'The Future of the British Caribbean Dependencies', *Journal of Interamerican Studies*, 31 (1989), p. 118.

34   *Turks and Caicos Current* (November–December 1982), p. 15.

35   Connell, 'Britain's Caribbean Colonies', p. 97; John Connell, 'The Turks and Caicos Islands: Beyond the Quest for Independence', *Caribbean Geography*, 3 (1991), pp. 35–36.

36   John Connell, 'Bermuda: the Failure of Decolonisation?', School of Geography, University of Leeds, Working Paper No. 492 (Leeds, 1987), pp. 26–31.

37   Connell, 'Britain's Caribbean Colonies', pp. 98–100.

38   Government of Bermuda, *The Implications of Independence for Bermuda* (Hamilton, 1995).

39   *Bermuda Times*, 21 April 1995.

40   *Royal Gazette*, 23 May, 27 July 1995.

41   John Connell, 'Bermuda: Aberrant or Exemplary Case?', *The Round Table* 341 (1997), pp. 37–50.

42   Aldrich and Connell, *France's Overseas Frontier*, pp. 220–232.

43   Stephen Henningham, 'The Uneasy Peace: New Caledonia's Matignon Accords at Mid-Term', *Pacific Affairs*, 66 (1994), pp. 519–537.

44 Rock Wamytan in *Pacific Report*, 9 (14), 29 July 1996, p. 4.
45 Werner von Busch *et al.* (eds), *New Politics in the South Pacific* (Suva, 1994), p. 98.
46 In the 1970s there was no interest in independence in Saba, based on what was already regarded as the negative experience of other Caribbean islands: Julia Crane, *Educated to Emigrate* (Assen, 1971), p. 97. Similarly in St Eustatius, there was no interest in the 1980s: E. Ayisi, *St Eustatius: The Treasure Island of the Caribbean* (Trenton, 1992), p. 75.
47 Simon Gillett, 'Developing St Helena', *Public Administration and Development*, 3 (1983), p. 159; see Robin Cohen, 'St Helena: Welfare Colonialism in Practice', in R. Cohen (ed.), *African Islands and Enclaves* (Beverly Hills, 1983), pp. 125–128.
48 Stephen Royle, 'Tugging at the Apron Strings', *Geographical Magazine*, 63 (June 1991), p. 16; Bishop of St Helena's Commission on Citizenship, *St Helena: The Lost County of England* (St Helena, 1996), p. 96.
49 The Bishop of St Helena's Commission on Citizenship, *St Helena*.
50 *Guardian*, 15 April, 19 June 1997; *Times*, 16, 26 April 1997.
51 Kenneth Chan, *Cocos (Keeling) Islands: The Political Evolution of a Small Island Territory in the Indian Ocean* (Honolulu, 1987), pp. 14–15.
52 *Australian*, 9 May 1994.
53 Gallagher, 'Portugal's Atlantic Territories', p. 357; Virginia Lockwood, *Tahitian Transformation* (Boulder, 1993), p. 95; Aldrich and Connell, *France's Overseas Frontier*, p. 245. Marquesans have intermittently sought to become a new territory, separate from the remainder of French Polynesia: S. Elbert and M. Kaiser, 'Ka'akai o te Henua 'enana: History of the Land of Men', *Journal of the Polynesian Society*, 98 (1989), p. 82. In the 1996 territorial elections one candidate in the Marquesas was elected on a platform that the Marquesas would remain French if Tahiti became independent.
54 Connell, 'Britain's Caribbean Colonies', pp. 91–92.
55 Helen Hintjens, *Alternatives to Independence: Explorations in Post-Colonial Relations* (Aldershot, 1995), p. 41; see also *Guardian*, 17 June 1997.
56 F. Bobin, 'Les Royaumes de Wallis et Futuna saisis par la doute', *Le Monde*, 15 April 1987, p. 9.
57 S. Pilioko, personal communication, September 1990.
58 Aldrich and Connell, *France's Overseas Frontier*, pp. 242–243; Robert Aldrich, 'France in the Indian Ocean: Declining Independence in Mayotte', in Robert Aldrich and Isabelle Merle (eds), *France Abroad* (Sydney, 1997), pp. 99–168.
59 Hima Douglas, 'Niue: The Silent Village Green', in A. Hooper *et al.* (eds), *Class and Culture in the South Pacific* (Suva, 1987), pp. 186–193.
60 *New Caymanian*, 16 October 1992.
61 Report of the Constitutional Commissioners, *Cayman Islands* (London, 1991), p. 12.
62 *New Caymanian*, 14 May 1993.
63 *New Caymanian*, 30 April 1993.
64 Report of the Constitutional Commissioners, *Cayman Islands*, p. 10.
65 *Royal Gazette*, 11 September 1991.
66 Lasana M. Sekou (ed.), *The Independence Papers: Readings on a New Political Status for St Maarten/St Martin* (St Maarten, 1990), pp. 45–51.
67 Bertram, 'The Political Economy of Decolonisation', p. 21.
68 Iaveta Short, 'The Cook Islands: Autonomy, Self-government and Independence', in Hooper *et al.* (eds), *Class and Culture*, p. 182.

69   Though, as an American Samoan Congressman suggested, commonwealth
      status 'provided CNMI, after 400 years of colonialism and foreign occupa-
      tion, with a political status based upon fundamental democratic principles
      and a government controlled and administered by the native Chamorros
      themselves': Eni Faleomavaega, *Navigating the Future* (Honolulu, 1995),
      p. 3. See also Samuel F. McPhetres, 'Challenges to Democracy in the Com-
      monwealth of the Northern Mariana Islands', in R. Crocombe *et al.* (eds),
      Culture and Democracy in the South Pacific (Suva, 1992), pp. 217–238.
70   R. Rogers, *Guam's Commonwealth Effort, 1987–1988* (Guam, 1988);
      R. Rogers, 'Guam's Quest for Political Identity', *Pacific Studies*, 12 (1988),
      pp. 49–70; and Laura Souder-Jaffery and Robert A. Underwood, *Chamorro
      Self-Determination* (Guam, 1987).
71   Lizabeth A. McKibben, 'The Political Relationship Between the United
      States and Pacific Island Entities', *Harvard International Law Journal*, 31
      (1990), pp. 257–287.
72   Robert Aldrich, *Greater France: A History of French Overseas Expansion*
      (London, 1996).
73   Michel Panoff, *Tahiti métisse* (Paris, 1989).
74   While these are characteristics of Creole societies in the Caribbean, the
      trilogy of *boudin, rhum* and *zouk* (spicy black pudding, rum and zouk music)
      has often become the reductionist symbol of Antillean life, corresponding
      more to the images created for tourists than with real culture in the
      Caribbean. See David Beriss, 'High Folklore: Challenges to the French
      Cultural World Order', *Social Analysis*, 33 (1993), p. 118.
75   On social legislation in the case of the Isle of Man, for example, see
      Prentice, 'The "Manxness of Man" ', p. 85. In a number of territories, such
      as this, attitudes to capital punishment and homosexuality are more con-
      servative than in the metropole.
76   Bobin, 'Les Royaumes de Wallis et Futuna', p. 9.
77   Carr, *Puerto Rico*, pp. 168–170.
78   Jane Moulin, 'Chants of Power: Countering Hegemony in the Marquesas
      Islands', *Yearbook of Traditional Music*, 26 (1994), pp. 1–19.
79   Mark Nuttall, 'Greenland: Emergence of an Inuit Homeland', in Minority
      Rights Group, *Polar Peoples: Self-Determination and Development* (London,
      1994), pp. 10–11.
80   On the Isle of Man, *Mec Vannin* (Manx Nationalist Party) expressed concern
      in the 1960s over 'the prospects of our survival as a nation, as a distinct Celtic
      community in its own right and with its own identity and independence. If we
      continue to attract new residents with plenty of money, the economic and
      financial problem is eased; but it will not help preserve our independence
      and national integrity': quoted in K. Atkinson, 'A Study of Post-war Immigra-
      tion to the Isle of Man', unpublished BA Honours thesis, Leeds, 1995.
81   John Connell, 'Politics and Tradition in Melanesia: Beyond the Struggle
      for Kanaky', in G. Trompf (ed.), *Islands and Enclaves* (New Delhi, 1993),
      pp. 101–144.
82   R. A. Underwood, 'Excursions into Inauthenticity: The Chamorros of
      Guam', *Pacific Viewpoint*, 26 (1985), pp. 160–184.
83   Guam Landowners Association, 'Guam', unpublished paper to United
      Nations Special Committee on Decolonisation Regional Conference (Port
      Moresby, June 1996), p. 1.
84   Sheila S. Clark, 'Ethnicity Embodied: Evidence from Tahiti', *Ethnology*, 33
      (1994), p. 224; Bernard Poirine, 'Tahiti: Is the Melting Pot Melting Down?',

310   NOTES (Pages 154–163)

Pacific Viewpoint, 35 (1994), pp. 62–63, 76–77. More generally, this distinctiveness can be perceived as 'everyday forms of peasant resistance – the prosaic but constant struggle between the peasantry and those who seek to extract labor, food, tax, rents and interest from them', even where such relationships are not economically exploitative. See James C. Scott, *Weapons of the Weak: Everyday Forms of Peasant Resistance* (New Haven, 1985).

85 Nancy Morris, *Puerto Rico: Culture, Politics and Identity* (Westport, 1995), pp. 50–52. During the 1993 plebiscite the pro-commonwealth party argued that with statehood future Olympic participation would not be under the Puerto Rico flag; the pro-statehood party guaranteed 'our two languages, anthems and flags'; and the pro-independence party stressed, 'Value our only flag, our only Homeland, our only Nation': *ibid.*, p. 64. See also Garcia-Passalacqua, 'The 1993 Plebiscite', p. 105.

86 On Bermuda, see Cyril Packwood, *Chained on the Rock: Slavery in Bermuda* (New York, 1975), and Moira Ferguson (ed.), *The History of Mary Prince: A West Indian Slave* (London, 1831/1987); on Sint-Maarten, see Sekou, *The Independence Papers*.

87 Christine Chivallon, 'Space and Identity in Martinique: Towards a New Reading of the Spatial History of the Peasantry', *Environment and Planning: Society and Space*, 13 (1995), pp. 289–309.

88 *National Caymanian*, 7 August 1992. Similar problems of establishing a national identity are apparent in the British Virgin Islands. See Colleen Ballerino Cohen, 'Contestants in a Contested Domain: Staging Identities in the British Virgin Islands', in C. B. Cohen, R. Wilk and B. Stoeltje (eds), *Beauty Queens on the Global Stage* (New York, 1996), pp. 125–145.

89 Jacques André, 'L'Identité ou le retour du même', *Les Temps Modernes*, 441–442 (1983), pp. 2026–2037.

90 Poirine, 'Tahiti', p. 59.

91 De Smith, *Microstates and Micronesia*, p. 31.

92 C. Gautier-Mayoral, 'Puerto Rico: Problems of Decolonisation and Democracy in the Late Twentieth Century', in C. Edie (ed.), *Democracy in the Caribbean: Myths and Realities* (Westpoint, 1994), p. 173.

93 Arnold Leibowitz, *Defining Status* (Dordrecht, 1989), pp. 58–59.

94 *Ibid.*, pp. 60–61.

95 *Ibid.*, p. 62.

96 John Connell, *New Caledonia or Kanaky? The Political History of a French Colony* (Canberra, 1987), pp. 398–399.

97 Guam Landowners Association, 'Guam', p. 2.

98 S. J. K. Blay, 'Self-Determination and the Crisis in New Caledonia: The Search for a Legitimate Self', *Asian Survey*, 28 (1988), p. 875.

99 Leibowitz, *Defining Status*, p. 56.

100 Hintjens, *Alternatives to Independence*, p. 30.

101 Rogers, 'Guam's Quest for Political Identity', pp. 66–67.

102 Albert Ramassamy, *La Réunion, décolonisation et integration* (Saint-Denis, 1987). See also Paulin Bruné, *Mon Dieu, que vous êtes Français: Essai sur la décolonisation par assimilation* (Paris, 1996).

103 Serge Mam-Lam-Fouck, *Histoire de la société guyanaise* (Paris, 1987), pp. 224–227.

104 Quoted in *France-Antilles*, 26 June 1987.

105 In New Caledonia this vote was heralded as a triumph for integration, and used to deter what was perceived to be Australian support for the FLNKS.

106 Peter Caruana, chief minister of Gibraltar, quoted in the *Times*, 10 June 1997.

107 Fergus, 'The Montserrat Independence Issue', p. 151. In 1993 the British Foreign and Commonwealth Office was evaluating the manner in which the Turks and Caicos Islands might again develop stronger ties with the Bahamas.

108 Constant has argued that regional cooperation beween territories in a local area, for example within the eastern Caribbean, also represents the 'invention' of a new path of decolonisation – alongside integration into the metropolis – that challenges conventional forms of decolonisation. See Fred Constant, 'Decolonisation Revisited: The Case of the Non-Sovereign West Indies', *Caribbean Affairs*, 3 (April 1990), p. 152.

109 One Samoan holding these views was persuaded by a member of the UN trusteeship mission – ironically, the French delegate – that 'the only way to play a ukelele was to practise until you could play': Malama Meleisea, *Change and Adaptations in Western Samoa* (Christchurch, 1992), pp. 53, 66.

110 De Smith, *Microstates and Micronesia*, pp. 69–70.

111 Richard Feinberg, 'The Solomon Islands' Tenth Anniversary of Independence: Problems of National Symbolism and National Integration', *Pacific Studies* (1990), p. 23.

112 Mike Faber, 'Small States and Left-Overs of Empire', *The Round Table*, 292 (1984), p. 19.

113 Gert Oostindie, 'The Dutch Caribbean in the 1990s: Decolonization, Recolonization?', *Caribbean Affairs*, 5 (1992), pp. 103–119.

114 Tony Thorndike, in *Montserrat Recorder*, 31 May 1991.

115 R. Hofte and G. Oostindie, 'Upside-Down Decolonization', *Hemisphere*, 1 (Winter 1989), p. 31.

116 Bertram, 'The Political Economy of Decolonisation', pp. 25–26.

117 Proponents of independence in Bermuda have never recently criticised any specific elements of the relationship with the United Kingdom.

118 Hofte and Oostindie, 'Upside-Down Decolonization', p. 28.

119 Helen Hintjens, 'France's Love Children? The French Overseas Departments', in H. Hintjens and M. Newitt (eds), *The Political Economy of Small Tropical Islands* (Exeter, 1992), pp. 64–75; see also Constant, 'Decolonisation Revisited', p. 158.

120 Tony Maingot, in *Montserrat Recorder*, 31 May 1991.

121 On Torres Strait, see S. Kehoe-Forutan, *Torres Strait Independence: A Chronicle of Events* (Brisbane, 1988); on Chatham Islands, see John Connell, 'Chatham Wants Better Deal from New Zealand', *Pacific*, 13 (November 1988), p. 60; and on the Isle of Wight, see the *Times*, 18 July 1996. Similar circumstances in many less developed countries, for example in the Polynesian island of Rotuma in Fiji, and in Bougainville, Papua New Guinea, have seen major secession movements.

122 Ruben Martinez, 'Independence for Puerto Rico: The Only Solution', *Caribbean Review*, 8 (Spring 1979), p. 15. Even the governor of Puerto Rico, Rafael Hernandes Colon, has observed: 'Puerto Rico presents in reality a set of collective symptoms indicating a deep state of trouble: inequalities in the distribution of income and a relatively low participation in production; high cost and low participation in housing, health and education. High criminality, alcoholism, drugs, divorce and suicide are other great expression of social pain': quoted in Leibowitz, *Defining Status*, p. 5. See also Carr, *Puerto Rico*, pp. 177, 184; Martinez, 'Independence for Puerto Rico', pp. 56–57; Martin, 'Independence', p. 174.

123 Quoted in Hofte and Oostindie, 'Upside-Down Decolonisation', p. 31.
124 Quoted in *Pacific Islands Monthly*, 54 (January 1984), p. 41.
125 Quoted in Maurice Satineau, *Contestation politique et revendication nationaliste aux Antilles françaises* (Paris, 1986), p. 143.
126 In a number of territories the threat of 'socialism' has been used by opponents of independence in attempts to discourage support, as in Guam (Rogers, 'Guam's Quest for Political Identity') and New Caledonia (Aldrich and Connell, *France's Overseas Frontier*).

5 Military Bases, Geopolitical Concerns

1 Portugal has however allowed the United States to use an air base at Lajes in the Azores, in return for which it receives substantial military and financial aid.
2 On how the United States stepped into Britain's shoes in international affairs from the 1940s onwards, see William Louis and Ronald Robinson, 'The Imperialism of Decolonization', *Journal of Imperial and Commonwealth History*, 22 (1994), pp. 462–511; Bernard Porter, *Britain, Europe and the World, 1850–1986: Delusions of Grandeur* (London, 1987), chapter 5.
3 David Goldsworthy, 'British Territories and Australian Mini-Imperialism in the 1950s', *Australian Journal of Politics and History*, 41 (1995), pp. 356–372.
4 See Robert Aldrich and John Connell (eds), *France in World Politics* (London, 1989).
5 H. C. Bach and Jørgen Taagholt, *Greenland and the Arctic Region: Resources and Security Policy* (Copenhagen, 1982), pp. 60, 65.
6 Robert Aldrich, 'Rediscovering the Pacific: A Critique of French Geopolitical Analysis', *Journal de la Société des Océanistes*, 87 (1989), pp. 57–71.
7 Julia Chang Bloch, 'Hawaii: America's Secret Weapon in the Pacific Century', *Centerviews* (March–April 1989), p. 4.
8 See, for instance, Philippe Leymarie, *Océan Indien* (Paris, 1981).
9 Clive Archer, 'The United States Defence Areas in Greenland', *Cooperation and Conflict*, 23 (1988), pp. 123–144.
10 Jens Brøsted, 'Greenland between Might and Right', *Scandinavian Review*, 74 (Summer 1986), pp. 13–17.
11 Bach and Taagholt, *Greenland and the Arctic Region*, p. 60.
12 Jørgen Taagholt, 'Greenland and the Faroes', in Clive Archer and David Scrivener (eds), *Northern Waters: Security and Resource Issues* (London, 1986), p. 184. See also his 'Greenland's Future Development: A Historical and Political Perspective', *Polar Record*, 21 (1981), pp. 23–32.
13 Clive Archer and David Scrivener, 'Frozen Frontiers and Resource Wrangles: Conflict and Cooperation in Northern Waters', *International Affairs*, 49 (1982), p. 67.
14 *Europa World Year Book* (London, 1996), p. 1050.
15 Taagholt, 'Greenland and the Faroes', p. 183.
16 Paul Claesson (ed.), *Grønlands Middelhavets Perle* (Copenhagen, 1983), in Archer, *op. cit.*, p. 139.
17 J. Brøsted and M. Fægteborg (eds), *Thule: fangerfolk og militæranlæg* (Copenhagen, 1985), as summarised in Archer, 'The United States Defence Areas' p. 135; Brøsted, 'Greenland between Might and Right', p. 15.
18 Archer, 'The United States Defence Areas', pp. 137, 135.
19 Brøsted, 'Greenland between Might and Right', pp. 16–17. The environ-

mental degradation around long-abandoned bases, such as Narsarssuaq, remains considerable: 'There is still enough heavy metal lying around to make Narsarssuaq a first-rate tourist hangout for William S. Burroughs': Lawrence Millman, *Last Places* (New York, 1990), p. 143. All waste material disintegrates exceptionally slowly in Arctic regions. In 1997 the Greenland premier offered to store both US and Russian nuclear warheads 'to make our contribution to world peace'. During the Cold War Greenland secretly provided storage of US nuclear warheads, even though Denmark had voted in 1957 to ban all nuclear materials from its soil. Both these positions created tension with Denmark (see *Independent*, 23 June 1997).

20   James Dietz, *Economic History of Puerto Rico* (Princeton, 1986), p. 83.

21   Quoted in Ronald Fernandez, *The Disenchanted Island: Puerto Rico and the United States in the Twentieth Century* (New York, 1992), pp. 57, 68, 137.

22   Humberto Garcia Muniz, 'US Military Installations in Puerto Rico: Controlling the Caribbean', in Edwin Meléndez and Edgardo Meléndez (eds), *Colonial Dilemma: Critical Perspectives on Contemporary Puerto Rico* (Boston, 1993), pp. 53–65; Sara Grusky, 'The Changing Role of the US Military in Puerto Rico', *Social and Economic Studies*, 36 (1987), pp. 37–76.

23   Fernandez, *The Disenchanted Island*, pp. 237–238.

24   Sara Grusky, 'The US Navy and Vieques, Puerto Rico: Conflict and Coexistence', *Canadian Journal of Latin American and Caribbean Studies*, 16 (1991), pp. 105–122.

25   Fernandez, *The Disenchanted Island*, p. 238.

26   Aldabra, Desroches and Farquhar were returned to the Seychelles in 1976.

27   Joel Larus, 'Diego Garcia: Political Clouds over a Vital US Base', *Strategic Review*, 10 (1982), p. 45.

28   André Oraison, 'Les Avatars du B.I.O.T. (British Indian Ocean Territory): Le Processus de l'implantation militaire américaine à Diego Garcia', *Annuaire des Pays de l'Océan Indien*, 6 (1979), p. 199.

29   Larus, 'Diego Garcia', p. 47.

30   The arduous (but ultimately successful) efforts by a British journalist to gain access to Diego Garcia are described in Simon Winchester, *Outposts* (London, 1985), pp. 27–58; see also John Todd, *Race for the World* (London, 1994), pp. 330–337.

31   Larus, 'Diego Garcia', pp. 51–52.

32   Jooneed Khan, 'Diego Garcia: The Militarization of an Indian Ocean Island', in Robin Cohen (ed.), *African Islands and Enclaves* (Beverly Hills, 1983), pp. 179–181. See also K. S. Jawatkar, *Diego Garcia in International Diplomacy* (London, 1982).

33   Larus, 'Diego Garcia', p. 48; see Winchester, *Outposts*, p. 36.

34   Oraison, 'Les Avatars du B.I.O.T.', pp. 184, 202. The argument that Mauritius was not aware of London's intention to lease the islands to Washington has been contested. See Oraison, 'Les Avatars du B.I.O.T.'; Joel Larus, 'Negotiating Independence? Mauritius and Diego Garcia', *The Round Table*, 294 (1985), pp. 132–145; Timothy P. Lynch, 'Diego Garcia: Competing Claims to a Strategic Isle', *Case Western Reserve Journal of International Law*, 16 (1984), pp. 101–123.

35   Vivian L. Forbes, 'British Indian Ocean Territory: Chagos Archipelago', *The Indian Ocean Review* (March 1992), p. 18; Iain Walker, *Zaffer Pe Sanze: Ethnic Identity and Social Change Among the Ilois in Mauritius* (Vacoas, 1986).

36   John Madeley, *Diego Garcia: A Contrast to the Falklands* (London, 1985).

37   Quoted in *Sydney Morning Herald*, 4 January 1988.

38   Joel Larus, 'Rethinking Diego Garcia', *The World Today*, 43 (December 1987), p. 205.
39   *Sydney Morning Herald*, 20 July 1990.
40   Donald R. Shuster, 'Palau's Compact: Controversy, Conflict and Compromise', *ISLA*, 2 (1994), pp. 207–236; Gary Smith, *Micronesia: Decolonization and US Military Interests in the Trust Territory of the Pacific Islands* (Canberra, 1993).
41   Quoted in *Pacific*, 21 (November 1996), p. 12. A general overview is given in Donald H. Rubinstein and Vivian L. Dames (eds), *Uncle Sam in Micronesia* (Guam, 1991).
42   Agnes McPhetres, 'The Northern Mariana Islands: US Commonwealth', in R. Crocombe and A. Ali (eds), *Politics in Micronesia* (Suva, 1983), p. 154; Zoel de Ishtar, *Daughters of the Pacific* (Melbourne, 1994), pp. 91–97.
43   See Aldrich and Connell (eds), *France in World Politics* (London, 1989), chapters 5–6.
44   See Robert Aldrich and John Connell, *France's Overseas Frontier* (Cambridge, 1992), chapter 9; Nic Maclellan, 'Liberty, Equality, Fraternity? French Military Forces in the Pacific', *Interdisciplinary Peace Research*, 2 (1990), pp. 3–26. For some commentators, the views expressed in the 1980s about the geopolitical necessity and advantages of a French presence in the DOM-TOMs remain unchanged. See Saint-Croix Rauzduel, 'Les DOM-TOM: Enjeux Strategiques pour la France', *Caribbean Studies*, 28 (1995), pp. 304–325.
45   See Robert Aldrich, *France and the South Pacific since 1940* (London, 1993), chapter 9. See also Bengt and Marie-Thérèse Danielsson, *Poisoned Reign: French Nuclear Colonialism in the Pacific* (Harmondsworth, 1986). However, questions have been raised about the evidence presented in the Danielssons' book; see Jean-Marc Regnault, *La bombe française dans le Pacifique: l'implantation, 1957–1964* (Papeete, 1994).
46   Regnault, *La bombe française*; Bernard Poirine, *Tahiti: La fin du paradis?* (Paris, 1994).
47   The residents of Britain's remaining South Pacific territory, tiny Pitcairn Island, the closest inhabited land to the French testing site, considered a lawsuit against the British government for failing to protect them, as British nationals, against French nuclear testing: *Guardian Weekly*, 8 October 1995.
48   Mururoa and Fangataufa were ceded by the French Polynesian government to metropolitan France in the early 1960s; in terms of international law, they could remain French territory even if the rest of French Polynesia became independent.
49   Stewart Firth, *Nuclear Playground* (Sydney, 1987); Jane Dibblin, *Day of Two Suns: US Nuclear Testing and the Pacific Islanders* (London, 1988).
50   Grusky, 'The US Navy and Vieques', p. 111.
51   Hank Driessen, *On the Spanish–Moroccan Frontier: A Study in Ritual, Power and Ethnicity* (Oxford, 1992), p. 185; Matthew Carr, 'Policing the Frontier: Ceuta and Melilla', *Race and Class*, 39 (1977), p. 66.
52   Gareth Stanton, 'Military Rock: A Mis-Anthropology', *Cultural Studies*, 10 (1996), pp. 270–287. This is made vivid in Harry Ritchie, *The Last Pink Bits* (London, 1997).
53   *Independent*, 31 May 1977.
54   Robert Hughes, *The Fatal Shore* (London, 1987), pp. 58–64.
55   D. P. J. Wood, 'The Smaller Territories', in B. Benedict (ed.), *Problems of Smaller Territories* (London, 1967), p. 30. An official enquiry into Australian

defence, in the 1980s, had a secret annex discussing the contingency of a 'Falklands-style occupation' of Christmas Island by Indonesia. The strategic location of Christmas Island has sometimes been disadvantageous; it was captured by Japan in the Second World War and, in the 1990s, became a target destination for Asian 'boat people' seeking entry to Australia.

56   See the section on Australia's 'managing off-shore contingencies' in the Cocos (Keeling) Islands and Christmas Island in Ross Babbage, *A Coast Too Long: Defending Australia Beyond the 1990s* (Sydney, 1990).

57   See chapter 6.

58   See Martijn Wilder, *Antarctica: An Economic History of the Last Continent* (Sydney, 1992).

59   A US Senate investigation into early proposals for a casino on Tinian (Northern Marianas) showed how Japanese *yakuza* (gangsters) sought to infiltrate the proposed casinos. The investigation concluded that every applicant for a casino licence had

> either ties to the Yakuza, other integrity issues or an inability to raise capital. . . . The money used to finance some projects was directly or indirectly from various branches of the Yakuza. . . . In political and government circles there is either a willingness to do business with the Yakuza or to look the other way. . . . One FBI agent in Saipan characterized the drug problem as endemic involving elected officials, government officials and prominent businessmen. . . . Most importantly, doing business in Tinian gave the Yakuza a back-door entry into the US. . . . Another casino applicant was the owner of a bank in the Mariana Islands (and) a member of a Yakuza family.

Quoted in Ron Crocombe, *The Pacific Islands and the USA* (Suva, 1995), p. 90.

60   Douglas Farah, 'East Caribbean Back as Key Transit Zone', *Washington Post* (reprinted in *Guardian Weekly*, 6 October 1996, p. 17); Leslie Plommer, 'Islands Link Drug Cartels to Europe', *Guardian*, 12 May 1997, p. 12; see also chapter 3.

61   Paul Sutton and Anthony Payne, 'The Off-Limits Caribbean', *Annals of the American Academy of Political and Social Science* (1994), pp. 87–95; Ivelaw L. Griffith, 'Drugs and World Politics: The Caribbean Dimension', *The Round Table*, 332 (1994), pp. 419–431 and 'Drugs in the Caribbean: An Economic Balance Sheet', *Caribbean Studies*, 28 (1995), pp. 285–303.

6 Disputed Territories, 'Colonial' Conflicts

1   Several other territories, such as Wei-hai-wei, in northern China were also leased by foreign powers because of their value as natural harbours and trading outposts, but were generally returned to China after the Second World War. China regards Taiwan as an integral part of the republic, and thus has had a 'four Chinas' policy to accommodate the return of the two non-incorporated territories.

2   B. V. Pires, 'Origins and Early History of Macau', in R. D. Cremer (ed.), *Macau: City of Commerce and Culture* (Hong Kong, 1987), pp. 7–22.

3   R. D. Cremer, 'From Portugal to Japan: Macau's Place in the History of World Trade', in *ibid.*, pp. 23–38.

4   Paul Fifoot, 'One Country, Two Systems: Mark II: From Hong Kong to Macao', *International Relations*, 12 (1994), pp. 25–58, provides an overview of the legal status of Macao from the 1500s to the present.

5   *Ibid.*, p. 29.

6   A remark by the secretary of the Chinese State Council's Hong Kong and Macao Affairs Office in 1985, however, provoked a surprising comment from Macao's governor:

> There is a lot to be discussed, including the time of the changeover. Must we go to the negotiating table to take the Chinese orders because China is such a powerful country? After 500 years of colonial rule, we are tired. Maybe we cannot wait for 12 years. We can leave within one or two years. Why should we stay for the period the Chinese dictate to us?

Quoted in *Far Eastern Economic Review*, 22 August 1985.

7   For instance, on capital punishment, which is permitted in China but not currently allowed in Macao.

8   These and other arrangements are discussed in Fifoot, 'One Country, Two Systems'; and Lo Shiu Hing, *Political Development in Macau* (Hong Kong, 1995).

9   Jonathan Porter, 'The Transformation of Macau', *Pacific Affairs*, 66 (1993), pp. 7–20; see chapter 3.

10   Peter Beck, *The Falkland Islands as an International Problem* (London, 1988), is an even-handed account. For the Argentinian view, see Angel M. Oliveri López, *Malvinas: La Clave del enigma* (Buenos Aires, 1992), as well as Adrián F. J. Hope, 'Sovereignty and Decolonization of the Malvinas (Falkland) Islands', *Boston College International and Comparative Law Review*, 6 (1983), pp. 391–446.

11   G. M. Dillon, *The Falklands, Politics and War* (London, 1989), p. 59.

12   *Ibid.*, p. 64.

13   Quoted in *ibid.*, pp. 65–66.

14   On the question of oil, see Lowell S. Gustafson, *The Sovereignty Dispute over the Falkland (Malvinas) Islands* (New York, 1988).

15   On this alternative, see Peter J. Beck, 'The Future of the Falkland Islands: A Solution Made in Hong Kong?', *International Affairs*, 61 (1985), pp. 643–660.

16   Lawrence Freedman and Virginia Gamba-Stonehouse, *Signals of War: The Falklands Conflict of 1982* (Princeton, 1991).

17   Quoted in *ibid.*, p. 324.

18   Among the many studies and memoirs, see, for instance, the account of the British governor at the time of the war, Rex Hunt, *My Falkland Days* (London, 1992); and that of the then Argentine foreign minister, Nicanor Costa Méndez, *Malvinas: Esta es la historia* (Buenos Aires, 1993). On popular reactions, see James Aulich (ed.), *Framing the Falklands War: Nationhood, Culture and Identity* (Milton Keynes, 1992); Klaus Dodds, 'War Stories: British Elite Narratives of the 1982 Falklands/Malvinas War', *Environment and Planning. Society and Space*, 11 (1993), pp. 619–640 (which has a detailed bibliography); and also his 'Enframing the Falklands: Identity, Landscape and the 1982 South Atlantic War', *Environment and Planning. Society and Space*, 16 (in press).

19   'Rule Britannia', a programme produced by Argentinian film-makers for Britain's Channel 4 in 1994, provides interviews with Dalyell and summarises the Argentinian view of the war.

20   See Peter J. Beck, 'Looking at the Falkland Islands from Antarctica: The Broader Regional Perspective', *Polar Record*, 174 (1994), pp. 167–180.

21   Klaus Dodds, 'The End of a Polar Empire? The Falkland Islands Depend-
      encies and Commonwealth Reactions to British Polar Policy, 1945–61',
      Journal of Imperial and Commonwealth History, 24 (1996), pp. 391–421.
22   *Herald* (Glasgow), 1 April 1997.
23   *Sydney Morning Herald*, 4 April 1992.
24   *Sydney Morning Herald*, 2 April 1987.
25   Quoted in Freedman and Gamba-Stonehouse, *Signals of War*, p. 205.
26   Various aspects of this question are examined in Alberto R. Coll and
      Anthony C. Arend (eds), *The Falklands War: Lessons for Strategy, Diplomacy,
      and International Law* (Boston, 1985).
27   At least some Britons shared this view: 'We are left to conclude that the
      continued occupation of the Falklands represents imperialism in its most
      primitive, least rational form', according to Hugh Tinker, 'The Falklands
      After Three Years', *The Round Table*, 296 (1985), pp. 339–344.
28   This interpretation is advanced in Channel 4's 'Rule Britannia' (see note
      19).
29   Quoted in Freedman and Gamba-Stonehouse, *Signals of War*, pp. 122,
      157 and 154. Dissenting from the usual view of Falkland Islanders as heroic
      defenders of their land and freedom, Ian Bruce, a former member of
      the British Task Force during the war, has commented: 'No-one really
      gave a damn about the islanders, who turned out to be a surly and selfish
      bunch in the main when all is said and done. That is why the major British
      military base is located 30 miles from Stanley': *Herald* (Edinburgh), 1 April
      1997, p. 13.
30   Yann-Huei Song, 'The British 150-Mile Fishery Conservation and Manage-
      ment Zone around the Falkland (Malvinas) Islands', *Political Geography
      Quarterly*, 7 (1988), pp. 183–196.
31   *Guardian Weekly*, 9 November 1986.
32   *Guardian*, 20 April 1987.
33   *Times*, 16 March 1987, p. 10; 17 March 1987, p. 8.
34   The blueprint for Falkland Islands development was a report first pre-
      pared in 1976 by Lord Shackleton; few of the recommendations were
      implemented until after the war, when the report was updated. See Lord
      Shackleton, *Falkland Islands Economic Study 1982* (London, 1982).
35   *Sydney Morning Herald*, 12 June 1989.
36   *Sydney Morning Herald*, 25 November 1991.
37   *Sydney Morning Herald*, 1 November 1994; *Guardian Weekly*, 18 June 1995.
38   *Independent*, 6 June 1997.
39   For an overview, see D. S. Morris and R. H. Haigh, *Britain, Spain and Gibraltar,
      1945–90: The Eternal Triangle* (London, 1992); and Thomas D. Lancaster
      and James L. Taulbee, 'Britain, Spain, and the Gibraltar Question', *Journal
      of Commonwealth and Comparative Politics*, 23 (1985), pp. 251–266.
40   The treaty is quoted, and issues of international law concerning Gibraltar
      discussed, in Gino J. Naldi, 'The Gibraltar Dispute and Some Possible
      Solutions', *Netherlands International Law Review*, 31 (1984), pp. 31–58. On
      the history of the legal status of the colony, see Howard S. Levie, *The Status
      of Gibraltar* (Boulder, 1983).
41   Philip Dennis, *Gibraltar and its People* (Newton Abbot, 1990), p. 228.
42   John A. Jones, 'The Voice of Gibraltar in the United Nations 1963–1964',
      Iberian Studies, 10 (1981), pp. 67–74.
43   Joshua Hassan, 'Gibraltar's Political and Constitutional Future', *The
      Parliamentarian*, 68 (April 1987), p. 58.

44   Gibraltar became part of the European Community when Britain joined the organisation, not strictly as a territory of Britain but because its foreign policy was the responsibility of Britain; Gibraltar remained exempt from a number of Community/Union regulations.

45   *Guardian Weekly*, 13 December 1987.

46   *Guardian Weekly*, 13 March 1988; *Le Monde*, 23 March 1988; *Tribune*, 24 August 1988; *Guardian Weekly*, 5 February 1989.

47   *Le Monde*, 10 December 1994.

48   *Guardian*, 16 January 1992.

49   *Guardian*, 20 May 1990; *Newsweek*, 23 June 1992.

50   A number of Moroccans have found work in Gibraltar, and there has been some problem with Moroccans (and other Africans) attempting to enter Europe illegally by taking boats or rafts across the Straits of Gibraltar. Moroccans in Gibraltar have been the object of continuing incidents of racism and violence. See Gareth Stanton, ' "Guests in the Dock": Moroccan Workers on Trial in the Colony of Gibraltar', *Critique of Anthropology*, 11 (1991), pp. 361–379; see also an article on the 'boat people' of the Straits of Gibraltar in *Le Monde*, 16 October 1991.

51   Report on the Australian ABC news programme 'Foreign Correspondent', 22 August 1995.

52   *Sydney Morning Herald* and *Australian*, 18 May 1996.

53   *El Pais*, 1 July 1991.

54   Naldi, 'The Gibraltar Dispute', p. 52.

55   Quoted in A. J. R. Groom, 'Gibraltar: No End to "Empire" ', *The Round Table*, 323 (1992), p. 283. In Spain's 1997 proposal for co-sovereignty there was some hint that independence was conceivable, though if the status were to change, the 'Andorra option' of joint sovereignty seemed more plausible: Anon., 'New Thinking over Gibraltar?', *The Economist*, 343, 15 February 1997, p. 52. See also Harry Ritchie, *The Last Pink Bits* (London, 1997), pp. 154–156; *Independent*, 10 June 1997; *Guardian*, 18 June 1997.

56   Domingo Del Pino, *Marruecos entre la tradición y el modernismo* (Granada, 1989), pp. 270–273.

57   For general overviews, see Mohamed Naciri, 'Les Villes méditerranéennes du Maroc: entre frontières et périphéries', *Hérodote*, 45 (1987), pp. 121–144; Robert Rézette, *Les Enclaves espagnoles au Maroc* (Paris, 1976); and, on Melilla, Henk Driessen, *On the Spanish–Moroccan Frontier* (Oxford, 1992).

58   The border of Melilla was extended inland to the farthest point reached by a cannon ball fired from the city's fort.

59   In strict legal terms, Spain had only a 'zone of influence' over northeastern Morocco.

60   Driessen, *On the Spanish–Moroccan Frontier*, pp. 41, 45, 70.

61   *Ibid.*, pp. 79, 102, 156.

62   *Guardian Weekly*, 29 December 1985.

63   Albert t'Serstevens, quoted in Rézette, *Les Enclaves espagnoles*, p. 62.

64   Naciri, 'Les Villes méditerranéennes', p. 132; see Rézette, *Les Enclaves espagnoles*, pp. 96–97.

65   Quoted in Rézette, *Les Enclaves espagnoles*, pp. 164, 166.

66   Quoted in *ibid.*, p. 158.

67   *Ibid.*, pp. 162–165; Isla Maclean, 'Africa's Forgotten Colonies', *Africa*, 93 (May 1979), pp. 51–52, 57.

68   Driessen, *On the Spanish–Moroccan Frontier*, p. 113.

69 Quoted in Janice Valls-Russell, 'Problems of Sovereignty: Spain's Rocky Straits', *The New Leader*, 17 November 1986, pp. 6–8.
70 *Le Monde*, 21 May 1987, quoted in Jean de La Guérivière, 'A l'Ombre des presidios', *Géo*, 140 (October 1990), p. 218.
71 Driessen, *On the Spanish–Moroccan Frontier*, pp. 170–176; *Le Monde*, 11 July 1986; *Le Figaro*, 10 October 1986, 24 November 1986, 4 February 1987; *Libération*, 3 February 1987.
72 *El Pais*, 27 May 1991.
73 Meir Serfaty, 'Political Pragmatism in Spain', *Current History*, 86 (November 1986), p. 379.
74 Driessen, *On the Spanish–Moroccan Frontier*, p. 137.
75 José García Cosío, 'Histórica Españolidad Indestructible', in *Ceuta: Ciudad Abierta – 23 Crónicas Periodísticas* (Madrid, 1987), pp. 24–25.
76 Miguel Angel García Brera, 'Los Museos Militares', in *Ceuta*, p. 47.
77 *Guardian Weekly*, 29 December 1985; Driessen, *On the Spanish–Moroccan Frontier*, p. 14; De La Guérivière, however, estimated in 1992 that there were 2000 legionnaires in Melilla and a similar number in Ceuta: 'A l'Ombre des presidios', p. 215.
78 See, for example, the discussion of the 'ceremony of the national flag' in Driessen, *On the Spanish–Moroccan Frontier*, pp. 111–119.
79 Quoted in Valls-Russell, 'Problems of Sovereignty', p. 7.
80 Jean-Pierre Péroncel-Hugoz, 'Ceuta et Melilla', in Jean-Pierre Péroncel-Hugoz (ed.), *Villes du Sud* (Paris, 1990), pp. 95–102.
81 Robert Swann, 'Gibraltar: The Cheerful Mongrel', *New Society*, 5 (127), 4 March 1965, p. 7.
82 Maclean, 'Africa's Forgotten Colonies', p. 52; Rézette, *Les Enclaves espagnoles*, p. 165.
83 Quoted in Del Pino, *Marruecos*, p. 277.
84 Moulay Ahmed Alaoui, quoted in de La Guérivière, 'A l'Ombre des presidios', p. 214.
85 *El Pais*, 7 March 1994.
86 See Tony Hodges, *The Western Saharans* (London, 1984); Anthony G. Pazzanita, 'Morocco versus Polisario: A Political Interpretation', *Journal of Modern African Studies*, 32 (1994), pp. 265–278 and 'The Western Sahara Referendum: A Question of Deadlock', *Journal of South Asian and Middle Eastern Studies*, 19 (1995), pp. 31–56.
87 Pierre Vérin, *Les Comores* (Paris, 1994), provides a general overview.
88 Olivier Gohin, 'Mayotte française: Aspects internationaux, constitutionnels et militaires', *Annuaire des pays de l'Océan Indien* 12 (1990–91), pp. 115–138. See also Robert Aldrich, 'France in the Indian Ocean: Declining Independence in Mayotte', in Robert Aldrich and Isabelle Merle (eds), *France Abroad* (Sydney, 1997), pp. 99–168.
89 See Ahmed Wadaane-Mahamoud, *Mayotte: Le Contentieux entre la France et les Comores* (Paris, 1992); and Pierre Pujo, *Mayotte la française* (Paris, 1993).
90 Samantha Weinberg, *Last of the Pirates: The Search for Bob Denard* (London, 1994). See also Malyn Newitt, *The Comoro Islands: Struggle Against Dependency in the Indian Ocean* (London, 1984).
91 See Sophie Blanchy-Daurel, *La Vie quotidienne à Mayotte* (Paris, 1990).
92 The independent Comoros covers 1862 square kilometres and has a population of 450,000.

93 Yves Salesse, *Mayotte: L'Illusion de la France: Propositions pour une décolonisation* (Paris, 1995); Jean Fasquel, *Mayotte, les Comores et la France* (Paris, 1991).

94 Nevertheless, disputes do arise. Rockall Island, a minuscule rock outcrop located between Iceland and the British Isles, was taken over by Britain only in 1955. Ireland rejects the British claim, and may take Britain to the World Court over the issue. Iceland and Denmark also dispute British sovereignty. The area around the island could hold petroleum reserves. See the *Times* and the *Guardian*, 12 June 1997.

95 One Canadian politician has suggested that Saint-Pierre-et-Miquelon 'should develop some sort of political status with Canada to end the last vestige of an old empire on the North American continent': *Halifax Chronicle Herald*, 1988; quoted in Stephen Royle, 'The Small Island as Colony', *Caribbean Geography*, 3 (1992), p. 267.

96 Jillian Spruyt and Howard B. Baker, 'Britain's True Land's End', *Geographical Magazine*, 69 (March 1997), pp. 46–47.

7 The End of Empire?

1 Richard Howitt, John Connell and Philip Hirsch, 'Resources, Nations and Indigenous Peoples' in R. Howitt *et al.* (eds), *Resources, Nations and Indigenous Peoples* (Melbourne, 1996), pp. 1–30.

2 Chris Gibson, 'Aboriginal Self-Determination in the Jawoyn Nation', unpublished BA Honours thesis (Sydney, 1995).

3 Bangladesh (East Pakistan) and Tuvalu (from the Gilbert and Ellice Islands) provide the only other two post-war examples of the fragmentation of existing states (other than short-lived federations).

4 The status of conflicts, such as those in Bougainville and Irian Jaya, as an 'internal' affair in UN terms, has meant that most such conflicts have been all but inaccessible to international review (even though nations such as France and the United States have deployed troops and military aid overseas when states – such as Chad and Liberia – facing insurgencies and internal unrest have sought external support).

5 Clifford Geertz, *The Interpretation of Cultures* (New York, 1973).

6 Ernest Gellner, *Nations and Nationalism* (Oxford, 1983).

7 Ian Nairn, *The Break-up of Britain: Crisis and Neo-Nationalism* (London, 1981).

8 R. Green *et al.*, *Namibia: The Last Colony* (Harlow, 1981), p. 2.

9 I. Lustick, *Unsettled States, Disputed Lands* (Ithaca, 1993), p. 443.

10 J. Agnew and S. Corbridge, *Mastering Space: Hegemony, Territory and International Political Economy* (London, 1995), p. 3.

11 K. Ohmae, *The End of the Nation-State, The Rise of Regional Economies* (London, 1995); Myo Thant, Min Tang and Hiroshi Kakazu (eds), *Growth Triangles in Asia* (Manila, 1994).

12 I. Clark, *The Hierarchy of States: Reform and Resistance in the International Order* (Cambridge, 1992).

13 J. Camilleri and J. Falk, *The End of Sovereignty? The Politics of a Shrinking and Fragmenting World* (Aldershot, 1992); Mathew Horsman and Andrew Marshall, *After the Nation-State: Citizens, Tribalism and the New World Disorder* (London, 1994).

14 Michael Hechter, *Internal Colonialism: The Celtic Fringe in British National Development, 1536–1966* (London, 1975).

15 D. Drakakis-Smith and J. W. Williams (eds), *Internal Colonialism: Essays Around a Theme* (Edinburgh, 1983).

16 Robert Jackson, *Quasi-States: Sovereignty, International Relations and the Third World* (Cambridge, 1990).

17 Michael Fowler and Julie Bunck, 'What Constitutes the Sovereign State?', *Review of International Studies*, 22 (1996), pp. 381–404.

18 Leslie Sklair, *Sociology of the Global System* (Baltimore, 1991); Arjun Appadurai, 'Disjuncture and Difference in the Global Cultural Economy', *Public Culture*, 7 (June 1990), pp. 295–310. Most territories have slowly disentangled themselves from any colonial moulds; decades ago the BVI, all of whose exports go to the USVI and whose currency is the US dollar, had 'virtually left the Empire without bothering to tell us': *Sunday Times*, 25 January 1976. The Cayman Islands followed, whilst literally and figuratively Martinique is becoming dominated more by McDonald's than by rum distilleries: William Miles, 'Déja Vu With a Difference: End of the Mitterrand Era and the McDonaldization of Martinique', *Caribbean Studies*, 28 (1995), pp. 339–368.

19 Jane Moulin, 'What's Mine is Yours? Cultural Borrowing in a Pacific Context', *The Contemporary Pacific*, 8 (1996), p. 138; see also J. Naisbitt, *Global Paradox: The Bigger the World Economy, the More Powerful its Smaller Players* (New York, 1994).

20 Anthony Smith, *Nations and Nationalism in a Global Era* (Cambridge, 1995), p. 25.

21 *Ibid.*

22 *Ibid.*, p. 27. See also James Anderson, 'On Theories of Nationalism and the Size of States', *Antipode*, 18 (1986), p. 224.

23 This process continues; for example, in the Torres Strait Islands, clustered between Australia and Papua New Guinea, a new regional government has been modelled on that of other island territories linked to Australia. See G. Lui, 'Torres Strait: Towards 2001', *Race and Class*, 35 (1994), pp. 11–20; P. Poynton, 'Dream Lovers: Indigenous People and the Inalienable Right to Self-Determination' in R. Howitt *et al.* (eds), *Resources, Nations and Indigenous People*, p. 52.

24 See Zohl de Ishtar, *Daughters of the Pacific* (Melbourne, 1994).

25 Juan Garcia-Passalacqua, 'The Grand Dilemma: Viability and Sovereignty for Puerto Rico', *Annals of the American Academy of Political and Social Science*, 535 (1994), p. 154.

26 Robert A. Underwood, 'Excursions into Inauthenticity: The Chamorros in Guam', *Pacific Viewpoint*, 26 (1985), p. 171.

27 Some of the few places in the world without television are dependent territories – Tokelau, Pitcairn and Tristan da Cunha – though they are not without videos.

28 Alison Quentin-Baxter, 'Sustained Autonomy – An Alternative Political Status for Small Islands?', *Victoria University of Wellington Law Review*, 24 (1994), p. 16.

29 For example, see Helen Hintjens, 'Regional Reform in the French Periphery: The Overseas Departments of Réunion, Martinique and Guadeloupe', *Regional Politics and Policy*, 1 (1991), p. 70.

30 See Eric Hobsbawm, 'Introduction: Inventing Traditions', in Eric Hobsbawm and Terence Ranger (eds), *The Invention of Tradition* (Cambridge, 1983), chapter 1.

31 Jackson, *Quasi-States*, p. 92.

32 Peter Lyon, 'Introduction', *The Round Table* (1985), p. 3.

33 Jackson, *Quasi-States*, p. 97.

34   In Botswana there was a 'conventional' view that independence meant
     nothing because there was little possibility of independence of action, given
     the country's geographical position. See C. R. Hill, 'Botswana: Independ-
     ence – Myth or Reality?', *The Round Table*, 245 (1972), pp. 55–62.
35   Geoff Bertram, 'The Political Economy of Decolonisation and Nationhood
     in Small Pacific Societies', in A. Hooper *et al.* (eds), *Class and Culture in the
     South Pacific* (Auckland, 1987), p. 29.
36   E. Dommen, 'External Trade Problems of Small Island States in the Pacific
     and Indian Oceans', in R. T. Shand (ed.), *The Island States of the Pacific and
     Indian Oceans* (Canberra, 1980), p. 195.
37   S. Winchester, *Outposts* (London, 1980), p. 309.
38   Quoted in John Connell, *Sovereignty and Survival* (Sydney, 1988), p. 83.
39   John Connell, 'The Turks and Caicos Islands: Beyond the Quest for Inde-
     pendence', *Caribbean Geography*, 3 (1991), p. 60.
40   Stewart Firth, 'Sovereignty and Decolonization in the Pacific Islands'
     (unpublished manuscript, Sydney, 1995), p. 27. In the Caribbean it is
     possible to consider the present political context as one where 'not yet fully
     decolonized' is a concept 'devoid of an expiration date': Gert Oostindie,
     'Ethnicity, Nationalism and the Exodus', in G. Oostindie (ed.), *Ethnicity in
     the Caribbean* (London, 1996), p. 209.
41   Gert Oostindie, 'The Dutch Caribbean in the 1990s: Decolonization,
     Recolonization?', *Caribbean Affairs*, 5 (1992), p. 118.
42   See, for example, T. Gaffaney, 'Linking Colonization and Decolonization:
     The Case of Micronesia', *Pacific Studies*, 18 (1995), pp. 23–59.
43   One Melanesian submission to the UN Special Committee on Decolonisa-
     tion stressed that colonial problems exist in West Papua (Irian Jaya),
     Kanaky (New Caledonia) and Bougainville (Papua New Guinea); it claimed:

> In the 1990s a new type of colonisation thrives in Melanesia, although
> the sources of colonial oppression take on a different form than they
> did in the 1950s. The tragedy for the people of Melanesia is that the
> Committee of 24 is locked into a vision of colonialism that history has
> abandoned. Pitcairn Island is not the issue. The Pitcairn Islanders can
> participate in free elections that accord with modern democratic
> principles. There are peoples in Melanesia who have never been given
> the right of a free and unimpeded vote on the issue of self-deter-
> mination. The extent to which the Committee of 24 closes its eye to
> this reality is the extent of the failure and hypocrisy of the world
> community. (*Times of Papua New Guinea*, 10 June 1993, p. 4).

44   Richard Woolcott (former head of the Department of Foreign Affairs and
     Trade), quoted in the *Australian*, 22 April 1995.
45   This has not always been easy. On the one hand, ex-colonial powers have
     not usually wished to revive old (and costly) ties. On the other hand,
     states seeking additional aid tend to rail against the structure of aid, the
     continued 'exploitation' of the transnational corporations domiciled in
     the state that is delivering aid, and other problems stemming from an
     unequal relationship. See John Connell, *Papua New Guinea* (London,
     1997), chapter 11.
46   Oostindie, 'The Dutch Caribbean', and 'Ethnicity, Nationalism and the
     Exodus'.
47   A. Ramassamy, *La Réunion, décolonisation et intégration* (Saint-Denis, 1987),
     p. 8.

48 Quoted in Edgardo Meléndez, 'Colonialism, Citizenship and Contemporary Statehood', in Edwin Meléndez and Edgardo Meléndez, *Colonial Dilemma* (Boston, 1993), p. 48.
49 G. Bertram, ' "Sustainable Development" in Pacific Micro-economies', *World Development*, 14 (1986), pp. 809–822.
50 Benedict Anderson, *Imagined Communities* (London, 1983).
51 Quoted in John Connell, *New Caledonia or Kanaky?* (Canberra, 1987), p. 445.

Index

Lightning Source UK Ltd.
Milton Keynes UK
UKOW02f1013290116

267378UK00002BA/221/P